The Art of Freedom

The Art of Freedom

On the Dialectics of Democratic Existence

Juliane Rebentisch

Translated by Joseph Ganahl

polity

First published in German as *Die Kunst der Freiheit. Zur Dialektik demokratischer Existenz* © Suhrkamp Verlag, Berlin, 2011

This English edition © Polity Press, 2016

The translation of this work was funded by Geisteswissenschaften International – Translation Funding for Humanities and Social Sciences from Germany, a joint initiative of the Fritz Thyssen Foundation, the German Federal Foreign Office, the collecting society VG WORT and the Börsenverein des Deutschen Buchhandels (German Publishers & Booksellers Association).

Polity Press
65 Bridge Street
Cambridge CB2 1UR, UK

Polity Press
350 Main Street
Malden, MA 02148, USA

All rights reserved. Except for the quotation of short passages for the purpose of criticism and review, no part of this publication may be reproduced, stored in a retrieval system, or transmitted, in any form or by any means, electronic, mechanical, photocopying, recording or otherwise, without the prior permission of the publisher.

ISBN-13: 978-0-7456-8212-9
ISBN-13: 978-0-7456-8213-6 (pb)

A catalogue record for this book is available from the British Library.

Library of Congress Cataloging-in-Publication Data

Names: Rebentisch, Juliane, 1970- author.
Title: The art of freedom : on the dialectics of democratic existence / Juliane Rebentisch.
Other titles: Kunst der Freiheit. English.
Description: English edition. | Malden, MA : Polity Press, 2016. | Includes bibliographical references and index.
Identifiers: LCCN 2015032565| ISBN 9780745682129 (hardback) | ISBN 9780745682136 (paperback)
Subjects: LCSH: Democracy--Philosophy. | Liberty--Philosophy. | Aesthetics. | BISAC: PHILOSOPHY / Aesthetics.
Classification: LCC JC423 .R325713 2016 | DDC 320.01/1--dc23 LC record available at http://lccn.loc.gov/2015032565

Typeset in 10.5 on 12 pt Sabon
by Toppan Best-set Premedia Limited
Printed and bound in the United Kingdom by Clays Ltd, St Ives PLC

The publisher has used its best endeavours to ensure that the URLs for external websites referred to in this book are correct and active at the time of going to press. However, the publisher has no responsibility for the websites and can make no guarantee that a site will remain live or that the content is or will remain appropriate.

Every effort has been made to trace all copyright holders, but if any have been inadvertently overlooked the publisher will be pleased to include any necessary credits in any subsequent reprint or edition.

For further information on Polity, visit our website:
politybooks.com

Contents

Acknowledgments   viii

Origins of the Text   ix

Introduction: Aestheticization – An Apologia   1

Part I: An Antique Diagnosis of a Crisis   15

1. The Provocative Beauty of Democracy: Plato   17
   1. Freedom and Indeterminacy   18
   2. The Slavery of the Tyrant   21
   3. The Unstable Democrat   23
   4. Clear-sighted, Processual, and Totalized Weakness of Will   25
   5. Weakness of Will or the Freedom from Oneself   29
   6. The Unfree Opportunist   32
   7. Many Jobs and Much Trespassing   35
   8. The Occurrence of an Inner Nature or the Freedom Toward Self   38
   9. Democrats and Theater Types   40
   10. Theatrocracy: The Fearlessly Judging Multitude   44
   11. Masses and Mimesis   49
   12. Self-Difference and Perfection   52

Part II: The Ethical-Political Right of Irony   57

2. The Morality of Irony: Hegel   59
  1. The Beginning of Morality in Socratic Irony   60
  2. Socrates' Divisive Work   62
  3. Irony and the Practice of Truth   66
  4. Hegel's Critique of Kant   68
  5. A Socratic Reformulation of the Moral Principle   71
  6. Critique of the Romantics   75
  7. Abstract and Subjective Freedom   79
  8. Evil and the "Natural Will"   82
  9. The Dialectic of Freedom   85
  10. A Less Rigorous Concept of Self-Determination   87
  11. Conflicts with and in Morality   90
  12. Hegel's Expulsion of Subjective Freedom from Ethical Life   94
  13. The Riddle of Socratic Virtue and the Historicity of the Good   97

3. The Ethics of Aesthetic Existence: Kierkegaard   100
  1. The Negative Freedom of Socratic Irony and its Romantic Superseding   102
  2. Self-Improvement and Forgetfulness-of-Self   104
  3. The Impotent Seducer   108
  4. The "Helmeted" Will and its Desperation in the Face of the Aesthetic   112
  5. Repentance and Duty: The Freedom to Choose What One Already Is   114
  6. One Sexism for Another   119
  7. The Love of Divorced Society Ladies   122
  8. Aesthetic and Aristocratic Exception   128
  9. Common Sinners   131
  10. The Leap of Faith   134
  11. Repetitions   139

4. Sovereignty in Romanticism: Schmitt   145
  1. Aestheticization and Neutralization   146
  2. A Look at an Orange   149
  3. Alien Power   152
  4. The Other in the Own and Decision   154
  5. Political Anthropology   159
  6. Schmitt and Kierkegaard   162
  7. Political Theology   165

8. "Concrete Life" and Decision	167
9. Schmitt's Rousseauism	171
10. Politics as a Critique of Politics	174

Part III: Democracy and Aestheticization — 181

5. The Spectacle of Democracy: Rousseau — 183
1. The Irony of the Actor — 185
2. The Public Expression of Indeterminacy — 189
3. The Actress and Her Parodies — 193
4. The Golden Mean — 196
5. "Thy Magic Powers Reunite What Custom's Sword Has Divided": The Feast of the Brothers — 198
6. All Brothers are also Men: The Problem of Male Self-Difference — 201
7. The Two Paradoxes of the Social Contract — 206
8. The Sovereignty of the Legislator and the Judgment of the "Common Man" — 210
9. Another Kind of Equality — 215
10. A Politicizable Boundary — 218
11. The Two Bodies of the People — 220
12. Representation and the Coding of Contingency — 224

6. The Anaestheticization of the Political in Fascism: Benjamin — 229
1. Charisma versus Ratio — 231
2. Politicizing Art — 232
3. Astonishment, Not Sympathy — 234
4. The Look of the Stranger — 237
5. Alienation — 238
6. Adaptability and Revolution — 241
7. Charisma and Democracy — 243
8. Political Theater — 245

7. Post-Democracy and the Anaesthetizing of the Political: A Look Forward — 248

Notes — 260

Index — 306

Acknowledgments

This book would have been literally unthinkable if it had not been for all the support I received in the course of writing it. My appreciation goes, first of all, to the Deutsche Forschungsgemeinschaft for their generous support, as well as to my colleagues from Special Research Area 626, "Aesthetic Experience and the Dissolution of Artistic Limits." I also thank the New School for Social Research, the Cluster of Excellence "The Formation of Normative Orders" and the Philosophy departments at the Universities of Potsdam and Frankfurt am Main. These contexts made a decisive contribution to the formation of this undertaking. My gratitude goes especially to Christoph Menke, Thomas Khurana, Dirk Quadflieg, Francesca Raimondi, and Dirk Setton for their continuous suggestions, which opened many paths while sparing me a number of wrong turns. I am especially grateful to Dirk Quadflieg for reading my drafts during the most decisive phases of writing. For stimulating conversations and discussion I would also like to thank Armen Avanessian, Christian Becker, Beatrice von Bismarck, Astrid Deuber-Mankowsky, Helmut Draxler, Eva Gilmer, Stephan Greene, Anselm Haverkamp, Carl Hegemann, Axel Honneth, Rahel Jaeggi, Gertrud Koch, Hans-Peter Krüger, Hans-Thies Lehmann, Bettine Menke, Ute Meurer, Andrew Norris, Terry Pinkard, Gerhard Rebentisch, Ludger Schwarte, Martin Seel, Dieter Thomae, Sandra Umathum, Christiane Voss, Albrecht Wellmer, and Antje Wessels. All of them in their own way influenced my reflections on the questions discussed in this book. I owe to Diedrich Diederichsen my belief that it would be truly possible to complete this project.

This book is dedicated to my parents, Evelyn and Gerhard Rebentisch.

Origins of the Text

An abbreviated version of chapter 1 first appeared as "Der Demokrat und seine Schwächen: Eine Lektüre von Platons *Politeia*," *Deutsche Zeitschrift für Philosophie*, vol. 57, no. 1 (2009), pp. 15–36.
Two passages in chapter 2 appeared, respectively, under the titles "Hegels Missverständnis der ästhetischen Freiheit," in C. Menke & J. Rebentisch, eds, *Kreation und Depression: Freiheit im gegenwärtigen Kapitalismus* (Berlin: Kadmos, 2012), pp. 172–90, and "Die Moralität der Ironie: Hegel und die Moderne," in J. Rebentisch & D. Setton, eds, *Willkür, Freiheit und Gesetz II* (Berlin: August, 2011), pp. 141–81.

In addition, a number of passages from various chapters are based on already published studies:
Chapter 3 contains considerations first developed in the following essays: "Kunst – Leben – Liebe: Ästhetische Subjektivität nach Kierkegaard," in S. Gaensheimer & N. Schafhausen, eds, *Bühne des Lebens/Rhetorik des Gefühls* (Cologne: Walther König, 2006), pp. 15–32.
Chapter 6 contains considerations first developed in the following essays: "Theatrokratie und Theater: Literatur als Philosophie nach Benjamin und Brecht," in E. Horn, B. Menke, & C. Menke, eds, *Literatur als Philosophie – Philosophie als Literatur* (Munich: Fink, 2005), pp. 297–318; "Demokratie und Theater," in F. Ensslin, ed., *Spieltrieb: Was bringt die Klassik auf die Bühne?* (Berlin: Theater der Zeit, 2006), pp. 71–81.

Chapter 7 contains considerations first developed in the following essays: "Zur Unterscheidung von Politik und Polemischem" in H. Blumentrath, K. Rothe, S. Werkmeister, M. Wünsch, B. Wurm, eds, *Techniken der Übereinkunft: Zur Medialität des Politischen* (Berlin: Kadmos, 2009), pp. 99–112; "Erscheinen: Bruchstücke einer politischen Phänomenologie," in *Demonstrationen: Vom Werden normativer Ordnungen*, Frankfurter Kunstverein/Exzellenzcluster "Die Herausbildung normativer Ordnungen," Nuremberg; Verlag für moderne Kunst: "Masse – Volk – Multitude: Zur Quelle demokratischer Legitimität," *WestEnd*, vol. 8, no. 2 (2011), pp. 3–8.

Finally, sections of two chapters have been previously published in English under the following titles:

Chapter 2: "The Morality of Irony: Hegel and Modernity," *Symposium*, vol. 17, no. 1 (Spring 2013), pp. 100–30. Translated by Daniel Smyth.

Chapter 5: "Rousseau's Heterotopology of the Theatre," in E. Fischer-Lichte & B. Wihstutz, eds, *Performance and the Politics of Space* (New York: Routledge, 2013), pp. 142–65. Translated by Gerrit Jackson.

Introduction:

Aestheticization – An Apologia

From the perspective of practical philosophy, aestheticization is normally viewed as a worrisome phenomenon. The term stands for a crisis that affects our entire life-world. In this context aestheticization does not merely refer to some phenomenon on the surface of society. On the contrary, it is regarded as a crisis because it penetrates the deep structures of the way we understand both ourselves and our political culture. It replaces ethics with an individualistic aesthetic, and politics with the spectacular staging of politics. The concept of aestheticization therefore indicates a profound transformation of ethics and politics, one through which the latter becomes aesthetic and thus assumes an alienated form. Aestheticization means "basically that the non-aesthetic is made aesthetic or is grasped as being aesthetic."[1] First of all, this suggests a theory of difference. If the process of aestheticization is viewed as a transformation leading to a deformation of ethics and politics, then the aesthetic is presupposed as having nothing to do with the true essence of ethics and politics. Yet the fact that ethics and politics can be aestheticized at all indicates that there is indeed an internal connection between ethics, politics, and the dimension of the aesthetic. The critique of aestheticization, therefore, asserts not only a difference but also a connection. Here the aesthetic does not appear as an external threat to ethics and politics, but as a kind of deformation undermining them from within by hollowing out their normative substance. For critics of aestheticization, therefore, everything revolves around the delimitation and the exclusion of the aesthetic, and yet their discussion of the aesthetic takes place in the realm of the non-aesthetic. In this sense the critique of aestheticization documents the entry (or re-entry) of the distinction between aesthetic and non-aesthetic into the non-aesthetic. It does not address the aesthetic as a sphere that confronts the non-aesthetic from the outside, but as a dimension operative within the non-aesthetic. And once this dimension is recognized, it changes everything.

In the following I will address what is in fact at stake in the ethical-political rejection of the aesthetic. This also means recognizing that "the aesthetic" in no way indicates a unified phenomenon in the context of the respective discourse; instead, it functions as a general concept for a whole range of phenomena as diverse as pleasure, taste, irony, distance, mutability, cultural diversity or "colorfulness," staging [*Inszenierung*], rhetoric, and semblance. The purpose of this investigation is not to derive a consistent concept of the aesthetic from all this. Any attempt to do so would be questionable for two different reasons. First, given the ethical-political interest underlying the critique of aestheticization, one can and should not foreclose the possibility that the term "aesthetic" might in some cases only be used as a rhetorical tool for excluding certain elements from ethics and politics which are not aesthetic in the original sense of the term. Second, a one-sided discussion of what gets dismissed as aesthetic in the critical discourse on phenomena of aestheticization would not be sufficiently inclusive, despite the diversity of the topics addressed. Upon closer inspection, we can see that the critique of aestheticization in no way condemns all aesthetic practices. For precisely where it rejects clearly aesthetic phenomena such as the theater, it also defends other aesthetic practices seen as conforming to given conceptions of ethics and politics. The critique of aestheticization therefore clearly represents a specific intermingling of ethical, political, and aesthetic motifs. In order to analytically untie this knot, we do not need, at least not in the first instance, to discuss all the seemingly aesthetic phenomena addressed by the critique of aestheticization. Instead, we need to take up the ethical-political problems motivating this critique and explain the systematic context within which its various motifs appear. The following investigation will thus not primarily address aesthetic theory but practical philosophy. Its aim is to awaken skepticism about the one-sided, negative definition of the transformation of ethics and politics that goes by the name of aestheticization, and to explore its productive meaning for the understanding of both these spheres.[2] In this sense, the following is intended as an apologia for aestheticization – an apologia, that is, for the ethical-political right of the "aestheticizing" transformation of ethics and politics itself.

A systematic discussion of the problem of aestheticization is more important than ever, not least due to the current relevance and radiance of this concept in recent discussions on so-called postmodernism. The "aestheticization of the life-world" is one of the most prominent formulations employed over the last two to three decades in order to find a tangible concept to capture the visage of contemporary Western societies. It is associated with the claim that the typical member of such societies is a homo aestheticus for whom aesthetic criteria such as taste, pleasure, and shaping have become so decisive that their effects can be seen in nearly all spheres of life. Even two decades ago, this finding seemed so obvious that the philosophical discussion of the matter focused solely on how to evaluate this fundamental shift: One side saw the rising domination of simulacra, which degrade contents into mere images, actions into performances, and self-understandings into poses.[3] The other side defended a generalized constructivist relation to self and world, which manifests itself in the freedom to shape ever more spheres of life.[4] However, the philosophical debate over the status of a supposedly obvious societal development remained unfounded as long as it was still possible to question the actual scope of this development.[5] As a result, attempts to empirically substantiate the thesis of the aestheticization of the life-world quickly came in for criticism. For instance, Gerhard Schulze's thesis of an "experience society"[6] brought about by affluence was accused of falsely generalizing a phenomenon located in the more privileged part of society.[7] Today, the parameters of the debate seem to have shifted: A much more prominent role is played by studies that show that aesthetic motifs such as creativity, spontaneity, and originality are no longer a sign of a sphere of freedom lying beyond the necessities of social reproduction, but have become an important productive force in their own right within the capitalist economic system. According to this research, these motifs have turned into crucial social demands representing an increase of constraints rather than freedom.[8] In any case, sociology seems to have become the central location for serious debate on how to appropriately describe, explain, and evaluate the crucial position of aesthetically connoted criteria both for individuals and for the organization of society in Western democracies. Yet as relevant as these debates may be – and I will return to the current state of this debate at various points[9] – I believe that philosophy has been wrong to retreat from them. After all, the diagnosis of aestheticization implies an assumption about the genuine, undistorted essence of ethics and politics, which is not a mere empirical but also a systematic question. The specific approach of philosophy in the context of contemporary diagnoses, however, can only become fully visible once we turn away from the business of diagnosing the present and turn to the history of philosophy. For the concept of aestheticization was already established in the first half of the twentieth century, which makes it relevant not only for postmodernism, but also for the theory of modernity. In fact, the discussion of aestheticization goes back even further. Contrary to the impression raised by recent debates, therefore, aestheticization in no way represents a merely contemporary problem; and traditionally the concept is much more philosophical than is suggested by the largely (cultural) sociological character of the current discourse. In fact, the philosophical discussion of the challenges posed by certain aesthetic motifs for the understanding of ethics and politics even goes back to antiquity. The history of practical philosophy is a history of crisis-diagnoses which have sought to combat the invasion of the aesthetic and its disintegrating effects into the spheres of ethics and politics. This is true despite the fact that the concept of aestheticization was not always employed explicitly.

At first sight it may seem remarkable that the ethical-political critique of various figures of the aesthetic shows up at extremely significant points in the history of practical philosophy. This demonstrates that the problem of aestheticization is anything but a marginal problem which, in line with the currently typical subdivision of philosophy, could be banished into a separate sphere called aesthetics. Instead, the problem shows up in places where core concepts of practical philosophy themselves are at stake. Conversely, the significance of discussions on the aesthetic in the philosophical tradition reveals the systematic burden that the current aestheticization discourse must bear – at least, that is, when it takes itself seriously. Without a reflection on the long history of this discourse we will hardly be able to adequately bear the load. If we neglect to do so, the claim that the "aestheticization of the life-world" represents a new phenomenon and a new epoch will remain questionable. Without a detailed discussion of the problems that practical philosophy has historically ascribed to "the aesthetic," our judgment of current developments will be in danger of either merely carrying over old prejudices into the present, for example by criticizing a supposedly novel domination of simulacra, or we will end up becoming a part of an old problem rather than a part of the solution, for example by becoming proponents of a supposedly new, constructivist relation to ourselves and the world. Therefore, the postmodern philosophical debates on the suggestive formulation "aestheticization of the life-world" are also philosophically unfounded. In order to clarify the philosophical assumptions that at least indirectly influence these debates, we require a historical and systematic discussion of the history of the philosophical critique of aestheticization.

As I have already indicated, this history begins in antiquity, or more precisely, with Plato's critique of democratic culture in *The Republic*. Plato mistrusts the "colorful" plurality of life-forms in a democracy, as well as the "dazzling" democrats that have learned from (theater) poets that it is possible to adopt several roles in life. He even sees a major problem in the fair appearance of democratic culture and its privileged life-form. For according to Plato's diagnosis, the logic of appearances constitutes the essence of democracy itself: The ethical commitment to the good gets replaced by an aesthetic stylization of existence, while good government (i.e., government that is committed to the good) gets replaced by an uncontrolled spectacle that seduces the people. For Plato, this logic is a small, dangerously subtle step on the path from democracy to tyranny. What is astounding about this antique diagnosis is how familiar its central motifs are even today. Indeed, they were adopted in the philosophical discourse at the beginning of modernity (around 1800) and have continued to play an important role into the twentieth century and beyond. Along with the growing political importance of democracy, the influence of the critique of an aestheticized democratic culture established by Plato has grown as well, regardless of whether we are dealing with a fundamentally negative or positive stance toward democracy. But why does Plato, of all thinkers, prove to be the decisive source when it comes to the problems of modern democracy, or rather the problems associated with its aestheticized culture? After all, the model of democracy in antiquity cannot be applied to modern democracies; just as the antique arts, which Plato criticized for their subversive influence on morals, can scarcely be equated with modern art forms. Nevertheless, it is no accident that modern philosophical thought on the matter draws on the work of Plato.

Plato invented a type of critique which would become so crucial for modernity that, despite the obvious differences between antiquity and modernity, a good deal of conceptual effort has been undertaken in order to pick up on this type of critique. Plato connects his analysis of various forms of government with his investigation of – to put it in modern terms – forms of subjectivization. The connection between government and self-government takes on greater significance in modernity, even though the organization of the state is no longer regarded as mirroring the soul, as is suggested at several points in *The Republic*. However, if we take a closer look at Plato's account of the constellation of government and self-government, we will find it to be far more interesting and complex than what is suggested by the customary reading of his work. For there is in fact a third point in this constellation. Government and self-government are not merely similar to each other, they form in fact an analogous unity via their respective relation to a value that is central to both. In the case of democratic culture, this is the value of freedom. Unlike Plato's claim that the ideal state mirrors the soul, his thesis on the relationship between ethics and politics has remained crucial to the modern critique of aestheticization. The key to the modern debate on aestheticization is likewise the problem of freedom. If the diagnosis of aestheticization refers to democratic culture – sometimes more explicitly, sometimes less – then the freedom that defines this culture is the systematic problem with which it is both ethically and politically concerned. The concept of democratic freedom, therefore, not only refers to the kind of freedom which is realized in political institutions and procedures. Rather, in the context of the critique of aestheticization, democratic freedom in this political sense is grasped as a culture of freedom that concerns the conduct of life as a whole. The question at hand is how to theoretically grasp what it means to be a free subject, and in which societal form this freedom can best be realized. In the framework established by the problem of freedom, there is a close connection between the topics of the subject and the state, self-government and government, ethics and politics.

The very fact that such a historically influential philosophical discourse is concerned with the critique of an aestheticization of the democratic culture of freedom already indicates that addressing this discourse will allow us to gain insights into the constitution and the tensions of democratic freedom usually overlooked or brushed aside by the justifications of democratic freedom, which are generally blind to the dimension of the aesthetic. But such tensions are also overlooked by republican thought in the tradition of Friedrich Schiller, which celebrates the aesthetic as a figure of unity and reconciliation both in an ethical and a political sense.[10] As this book will show, it is precisely in their rejection of – or skepticism about – the close relation between the culture of freedom and the problem of its aestheticization that critics of aestheticization display a very precise sense of the risk and the challenges of such a culture, which makes their work conceptually fruitful for an apologia for aestheticization. In other words, the critique of aestheticization proves to be a remarkably productive resource for the project of redefining the meaning of aestheticization for the ethical-political understanding of the democratic culture of freedom. This is the standard by which any attempt at a positive account of the changes in the understanding of ethics and politics that go by the name of aestheticization will have to measure itself. To the extent that the ethical-political legitimacy of an "aestheticizing" transformation of ethics and politics can be defended within the framework of the problem of freedom, it will be necessary to demonstrate this by means of a critique of the critique of aestheticization. This entails the examination of both the way the critique operates as well as of its prerequisites. In each case we will have to ask, what is rejected as an aestheticization of the understanding of freedom for ethical and political reasons, and is the rejection plausible? Which understanding of freedom is ethically and politically defended, and is this understanding immune to critique?

Regardless of whether the critique of aestheticization associates the problem of "aestheticized culture" with democracy itself, thus fundamentally rejecting the latter, or whether aestheticized culture is viewed as a danger to which democracy needs to immunize itself – in both cases the point of dispute lies in the understanding of freedom that is associated with aesthetic motifs. What is called the aesthetic is usually a form of freedom that contradicts social practices, their normative orders, and the corresponding identities or roles. It does so by giving private motives – moods, pleasure, taste – such clear priority over conformity to a given social order that they come to dominate the way that individuals determine their own lives. The understanding of freedom around which the debate on aestheticization revolves questions the constitutive connection between the social and the individual good – the claim that the latter can only exist in and through participation in the former. Critics of aestheticization fear that a privatistic model of freedom, if it succeeds in establishing itself in society, will have a disintegrating effect on the political community. At best, social bonds will be replaced by "aesthetic" relations; and where there are no longer any social bonds, the staging of community becomes a politically decisive force. Yet the staging of community, as critics of aestheticization go on to argue, does not create community. On the contrary, not only does it barely conceal the fact that it is only necessary because the collective has been undermined from within by the aesthetic self-understandings of its (non-)members, but it is only capable of producing a community to the degree that it simultaneously establishes a divide between those who produce the community and those who – again in the form of moods, pleasure, and taste – experience it. The political community thus disintegrates into a spectacle and an audience.

Because of aestheticization's supposedly disintegrating effects, the aesthetic form of freedom has been denounced as "degenerate freedom" (Plato) or as "caprice" or "arbitrariness" [*Willkürfreiheit*] (Hegel). In order to dispel the danger that aesthetic freedom poses for the political community, critics of aestheticization all seek to show that this form of freedom represents a self-misunderstanding. On this view, aesthetic freedom not only represents a "degenerate" form of freedom from the perspective of the political community that needs to be protected from its effects. In order to really strike at the corresponding understanding of freedom, it must also prove to be deficient in places where we would not usually seek out its effects on the community, i.e., in the life of individuals. According to critics of aestheticization, it is already at this level that the freedom claimed by the individual vis-à-vis the social order turns into unfreedom. This must be proven, therefore, with respect to the dazzling types, those who have "mastered the art of living" [*Lebenskünstler*]. If it can be shown that the incongruence between individual and social good, which becomes visible in aesthetic existence, leads to unfreedom, then the critics of aestheticization will also have shown why the further effects of this life-form on the community must be combated. The effort to preserve the social order is then not for the sake of the order, but for the sake of the freedom of its members.

In this history of the philosophical critique of aestheticization, very different conceptual presuppositions have been employed in order to deliver this proof. And it is here that the gap between modernity and antiquity also becomes particularly visible. Whereas Plato employs a metaphysical conception of the good, Hegel points to the constitutive role of social practices for individual freedom. Therefore, Plato formulates his critique in the name of a conception of the good that is as problematic as it is metaphysical, and according to which there is an objective, individual, and social good, making any actions that contradict this good a form of alienation from the good. However, since Hegel's objection to the romantic ironist, this critique has taken the shape of a reference to the constitutive role of social practices for the unfolding of individual freedom. Without question, this last remark is still justified today. It captures extreme constructivist positions that reduce the possibility for shaping one's own life to a question of individual ethics,[11] as well as all those who argue that Foucault's demand "not to be governed like that"[12] refers to the entirety of life – just as if a life beyond all social determination were desirable or even possible. Not only is everybody always involved in social practices, any understanding of the self requires social recognition in order to be realized.[13] But this can only count as an objection to all the dazzling figures that stand at the center of the critique of aestheticization if their lives necessarily entail a repression of the constitutive role that the social world plays in the self-understanding of the individual. That, of course, can be disputed.

As I will show in the following, by associating "aesthetic" freedom with freedom from the social *in toto*, the critique of aestheticization conceals another, more productive interpretation: The distance from the social – as is often made especially visible by the self-transformations undergone by *Lebenskünstler* contrary to the expectations of society – does not necessarily entail a kind of distance from all social determinacy that is as abstract as it is imaginary. We could also grasp this distance in a different way: not as a *model* for the life of the subject, but as a productive *element* of it. Referring to aesthetic existence, to dazzling life-forms, does not mean demonstrating and defending abstract freedom from the social, but rather the mutability of the social. The aestheticization of freedom would then no longer stand for the misunderstanding of a kind of freedom *from* the social in a kind of non-dialectic opposition to freedom *in* the social. Rather, it would express the tension at the heart of every individual's life. Whoever lives within the misunderstanding of solipsistic self-production is just as unfree as those who have never had the experience of distance from themselves, their social roles, and the corresponding expectations. It is only possible to mediate between both sides of this tense relationship if we grasp them as elements in a process in which we can change both ourselves and the social practices of which we are a part. As will be shown in more detail, this mediation demands an art of freedom, which goes beyond a mere craft [*Handwerk*],[14] and thus beyond the idea that self-determination is to be conceived as a kind of skill we can first learn and then master.[15] For the subject performing such an art must always call itself into question in the course of this process. The changes in the self are not brought about by a meta-subject standing above the subject's own social identity. Instead, it is rooted in the immediate experience of self-difference, which compels the subject to reconceive of itself, its self-understanding, and the meaning of its subjectivity from a distance.

The dialectic determination of freedom in the sense of an antagonism at work in the heart of this concept, which connects the capacity for subjective self-determination with an aspect that has "not yet been subjected to the centralizing authority of the consciousness,"[16] does not imply abandoning the normativity that necessarily characterizes ethics and politics. On the contrary, it is only because individuals in their lived interaction with the world can end up in a relation of difference to themselves, and thus also to their roles as participants in social practices, that the normative question about the individual and social good can be raised at all. The experience of such difference, in other words, is a necessary condition for the self-determined appropriation or transformation of the social practices by which we are always already determined. Recognizing the possibility of such questioning as a good in itself, and thus also the possibility of changing given determinations of the good, means giving this possibility priority over every substantive determination of the good.

The form of government that has integrated the possibility of questioning given determinations of the good into the concept of the good itself is – as Plato clearly recognized – democracy. It is the only form of government in which it is allowed to publicly criticize everything, to publicly call everything into question – including the shape of democracy itself. Because it remains open, despite all the risk involved, to re-determinations of the good, and thus to the possibility of a more just order, democracy remains – to cite Jacques Derrida's now famous formulation – "to come."[17] Yet this is not meant, as Derrida is often misunderstood, as an eternal suspension until the arrival of a coming messiah of democracy. On the contrary, our determinations of the good are all that we have for realizing our freedom in the here and now. Democratic openness to future events does not mean openness for the sake of openness; nor is this a fundamental criticism of normative determinations in general. Rather, it emphasizes the possibility of their historical revision. For precisely this reason, democracy, to cite a formulation of the French theorist of democracy Claude Lefort, is the *"historical society par excellence."*[18] We could also say that the democratic culture of freedom is moved both politically and ethically by that dialectic at the core of the concept of freedom defended here. The point of defending the motifs of freedom that have been hastily rejected or condemned in advance by critics of aestheticization does not, therefore, merely mean defending an "aesthetic culture" that is somehow desirable for democracies, as if this were some mere cultural addition. What is at stake is nothing less than the understanding of the ethical-political structures of freedom in general.

Yet due to its insight into the historicity of the good, democracy also has an internal connection to what has been criticized as the "aestheticization of the political." We can argue plausibly that participants in social practices are always potential non-participants, and thus also that members of society are potential non-members, such that the meaning of social practices can be called into question at any time. If this is the case, then the immediate result will be a critique of pre-political conceptions of the order and unity of the political collective. Neither the order nor the unity of the community can merely be presupposed, rather its character is revealed to be a political determination. Furthermore, this means that the unity of the community, along with the order within which it is grasped, must be politically created, produced, and staged. Because democracy knows neither order nor unity beyond political representation, it not only stands in clear opposition to Plato's anti-democratic conception of the natural political order. Instead, it also concerns the idea of collective self-government, an idea that is central to the modern understanding of democracy – and this has far-reaching consequences. For if it is true that the self of collective self-government cannot be assumed to be a unified will, but must first be brought forth by political representation, then this means that the *demos* of democracy can never exist beyond the separation thereby established between representatives and the represented, producers and recipients, the rulers and the ruled. The *demos* can therefore never exist outside relations of power and domination; it never exists as such. At the same time, however, this is precisely the way that democracy preserves its openness to the future. For the democratic answer to the problem of sovereign power does not consist in concealing the latter, but in exhibiting it and thus exposing it to an examination of its legitimacy. This is the whole point of a democratically understood "aestheticization of the political." On the democratic political stage, the representatives of the *demos* must justify themselves before those whose will they represent; they must face a heterogeneous audience whose members always potentially have or develop alternative conceptions of the democratic general will, which can ultimately be asserted publicly as a (countervailing) power in opposition to the currently prevailing conception.

Of course, a defense of the aesthetic – in this context it would be more specific to say the "theatrical" – dimensions of democratic politics faces a particularly daunting challenge posed by those critics of aestheticization who are resolute defenders of democracy. Indeed, the issue of aestheticization and democracy has been historically addressed from very different perspectives on democracy, which reveals a further distinction between the discourse in antiquity and modernity: For Plato the democratization and aestheticization or theatricalization of the culture represent one and the same process, whereas the modern theory of democracy, at least in the Rousseauian tradition, is guided by the opposite intuition, seeing aestheticization or theatricalization as a perversion of democratic culture, and thus as a threat of decline against which democracy must be defended. The surprising similarity between the critical motifs found in Rousseau's defense and Plato's critique of democracy is, however, highly informative. It shows us the anti-democratic features of Rousseau's image of the democratic community and thus plays into the hands of an argumentation that defends the dimensions of the aesthetic – with and against Plato – as a constitutive element of democratic life.

If we are to defend the aestheticization of the democratic culture of freedom both ethically and politically, we cannot merely impose this defense on the anti-aestheticization discourse from the outside; rather we must demonstrate the implications of this critique by means of a critique of the critique of aestheticization. The discussion of this critique is relevant not only because it points out the connection between ethical, political, and aesthetic motifs in the discussion of the understanding of democratic freedom, but also because it addresses a whole series of (partially related) problems: weakness of will, evil, indifference, forgetfulness-of-self, reification (of the other and of the world), opportunism, charismatic rule. These are all problems that an apologia for aestheticization must address if it does not want to become yet another symptom of the ethical-political problem diagnosed by critics of aestheticization. The discussion of the critique of aestheticization not only gives depth and contours to a corresponding concept of freedom, it moves us to develop such a concept in the first place. For the rejection of aestheticization, as I will demonstrate with reference to selected historical examples from the tradition of this critique, reveals deficits that can only be removed by a dialectic concept of freedom.

We now have a rough idea of the road map for the following chapters. In part I, I will reconstruct and critique the motifs of Plato's critique of aestheticization and democracy often employed by modern critics of aestheticization. The subsequent parts address the ways in which the modern discourse has responded to Plato and the problems he raised. On the basis of the connection between ethical and political arguments reconstructed in part I, part II will present the modern responses, not as they arise chronologically, but rather how they correspond to the logic of Plato's system. Thus I will first address the question of what it means to live a life in freedom before turning to the concept of democracy essentially linked to this ethical problem. This connection has remained crucial for modern critiques of aestheticization as well, though it has been accentuated in different ways, emphasizing either a theory of subjective freedom or of democracy. For this reason, part II will initially address those modern critiques of aestheticization that depart from the problem of subjective freedom. Here the critique of romanticism proves particularly relevant, for various motifs found in the Platonic critique of the aesthetic life-form and its underlying understanding of freedom emerge in altered form in the critique of the romantic ironist. Even at this early stage – in the discussion of the relation between irony and ethical life (Hegel), as well as between irony and individual (Kierkegaard) or political (Carl Schmitt) sovereignty – numerous links to the issue of democracy and democratic political culture emerge. The latter stand at the center of the discussion in part III, though not without reference to the theory of freedom. One of the aims here will be to give a more precise definition – with regard to the politics of representation – of the "aestheticized" notion of democratic culture defended in this book and to distinguish it from other constellations of aesthetics, ethics, and politics. In this context we will have to discuss Rousseau's positive vision of the Republican festival, which he opposes to the theatricalization or the aestheticization of the political, as well as the relation between Walter Benjamin's famous critique of the "aestheticizing of politics, as practiced by fascism" and the general line of argumentation found in the tradition of the critique of aestheticization. In conclusion, I will take a look ahead and distinguish the previously developed understanding of democratic culture from a contrary tendency that currently goes by the name of "post-democracy."

However, the close referential connection between ethical and political motifs we find in all three parts indicates that the structure of the book, contrary to Plato's system, is merely for heuristic reasons. For the defense of the "aestheticizing" transformation of ethics and politics also concerns the relation between the two. Whereas Plato gives priority to ethics over politics – the arrangement of the political order that is to ensure a good life for all follows from the knowledge of what suits the individual – the order of reasons now enters into a different constellation. The point is not merely to stand this hierarchy on its head, not to put politics before ethics, but to dissolve the hierarchy of ethics and politics from the perspective of a dialectic of freedom that penetrates both spheres alike, though each in a different way.

PART I

An Antique Diagnosis of a Crisis

1

The Provocative Beauty of Democracy: Plato

For Plato, as for all classical philosophers, "politeia" does not so much characterize a community's constitution as it does its way of life. This way of life, however, is said to depend on what counts as its highest good.[1] According to the classics, this is what ties together the different perspectives of ethics and politics. Plato claims that in a democracy with its corresponding way of life or – as we would call it today – culture, this supreme good bears the name of "freedom." Therefore, the true object of Plato's reflections on democracy, for which he uses Socrates[2] as his mouthpiece in Book Eight of *The Republic*,[3] is the idea of freedom that is constitutive of democratic culture. Although – as Plato has Socrates observe coolly – some might regard democracy as especially colorful and perhaps even as the "fairest regime" (Rep 557c) given that it allows for ethical diversity and the freedom to choose one's own way of life, it is nevertheless second bottom in Plato's hierarchy of forms of government, just above tyranny. For Plato, democracy's fair appearance is misleading, and he argues that the democratic "thirst for freedom" (Rep 562c) necessarily leads to unfreedom. It privileges the desires, thereby undermining rational judgment, destabilizing the will, and producing individuals who are weak in every respect – even politically. Plato condemns the man who is "well disposed toward the multitude" (558c) as a man of dazzling weakness and the colorful diversity of democratic culture as a sure sign of its decline. Democratic aestheticization is consequently a harbinger of tyranny.

This is not a diagnosis to which we will readily agree. However, even in the context of an apologia for democracy and its beauty, we are well advised to examine the concept of democratic freedom in the contrasting light of a radically opposed position. For it is often the case that those who seek to banish a concept from our practical and theoretical consciousness have a particularly strong sense of its implications.

1. Freedom and Indeterminacy

Curiously enough, Plato's investigation of democracy focuses on freedom rather than equality, though he does not provide any further justification for doing so. Instead he has Socrates quote democrats' self-understanding, i.e. the widespread opinion that freedom constitutes democracy's highest good (Rep 557b and Rep 562b). He begins his discussion with an empirical observation of the self-understanding of democratic culture that is implicit in democratic discourse. He views the democratic principle of equality as a mere corollary of *exousia*, i.e. democratically granted freedom, according to which one has the "licence...to do whatever one wants" (Rep 557b). This license is granted to all persons regardless of their status or birth, to "equals and unequals alike" (Rep 558c). Democratic equality has no substance and is not founded on similarities; it is entirely formal, applying to anyone and everyone living in freedom. Yet Plato's first objection concerns the implication that anybody can invoke the principle of democracy in order to speak in its name. After all, *exousia* implies the permission to speak freely, even for those who seek to persuade and seduce the masses.[4] This necessarily creates an opening that can be exploited by charismatic figures who equate their own will with that of the democratic community as a whole, thereby presuming to have authority and potentially subverting the dominant authorities. In a democracy, as Plato has Socrates explain, nothing is obligatory. The democratic idea of freedom compels nobody to exercise authority or to submit to it against their will. People need not fight in wartime, and they may wage a private war in peacetime. They need not be forbidden from holding political or judicial office (Rep 557e). In a democracy, even citizens punished with death or exile can be pardoned (Rep 558a). In principle, anyone who wishes to found a state can simply pick and choose a constitution at will, as if they were in a "bazaar" (*pantopolion*). Given the freedom (*exousia*) it allows, democracy can entail "all species of regimes" (Rep 557d).

It is striking how topical this classical diagnosis remains even – or perhaps especially – today.[5] Hardly any state today would not claim to be democratic. The modern age has not only witnessed constitutional monarchies and parliamentary, presidential, liberal, and welfare-state democracies, but also people's democracies in the Soviet Union or in China, as well as various military dictatorships which have adorned themselves with the title of democracy. Here we might think of Franco's so-called organic democracy in Spain or Trujillo's "Neo-Democracy" in the Dominican Republic. "Democracy" apparently specifies neither a particular form of government nor a particular kind of constitution, rather the term is characterized by its very indeterminacy. This is not the result of some theoretical incapacity; the indeterminacy of democracy, i.e. its dependence on performative and formative acts, must be grasped as one of its essential features. Doing so has always been one of the major challenges facing any theory of democracy.

According to Plato, the indeterminacy of democracy is originally due to *exousia*, i.e. the democratic freedom to do as one wishes. The term goes back to the impersonal expression *exesti* ("it is permitted, lawful") and associates freedom with opportunities or freedom of action. This meaning bears an astounding resemblance to our contemporary, liberal idea of negative freedom, though the modern concept of subjective rights, which associates the liberal concept of negative freedom with the protection of individual ways of life from external threats, is foreign to the concept of *exousia*.[6] Aside from this difference, both the political discourse of antiquity and the liberal concept of negative freedom raise the same difficult question: What is the scope of a concept of freedom founded on the freedom to act as one pleases?[7] Even the neutral meaning of *exousia* can potentially be abused and turned into *hubris*, licentiousness, recklessness, arrogance; in short, transgressions cannot be excluded from its conceptual horizon. According to Plato, this is precisely what makes *exousia* problematic not only for the community as a whole, but also for the lives of individuals within that community.

At the level of the community, which, because of its democratic foundations, cannot defend itself from power-hungry rogues, "an extreme of liberty" (Rep 564a) within democratic *exousia* will lead at some point to "an extreme of subjection," i.e. tyranny (ibid.). Moreover, and more importantly for our purposes, Plato cautions that we should distrust the fair appearance of democratic culture even before it turns into tyranny. He has Socrates claim that, like a "cloak (*himation*) decorated in all hues," democratic culture is "decorated with all dispositions" and that many "would judge this the fairest of regimes," just as would "boys and women looking at many-colored things." But unlike women and children, the philosopher cannot be content to take pleasure in the colorful diversity of a culture in which everybody lives as they please. The task of the philosopher is instead to see through the fair appearance of the democratic patchwork. Beneath this fair appearance, the philosopher finds nothing of substance, and this constitutes democracy's most severe flaw. Not only is a democratic constitution a mere cloak (or disguise) that can be tailored at will, the way of life privileged by democratic society essentially lacks any substance. Both its form of government and its way of life can take on the most diverse appearances. At the level of democratic culture, those who can easily assume different identities most clearly embody the democratic idea of freedom. Democratic "man" is characterized by his "versatility," and "the attractiveness of his combination of a wide variety of characteristics" matches "the variety of the democratic society. It's a life which many men and women would envy, it contains patterns of so many constitutions and ways of life" (Rep 561e).

In this sense as well, Plato's diagnosis is astoundingly topical. The presence of those who have mastered the art of living (*Lebenskünstler*), as well as the general recognition their experimental lifestyles enjoy, count as the hallmark of modern Western democracies.[8] Similar to the problem of democratic government, Plato sees the major problem of democratic self-government in the indeterminacy that is only partially cloaked by its various manifestations. In both cases he sees the source of this problem in an exaggerated notion of freedom, which dominates both government and self-government and thus unifies the dimensions of ethics and politics in the democratic way of life. It is only logical, therefore, that Plato should base his critique of democracy on this understanding of freedom.

The ethical problem of self-government is especially significant in this connection. If the essence of a society is defined by what is considered its highest good, then the way of life that embodies this good most completely will be its most definitive way of life. A critique of democracy must show that its dominant form of life does not live up to the ideal of a truly good life. In other words, it will have to demonstrate that this form of life does not fulfill its claim to enable freedom. Democratic freedom must be proven deficient with regard to the very masters of the art of living who embody this freedom most completely. Therefore, a defense of democracy, its understanding of freedom, and the diversity of its culture must begin by addressing this argument. The point is not merely to defend democrats' propensity for experimentation and their interest in innovation against the conservative mindset of the traditionalists, as has so often been done. Instead, it is a matter of finding the proper understanding of freedom in the first place.

2. The Slavery of the Tyrant

In an initial, preparatory step, the critical thrust of Plato's complex objection to the democratic form of life becomes especially apparent when he seeks to demonstrate the inner connection between democracy and its opposite, tyranny. On the level of self-government, just as on the level of government, the figure of the tyrant is paradigmatic of that unfreedom to which democratic freedom's own lack of restraint must ultimately lead. Although a tyrant never imposes restrictions upon himself and thus represents an extreme case of a person who does whatever he wants, Plato argues that he cannot be called "free." The tyrant's incapacity for moderation and restraint instead makes him a slave to his own desires. A life determined exclusively by desires therefore depends on things to whose existence and stimuli we react in a merely passive way; it focuses solely on individual things, rather than on the principles that transcend these individual impressions. This is a life that is necessarily unstable. At best it follows temporary plans in the service of desires produced by incidental stimuli in the world. A person who merely follows his momentary desires is not "his own master"; due to his weakness he is hardly distinguishable from what Plato has Socrates derogatorily call "women and slaves" (Rep 431b, c).

Because desire can assume very different forms, those who allow themselves to be driven by this "multiform creature" (Rep 590a) have not only lost control *over* themselves, but they have also lost themselves entirely. This claim assumes, of course, that our notion of the self entails a certain continuity of orientations and thus a considered will; as a will which is essential for our self-understanding, it reaches beyond our situational will, which merely aims to satisfy momentary desires.[9] Because the tyrant confuses freedom with the satisfaction of momentary desires, he wallows in the "shallow present"[10] of immediate desires and is powerless to resist the influences that determine him. Although Plato does not doubt that the tyrant is capable of rational thought, he views the latter as being restricted to the strategic aim of best satisfying the desires that have been awakened within him. In Plato's eyes these considerations never concern the existential question of whether we should wish to have these desires in the first place. According to Plato's influential account, the tyrant lacks the elementary ability to judge his own intentions; he can neither affirm nor suppress them. He can neither give direction to his wants nor assert control over his own will. And yet because it is only under this condition that we can speak of free will at all, the tyrant proves to be unfree in the very moment he believes he has attained the summit of freedom. A number of contemporary theories of free will rightly claim that a life deprived of any anchoring in the rational beliefs according to which we judge our own intentions necessarily represents a kind of loss of self [*Selbstvergessenheit*]: a life in which we are merely pushed along by what is awakened inside of us by diverse, unfiltered impressions.[11] The only way we could regard ourselves as the "subject" of such a life is as an *object* of domination, as slaves to our uncontrolled and random desires. Indeed, an egomaniacal drive to satisfy our momentary desires has little to do with self-determination.

We can agree with Plato that a life – inasmuch as we can conceive of it as anything other than a thought experiment – determined entirely by the particularity of incidental stimuli, without any grounding in a general principle that transcends these individual impressions, fails to fulfill the condition of free will. But how should we conceive of such a grounding in a general principle? According to Plato, the continuity of the orientations that give contour to our individual personalities should be based on objective knowledge, which would make this continuity immune to situational temptations and thus to the possibility that we might betray our own beliefs. So it is only logical that in *The Republic* the tyrannical character's lack of moderation is largely seen to be the result of poor education, and hence rooted primarily in a lack of discipline. He is unaware of what is truly good (for him), and his temperament does not allow him to make any effort to educate himself. Plato maintains that whoever attains knowledge of what is truly good can no longer be shaken in his convictions. Because self-determination requires that we somehow acquire knowledge of what is objectively good, Plato sees reason as representing the principle of autonomy vis-à-vis the heteronomy of desire; therefore, it also represents a kind of freedom that can be equated with personal sovereignty.

However, the opposition Plato asserts between freedom and dependence is questionable, as is the manner in which he identifies freedom with the unshakeable stability of the will. This excludes the possibility that even our well-considered beliefs can be undermined by other persons and other events, which occasionally cause us to revise our beliefs. Indeed, Plato's conception of freedom is irreconcilable with a notion of freedom that accounts for the productive influence of those moments in which we are unexpectedly determined by outside influences. He ignores the possibility that we sometimes recognize what is best – for us – only in moments of supposed weakness, thus abandoning our previous beliefs and opening ourselves to an experience that constitutes the beginning of a different understanding of, and relationship to, ourselves.[12] Plato cannot conceive of a situation in which our weaknesses can prove to be our strengths and vice versa; there can be no such revisions for those who know what is truly good. Any fundamental changes must be considered a sign of weakness.

3. The Unstable Democrat

This perspective is what defines Plato's judgment of the democrat. Plato regards the possibility of viewing ourselves differently in the light of new influences as the essence of the democratic way of life. Accordingly, he criticizes democratic *exousia*, in contrast to its tyrannical variety, not merely as a lack of discipline, but as an equally dubious, arbitrary form of self-interpretation. Just as democracy is not yet tyranny (it merely makes tyranny possible), a democrat is not identical to a tyrant. Unlike the excessive tyrant, democrats are capable of moderation, though this is not the sole principle that defines them. According to Plato, democrats are somewhat lax when it comes to knowing what is good for them; they do not suffer from a fundamental lack of restraint, but from a lack of consistency. Plato thus seems to view the democratic man as suffering from weakness of will (*akrasia*). But this would also mean that Plato acknowledges a phenomenon in *The Republic* that he still denies in *Protagoras*, where he rejects the notion that a person who knows what is best for himself can have any motive for not doing what is good. "This inferiority of a man to himself is merely ignorance, as the superiority of a man to himself is wisdom."[13] What might appear at first sight to be a contradiction turns out to be quite consistent. Whereas the argumentation in *Protagoras* assumes that a person's rational faculties have been fully developed, the argumentation in *The Republic*, which we can regard as a piece of educational literature, begins with a scenario in which this condition has not yet been fulfilled.

Plato leaves no doubt that when the future democrat receives a lesson in thriftiness, though not "meanness" (Rep 572c) from his oligarchic father, then this is hardly more than a weak reflection of an aristocratic emphasis on reason and truthfulness. Plato therefore does not contradict his claim in the *Protagoras* that those who are aware of what is truly good can no longer be swayed. But by assuming that reason plays only a marginal role in the democrat's education, Plato can now account for the fact that people can willingly act contrary to their own rational beliefs, a phenomenon he largely ignored in the *Protagoras*. Plato therefore no longer sees weakness of will as the result of a lack of knowledge, but as a conflict between reason and desire. If education cannot manage to produce harmony between the various parts of the soul, thus failing to establish a hierarchy under the rule of reason, then these parts will remain in constant conflict with each other. If reason loses out in this struggle, a person will act contrary to his own better knowledge.[14]

And that, according to Plato, is the democrat's problem. Although he has been instilled with the values of temperance and economy, he comes under the influence of wasteful, villainous, and thus potentially tyrannical individuals – Plato calls them "winged drones" – who squander their wealth. But unlike an oligarch, these individuals do not fulfill any function in the state. Both of these influences struggle to gain control of the democrat's soul: The antagonistic principles of reason (though only poorly developed in the democrat as a result of his being brought up on thriftiness) and desire battle it out on a level playing field, and sometimes the one, sometimes the other prevails (cf. Rep 559d–560b). Plato thus characterizes the democrat as representing the indifferent principle of equality, and his own soul characterizes the principle of democracy. Decisions based on reason carry no more weight than those based on desire, which implies that reason and passion cannot be strictly distinguished and set in abstract opposition to each other. Even actions based on desire can be founded on reasons, yet the latter are related to a certain situation and conflict with a consideration of reasons that goes beyond the immediacy of the situation – a consideration that stands in the background of our (reasoned) beliefs. At any rate, the democrat occasionally allows the situational reasons of desire to triumph over more comprehensive, rational reasons. The democrat's character is neither truly soberminded nor entirely unrestrained, rather he "effected what he thought was a very reasonable compromise between the competing attractions of the two lives" (Rep 572c).

For Plato, however, this does not make the democrat a well-balanced character, but rather an utterly unstable individual, shifting back and forth between different ways of life depending on the situation, similar to a tyrant. But unlike the tyrant, who is merely driven by his momentary desires, the democrat does not lack convictions that transcend a given situation and enable him to judge his own desires. Yet the very fact that he can be affected by stimuli that conflict with his convictions implies the willingness to relativize and perhaps even revise these convictions. Unlike the tyrant, who refuses to justify his various actions, the Platonic democrat continues to interpret his own unstable behavior. Because of the specific constellation of desire and reason in his soul, he must not only bring various principles to bear depending on the situation, but also new interpretations of his own self. What results is an image of the democrat as an equally colorful and fickle character. What makes him so seductive is not – as Derrida suggests in his reading of *The Republic*[15] – the charismatic virility typical of roguish or tyrannical characters who are driven by their desires. The democrat's seductiveness instead lies in his ability to transform himself, entirely outstripping the multiform nature of the desires that toss about the impulsive, tyrannical character. The democrat has a far broader palette of possibilities at his disposal: excess and asceticism, laziness and ambition, extravagance and economy.

> [He] lives from day to day, indulging the pleasure of the moment. One day it's wine, women and song, the next water to drink and a strict diet; one day it's hard physical training, the next indolence and careless ease, and then a period of philosophic study. Often he takes to politics and keeps jumping to his feet and saying or doing whatever comes into his head. Sometimes all his ambitions and efforts are military, sometimes they are all directed to success in business. There's no order or restraint in his life, and he reckons his way of living is pleasant, free and happy, and sticks to it through thick and thin. (Rep 561c,d)

4. Clear-sighted, Processual, and Totalized Weakness of Will

What is remarkable about Plato's image of democrats is their lack of the contrition that usually follows when the will is weak and our actions contradict our better judgment. Plato's democrat does not appear to show the remorse typical of those weak-willed individuals who return to their guiding principles after temporary lapses of self-restraint. While a person with a weak will allows himself to be temporarily overwhelmed by desire (and by the reasons for fulfilling them at that very moment) without abandoning his basic convictions, democrats appear to entirely ignore their convictions. This is not a mere temporary deviation from one's self-understanding, but an implicit reinterpretation of it in the light of temporarily prevailing desires. To describe the kind of weakness of will expressed by inconsistent wanting rather than uncontrolled acting, Martin Seel has proposed the term "processual *akrasia*": "The conflict that causes us to be weak is not a conflict between what I *actually* want and what I want *now*, but between what I want inside and outside the situation in which I deviate from my original intentions. It is a collision between conflicting *understandings* of myself."[16]

But even in the second case, we can only speak of weakness of will if I remain unswayed in my basic convictions, even though my temporary self-understanding may conflict with my actual self-understanding. In moments of weakness, I am mistaken about myself: When faced with a temptation, I construct a new understanding of myself that is better suited to the situation at hand; but by doing so, I am mistaken about what I actually want, and thus about who I actually am.[17] For this reason I am not aware of any weakness when I act, which distinguishes processual *akrasia* from cases in which I know my actions are not good for me, e.g., smoking a second pack of cigarettes a day. But even in cases of processual *akrasia*, I feel remorse once I have realized that I have been weak and have fooled myself into thinking otherwise. My hedonistic self-image from last night may appear quite inappropriate the next morning once I am confronted with my promise to others, and especially to myself, to assume certain responsibilities. Whereas in the case of clear-sighted *akrasia* the subject comes into conflict with himself in the very moment of his weakness, in the case of processual *akrasia* this conflict is temporally extended and in a certain sense de-dramatized: The morning after I am no longer the person I was the night before.

In spite of this distinction we should not lose sight of the commonalities between both varieties of weakness of will. First, even clear-sighted *akrasia* can be considered a case of competing relations-to-self. The unrestrained actions in which I deviate from my guiding principles manifest a side of myself that is irreconcilable with my other convictions. In other words, even in the case of clear-sighted *akrasia*, I experience at least a minimal divide within myself. Second, even processual *akrasia* points to a conflict reminiscent of clear-sighted *akrasia*. In fact, the "akrasian" conflict – acting against our better knowledge – is only temporarily shifted into the theoretical sphere. After all, self-deception can refer to the way I ignore my own convictions and cling to a contrary belief.[18] As long as I do so, there is no conflict between the akrasian action and my actual convictions. I only recognize the conflict once I dissolve the self-deception. Clear-sighted and processual *akrasia* are not fundamentally distinct;[19] rather, they represent two manifestations of a conflict that points to a divide, however minimal, within the self. Whereas the conflictual nature of the conflict may be more pronounced in the case of clear-sighted *akrasia*, the case of processual *akrasia* underscores the essence of this conflict in a more or less dramatic form: a rivalry between incompatible self-understandings.

Plato's democrat, however, seems strangely unaffected by any such conflicts. He does not feel the remorse that, in the case of processual *akrasia*, ultimately reveals an already latent conflict – obscured by our self-deception – between our true and our akrasian self-image. Although even Plato states that the democrat's intoxication is followed by a period of asceticism, he does not claim that the ascetic self-image is the normal self-image to which his intoxication is a mere exception. The democrat does not merely abandon his changing self-interpretations in the light of his prevailing self-image; rather, he only exists in and through his changing self-interpretations. Like a chameleon, he is constantly in flux. If we can speak of processual *akrasia* at all in this case, we will immediately have to concede that democrats totalize this *akrasia* to a degree that makes it questionable whether their acts can still be considered cases of *akrasia* at all. The democrat does not seem to be adequately characterized as suffering from weakness of will, which is perhaps the reason why the problem of a weak will is hardly ever discussed in connection with democratic culture. Because flexible adaptation to constantly shifting circumstances has become the norm in developed Western societies, we can hardly regard deviations from our convictions, self-revision, and self-transformation as signs of weakness. Unlike opportunism or apathy, we do not generally regard weakness of will as a characteristic pathology of democratic societies. And there is a significant difference between these phenomena and weakness of will: Whereas the latter presupposes a will that can be weak in a given situation, opportunism and apathy refer to problems affecting will-formation itself.[20]

This is where Plato seems to locate the problem of the democrat. The latter does not seem to have any decisive will that could become weak in a given situation; he does not seem to have any real convictions that he could cling to in the face of temptation and thus prove the strength of his will. Every position on himself and the world enjoys the same status and can be tossed aside or suspended at the next opportunity. He is therefore free of both self-deception and remorse. The Platonic democrat not only has a weak spine like Akrates, he does not seem to have any palpable character at all. He stands for nothing, not even – unlike the tyrant – for excess. He neither identifies with nor stands behind any of his own intentions, which means that his self-understanding and relation-to-self cannot be affected by any of them. He changes his orientations like he changes his shirt and calls it liberty.

From Plato's perspective, the democrat's failure to understand his self is just as severe as that of the tyrant. And like the tyrant, who is driven solely by his desires, the democrat also fails to understand the liberty he demands. Here as well, Plato's diagnosis is in line with contemporary theories of freedom. Both Peter Bieri and Harry Frankfurt believe that if we do not identify with any of our individual aims and remain forever uncommitted, we will never experience freedom. Only if we make "substantive decisions" (Bieri) about what we actually want and thus who we actually are can we give our intentions a specific direction and thus become the subject of our own will. Only to the extent that we succeed in doing so can we regard our own will as free.[21] But contrary to Bieri's suggestion, in none of these decisions is the entirety of our own self at stake, at least not necessarily. Martin Löw-Beer rightly points out that in most cases, the question is what (or who) I want (to be) in the one or the other sense.[22] Even then, the Platonic democrat's conception of freedom remains a provocation for any theory that one-sidedly binds freedom – in a latently Platonic fashion – to the notion of resolute identification.

Unlike the tyrant, after all, a democrat makes decisions about what he wants to do and how he wants to be. Unlike the tyrant, he relates to the intentions that he sometimes affirms and sometimes represses. What he lacks is not the ability to form a will, but to fully identify with it – "wholeheartedly" in Harry Frankfurt's terms.[23] Because democrats do not consistently identify with any of the beliefs they express through the decisions they make, none of their beliefs last much longer than the moment of decision. For Plato, therefore, this represents a convergence of tyrannical intemperance and democratic inconstancy; it is nearly impossible to distinguish between someone who associates with an orientation for only a very brief moment in order to then abandon it for an entirely different one, and somebody who lets himself be driven solely by his impulses.[24]

However, it is just as difficult for us to conceive of a life without any sense of future commitment – i.e. a life without any conception of what it means to desire something over any extended period of time, a life in total indifference – in any pure form as it is to conceive of a life dedicated solely to the satisfaction of immediate desires. Both cases represent hyperboles Plato employs in order to reject *exousia* as ultimately leading to unfreedom. Just as is true of the unrestrained tyrant, Plato constructs the figure of the inconstant democrat in order to argue for his own problematic and overly theoretical notion that liberty is founded upon knowledge of what is truly good. Whoever knows what is truly good will be immune to the temptations that enslave the tyrant to his own desires; moreover, because this knowledge cannot be challenged by anything or anyone, the truly knowledgeable – who according to Plato are truly free – are not susceptible to the inconstancy that afflicts the democrat. At the same time, however, they remain excluded from any possibility of revising their convictions.

5. Weakness of Will or the Freedom from Oneself

There is good reason to suspect that Plato's caricature of the democrat prematurely classifies crucial aspects of human freedom as unfreedom. Because of the way he views our relation to general convictions, which is necessary for the concept of free will, Plato cannot account for the fact that convictions can change. What is certainly true for the strength of the will – viz. our will is strong inasmuch as we remain true to our principles in the face of external and internal resistance – is in no way a sufficient explanation of free will. After all, free will means that we can want this or that, that we have the freedom to decide what it is we actually want.[25]

Furthermore, the phenomenon of weakness of will demonstrates that we sometimes want this *and* that, even if the two options are mutually exclusive. However, such conflicts merely reveal the more or less latent drama involved in any decision about our identity. They refer to what Jacques Derrida terms the "madness" of moments of decision.[26] Yet this "madness" is not due to the impossibility of deciding between two alternatives that are both mutually exclusive and equally convincing. Such an impossibility can hardly be regarded as the norm when it comes to making practical decisions. Nor does it count as a case of weak will, since *akrates* represents an instance in which we are convinced of one alternative and yet choose another; therefore, the two things we want simultaneously lie on different levels. Decisions on our identity have an element of "madness" in a different and more everyday sense – even and especially when we have good reason to choose the alternative. This is because decisions of this sort, as considered as they may be, are structurally finite. There is necessarily an element of hastiness in the moment of decision. As Derrida emphasizes, responsibility and decision can never be founded entirely on knowledge. There is always a leap, a discontinuity between the sphere of knowledge on the one side and the sphere of decision or responsibility on the other.[27] And it is precisely this kind of discontinuity that comes to the fore in instances of weakness of will. Our certainty about our own principles must open itself to something that lies beyond the calculations based on these principles. Here we are faced with the insistence or weight of an intention that lies outside the self-image we have chosen for ourselves on the basis of concrete reasons. From that perspective, our self-image might even entirely disqualify as a reason for action. My urge to smoke, for instance, does not appear as a reason to act from the perspective of my identity as a non-smoker; instead it represents a mere urge. This is what makes up the true irrationality of an act performed out of weakness of will.

We should, however, follow Donald Davidson in emphasizing that this very structure also underlies a "form of self-criticism and reform...that has even been thought to be the very essence of rationality and the source of freedom."[28] Even in cases such as these, according to Davidson, "the agent has reasons for changing his own habits and character, but those reasons come from a domain of values necessarily extrinsic to the contents of the views and values to undergo change. The cause of the change, if it comes, can therefore not be a reason for what it causes."[29] We should not take this to mean that the changes I make to myself can be reduced to mere causality, but the considerations that are doubtlessly necessary for self-revision are motivated by a force whose insistence or weight moves me to reconsider the validity of the principles that have previously guided me. Davidson thus concludes his essay on the "Paradoxes of Irrationality" by claiming that a "theory that could not explain irrationality would be one that also could not explain our salutary efforts, and occasional successes, at self-criticism and self-improvement."[30]

Because cases of weakness of will demonstrate the separation between myself and the beliefs that guide me, a supposed weakness can in fact represent an initial impetus to realize that what I have taken to be the best (for myself) is in fact not the best (for myself). If, for example, I feel especially happy in a situation that appears to be a deviation from the perspective of my previous self-understanding, which happens to be dominated by an overdrawn notion of discipline, then this could be a first step in the right direction, i.e. toward a different self-understanding that is less constrained by internal and external forces. Therefore, an implicit reinterpretation of myself could represent the core of a comprehensively revised self-understanding that, on the basis of new and different considerations, might ultimately dethrone my previous orientations. In this case, what initially seemed to be weakness would have proven to be a strength.

But even if we later recognize the implicit reinterpretation of our self as a case of self-deception and our actions as a case of weakness, we would still have to concede that this moment of *akrasia* reveals the instability of our practical understanding-of-self and relation-to-self. This is also an indicator of the freedom we have toward ourselves, or rather the current conception of our self. These moments demonstrate that we are not one with ourselves. But not only is this never the case; it would not be desirable in the first place. If we could never step back from ourselves and open ourselves to other possible images of ourselves, we would not know what freedom is. We need to defend this freedom even if – after having been seduced into being someone we are not – we remorsefully return to the principles that we have had good reasons to follow. As Martin Seel puts it: "The fundamental instability of our practical relations-to-self and understandings-of-self is not only a flaw in our orientations; it also represents our openness for orientations that we have not yet acquired. Moreover, it represents the freedom to orient ourselves, which is not fulfilled by merely having certain orientations."[31]

This would mean abandoning the Platonic notion that what is good (for us) is something that we can attain through objective knowledge, and that freedom means acting in accordance with that knowledge. In fact, we can only gain access to the good, and thus to freedom, by constantly deciding what (who) we actually want (to be) in the light of changed circumstances and incidental opportunities. Inasmuch as wanting, unlike mere wishing, presupposes that what we want can in fact be attained, the moment of decision implies that we ask not only who we really are, but also what we can be and do in a certain situation, as well as what is best for us under the given circumstances. The ability to pose – in Ernst Tugendhat's terms – the "question of truth"[32] in this tripartite sense, the ability to engage in such a "reflected relation-to-self," is a requirement of freedom. To the extent that Plato claimed to know what is truly good, he failed to recognize that the possibility of asking what is truly good is itself a part of what is truly good; in fact it is prior to all substantive determinations of the good.[33] Unlike the metaphysical idea of an objective good, we can never be entirely certain whether that which we regard to the best of our knowledge to be the best (for us) today will ultimately prove to be the worse option once the circumstances have changed.

If, as Plato would have us believe, we can only – that is, only as long as our upbringing goes well – follow a single path, we would lack the freedom opened to us by the "question of truth," i.e. the freedom to decide that is itself a part of the experience of freedom. Furthermore, we would be deprived of the experience of being the subject of our own will and life in and through the decisions we make. In other words, we would lack the experience of freedom itself. As a life determined not by deities but by finite beings, this life is necessarily subject to changes. Freedom does not primarily mean making ourselves immune to changing conditions or unexpected stimuli in order to preserve our present convictions. This kind of strong will is only free in the sense that it takes over the authorship and responsibility for our own lives, provided that these orientations stand up to re-examination in light of changing circumstances and incidental opportunities. Because the conditions of our existence can change, and because we can change along with them, self-determination remains a task of which knowledge cannot relieve us. A post-metaphysical concept of freedom implies the consciousness of our fundamental ability to change our conception of the good, which also entails the consciousness of the latter's historical nature. Plato was right to view this consciousness as an integral part of the democratic culture of freedom. Contrary to Plato's caricature of sheer inconstancy, we need to defend this consciousness – decisively, so to say. After all, the very ontology of the good is at stake.

6. The Unfree Opportunist

Plato's critique of democracy is relevant to my own considerations, not only because his metaphysical conception of the good contrasts with an apologia for the democratic conception of freedom, but also because it draws attention to problems – even if it is for the wrong reasons – that such an apologia must not overlook. The Platonic caricature of the inconstant democrat remains politically relevant even today, for it represents a potential coincidence of the democratic character and the opportunist. In fact, at first sight, the opportunist even appears to represent the essence of a democrat. He is not only open to change, but he is also willing to revise his own orientations. The opportunist cares little for his prior convictions, for the winds have shifted and he now dances at the party of his former enemies. The fact that the democrat is followed by the opportunist's shadow obviously poses a problem for an apologia for the democratic understanding of freedom. The problem does not, however, lie in the fact that the opportunist changes his opinion depending on the circumstances. As we have seen, the possibility of self-revision stands at the very center of the democratic conception of freedom. The problem is that the opportunist never decides. He adopts whatever beliefs the "they" – as Heidegger would put it – of the *zeitgeist* dictate to him. He is a mere follower who jumps on the bandwagon, handing over responsibility for his own way of life to whoever happens to be in control. What he takes to be his own opinions are in fact entirely due to the influence of others; he simply absorbs them without examination. He never steps back from these influences enough to truly appropriate others' convictions by way of rational judgment.[34] Because he has handed over any decisions on his own beliefs to others, no belief has any real weight for him. What he thinks and believes, even what he is, is not up to him. He thus fails to become the subject of his own will; he fails to be a free human being.

However, we should not believe that we can so easily dismiss the difficulty of distinguishing between opportunists and good democrats. First, the critical distance that supposedly distinguishes the genuinely free democrat from the unfree opportunist runs the danger of appearing to be mere idealistic pathos. Nobody is constantly aware and critical of his own opinions.[35] One of the lessons taught to us by psychoanalysis is that it is not easy to detach from how we are accustomed to seeing ourselves, or to seal ourselves off from the influence of others. We often adopt beliefs without having critically examined them, and the accompanying changes to our self-understanding often occur without our noticing them. Changing circumstances and incidental opportunities can only enable us to re-define ourselves if they allow us to step back from ourselves, to become a problem for ourselves, and to pose the "question of truth." Neither do we constantly take up such a detached stance, nor can we simply resolve to do so. Yet, the unfreedom of the opportunist, who is largely uncritical of his own beliefs, demonstrates that freedom cannot exist without such moments of detachment, without our stepping back from our own convictions in order to relate to them in a new and *free* way.

The second problem concerns the pathos of decision making which is supposed to distinguish democrats from opportunists. Even the opportunist's fundamentally indifferent stance cannot be easily differentiated from the democrat's openness to change. After all, any time we step back from ourselves, we implicitly stop identifying with our own beliefs. In other words, we become somewhat indifferent toward them. Likewise, any serious consideration of various options means not having already decided for one or the other. However, the opportunist demonstrates that an indifferent stance can become a problem once it becomes totalized. If we forever remain critical observers of ourselves and our possibilities, if we remain stuck posing the "question of truth" without ever daring to give an answer, we will forever remain in a sphere beyond the sphere of freedom, similar to the uncritical opportunist. Both the problem of opportunism and that of apathy demonstrate that there can be no freedom without a decision about what is best (for us individually and for society). This is true even if we recognize the fundamental fallibility of our decisions – as well as the "madness" that goes along with nevertheless making such decisions "wholeheartedly." The democratic awareness of the fundamental fallibility of all substantive determinations of the (individual and social) good cannot relieve us of the task of determining to the best of our knowledge and belief what the good is – unless we wish to pay the price of abandoning freedom. The democratic awareness of fallibility which keeps democracy, and life in a democracy, open to the possibility of its own transformation does not aim for a space beyond decision, but for the possibility of correcting those decisions. Total indifference is not, contrary to what Plato would have us believe, a necessary consequence of the realization of our fallibility, even if that remains a possibility that the democratic understanding of freedom cannot exclude.

For a life that is free and self-determined in both an individual and social sense, moments of decision are just as inevitable as moments of detachment from decisions we have already made. Due to the dual character of freedom, I would like to employ the term self-determination for the idea of lived freedom, because "self-determination" refers to the fact that – particularly given the fundamental instability of our practical orientations – there is always something new to be decided. By contrast, the term self-realization, which is often used in connection with the individualism typical of Western democracies, has come to be customarily associated with the ideological notion of a core self that is to be objectively grasped and then unfolded, i.e. realized. According to this conception, we no longer bear responsibility for our own lives, but merely become conscious of supposed facts: "I am a person who…" Although this more recent meaning of self-realization is radically individualist, claiming independence from given roles and thus the ability to contradict social expectations, it is no accident that self-realization was able to become a central category during the largely depoliticized era of the 1970s and 1980s. Following the challenge represented by the social expansion of possibilities for individual lifestyles after 1968, there was a retreat to the ideology of individual (pre-)determination, compensating for the loss of social orientations.[36] Although the concept of self-determination, too, is somewhat problematic due to the history of its usage, it does contain a reference, unburdened by the ballast of the metaphysical subject, to the constantly precarious subject of self-determination, as well as to the constant task of taking responsibility for our own lives. This is assuming that we follow Tugendhat and no longer grasp self-determination as a matter of what the ego wants, but of who (i.e. how) it wants to be.[37]

7. Many Jobs and Much Trespassing

In employing this concept of self-determination, I am not arguing that a person is entirely free to determine his own life. Instead my aim is to redefine the idea of freedom *toward* ourselves, which is as crucial to the concept of individual self-realization as it is to the Platonic concept of freedom, putting aside all objectivist assumptions about the nature of the individual. Unlike the "milieus of self-realization" typical for our times, for Plato the idea of freedom toward oneself means that we can immediately convert our individual nature into a social identity that conforms to the social order. This once again demonstrates that for Plato, freedom is virtually the opposite of what we, that is we democrats, normally take it to mean. In the Platonic state, individual freedom consists in affirming what is supposedly clearly dictated to us, fulfilling the supposedly natural role assigned to us in society without complaint. Plato's idea of justice is based upon a principle of identity according to which each person is "to do one job, the job he was naturally most suited for" (Rep 433a). And this is something he should do both in his own interest and in that of the community. In accordance with this principle of identity, what is good for the individual should always already be linked to the social good, such that the former can only be had through the latter – and thus not as such (Rep 443c–e). To live a good and just life therefore means to fully realize one's *sole* natural determination, guided by a proper education, and thus to properly fulfill one's own role in the division of labor organized in and by the state. Arbogast Schmitt rightly points out that Plato does not mean to claim that each individual should restrict his own pursuit of individual happiness and subordinate himself to the good of the community. Instead each individual should learn to pursue his own true advantage, i.e. to realize himself. He is to do so by developing his capacities in an optimal way, recognizing the powers and limitations of each of these capacities and bringing them into harmony with each other.[38] But in order to be able to transfer such a division of labor within the soul to the state without the optimal development of each person's capacities conflicting with the aim of a division of labor based on various skills, Plato strictly relegates the idea of such a development to a person's natural predispositions. Individuals' factical inequality should determine the aim and scope of their development. According to Plato, justice reigns when everybody does what suits them – and what it is that suits them is determined by "nature" (*physei*). As Socrates states in the fourth book of the *Politeia*, "the man naturally fitted to be a shoemaker, or carpenter, or anything else, should stick to his own trade" (Rep 443c). Indeed, this could be regarded as an "adumbration of justice" (ibid.).[39]

The problem with Plato's claim is not that we are determined by our nature, rather it is the way he understands this fact. He assumes that there is a *single* natural determination, a truth that can be found within ourselves and then manifested in our social identity. Such a theory of predestination stands in stark contrast to the dubious democrat's identity changes. Plato uses the terms *polypragmosyne*[40] ["the readiness to engage in multifarious activities" or "busybodiness"] (Rep 434b) and *allotriopragmosyne* [meddlesomeness] (Rep 444b) to formulate his decisive accusation: doing many jobs at the same time and trespassing on each other's functions. Compared to the notion of natural determination, the experimental democrat is always doing far too much and thus always fooling about and interfering with others. He concerns himself with matters far beyond the satisfaction of his immediate needs: The democrat "spends as much money, time and trouble on the unnecessary desires as on the necessary" (Rep 561a). This is the reason that *exousia* is often linked to wealth and affluence.[41] It is also because of the democrat's material possibilities that he does not regard self-preservation as his sole purpose. His unnecessary desires become just as important to him as his necessary, i.e. natural, needs. He thus separates the question of the individual good from the goal of self-preservation. But the moment he takes his pursuit of happiness beyond self-preservation, the substance of the individual good becomes immediately unclear, since it no longer merely consists in satisfying needs, but also in the question of the nature of our existence in general. What, if not nature, determines what it means to exist? To the extent that he goes beyond what is naturally necessary, the democrat rejects the idea of natural determination, and thus also the coherence of the attendant relation-to-self. He does not accept nature as the ultimate truth (about himself); rather, he exposes his actions to external influences. Plato is convinced that by doing so, he will necessarily be alienated from himself.

When it comes to the idea of a direct coincidence between our inner nature and our social identity, which in Plato's view of the ideal just state represents the bond between the individual and society, the question is whether Plato's critique of the democrat is justified, or whether he hastily interprets that which should in fact be defended as a condition of a good life as alienation. By rejecting the idea of natural determination, the democrat does not reject the notion that we are determined by nature per se; rather, he understands – and lives

– this determination in a different way. Nature does not dictate a certain inner program for him to decode and implement; rather, it provides him with various desires and partially contradictory urges to which he must react flexibly in the process of will-formation. Sometimes he succumbs to these desires and urges, elevating them to the status of a will, and sometimes he suppresses them in the name of superordinate, considered reasons that transcend the given situation. These intentions, however, are never accessible to him as such, rather only in connection with the situations in which they arise. In this manner, he gives the pleasure of the moment its turn, as if by lot (*"te parapiptouse aei hoper lachouse"*) (Rep 561b, see note 18). They happen to him. The democrat can experience these desires and relate to them, but he cannot control whether they arise or not. Although there are desires that can only develop as a consequence of a formed will, Plato's portrait of the democrat is obviously referring to a different case in which the subject cannot control whether these desires arise.

In my opinion, if the term "inner nature" is to have any meaning at all, it must refer to desires that arise independent of the subject's will. Here something occurs in the subject that does not derive from his respective social identity, but that instead involves a dimension that the subject cannot control and in this sense precedes his will.[42] An inner nature is not, therefore, merely the other of culture; its appearing is not subject to the law of nature. These desires are instead "non-necessary desires." Not only are they culturally communicated, they only assert themselves in the context of culture, i.e. in socialized subjects. They do so, however, in a negative way, disrupting or interrupting the subject's self-understanding. They can be traced neither to a biological purpose nor to the will-formation of a moral subject. They just happen, because they are not at all determined by a relation to a general principle (a purpose or a norm). Instead, these inner occurrences emerge from the subject's relation to the particularity of a given situation. The force exerted by these desires is not to be viewed as a substantive essence that could be assigned to a unified subject (or his somatic core). Instead, they develop in constellation, deriving from the mimetic relation of the subject to the external world. And it is precisely because of this constellation-like character that the force exerted by these desires does not merely lie in the hands of the subject.

As Plato observes in the case of the democrat, desires "happen" not only in the sense that the subject cannot control whether they arise or not; rather, the emergence of desires can be considered an event in the sense that the person who perceives them was previously unfamiliar with this side of himself. He is surprised by them. Because something unexpected occurs in these moments, something that does not fit together with a person's previous self-understanding, it must produce a kind of crack in the person's self-image.[43] But to the extent that these inner occurrences are not immediately integrated into familiar patterns, they point to a potential in the subject's self-understanding that has not yet been exhausted.

8. The Occurrence of an Inner Nature or the Freedom Toward Self

According to this understanding, "inner nature" is not a program that can be translated into culture, or rather the culture of a social identity. On the contrary, it manifests itself in the crisis of this culture. The forces, intentions, and energies of our nature are, as George Herbert Mead emphasizes, possibilities of our self that lie beyond their respective social "presentation": "We do not know just what they are."[44] Contrary to Plato's doctrine of predestination, according to which our inner nature can be clearly decoded and thus seamlessly translated into a social identity, our inner nature as such is never transparent to us. Although we can relate to its various forms of appearance by giving it (or attempting to give it) a direction through the exercise of our will, we can never appropriate this nature as such. It remains accessible to us only in the form of an event in the sense already described. Therefore we cannot understand this nature as a kind of static immanence best disclosed in a state of detached self-reflection. We can only gain access to our inner nature via our always already existing relations to the surrounding world. Precisely because our inner nature as such cannot take on objective existence, but can only appear within a changing world, our inner nature can be a challenge to and a corrective authority for our current self-interpretation. The experience of new impulses or the more intense experience of previously suppressed impulses can motivate me to change my beliefs, and thus my life. The discontinuous events of my inner nature can represent an origin, though not in an absolute sense (i.e. as a return to an original state prior to all culture), but in the sense of an experience (of self) which can retrospectively be described as the beginning of a development, as the origin of a transformation.[45]

Consequently there is always a measure of ambivalence in my decisions about who I am and what I want, i.e. in my acts of self-determination. Insofar as I recognize myself as a person with this or that motive or desire, these decisions always represent an act of self-discovery; they also represent a decision about myself inasmuch as I thereby interpret and judge this discovery.[46] This ambivalence accompanies what Helmuth Plessner called the "eccentric positionality of humans": the "fundamental divide" between "existence that occurs" and "existence which is carried out." This divide runs straight through the "self" in such a way that "nobody knows whether they are still the person who cries and laughs, thinks and makes decisions, or whether it is that self that has been divorced from his self, the other within him, his counter-image, perhaps even his polar opposite."[47] Because of this divide, which Plessner terms a "falling-out with oneself, from which there is no exit and for which there is no compensation,"[48] the simultaneity of constative and performative structure is characteristic of all acts of self-determination. This in turn means that acts of self-determination necessarily occur in the name of a self that does not exist prior to those acts, at least not as such.[49] It is only through the act of self-determination that the subject brings itself to bear in this or that determination, in order to then retroactively identify with that determination. The process of subjectification that thereby takes place is, strictly speaking, not a subjective process at all, but rather an event. There is no safe place from which a unified subject can assert itself as master over its own desires.[50] Instead, our discussion of weakness of will has shown that the level of reflection cannot be shielded from the force of our desires, especially when it comes to those cases of self-revision that are of particular interest to us here. Whatever motivates us to revise our own beliefs, to make a new decision on our own self-understanding, does not count as a reason from the perspective of the beliefs we revise. Instead, it represents a reason that has been "disrobed" of its status as a reason[51] – a pure force that penetrates the sphere of reflection and ultimately sets it in motion by virtue of its own insistence and impact. With respect to the idea of autonomous subjectivity linked to the concept of self-determination, the potential autonomy of the subject cannot be located in a sphere of reflection cleansed of all heteronomy, but can only remain capable of (re-)producing itself through heteronomy (of our inner nature).

For this reason, the Platonic democrat is not absolutely free *from* himself, even if he is capable of distancing himself from his own current self-understanding, for he can never free himself from his own nature. The democrat does not create himself in the strong sense of the term; he does not simply invent himself *ex nihilo*, and thus he cannot count as a paradigm of radically constructivist notions which claim a person's essence to be a mere matter of voluntaristic decision.

In fact, without any ties to his own inner nature, the freedom of democratic man cannot be regarded as *his* freedom.[52] Therefore, even the democrat is free *toward* himself in a crucial sense: He makes his desires the gauge of his own self-understanding and makes revisions accordingly. Because we interpret our desires in every decision we make about what we actually want (and who we actually are), we cannot become or want anything that we not already potentially are or want according to our inner nature. But since this nature is never accessible to us as such, it remains a surplus despite all our attempts to realize it in our lives.

Because our inner nature is not transparent to us, our self-interpretations can of course be wrong. This becomes especially apparent in times of crisis in our self-relation, when our previous self-interpretation proves to be inappropriate, wrong, perhaps even alien in the face of the desires we have developed. The same is true when a successful self-relation reveals itself in a feeling of internal harmony, which, as Dieter Thomae has shown, is nothing but the way that freedom becomes psychologically manifest.[53] Therefore, the possibility of misinterpreting our nature is a necessary part of our freedom of self-determination. What we know about ourselves, about "our own nature," is just as fallible as what we think is best (for us). Just because our "own nature" remains fundamentally questionable, the question about what is best for us arises again and again.

This reference to what Plessner called the "eccentric positionality of humans" denies the possibility of a complete or completed identity between the natural (non-)foundation and the social form of the subject. Furthermore, the impossibility of determining the foundations of the subject is a never-ending source of change and innovation.[54] With this in mind we can take up a new perspective on Plato's criticism of the aestheticization at work in the democratic way of life. After all, Plato uses aesthetically connotated terms to describe the democrat not merely because of the latter's ability to transform himself; rather, the "variable" democrat also embodies the very character that Plato, in the third book of the *Politeia*, accuses the theater of bringing forth.

9. Democrats and Theater Types

Two lines of argumentation converge in Plato's characterization of the democrat: his objection to the democratic understanding of freedom and an argument for excluding theater and the poet from the ideal state. Plato rejects theater along with democracy not only because it proves to be a vehicle for "busybodiness" (*polypragmosyne*) and "meddlesomeness" (*allotriopragmosyne*). For he accuses theater not merely of seducing the audience into viewing a spectacle, but also of providing a stage for skilful imitation, thus inciting the audience to engage in imitation as well. Theater thereby becomes a rival to the educational program prescribed in *The Republic*. Plato emphasizes that imitation, as the central instrument of theater, is also an inevitable element in education, which is why its content and form must be closely monitored. According to the Platonic logic of identity, only naturally predetermined identities can be allowed to be objects of imitation. The young guardians, whose training takes up a large portion of the discussions in *The Republic*, may only be permitted to imitate the role models that suit the identity that has been determined for them: "men of courage, self-control, piety, freedom of spirit and similar qualities" (Rep 395c). In no case may those destined to become "men of worth" be allowed to "take the parts of women, young or old" (Rep 395d). The use of imitation, as Plato is aware, can "establish habits" that "become second nature" if one begins in the "earliest years" and carries it out "into adult life" (Rep 395c, d). For this reason, Plato praises epic narrative as a form of representation that, unlike the theater, preserves the identity of the narrator; moreover, the contents of these narratives can help cultivate the virtues of those who are meant to listen to them (cf. Rep 396e–398b). Epics are a nontheatrical form that serves to shape essentially unspectacular virtues. Plato therefore does not expel all "story-tellers and poets" from the city; those who are "severe" may remain (Rep 398a, b).

Yet the playwrights must go, for they represent a serious threat to Plato's educational program. By introducing role-playing and thus the duplication of persons and roles, they threaten to dissolve the self-identity of all members of society. Plato does not so much emphasize the possibility, symbolized by the mask, of a chasm between a person's actual self-understanding and his public appearance – or rather, the problem that the members of society are thereby no longer transparent to each other, which would later become a crucial concern for Rousseau (cf. ch. 5). On the contrary, he is concerned that individuals will vanish in their roles and that that their self will be dissolved by the masks they wear, since the actors' merely apparent mimesis could be accompanied by true mimesis. Therefore, a person might not only seek to represent others, but to become like them; their role might rub off on them. Because theater produces an enjoyment of mimesis, thus bringing about in its audience a disposition for what it imitates, both its form and content prove problematic.

For the simple reason that theater aims to entertain, playwrights put emphasis on spectacle: evil, passions, fantasy. Following the model presented by the actor, imitation will thus extend to what Plato regards as pedagogically worthless or even a threat to the community. Nothing is unworthy of imitation by actors or by those infected by the joy of acting – neither the male characters of tragedies who are enslaved by their passions, nor the ill, nor women, nor even dogs and sheep (Rep 397a). This last implication in particular makes the theater, in Plato's eyes, a state affair. The theater not only represents a threat to aesthetically uninteresting virtues, but, more fundamentally and thus more crucially, it alienates individuals from themselves and their respective tasks in the community by seducing them into transforming themselves into all kinds of arbitrary things. The playwright's infectious ability "to transform himself into all sorts of characters and represent all sorts of things" (Rep 397e, 398a) represents an extraordinary threat to the "natural order" of the Platonic state, founded on the self-identity of its members, because the principle of theatrical mimesis cannot be contained within the theater. Poets may have the skill to *imitate* a transformation into "all sorts of characters," but Plato fears that for an audience educated by the theater, the transformation can become real.

Yet, the theatrical mimesis in which anything and everything can be imitated – which is also a reason why Plato regards it as such a serious threat – merely displays the logic of all mimesis in its purest form. The subject of imitation is never a subject; it is a subjectless subject or a non-subject. The "actor's paradox," according to which actors can be *everything* because in essence they are *nothing*, is an exemplary illustration of the fact that the subject of imitation only becomes this subject in and through the act of imitation.[55] This, however, is precisely what calls into question Plato's doctrine of predestination. What a subject is and can be is never sufficiently certain, but can only crystallize by means of a mimetic relation to others and otherness. While Plato seeks to ensure that this exchange obeys the logic of identity, democracy proves to be downright theater-friendly because of its understanding of freedom; and the democrat is a man of the theater, a *polypraktor*. Due to his tendency toward *polypragmosyne*, which according to Plato always also represents *allotriopragmosyne*, his life is much more multifaceted than that of the self-identical members of Plato's ideal state, and bear much greater similarity to the polymorphic skills "artistically" displayed by the playwright. Instead of following the idea of natural determination, the way the democrat expresses himself depends on external circumstances – and therefore on the discontinuous influence of shifting circumstances and incidental opportunities. The democrat not only allows himself to be affected by the latter, but in certain cases he even adapts to them.

According to Plato, the democrat not only loses sight of the essence of his own being, he lives his life among mere appearances. Once he has "lost himself," he can only imitate others; he is condemned to live his life "as if." In Plato's eyes he appears, for example, only as if he is engaging in "a period of philosophic study" (Rep 561d), but on the basis of what has already been said, the democrat seemingly eliminates the distinction between being and appearance. There is no longer any being prior to imitation, the only path to one's true self is to constantly renew one's mimetic relation to others and otherness. The democrat does not, however, thereby eliminate the distinction between being and appearance as such; he only locates it elsewhere. What is external to the subject and what is an authentic part of him can only emerge again and again in the course of an individual life against the horizon of lived experience. Only then can we decide to identify with a certain self-understanding in a lasting way, or to abandon it because it has become so alien to us that it no longer seems a part of us, making us feel like actors playing ourselves.

If it is true that we can only gain access to our inner nature through interaction with a changing world, then the bond that Plato seeks to forge between the individual and the social good, thus making the two indistinguishable, must dissolve from within. Contrary to Plato's hopes, if individuals can never be entirely transparent to themselves, then their role in the community can never be so clear that they only need the proper education to grasp it. Platonic education instead proves to be a matter of grim discipline, and the guardians appear as prisoners of an ideology that hypostatizes the social as a natural given. By contrast, if the nature of the individual can never be fully decoded and translated into a social identity; if that which is "appropriate" to the individual can only emerge through lived interaction with the world, then the social order must necessarily assume an element of contingency. In one sense Plato saw this clearly: He has Socrates laconically observe what must sooner or later come to occur in a democracy under the influence of the democratic understanding of freedom: No previously dominant hierarchy can remain intact; the sons will rebel against the fathers, students against teachers, subordinates against their superiors. It can even "go to extremes," such that slaves and women are made equal to masters and men (Rep 562d–563b). The principle of identity, according to which all citizens "ought individually to devote their full energy to the one particular job for which they are naturally suited. In that way the integrity and unity both of the individual and the state will be preserved" (Rep 423d), is dissolved by self-relations: Because individuals do not let themselves be forced into predetermined roles, the natural order of the state loses its foundation and the structure of domination is shown to be capable of fundamental change.

But if we can defend the notion of democratic self-government against Plato's objections, then we can also renegotiate his critique of democratic government. I will now, therefore, return to Plato's critique of democratic government, once again focusing on his critique of aestheticization. It is already clear that the unfolding of the self in the dynamic sense just described requires a society that protects the possibility of posing the "question of truth" – with regard to the life of the individual and society – in a way that is prior to all substantive determinations of the individual or social good. In other words, it requires democracy.

10. Theatrocracy: The Fearlessly Judging Multitude

According to Socrates' narrative in *The Republic*, democracy emerges once the oligarchs have been dethroned. The "sheltered" "rich man" will easily be subdued by the "lean and sunburnt" "poor man" (cf. Rep 556d,e). "Then democracy originates when the poor win, kill or exile their opponents, and give the rest equal civil rights and opportunities of office, appointment to office being as a rule by lot" (Rep 557a). According to the formal principle of equality deriving from democratic *exousia*, any random individual has the right to govern. We are already familiar with Plato's concerns on this matter. He maintains that this "fine and vigorous beginning" is "the root from which tyranny springs" (Rep 563e). From "an extreme of liberty one is likely to get, in the individual and in society, a reaction to an extreme of subjection" (Rep 564a). As we have seen, Plato maintains that even when it comes to the individual's way of life, democratic freedom must be regarded as a form of unfreedom. He views the democrat's constantly changing appearances as mere symptoms of a weakness, of a profound lack of anchoring. Because democrats, according to Plato's caricature, stand (up) for nothing, and certainly not for a stable social order, the community will end up being dominated by the strongest. Plato therefore fears the class of roguish drones will take power in the state: "In a democracy practically all the leaders are drawn from it. Its more energetic elements do the talking and acting, the remainder sit buzzing on the benches" (Rep 564d). Sooner or later, the tyrannical drones will take power, because in a democracy the people are, in Plato's words, ignorant (cf. Rep 565b). More precisely, the people are unaware of what is truly good: the natural order of the state under an aristocracy. In a democracy there is method to this ignorance: Because democrats define freedom as a state in which they are not restricted by naturally predetermined roles, nobody is concerned with the actual character of those who run for office. In a democracy nobody "minds what the habits and background of its politicians are; provided they profess themselves the people's friends, they are duly honored" (Rep 558b). What counts instead is the impression that a candidate makes. For Plato, this means that a democratic people allows itself to be seduced, persuaded, and blinded by any person who claims to be a politician. In other words, the problem of democracy lies in the aestheticization of political culture.

In Plato's view the ignorance of the people causes the natural order of the community to break down into political actors and an audience. After all, if the power of government is not justified by nature, than it must first be established – an accurate observation. In a democracy, candidates for political office must literally produce themselves in front of an audience in order to receive a mandate for office, for only the consent of the audience legitimates political power. It is thus no accident that the poets have a role to play, as role models and supporters, in the effort to assemble "large audiences" and "sway" them to accept the most diverse political programs "with their fine persuasive voices" (Rep 568c). The ultimately decisive reason for the decline of democracy, therefore, is the fact that the sole criterion for judging such political staging is whether the latter happen to appeal to the people or not. Because democracy is founded on the public's spontaneous judgment of taste, it is bound to go under, allowing the drones to triumph, who know how to ensure "every variety and refinement of pleasure" (Rep 559d). The fate of democracy is thus sealed and will sooner or later turn into tyranny.

But once again, the question is whether Plato's conclusions are too hasty, and whether we can defend the judgment of a democratic people against such a caricature. Plato discusses the judgments of the *demos* not in *The Republic*, but in his later dialogue *Nomoi* (*The Laws*)[56] – interestingly enough in the context of his critique on the boundlessness of the arts, which he regards as the cause for the decline of Athens. The removal of constraints on the arts eliminates all constraints on the freedom of the audience, which, after enabling a democratic revolution, inevitably leads to its decline.

In *The Laws* Plato has the Athenian citizen report that the city's doom began with artists who, although talented, were "ignorant of the correct and legitimate standards laid down by the Muse," thus letting themselves be "gripped by a frenzied and excessive lust for pleasure" (L 700d). This not only violates the laws of art; rather, by "jumbling together laments and hymns" and imitating "pipe tunes on the lyre" (ibid.), these artists set a political process in motion in which the law of a thing came to be replaced by the law of effect. Even worse, the artists in their "idiotic way" (L 700e) turned the audience into a dominant social authority. By departing from what Plato naturally assumes to be its own eternal laws, by crossing genre lines and using hybrid forms of media, this new form of art encouraged an uneducated audience to judge the quality of art despite their lack of knowledge about traditional rules, instead basing their judgment solely on their own pleasure or displeasure. This kind of judgment, a question of taste, cares little for traditional rules and dismisses the cultivated tastes of the educated classes. From the latter's perspective, the audience is guilty of "breaking the rules and offending good taste." (L 700e)

Instead of the authority of good taste and its laws, including a quiet and obedient audience, (as the Athenian recounts nostalgically, the "mass of the people" could once "always be disciplined and controlled by a stick"), now there emerged spontaneous outbursts from the audience: "catcalls," "uncouth yelling," and "applause." This is how "a sort of vicious 'theatrocracy' arose" and usurped a "meritocracy." If, as the Athenian states,

> this democracy had been limited to gentlemen and had applied only to music, no great harm would have been done; in the event, however, music proved to be the starting-point of everyone's conviction that he was an authority on everything, and of a general disregard for the law. Complete license was not far behind. The conviction that they knew made them unafraid, and assurance engendered effrontery. You see, a reckless lack of respect for one's betters is effrontery of peculiar viciousness, which springs from a freedom from inhibitions that has gone much too far. (L 701a, b)

Plato is aware of the consequences: The impudent, bold, excessive freedom of the arts will give rise to a new culture of freedom, namely that of democracy. Therefore, Plato sees the origin of democracy in the theater, for it cultivates a lack of respect for traditional laws along with a general tendency toward aestheticization. Because democrats accept no law as being irreducible, not even the law of one's "own nature," a democracy is ruled by a both ethically and politically unreliable authority: spontaneous pleasure and aversion. However, as we saw in our discussion of Plato's critique of democratic self-government, democrats, unlike tyrants, do indeed relate to their own intentions in interaction with their surroundings. The dimension of a reflected relation-to-self is decisive for an apologia for political judgment in a theatrocratic democracy.

So again, "what is proper to a thing" is "what is best for it," as Socrates states in *The Republic* (Rep 586e). But as I have argued in the previous sections, this cannot be determined once and for all – e.g., in children – in order to then be brought to fruition through proper education in the form of a social identity (a certain position in the community). What is particular to an individual can instead only be shown in interaction with a changing world, in the sometimes more, sometimes less, turbulent course of a life. Only by being susceptible to impulses from others and otherness does a subject come into contact with what makes it a particular being, with its own inner nature. Only by going beyond ourselves and engaging with others and otherness can we (repeatedly) find ourselves. The expressions of our inner nature have the character of events, because they are not (pre-)determined by a general purpose or norm but in and through the particular nature of a situation. Indeed, the unconstrained art depicted in the *The Laws* is an extreme and thoroughly paradigmatic object, for the passionate reaction of pleasure or aversion is instigated by something for which there is no (or not yet) a concept, and for whose judgment there are consequently no (or not yet) rules.

Judgments about unconstrained art are therefore necessarily subjective and indifferent toward traditional authority. However, the experience of pleasure or aversion is not identical to the judgment of an art critic, which sets the new in relation to tradition and then either accepts it as progress or rejects it as regress. Even in everyday instances in which we are not dealing with objects of art, we do not approve of every spontaneous expression of our own desires, which is what we saw in the normal case of weakness of will. But such events – expressions of energies and forces manifested in a subject by virtue of its relation to something other – are excellent occasions to once again "fearlessly" pose the "question of truth," the question of the good. This might then lead us to replace our previously guiding principles with new ones, regardless of whether they concern art criticism, political convictions, or our own self-understanding. The openness of the subject that is not dominated by norms to others and otherness is therefore the condition of the possibility for the autonomy of the judging subject. The democratic subject in no way rejects all rules – here we are dealing with a thoroughly socialized and, as Plato would say, "well-mannered" subject – but is capable of changing the rules according to the circumstances on the basis of its experiences with strange, new, and particular things. This, we could object to Plato, is what makes up its freedom.

But for Plato, as we have seen, the problem lies in the fact that the democrat does not know the proper rules. Due to his upbringing the democrat knows what is better, but not what is really and truly good (for then he would be immune to outside influences and could not imagine changing). Plato maintains that whoever remains ignorant in this sense remains exposed to the poison of aestheticization and can be affected by the surface occurrences of the world, its impulses and effects, thus condemning that person to fall under the spell of mere appearances. But from a post-metaphysical perspective, all mortal subjects are ignorant in this regard, and matters look somewhat different against the background of a finite world. Under these circumstances, as we have seen, we must defend a concept of the good that allows us to ask about the good and thus question its prevailing determinations. This does not eliminate the distinction between being and mere appearance, but reveals it to be historically dynamic. What I believed was good yesterday can in the light of changed circumstances prove to be bad today. The finite nature of the knowledge upon which we base our actions once again demonstrates that in a post-metaphysical world the good can only appear to us historically. The fact that judgment, even political judgment, is basically fallible does not devalue judgment itself; on the contrary, its basic fallibility is a crucial part of freedom. Only because we can be influenced by new ideas and outside impulses, only because we can abandon our previous principles (that we have been brought up with) as a result of certain experiences can we judge freely.

If, firstly, the judgment of the theater audience about unruly art does not entirely consist of spontaneous impulses of pleasure or aversion, but can instead be understood as paradigmatic evidence that present criteria of judgment can be questioned in the light of new influences, alien impulses, and other perspectives; and if, secondly, we must defend this fact in the name of a post-metaphysical ontology of the good, then this will also affect our concept of judgment itself. This is the actual revolution represented by theatrocracy. Here we are not only dealing with a situation in which the multitude, condemned to silence by the authorities, dares to cast judgment on political affairs, the art of politics – a crowd, by the way, that does not merely consist of "free men," but also encompasses "those who are neither functionaries nor citizens."[57] Not only does a theatrocracy grant everybody the authority to judge, more importantly it transforms the concept of judgment itself, depriving it of its foundation in the problematic conception that the good is something that we, at least the best of us, can acquire as objective knowledge, the validity of which does not depend on individual experience. Instead, judgments about the good are opened up to historically variable experience. What is good can only prove to be such in practice, i.e. through lived interaction with the impulses we receive from a changing world. For the self-declared intellectual aristocrats in the Platonic tradition, however, this also means that their necessarily finite determinations of the good are now exposed to the fearless judgments of those to whom they must justify their actions.

Therefore, if we can defend the people's "lack of respect" for the unquestionable authority of traditional determinations of the good from a democratic perspective, then we do so by defining the masses as a multitude of judging individuals. This optimistic image, however, is faced with an entirely different image of the agitated mob, which drowns the cacophony of individual judgments in bellowing unanimity. This negative phenomenon, recalled by Plato's description of the theatrocracy, doubtlessly represents a problem for staunch democrats. However, here we are dealing with something entirely different from the fearlessness of the independently judging multitude feared by the aristocrats.

11. Masses and Mimesis

Similar to his caricature of the democrat as an inconstant opportunist, the picture Plato paints of the democratic rabble presents a serious challenge: the conformity of the masses. In a crowd [*die Masse*], an assembly of unfamiliar individuals of various backgrounds can come together to form a unit, the de-individualizing effect of which can produce a kind of homogeneity that supersedes any assimilation that could come about within social groups. Because it is not founded on an existing order, the crowd is in fact a phenomenon typical of democratic societies.[58] From a democratic perspective, the problem is not so much that a crowd lacks any social preconditions but that heterogeneous individuals, along with their capacity for judgment, disappear in the group. Just as was true of the opportunist, the crowd poses the problem of suspended judgment.

After all, the crowd does not judge, it gets agitated. It takes the aspect of mimetic relinquishing to an excess by joining it to the other members of the crowd. The result is that the members mutually infect each other with their affectivity. As the sociologist Gabriel Tarde argued in his study of the crowd in modernity,[59] such massive affective feedback draws individuals into the crowd to such a great extent that it overwhelms their individuality. The agitation of the crowd thus assumes an independent form, separate from the occasion that gave rise to it. The latter is pushed into the background by the crowd's enjoyment of its own increasing excitability. Whether they sway along with a charismatic leader[60] or take aim at a given victim, in each case the members of the crowd bring together what appears to be irreconcilable: "maximum openness and maximum isolation by virtue of self-referentiality."[61]

The leveling effect of the crowd provides us with nearly laboratory-like conditions for studying the fundamental role of imitation when it comes to socialization. "Things are not born alike, they become alike."[62] However, due to its closed ranks, the crowd cannot be taken as a model for imitation in general, because individuals are constantly exposed to diverse influences; they are the object of a number of what Tarde suggestively terms "radiations of imitation."[63] "Our social life includes a thick network of radiations of this sort, with countless mutual interferences."[64] This diversity is not only a source of individuality, but also of a certain resilience to external influences. Such resilience derives neither from a presupposed individuality nor from a kind of meta-knowledge about what is truly good, rather from previously adopted beliefs, from earlier imitation so to say.[65]

We do not always imitate fully consciously. Others' beliefs and habits often seep in without our noticing them, and the transition from conscious imitation, from a reflected will to a mechanical habit, often goes unnoticed.[66] But we often (repeatedly) become aware of what is unconsciously true for us when it comes under pressure from a competing influence. At this point an internal conflict arises, preceding our conscious judgment about our own beliefs. For Tarde, such conflicts are not only the motor of history, they are also the source of individuality and of the aesthetic dimension of social life. According to Tarde,

> the really fundamental social opposition must be sought for in the bosom of the social individual himself, whenever he hesitates between adopting or rejecting a new pattern offered him, whether in the way of phraseology, ritual, concept, canon of art, or conduct. This hesitation, this miniature internal battle, which is renewed a million times every moment of a nation's life, constitutes the infinitely minute and infinitely fruitful opposition that underlies history...For the very reason that the life of each social individual is composed of such numerous psychological oppositions, there has been a real accentuation of his individual characteristics, or his personality...We find, also, that the aesthetic side of the social life...is supported by this very interplay of infinite minute oppositions.[67]

If the dazzling figure we have described the democrat to be, both with and against Plato, is characterized by his openness to diverse influences, then the result will be an element of resistance to the effects of the crowd. The democrat will not resort to self-restriction and self-control as a means for combating the latter's leveling dynamic; rather – as Plato himself suspected – the monoculture of tyrannical (totalitarian) societies suits the effects of the crowd quite well.[68] The democratic antidote to the conformity of the crowd is not restriction and control, but openness to a diversity of influences. This kind of openness cannot entirely prevent the phenomenon of the crowd from arising: When we are a part of a crowd, perhaps we cannot and do not want to prevent it from sweeping us up with it (e.g., sporting events). However, the diversity of influences that otherwise determine our lives tends to limit the effects of the crowd to the time and place of its emergence.

Even Plato's democrat is a part of various social groups. He maintains contact with "men of war and money" just as he does with ascetics and poets. This makes him less a man of the crowd than a man of what we would now call one of the publics. Unlike the case of the crowd, a person can be a member of various different subpublics or special publics.[69] Being a member in various associations, being open for new and different things, with the concomitant necessity of repeatedly reflecting on one's own beliefs, all promote the individualization of individuals as well as their resistance to conformity. Democracy's ability to resist the (always possible) transition to tyranny lies precisely in its colorfulness, in its cultural pluralism.

The connection between diverse "radiations of imitation" on the one hand and individualization on the other clearly compels us to reject Plato's understanding of role models. Platonic role models claim their status independent of imitators, which would be impossible in a democracy, where role models gain their status only by relying on those who make them – more or less consciously – into role models. As long as we recognize them as such, they are our role models, our powerful "radiations of imitation." They are not so much representatives of a total concept as they are exemplars that show to us our own possibilities.[70] And they can lose this status to competing influences. By recognizing the difference between them and myself, I also recognize a difference within myself, one that under certain circumstances can cause me to make a new decision about myself, to undertake a new act of self-determination. Without the experience of such a difference within myself, there can be no free judgment, rather only blind imitation. The fact that we can never be entirely at one with ourselves (with our role models) is a necessary condition of our freedom. And the resulting tension between ourselves and society is the sole indicator of the uncorrupted life in and of a democracy. We must understand the repeated rejection of society as a way of accepting it.[71] Only by detaching ourselves from society can we relate to it consciously; only then is criticism possible, and only then can we distinguish our consent from conformity.

I would therefore like to conclude this chapter by returning to the Platonic thesis of an ethics-based connection between self-government and government, as well as to the diagnosis of the essential indeterminacy of democracy.

12. Self-Difference and Perfection

The fact that democratic culture assumes all decisions about what is good (for us) to be fallible is not only a sign of the basic fragility of our practical self-understandings and self-relations; rather, as I have attempted to demonstrate, this fragility also represents an opportunity to improve or perfect ourselves and our social practices. However, we should not infuse the concept of "perfecting" with a teleological meaning. As we saw with regard to the ethical problem of self-government, we cannot presuppose a unified subject whose essence gradually becomes more perfect and then ultimately attains perfection. The subject instead seizes itself – repeatedly and ever anew – out of the discontinuous and uncontrolled experiences of a distance from itself, i.e. out of experiences of self-difference. This obviously does not correspond to a teleological movement in which a unified self becomes increasingly enriched. It merely represents a dynamic movement in which what can count as a self is constantly put into question and constantly re-forms itself.[72] Although in our context the concept of self-perfection cannot be grasped in a teleological sense, it should point to the fact that the changes in self-relations and self-understandings that can occur within this dynamic cannot merely be grasped as causal leaps which we experience as passive spectators of an event that happens to us. The concept of self-perfection instead refers to the opportunity to change for the better (or what appears better *prima facie*), which is in turn a part of any reflection on the "question of truth." We can only seize this opportunity if we are open to changes in our world and if we let ourselves be affected by them. The chance to become more perfect, in other words, depends on the basic instability of our practical self-relations and self-understandings. Contrary to social models claiming that we actualize our inner nature, the possibility of perfecting our individual lives must be thought of as a process in which individuals can only acquire unity of self through mimetic expression to others and otherness, i.e. only through the experience of self-difference.

At the same time, however, this is a process in which social practices are also put in question. Indeed, I would misunderstand the changes in myself if I took them to be merely private changes. Through these changes I change the practices of which I too am a part. Occasionally this can occur without our noticing, while in other cases it can lead to collisions between myself and existing practices, a collision that can only be removed by making explicit changes to the world. Changes to the individual's self-understanding can have far-reaching social consequences.[73] That I now choose to understand myself differently can also mean that, in order to be able to live out my new self-understanding, I must enter into a struggle for recognition. In this case the world must change if I want to be able to continue living in it. Within these struggles, the distance of the community to itself becomes manifest, a self-difference that calls for a new and perhaps more just determination of the political order and thus also of what it means to be a member of society.

Precisely because democracy gives its own self-understanding the space to become more perfect, radical democrats, unlike Plato, do not regard the indeterminacy of democracy as a weakness. Although they might not view it as a strength per se, and despite the threats that must be taken seriously, they do view it as an opportunity. It is true that democracy cannot prevent political decisions about the democratic good – about the meaning of a just order – from later proving to be wrong and unjust; this possibility is in fact a condition of democracy's historical existence. Nor can it guarantee that the continuous process of judging, so essential to its historical existence, will always take place; in the opportunist's indifference or in the dynamic of the crowd, it certainly does not. But as we have seen, such suspensions of judgment are not a necessary consequence of democratic freedom. The democratic consciousness of fallibility, its openness to new occurrences, does not intend to suspend all determination in general, but to preserve the opportunity to correct them historically. The democratic ontology of the good – the realization that the good is only given to us historically – opens the life of (in) a democracy not only to the possibility of change, of history, but also to the possibility of improvement.[74] Therefore, faithful democrats are in fact the most suspicious about democracy's forms of appearance. Emphatic democratic moments are those in which a conflict forces the prevailing democratic self-understanding to reflect upon itself and perhaps to revise itself. These are mostly moments in which a political subjectivity emerges that does not already agree with the prevailing social formations on offer and thus initiates an argument about society's democratic self-understanding. The political heart of democracy should thus not be equated with an existing order; rather, its beating can be heard most clearly whenever democracy exposes its orders to the possibility of change for the better, to the possibility of becoming more just.

Consequently, the perfecting of democracy as a form of government should not be thought of as a way of asymptotically approaching a pre-established regulative idea, but as a process in which democracy constantly regains itself in and through the struggle over its essence. The essence of democratic government and self-government, the essence of the democratic culture of freedom, is this openness to what is coming, to the next and future self (our own and that of others), to a different social world. This, however, is not to be understood as a way of postponing or putting something off until something else comes along. Nothing can relieve us of the burden of taking responsibility for our present lives. In the name of our freedom we must determine here and now what is best for us as individuals and as a society. Our determinations of what is good and just are all that we have, that is, for the time being. However, we would not be entirely free if we were not constantly capable of stepping back – through experiences of others and otherness – from these finite determinations in order to acquire a new relationship to our (perhaps older, now reaffirmed) principles.

Without our noticing it, ethics and politics thereby enter into a constellation that fundamentally contradicts the Platonic order of reasons. Plato granted ethics priority over politics: The knowledge of what is suitable to each individual should bring forth a political order in which the good life is completely realized for all; it therefore cannot only be called entirely just, rather it also forms a perfect unity. By contrast, in democracy a dialectic of freedom penetrates both spheres, ethics and politics, and sets them in motion. Because the good is only given to us historically, making our practical orientations never entirely stable, we must constantly redefine what we want (to be) in lived interaction with the world. Because (for the same reason) the meaning of social membership and thus of a just order can never merely be taken as given, it must be posited politically, and thus continuously acknowledged,[75] whereby this meaning is also subject to the possibility of change. This not only sets both ethics and politics in motion, it also sets them in a tense relation to each other – one in which neither side can be subordinated to the other. Because a just order cannot be derived from a certain concept of an individual good life, nor a good individual life from a certain concept of a just order, and because both spheres overlap each other, tensions and conflicts can arise and need to be mediated. As we will see in more detail later (especially in ch. 5), this tension is constitutive for the democratic culture of freedom.[76]

What is astounding about Plato's critique of democracy is not so much the fact that it is particularly fruitful, though in a negative way, for a concept of democracy, rather how influential his aesthetic-critical motives have remained for our modern discourse on freedom and democracy. While the connection between an aestheticized shape of freedom and the problem of arbitrariness shows up in altered form in discussions about romantic irony, his critique of theatrocracy reappears, though inverted, in Rousseau's theory of democracy. As I mentioned in the introduction, for heuristic reasons and contrary to the historical chronology, my own discussion of the diverse variants of modern criticisms of aestheticization follows the Platonic system. I therefore discuss the question of what it means to live a life in freedom (part II) before moving on to the implications of the competing answers for a theory of democracy (part III). The close connection between ethical and political motives in both parts, however, will make evident that Plato's subordination of politics to ethics is untenable from the perspective of a democratic culture of freedom.

Although we cannot understand the modern criticism of aestheticization without grasping the revolving antique motifs that show up there, we must not ignore the obvious historical differences between antique and modern criticisms of aestheticization. For instance, in the case of romanticism, which I will be dealing with in the following chapters, the aestheticized way of life is no longer criticized from an aristocratic perspective but as an elite phenomenon. Historically and systematically decisive is the fact that the modern critique of the aestheticized form of freedom is, at heart, a criticism of modern subjectivism. This is the reason for the surprisingly central position of the critique of romantic irony in the ethical-political discourse of modernity. This critique is of eminently systematic significance for both Hegel and Kierkegaard, as well as for Carl Schmitt. For Hegel, it is what necessitates the transition from morality to "ethical life" [Sittlichkeit]; for Kierkegaard, the criticism of an aesthetic and ironic existence necessitates an initially ethical and then ultimately religious life; and for Schmitt, the criticism of political romanticism is what grounds his critique of liberalism. Despite the obvious differences between these authors, which we will discuss in more detail in the following chapters, their critiques of romanticism all have the same dual character, representing both a critique of culture and of a false philosophy of the subject. All three authors are, on the one hand, reacting to an aesthetic *zeitgeist*: that of the modern, truly democratic epoch.[77] On the other hand, their reactions are linked to the diagnosis that this *zeitgeist*, i.e. its understanding of freedom and the associated social upheavals, derives from the influence of a false philosophy of the subject. Again, this is a major reason why the critique of romanticism is so decidedly modern. It attempts to show that the romantic movement, especially significant for this *zeitgeist*, merely carries forward the very (modern) dualism between subject and object that these authors sought to overcome. The romantic conception of irony thus counts as the epitome of a subjectivist, and thus highly problematic, understanding of freedom. According to Hegel, Kierkegaard, and Schmitt, the significance of the connection between romanticism and the metaphysics of the subject is therefore not only epistemological, but also immediately practical and political. In this sense, however, the criticism of romantic irony cannot be reduced to the critique of a problematic philosophy of the subject. Furthermore, all three authors intertwine this critique with reservations about the understanding of freedom that prevails in the democratic era, to which each of these authors offers his own answer: Hegel with his conception of ethical life; Kierkegaard with his turn to Christian faith; and Schmitt with his anti-liberal theory of political sovereignty.

In the following three chapters, I argue that this understanding of freedom (including its aestheticized, ironic culture) can and must be defended against the accusation of subjectivism. Romantic irony cannot be regarded as a subjectivist self-misunderstanding capable of being therapeutically removed; rather, it must be understood as a structural element of the concept of modern (democratic) ethical life, an element that is as necessary as it is productive (cf. ch. 2). The aesthetic existence that the romantic ironicist embodies for Kierkegaard does not run into an abstract opposition with ethics, but becomes visible in its ethical dimensions (cf. ch. 3). Finally, the romantic self-understanding of liberal democracies can be understood as a self-understanding that opens up a perspective on the problem of sovereignty – a perspective, moreover, that allows us to reject Schmitt's aggressive anti-liberalism (ch. 4).

PART II

The Ethical-Political Right of Irony

2

The Morality of Irony: Hegel*

Hegel's critique of romantic irony occupies an immensely important place in his *Philosophy of Right*, for it is here that he seeks to demonstrate the necessity of a transition from morality to ethical life.[1] The question is how precisely we are to understand this transition and the role of irony in effecting it. One possible interpretation is that Hegel situates irony on the cusp between morality and ethical life because the corresponding understanding of freedom is constitutive of modern ethical life. I consider this the most convincing reading when it comes to making productive use of Hegel's *Philosophy of Right* in the context of a theory of modern ethical life, and it is a reading for which we can find support in Hegel's own work.[2] Here, however, I will be focusing on the elements of Hegel's argumentation that are decidedly critical of irony. What it means to understand irony as a constitutive element of modern ethical life is made particularly evident by the costs that arise if we regard Hegel as a critic of irony, as a theorist for whom irony is not something that should be taken up as a constitutive element of ethical life, but as an expression of a self-misunderstanding of human freedom requiring therapy.[3] Indeed, in certain parts of his work, there is no avoiding such an interpretation. In what follows, I aim to show that Hegel's critique of irony creates tension between, on the one hand, his declared project of developing a theory of modern ethical life in which subjective freedom and difference are respected, and, on the other hand, conservative

* A version of this chapter first appeared in English in *Symposium*, vol. 17, no. 1 (Spring 2013), pp. 100–30. Translated by Daniel Smyth.

arguments which oppose such a project. The latter result in no small part from the way that Hegel's critique of irony distorts the level of morality. I hope to show, with and against Hegel, that one can only remain faithful to the project of a theory of modern ethical life by correcting those aspects of his argument that are critical of irony.

To do so, however, I will not begin with Hegel's famous critique of the romantic ironist's advocacy of a freedom of choice alienated from all ethical life. For Hegel, romantic irony is merely an extreme case of the characteristic divergence of subjective freedom and ethical universality which afflicts morality as a whole. Insofar as romantic irony, according to Hegel, merely continues and exacerbates a much earlier development, any defence of romantic irony must likewise find an earlier foothold. The question is whether each step in Hegel's multifaceted claim is convincing: Is morality as a whole characterized by an increasingly radical opposition between subjective freedom and ethical universality?

1. The Beginning of Morality in Socratic Irony

For Hegel, interestingly enough, irony stands both at the end and the beginning of morality. There are, however, two different forms of irony in play here: Socratic irony lies at the origins of morality, romantic irony at its end. The fact that morality begins with Socratic irony is also noteworthy because Socrates clearly could not have been affiliated with the modern philosophy of the subject, which represents the main target of Hegel's critique of romanticism. Hegel nevertheless sees Socrates as playing an essential, indeed constitutive role in the "age of subjective reflection." In an aside about historical periodization, Hegel actually says: "The principle of the modern age begins ... with the disintegration of Greece in the Peloponnesian war."[4] And what the Peloponnesian war signified for politics, Socrates signified for "thinking consciousness" (cf. GPh 18:448/1:390). According to Hegel, it is with Socrates that "unrestrained ethical life" comes to an end: "The Athenians before Socrates were ethical, not moral men; they did what was rational in their relations without reflection, without knowing that they were virtuous men" (GPh 18:445/1:388). Morality, by contrast, is "ethical life combined with reflection" (ibid.).

Socrates gives rise to the explicit consciousness that everything that exists is mediated through thought. The good must likewise be recognized by the subject in order to realize itself as such. Yet, according to Hegel, Socrates' insistence that the good depends on being known by the subject – as the content of subjective thought – does not mean that the good is merely subjective or arbitrary. This is precisely what is supposed to distinguish Socrates from the Sophists. What Socrates seeks to produce and posit through thought is something objective, which supersedes all inclination and particularity (cf. GPh 18:444/1:387). On Hegel's reading, Socrates' understanding of the freedom of self-consciousness – which requires that I recognize anything that is supposed to be valid for me – should be grasped more precisely as requiring an individual's insight into the absolute validity of something objective, which transcends the specificity of the particular. Naturally, the good must be understood and accepted subjectively if it is to be realized as such; but the actual content of the good is seen to lie outside the realm of subjective reflection as something objectively given. It would thus appear that Hegel makes Socrates out to be an essentially Platonic figure.[5] Like Plato, Socrates advances an objective conception of the good and, accordingly, an overly theoretical conception of the subjective recognition of the good as knowledge.

Hegel does not, however, content himself with this picture of Socratic praxis.[6] In contrast to Platonic philosophy – a distinction that, for Hegel, is both immensely significant and consequential – Socrates never develops his philosophy into a system, but remains at the level of "individual doings" (cf. GPh 18:455/1:387). The fact that Hegel understands Socratic practice as an incomplete, preliminary stage along the way to a full picture of the philosophical system explains his highly ambivalent judgment of Socratic philosophy in general and Socratic irony in particular. Hegel commends Socrates, unlike the romantics, for assigning irony "a limited significance" (GPh 18:461/1:402) as a pedagogical instrument. For Hegel, the "truth" in Socrates' irony consists in his "putting himself forward as ignorant" (GPh 18:457/1:398) in order to entangle his interlocutor in a conversation, over the course of which the latter's prejudices about the various topics under discussion are first articulated and then dismantled, thus freeing his mind for the truth. Yet it would be a mistake to infer that Hegel thereby overlooks the fact that Socrates might well have been wholly serious in uttering his famous claim "I know that I know nothing." Indeed, Hegel is all too conscious of this possibility.

Most Socratic dialogues simply aim to generate confusion about the concept of the topic or object under discussion. Although this might lead to further serious reflection, unlike a proper philosophical system, it does not necessarily lead to a result. Though the Socratic method is essentially designed "to lead to the *true* good, to the universal idea" (GPh 18:461/1:402), it never succeeds in providing the positive content of the topic or object, but can only give negative clues and hints by ironically destroying prejudices. "This merely negative side" is, according to Hegel, the "main thing" for Socrates (GPh 18:466/1:406). Nevertheless, Hegel notes parenthetically that the productive dimension of Socratic negativity coincides with dialectic: "All dialectic treats as valid whatever is put forward as valid, and lets the inner destruction develop itself – universal irony of the world" (GPh 18:460/1:400). Compared to Hegel's conception of the task of philosophy, the merely negative force of ironic practice is obviously insufficient. The "flaw of the Socratic principle" in Hegel's eyes consists in Socrates' inability to give a concrete, positive determination of the good (GPh 18:468/1:407).

In the course of diagnosing this flaw, Hegel attributes to Socrates a deeply ambivalent position on Athenian ethical life. At the same time, he sees Socrates "at the forefront" (GPh 18:468/1:407) of a development that drives the "Greek spirit [*Geist*]" to its "flourishing" (GPh 18:469/1:408). Hegel views the introduction of subjective consciousness as being responsible for the "highest liveliness" of Athenian ethical life, because it leads to the latter's free and conscious recognition (GPh 18:469/1:408). Yet, this summit already shows signs of an impending fall, for which Socrates will again be the avant-garde. Because Socratic reflection does not attain to any positive determination of the good, rather merely casting doubt on prevailing laws and prohibitions, it effects a separation – indeed, an opposition – between a given form of ethical life and reflective freedom.

2. Socrates' Divisive Work

According to Hegel, Socrates endeavors to drive a wedge between ethical universality and reflective freedom by presenting particular counterexamples to the pre-critical acceptance of the universal validity of prevailing laws and prohibitions. Contrary to the commandment "Thou shalt not lie," he asserts that lying is not reprehensible in all cases – if, for example, one is protecting an innocent person from persecution. What seemed to have absolute validity now suddenly appears to have only relative validity. This, for Hegel, represents the beginning of morality, for the core of the moral mindset, which "rattles about in this enduring contradiction" (GPh 18:487/1:419) and consists in attending to singular cases of conflict between universally formulated duties and weighing them against each other. We shall return later to the question whether the description of moral conflicts as collisions of universally valid duties is ultimately accurate (cf. sec. 7).

On Hegel's interpretation, however, such reflections inevitably open the door to sophistry. If particular cases are permitted to restrict the universal validity of a principle, then it will be perceived as a particular claim that is sometimes valid and sometimes not, thereby destroying the authority of the principle together with its universality (cf. GPh 18:481/1:418). Furthermore, everything is seen to depend on manipulable circumstances, for with enough rhetorical skill, any state of affairs can be presented and interpreted at will, such that any rule can be suspended on any occasion. In Hegel's view, because Socratic philosophy merely preaches purely negative freedom in opposition to the validity of prevailing principles, it is powerless in the face of this threat and can easily be replaced by contingent private interests (cf. GPh 18:486–87/no corresponding passage in English edition, but see 1:429), i.e. by merely subjective whim. The failure of Socratic philosophy to provide a positive determination of the good renders it incapable of coping with an "ambiguity" on which "everything [has] turn[ed]" in philosophy ever since Protagoras (cf. GPh 18:430/1:373f.). Protagoras' famous dictum that man is the measure of all things can thus be understood in two different ways. It can be taken to pertain to man's "rational nature," his "universal substantiality" (ibid.), but it could also be taken to address man's "contingent humanity" and "specific particularity" (ibid.). The decision to analyze the sentence one way or the other is thus tantamount to deciding between reason and arbitrariness. And in the context of Socratic philosophy, according to Hegel's critique, this decision itself can only be made arbitrarily, for it rests on the "contingency of character" (GPh 18:490/1:421).

The negativity of Socratic philosophy in its pursuit of truth ultimately brings it into perilous proximity to a mode of Sophistry guided by private interest. For Hegel, this dangerous affinity manifests itself not only in the historically dubious development of Socrates' followers Alcibiades and Critias – the one a "genius of folly," the other "the most influential of the thirty tyrants" (GPh 18:515/1:421) – but also in the aggressive reactions that the historical Socrates brought upon himself. And with good reason, if one follows Hegel, who views the extremely unflattering depiction of Socrates as a Sophist in Aristophanes' *The Clouds* as being profoundly true.[7] Aristophanes recognized the danger implicit in any insight into the "nullity" of "what natural consciousness holds as the truth" (GPh 18:484/1:428). Accordingly, Hegel not only understands the assault of "common sense" on Socrates' "Thinkery," with which Aristophanes closes his play,[8] but also the complaint that the Athenian people raised against the historical Socrates. As Aristophanes' portrayal shows, Socrates truly did alienate his students from traditional ethical life. By planting doubts in his students' minds about the universal validity of laws and prohibitions, Socrates provoked dissatisfaction with the life their parents had planned for them. This, according to Hegel, is to poison "the mother's milk of ethical life" (GPh 18:505/1:437). Anyone who violates this "first immediate ethical relation" violates ethical life in its "essential form" (ibid.). Moreover, Hegel continues, it is perfectly justified to accuse Socrates of heresy; after all, Socrates admittedly occupies an intermediate position – both historically and according to his own self-understanding – between the former "naïve" ethics of Athens and his own principle of subjective freedom. Thus the Socratic "*daimon*" – a voice Socrates perceives as simultaneously foreign and inward – occupies an intermediate position between the oracles of the ancient world and the new principle of conscience. As a nonetheless individual authority, however, the Socratic "*daimon*" is structurally inimical to the ancient divine world, a harbinger of the profound revolution that culminates in the wholesale replacement of the oracle with "the individual self-consciousness of each man" (GPh 18:503/1:435).

Just as Hegel sees a partial truth in the "naïve ethics" of Athens, despite its pre-reflective status, he does not completely reject the principle Socrates embodies, despite his critique of its negativity. Rather, he grants that there is an element, though only an element, of truth to this principle. It is thus quite consistent for Hegel to regard Socrates' fate as tragic not because he supposedly died for his freedom[9] – that would not be genuinely tragic, but rather heroic. Hegel instead regards Socrates' fate as tragic because it is the inevitable consequence of a conflict between two equally justified principles: "In the truly tragic," Hegel writes, "there must be justified ethical principles on both sides which come to collide; this is how it is with the fate of Socrates. His fate is not just his personal, individual, romantic fate; rather it is the tragedy of Athens, the tragedy of Greece that plays itself out there, that presents itself in him" (GPh 18:447/no corresponding passage in English edition). In this conflict, both sides lose – albeit in an asymmetrical way. Socrates dies, of course, but the physical destruction of the person cannot eliminate the principle he advanced. On the contrary, Socrates' principle ultimately triumphed as the "higher principle" (GPh 18:516/1:448). Athens itself, Hegel says, ultimately collapses due to its inability to integrate the principle of subjective freedom into the universality of ethical life. The death of Socrates, like the downfall of Athens, is for Hegel the effect of a single tragic collision between two justified but equally deficient principles that have not yet been sublated into a third. Accordingly, modern ethical life is supposed to distinguish itself from ancient ethical life by incorporating subjective freedom: "In our constitution," Hegel writes, "the universal of the states is a stronger universal, yet one which permits individuals to have freer play; they cannot become so dangerous for this universal" (GPh 18:507/1:439). It remains to be seen whether, as Hegel claims, subjective freedom can be sublated and preserved in modern ethical life in a way that no longer threatens the universal while still having room to unfold. The position of subjective freedom in Hegel's conception of modern ethical life depends in no small part on his account of the levels of morality that reach their apex in romantic irony.

According to Hegel, the opposition between subjective freedom and ethical universality is not just responsible for the "tragedy of Greece"; it is also characteristic of those forms of morality that dominate the modern self-understanding. The fact that the principle of subjective freedom managed to prevail historically hardly constitutes a reason to forget its previously diagnosed problems. Quite the opposite. The problems with morality that arise from the original sin of falsely supposing that subjective freedom is opposed to ethical universality only grow more acute. Yet, as we have seen, Hegel sees these difficulties already in the fluid transitions between Socrates and the Sophists. On Hegel's reading, Socratic philosophy questions the absolute validity of ethical laws and prohibitions by examining particular circumstances in order to relativize the supposed universal validity of conflicting laws and prohibitions and to weigh them against each other. This account of Socratic reflection entails that conscience and duty, individual and ethical norms, are both subject to unequal presuppositions and opposed to each other. Because Socratic philosophy merely preaches reflective freedom from universally valid laws and prohibitions, Hegel concludes that (1) it is structurally indifferent to these laws and prohibitions, which is why (2) it cannot control whether reflective freedom is governed by the desire for truth or the desire for private advantage. Therefore, (3) the moral consciousness of the interpretability of laws and prohibitions subjects the latter to the arbitrary will of the interpreter and, accordingly, (4) duty is subordinated to conscience, and ethical norms to the individual. This line of argument brings us quite close to Hegel's critique of the overweening arbitrariness of romantic irony. The distinction between Socrates and the romantics is merely one of degree. The romantics simply radicalize the problems of morality that have their origin in Socrates.

3. Irony and the Practice of Truth

Although we are still not in a position to judge whether Hegel's portrayal of Socratic and moral reflection is entirely accurate (a question we will return to in sec. 5), it is apparent that Hegel's interpretation of Socratic philosophy lacks any reference to the intersubjective space of (giving and asking for) reasons, which provides the framework for the opposition between truth and illusion, knowledge and opinion, public and private interest. It is noteworthy, for example, that Hegel considers the dialogical form of Socratic philosophy only insofar as its function is to unsettle the ethical convictions of the interlocutor, but not as a medium for an intersubjective practice of truth.[10] Yet if we view Socratic philosophy from this latter perspective, we could make several objections to Hegel's interpretation. If we understand Socratic practice as such a practice of truth, it becomes clear that it by no means eliminates all reference to truth (nor to the good). Nor can this reference simply amount to an incomplete version of Platonism, as Hegel suggests. The practice of giving and asking for reasons does not aim at a truth (or good) that is given independently of that practice, as the Platonists would have it. Rather it reveals that the truth (the good) is and can only be given in and through the practice of giving and asking for reasons. This kind of practice by no means prevents determinations of the (relevant) good from becoming universal. Should they manage to do so, then they clearly ought not to be considered merely subjective, arbitrary determinations. Nevertheless, such determinations remain finite. We can perhaps summarize a few of the basic insights of post-metaphysical philosophy of language by saying that the truth (the good) must always be rediscovered anew in the space of (giving and asking for) reasons. This is because (1) the possibility of error, illusion, or self-deception belongs to the very mode of existence of finite beings, equipped as they are with only limited perspectives on themselves and the world, and yet imbricated in a history with an open future; (2) the plurality of social perspectives challenges the very idea of an ultimate perspective from which the whole, genuine, and actually true truth is open to view; (3) the intersubjectivity of language, which is the locus of all possible truth, is at the same time the locus of what Heidegger called "idle talk" and unreflectively accepted opinion. This is why truth must constantly be recovered from this dimension of human life by questioning (and responding to these questions with justifications of) what can count as true in a particular context.[11] Precisely because Socratic practice – unlike Platonic practice – abstains from presenting a concept of the truly good, it appears to provide a paradigm for such a practice of truth by disclosing an intersubjective and thus essentially historical space for the truth (about the good).

Hegel, by contrast, is only capable of seeing the false isolation of subjective consciousness from ethical universality. For him Socratic negativity represents only one moment in spirit's historical development, which must be sublated in order to give rise to a positive determination of the good. There are serious drawbacks to this misconception, which also affect some of the fundamental intuitions of Hegel's own philosophy, which famously emphasizes the need to think through intersubjectivity and historicity. This misconception paves the way not just for those strands of Hegel's philosophy that force us to expel all intersubjectivity from ethical life, but also for those that compel the philosopher of history to position himself "on the side of the unchangeable in the midst of history," as Adorno put it.[12] To the extent that Hegel associates the dimension of intersubjectivity with the collective hegemony of norms rather than with the dynamics of a practice of truth, he can only celebrate the liveliness of a prevailing mode of ethical life insofar as all disputes about its substance have been eliminated and intersubjective debates about the truth have been laid to rest in the affirmative reproduction of prevailing norms.[13] The role of subjective freedom is thereby reduced solely to the potential for recognizing that, from a certain perspective, the universal and the particular are *always already* mediated in ethical life. I will return to these motifs later (sec. 12).

The problematic strands of Hegel's philosophy already become visible in his interpretation of Socrates. Although he is aware of the contradiction that a prevailing form of ethical life, which is something concrete, nevertheless aspires to be universally valid, his strategy for resolving this contradiction – i.e. marginalizing particular cases – contrasts starkly with that of Socrates. He writes that "the inconsistency of making what is limited into an absolute certainly becomes unconsciously corrected in the ethical man; this correction lies in the ethical status of the subject, in the whole of communal life. There can be extreme cases of collision, which are unfortunate; but these are uncommonly rare cases" (GPh 18:477/1:415). He goes on to say that "the laws, the ethical norms, the regime, governance, the actual life of the state have within themselves the corrective for the inconsistency involved in pronouncing such a determinate content to be absolutely valid" (GPh 18:489/1:420). According to Hegel, the "restriction of the universal" must be recognized in a concrete mode of ethical life so that "it holds fast and does not become contingent" – namely, as the "spirit of a people" (GPh 18:488/1:419–20).[14]

Such arguments contrast with Hegel's project of developing a theory of modern ethical life that preserves a space for subjective freedom, insofar as subjective freedom is only allowed a place in ethical life to the extent that it coincides with prevailing ethical norms. If we are to reject such arguments, we must dispute the diagnosis that represents their primary motivation. In other words, we must refute the suspicion that Socratic reflection falsely relativizes laws and commandments. This is the only way to show that moral reflection does not necessarily give rise to the opposition between subjective freedom and ethical universality that Hegel diagnoses – with problematical consequences for his own project.

Yet in doing so, we must not overlook the possibility that Hegel's objection – that morality implies insufficient mediation between subjective freedom and ethical universality – may be justified when applied to the most prominent modern form of morality: the Kantian moral principle. Because of his misconception of Socratic morality, Hegel was not able to suggest an alternative formulation of the intuitions connected with the moral principle on the basis of his critique of Kant. Instead, he is obliged to view the whole of morality as an increasingly explicit manifestation of a one-sided subjectivism. In what follows, I will therefore attempt to show – both with and against Hegel – that there is a defensible alternative to Kant's interpretation of the moral principle – one that retains the spirit of Hegel's critique of Kant while contradicting Hegel's critique of both Socratic and romantic irony. Both forms of irony – the Socratic and the romantic – illuminate aspects of morality that should not be superseded by a conception of modern ethical life, but rather integrated as constitutive elements into such a conception.

I will proceed in three steps. First, I will briefly recapitulate Hegel's critique of Kant (sec. 4) in order to use it as a framework for an alternative understanding of Socratic morality (sec. 5). We will then be in a position to see romantic irony in a different light (secs 6 through 11).

4. Hegel's Critique of Kant

The guiding thesis of the *Philosophy of Right* is that something is right, or someone is in the right, if the claim of the relevant issue or person is an expression of freedom. Within morality, according to Hegel, this idea represents the principle that something is right or justified when the subject can recognize it as "its own" (Rph §107).

The recognition of something as right or justified is therefore supposed to simultaneously express a kind of reflective self-appropriation on the part of the recognizing subject. Yet as we have seen, on Hegel's diagnosis, this understanding of right necessarily leads him to posit an abstract opposition between subjective freedom and ethical universality. At least initially, Kant appears to differ from this diagnosis in that he links the notion of reflective self-appropriation to the idea of instituting and obeying universal laws. But for Hegel, this in no way resolves the problematic opposition between subjective freedom and ethical universality. On the contrary, the Kantian moral principle only renders it more acute.

Hegel's critique of Kant's moral principle of autonomy, both as it is developed in his Jena writings and repeated in his *Philosophy of Right*, focuses on what he terms its "empty formalism" (Rph §135). Indeed, the formal requirement that autonomy of the will means acting on maxims that can simultaneously be conceived of as universal laws necessarily fails to determine the content of the maxim itself. This leads Hegel to conclude that, in principle, there cannot be anything "which could not be made into an ethical law."[15] Rather, any arbitrary content, "any determinacy," has the potential "to be taken up into the form of the concept" and thus to be logically or semantically posited as universal. But which of these innumerable determinacies can truly aspire to universality in a normative sense cannot, according to Hegel, be determined on the basis of such a formalism. In presuming that even "the most common understanding" can decide this question "without any instruction," however, Kant presupposes that a correlative determination is already available.[16] For example, the fact that stealing, considered as a universal law, is incompatible with the requirement of private property presupposes that it is already clear (posited) that there should *be* private property. But in that case the "sublime faculty of autonomy in the legislation of practical reason" in truth merely boils down to the "production of tautologies" (JS 460). In this case, if there is to be private property, there must be private property (cf. JS 463). From a Hegelian perspective, the question of how a moral law can be binding gives rise to a paradox. Terry Pinkard summarizes the problem by pointing out that the paradox derives from Kant's demand that we have a reason to impose a principle (the moral law) on ourselves. If there is a previously given reason to adopt this or that principle, then we have not imposed that reason upon ourselves. Yet in order for that reason to be binding (to use Kant's formulation), we must be able to claim that we have imposed it upon ourselves. In brief, Kant presupposes a lawless agent who gives laws to himself on the basis of other laws, which must precede that act of legislation, but which are also supposed to follow from it.[17]

The real danger that Hegel sees in the paradox of Kantian self-legislation does not merely consist in the fact that it is tautological, i.e. that when it comes to prevailing ethical norms, it seems *obvious* to the subject which specific content should be made into a universal law. Hegel sees an even greater problem in the "unethical" status of Kantian self-legislation (JS 463). For even conditioned, arbitrary contents can be "slipped into" an absolute, logical form by "sleight of hand" (JS 464). According to Hegel, this unavoidable multiplication of different yet purportedly universal determinacies has the distinctly unethical effect of making "that which is ethically necessary ... into something contingent": "yet contingency in ethical life ... is unethical" (JS 467).

We could of course point out, as many Kantians naturally do, that the contents of the Kantian moral principle are not generated by reason's self-legislation. Rather, reason examines these contents empirically in order to judge their legality.[18] But there is a problem with this reading of Kant, one which appears to bring him a step closer to Hegel insofar as the moral principle is regarded as secondary to the practices it presupposes. Where does the latter obtain its criteria of judgment? Hegel's objection thus merely re-emerges on a new level, for the moral principle can *never* operate in a normative vacuum. The criterion for evaluating our actions must ultimately have its source in these actions themselves. We could, however, make a further attempt to defend Kant against Hegel's criticism by arguing that the Kantian moral principle does not operate on the basis of a determinate and substantive internal standard, but solely on the basis of a formal question concerning the universalizability of contents. This is a question that clearly does not merely pertain to the "grammatical form of normative generalizations, but [to] universality of the will."[19]

But in this case, Kant falls prey to Hegel's first objection that this principle is entirely tautological. And this, in my view, is the ultimate essence of Hegel's critique of Kant. It consists in the realization that the ethical background necessarily comes into play in the categorical imperative. What is called the universality of the will is therefore *de facto* not entirely universal; it remains bound to the concrete character and thus to the particularity of a prevailing mode of ethical life.[20] For precisely this reason, Kant's categorical imperative can function only in the context of an absolutely untroubled, or as Hegel puts it, "naïve" ethical life of unquestioning agreement. In other words, it can only function as a tautology.

If Hegel is right that the mediation of the universal and the particular represents the central question of morality, and that Kant fails to provide a satisfactory mediation of the two, then the question arises whether – and if so, how – we might reformulate the moral principle in light of this objection. One can hardly look to Kant for such a reformulation of the relevant Kantian intuitions. In my view, we must instead attend to what Kant uncritically presupposes: the commonality of our understanding of the world and of ourselves in moral reflection. That in turn leads us back to Socrates.

5. A Socratic Reformulation of the Moral Principle

Socratic reflection, as Hegel presents it, questions the validity of universal principles in light of various concrete situations in which different demands – which are presumed to be universal – come into conflict with each other. When that happens, it appears our task is to weigh these demands against each other and, if necessary, to relativize their respective claims to universality. This notion of Socratic reflection differs from Kant's account with regard to where it locates the problem of grounding moral principles. The central question for Socrates does not seem to be how moral norms can be grounded or justified, but rather how, assuming they are valid in our practices, we can justify exceptions to them. Yet closer examination reveals, as we shall shortly see, that such a description is not only wrong, but also insufficiently radical. Socrates does not merely seek to reject universal norms by advocating the validity of exceptions in certain situations. The systematic essence of his focus on cases of exception goes deeper, claiming that only once we attend to such exceptions can we get sight of how all moral judgment is dependent on particular situations. Once we grasp this dependency in a Socratic manner, it becomes clear that the universality anticipated in moral judgments is not primarily located on the level of moral norms themselves. It is rather to be found in what Albrecht Wellmer has called the "communicative substructure" of Kantian ethics: the level that concerns our understanding of the world and of ourselves, an understanding that underlies how we interpret any given situation.[21]

A decisive first step toward what I would term a Socratic reformulation of the moral principle involves recognizing the fact that even universal formulations of moral norms always indicate particular situations. Any consideration of their genesis confirms this fact. As Wellmer emphasizes, moral norms are formed negatively, i.e. by negating non-universalizable maxims. Once I establish that I cannot want a maxim – for example, to lie whenever it benefits me – to be a universal law, it follows that it would be morally wrong for me to act on it anyway. But before we reformulate the result of this reasoning as a moral norm – e.g. "one ought not to lie" – we should (despite Kant's imprecision on this point) pause to reflect on how the universal form of this norm is generated. Because this norm arises from the negation of determinate grounds for action – lying to further private ends and interests – it would be wrong to construe it as a prohibition of the action type in question, as lying *tout court*. And for this reason, exceptions to universal formulations of moral norms can indeed be morally justified – e.g. lying in order to protect an innocent person from persecution – without thereby undermining the validity of the categorical imperative that "one ought not to lie (for private interests)."[22] So it turns out to be misleading to even talk about "exceptions" to moral norms.

Similarly, we are now in a position to show that it is equally misleading for Hegel to portray Socratic reflection as seeking to relativize the validity of universally formulated principles out of sentimental attachment to exceptional cases. If we take into account that a universal formulation of moral norms implies a negation of *determinate* grounds for action, then it becomes clear, in accordance with Hegel's compressed account, that moral reflection does not involve a collision between two equally valid but conflicting norms – "one ought not to lie" versus "one ought to protect the innocent from persecution." Rather, closer consideration – i.e. further Socratic reflection – reveals that we need not acknowledge any real exceptions to the rule "one ought not to lie" in concrete practical situations, since we simply are not dealing with instances of its application. The lies in discussion are not told in order to advance individual interests, but for a morally obligatory reason.[23] We can summarize the crucial systematic point in this context by noting that moral norms make reference, both in their genesis and in their validity, to modes of action in determinate situations.

Nevertheless, it is still uncertain whether particular modes of acting can be universalized or not. This holds true for morally complex cases as well as for those Wellmer terms "morally elementary."[24] Defending the universalizability of a person's actions in a morally complex situation necessarily involves recourse to a particular – or particular type of – situation. In *this* situation or in a situation *like this one*, we are obliged (or permitted) to do such and such. Assessing the universalizability of modes of action in morally complex situations can, however, lead to what Wellmer describes as "the dilemma that the *domain of application* for such a maxim gets *smaller* the *more precisely* I characterize the relevant type of situation, and that it becomes more *indeterminate* the more *universal* my characterization."[25] Yet according to Wellmer, this dilemma – that modes of action cannot be formulated as rules in complex situations in the same way they can in elementary ones – shows only that "the *power of judgement* [plays] a much more fundamental role in the application of moral norms than Kant would like to admit."[26] Moral arguments arise wherever there are moral problems, that is, wherever questions about the appropriateness and relative completeness of situational descriptions give rise to moral discourse in the first place.[27] Once these questions are resolved, the problem is generally neutralized, as it is clear what is to be done. Indeed, fundamental moral norms are not what usually spark controversy in cases of moral conflict, but rather characterizations of the situations or types of situations to which they are to be applied. Socratic dialogues provide excellent examples of this: Socrates asks his interlocutors whether he has described a situation correctly and completely; the others then supplement the description or – as is usually the case – nod in agreement. If, therefore, cases of moral conflict call into question not moral norms but rather the perception and description of the relevant situations to which they are to be applied, then, Wellmer argues, there is no clean way of separating justificatory from applicatory discourse when it comes to moral judgments. He even advances the stronger claim that the problem of justification specific to moral judgment is primarily a problem of application.[28] The problem of justification always refers either explicitly or implicitly to the interpretation of the situations in which the moral quality of a mode of action is in question.[29] The question of whether my maxim can become a universal law cannot be treated apart from the question of whether my representation of the corresponding practical situation is complete, apt, and true (rather than a Sophistical distortion). Even within moral reflection itself, therefore, the universality of moral judgment must necessarily be traced back to what Kant assumes to be entirely unproblematic: The level of our shared, intersubjective understandings of the world and ourselves.

The moral standpoint thus clearly does not summarily call into question the validity of all laws and commandments, as though it purported to stand above all practices. That would indeed represent a kind of reflective formalism bordering on insanity, having "crossed over" the "threshold of social pathology."[30] Ethical laws and commandments only become the object of moral discourse in very concrete moral conflicts. It would be wrong, however, to construe these conflicts as collisions between two universally formulated norms – collisions which can only be neutralized by relativizing (at least) one of the norms in question. Such a description is, as we have seen, misleading. There are really only two circumstances that lead to moral conflicts in the proper sense. A moral conflict may arise if there are competing views about the appropriateness or completeness of a given description of the relevant situation. The other circumstance in which moral conflict may ensue concerns the level of agents' understanding of the world and of themselves, for this level underlies and supports the interpretation of any given situation. Differences in worldview or self-understanding may therefore lead to differences of interpretation of a given situation. In such cases, this "communicative substructure" – the shared understanding of self and world – serves not only as a presupposition of moral discourse, but also as its object and aim. Though this second type of conflict may well play a latent role in the debate between Socrates and the Sophists, it becomes fully manifest in the individualism of the romantic ironists.

Romantic irony, on my view, sheds light on the scenario that emerges from the Socratic reformulation of the moral principle with regard to the second sort of moral conflict – i.e. conflicts deriving from differences in our understanding of the world and ourselves. For this reason, Hegel is quite right to situate romantic irony on the threshold of his own conception of modern ethical life. If modern ethical life is not informed and shaped by romantic irony, it ceases to exist altogether (or at least it ceases to be modern). In order to grasp this point, we must insist – both with and against Hegel – that ethical life does not overcome or supersede the purportedly deficient forms of romantic irony and the morality connected with it, but actually sublates and preserves these forms within itself. It is precisely by considering the romantics' individualism that we can show – in agreement with Hegel – that the logic of morality is by no means to be understood as abstractly opposing subjective freedom to ethical universality. Such considerations, as I will now attempt to show, instead reveal the necessity of dynamic mediation between these two sides. Remarkably, it is the ironists – Socrates on the one side, the romantics on the other – who guide us toward a reformulation of the moral principle which both takes account of Hegel's critique of Kant while remaining true to Hegel's intention of dynamically mediating between the universal and the particular, even where Hegel himself falls prey to a conservative impulse.

Yet in order to bring this third path into view (sec. 2), we will first need to discuss Hegel's critique of the romantics in more detail (secs 6–10).

6. Critique of the Romantics

From Hegel's perspective, romantic irony represents a radicalization of the opposition between subjective freedom and ethical universality that began with Socrates. Hegel considers Socratic morality incapable of excluding the sort of private interest that subtly influences how we interpret competing duties. He therefore sees in Socratic praxis the origin of a conflict between subjective freedom (private choice) and ethical universality – even if this conflict is temporarily concealed by Socrates' own individual virtue. In this context, Kant appears merely as a further developmental stage in the ever-increasing radicalization of this conflict. For Hegel, the purported universal validity of the Kantian moral principle is, on account of its merely formal grounding, a mere pretence that prevents insight into the nature of this conflict. The romantics, by contrast, have the dubious advantage of at least allowing the conflict between subjective freedom and ethical universality to clearly come to light.

It is for this reason that the romantics – Friedrich Schlegel in particular – have a systematic significance for Hegel, as they make explicit the increasing separation between subjective freedom and ethical universality that began with Socrates. The truth is supposed to reveal itself in romantic irony, for the way the latter presents the problem of morality requires that we transition to a level that supersedes it. This necessary transition is supposed to reveal itself in the fact that the standpoint of morality, in which the corresponding conception of freedom manifests itself in its pure and unadulterated form, must necessarily collapse into its opposite and thereby destroy itself. The opposite of morality, however, is evil.

Hegel's *Phenomenology of Spirit* had already asserted the necessity of this transition from the standpoint of morality into evil.[31] On Hegel's interpretation, the moral standpoint implicitly contains a complete inversion of the original concept of duty. While "naïve ethical life" places the ethical consciousness of duty above self-consciousness, the conditions of morality effectively reverse this relation. Holding fast to a purported duty is then labeled evil, while acting out of self-certainty becomes a duty and an instance of conscientious behavior. Because Hegel is unable to view moral reflection as anything other than an element in the arbitrary relativization of ethical laws and prohibitions, he interprets it as an "inverted" [*verkehrte*] position in both senses of the term (both "inverted" and "incorrect") and thus as a form of hypocrisy. For Hegel, evil consciousness, which openly postulates that "I am [evil]," (PhG 405) has the crucial function of resolving the "inversion" of moral hypocrisy by "pressing [it] to its ultimate consequence" and thus distilling the pure "spiritual shape of conscience."[32] All that remains of conscience and its hypocritical commitment to universality is the self-certainty of the subject in evil consciousness. And this is precisely what Schlegel's irony amounts to on Hegel's interpretation. It is the "acme of the subjectivity that conceives of itself as the ultimate [authority]" and is thus identical with "evil, and indeed with the evil which is completely universal in itself" (cf. Rph §140). For the romantic ironists, even those things that are "ethically objective," even "law and object [*Sache*]," are merely moves in a game that has expressly ceased to revolve around anything more than self-satisfaction [*Selbstgenuss*] (ibid.). Therefore, by taking on the form of evil, in which individual subjectivity quite explicitly posits itself as the absolute standing against all ethical authority, morality becomes the complete opposite of itself: immorality. Hegel claims to have thereby proven the necessity of overcoming morality in and through a theory of ethical life.

Hegel's interpretation of romantic irony as the culmination of a subjectivism in which arbitrary choice reigns supreme traces back to his claim that romantic irony must be understood as a practical application of Fichte's philosophy of subjectivity. Thus, Hegel already saw Fichte as "Kant's perfecter."[33] Fichte, in contrast to Kant's own "inverted" philosophy, had expressly made the ego "into the absolute principle of all knowledge, all reason and cognition."[34] But this would mean, among other things, that "every content which is to have value for the *ego* is only posited and recognized by the *ego* itself" (Ä I 93/64). The consequence of such a subjectivist philosophy, as Hegel claims in a section of his *Lectures on Fine Arts* dealing with the influence of Fichte's philosophy on the romantic conception of irony, is that the ego becomes the "lord and master of everything," and

> in no sphere of morals, law, things human and divine, profane and sacred, is there anything that would not first have to be laid down by the ego, and that therefore could not equally well be destroyed by it. Consequently everything genuinely and independently real becomes only a show, not true and genuine on its own account or through itself, but a mere appearance due to the ego in whose power and caprice and at whose free disposal it remains. (Ä I 94/65)

As much as Hegel sees traces in Fichte's work of the problems he discusses in connection with romantic irony, the practical consequences of Fichte's philosophy of the subject only become apparent in romantic irony, which is why the latter is of greater significance for his practical philosophy. While Fichte held fast to the objective validity of the ethical – if only on conceptually inconsistent grounds[35] – Schlegel degraded the ethical to a product of subjective beliefs and thereby made "the subject's choice the principle of the practical [realm]" (Rph §140, 285–6/180–1). From this perspective, romantic irony appears to be a dangerous means for subverting ethical substance. For it would seem to regard nothing as holy apart from the capricious and arbitrary choices of the subject itself. As Hegel notes in *Aesthetics*, romantic irony's lack of measure and limits distinguishes it significantly from comedy. While comedy only directs its destructive power at that which is "inherently null," i.e. "a false and contradictory phenomenon, a whim, e.g. an oddity, a particular caprice in comparison with a mighty passion or even a *supposedly* tenable principle and firm maxim," the destructive power of irony even threatens "what is in fact moral and true, any inherently substantial content" (Ä I 97/67). The ironist sees in everything "which otherwise has value, dignity, and sanctity for mankind just a product of his own power of caprice, whereby he is at liberty either to grant validity to such things, to determine himself and fill his life by means of them, or the reverse" (Ä I 95/65f.). "He," Hegel continues,

> who has reached the standpoint of divine genius looks down from his high rank on all other men, for they are pronounced dull and limited, inasmuch as law, morals, etc., still count for them as fixed, essential, and obligatory. So then the individual, who lives in this way as an artist, does give himself relations to others; he lives with friends, mistresses, etc.; but, by his being a genius, this relation to his own specific reality, his particular actions, as well as to what is absolute and universal, is at the same time null; his attitude to it all is ironical.

This, Hegel concludes, comprises

> the general meaning of the divine irony of genius, as this concentration of the ego into itself, for which all bonds are snapped and which can live only in the bliss of self-enjoyment. This irony was invented by Friedrich von Schlegel, and many others have babbled about it or are now babbling about it again. (Ä I 95/66)

Hegel's central objection to the romantic ironist is that his supposed freedom of choice, in truth, signifies nothing more than a form of unfreedom, especially for the ironist himself. Hegel traces the transition from the romantic pretention to freedom in actual unfreedom back to a category mistake: The romantics misunderstand their respective empirical I as being pure, i.e. "abstract and formal" (Ä I 93/64), thereby negating "every particularity, every characteristic, every content" (ibid.), thus everything that makes the I concrete. Such a misunderstanding would indeed have far-reaching consequences. Because the romantic ironist takes his freedom to be something absolute in contrast to his own determinacy, he is compelled to believe that the only way to preserve himself and his own freedom is to deny all determination by the world and to avoid all commitments in and to it. This is the reason for his fundamental alienation from all practices. For practices necessarily involve determinations – either in the form of a confrontation with pre-established situations or in the form of decisions about how to act in view of circumstances and standards. One could therefore only live out the infinity of an absolute and abstract freedom by retreating from practices into a sphere of pure possibility. The "disposition" formed by such an understanding of freedom would be "dead, even if its aspiration is to be beautiful," "for inertia would rather not emerge from that inward brooding in which it reserves a universal possibility for itself" (Rph §13, Addition).

Such a conception of freedom would, furthermore, necessarily run into the contradiction that it "cannot even attain what it wants to attain. Someone who wants to protect abstract freedom still has no choice but to exist concretely."[36] In particular, to the extent that all determination is supposed to be taken up into the subject, the sole foundation of determination that remains for the ironist is his "natural individuality" and its contingent excitations, i.e. his drives and inclinations. And these excitations are always dependent upon changing outer stimuli. Consequently, the truth of such freedom of choice ultimately consists in nothing other than unfreedom, viz. in the dependency of the ironist on contingent stimuli, by means of which he allows himself to be heteronymously determined. At the same time, an exclusive orientation toward "natural individuality," changing moods and states of mind, would lead to a process of unending self-reflection without any grounding. To the extent that he regards all substance to be "empty" and "vain," the I, thrown back upon its own incidental particularity, would itself become empty (cf. Ä I 96/67).

For Hegel, this explains the romantic longing for reality and the absolute, a longing that, due to the fact that the "vain" romantic subject remains trapped within itself, can never be fulfilled. The longing for substance in the romanticist's beautiful soul (especially in Novalis, see GPh III 418), which grows out of the deficiencies of an overly subjectivist understanding of freedom, thus finds its consummate expression. According to Hegel, this soul is characterized by the contradiction that

> on the one hand, the subject does want to penetrate into truth and longs for objectivity, but, on the other hand, cannot renounce his isolation and withdrawal into himself or tear himself free from this unsatisfied abstract inwardness. Now he is attacked by the yearning which also we have seen proceeding from Fichtean philosophy... That longing, however, is only the empty vain subject's sense of nullity, and he lacks the strength to escape from this vanity and fill himself with a content of substance. (Ä I 96/66f.)

According to this line of argumentation, the problem with romantic irony is that it turns freedom into unfreedom in a way that is not even clear to itself – a kind of unfreedom that also manifests itself in the alienation from the normative dimension of ethical life in general. This causes the separation of subjective freedom and ethical universality to reach its apex.

7. Abstract and Subjective Freedom

Regardless of whether Hegel's objection to the abstract conception of freedom does justice to the romantics, he both demonstrates the contradictions entailed by such a conception and points out its practical consequences. As Hegel was aware, praxis is never merely indifferent to the theory applied to it. He thus interprets the occasionally depressed mood of the romantics as a symptom of a misguided self-understanding. This is the point Kierkegaard develops in his famous *Journal of a Seducer*, which in many places picks up on Hegel's analysis of the romantic ironist's psyche (cf. ch. 3, sec. 3). Like Hegel, Kierkegaard claims that romantics' abstract conception of freedom is the source of a kind of narcissism that manifests itself in more or less aggressive resistance to the recognition of a concrete external reality that determines (and constantly re-determines) our self. No reality is ever good enough once it is measured against our own infinity. The flipside of this aggression is that feeling of inner emptiness that Kierkegaard calls boredom.

Axel Honneth in particular has pointed out that the connection between an abstract understanding of freedom and a narcissistic personality disorder continues to be of concern.[37] Not only do Western societies show a rise in narcissistic personality disorders and the attendant feelings of emptiness, lacking self-worth, and motivation. Recent social research also traces these symptoms to an abstract conception of freedom. These disorders can be viewed as a reaction to an overly subjectivist ideology that corresponds to a "new spirit of capitalism,"[38] according to which individuals are called on to shape their lives "freely," i.e. independent of all social preconditions.[39] Various symptoms of depression are therefore linked to the difficulties faced by individuals in their attempt to live up to this abstract idea of freedom within a concrete reality with all its actual limitations. Narcissism is of course not a form of self-love, but a kind of entrapment within an ideal image of one's own self, an image which cripples and renders the narcissist powerless. He can only be healed by recognizing the objective limits of his power. This is also the first step in awakening the narcissist's potential politicization, since social conflicts remain concealed as long as the freedom of the individual is considered independent of all social preconditions.[40]

Though it is right to criticize an abstract and overly subjectivist notion of freedom, the decisive question for our purposes – an investigation into the role of irony in making the transition from morality to ethical life – is whether it is convincing to conceptualize romantic irony as its paradigm. Hegel's "misunderstanding of romantic irony as empty subjectivity"[41] has often been criticized. Indeed, Hegel not only fails to recognize the aesthetic dimension of romantic irony, especially when it comes to its foundations in a notion of aesthetic autonomy. This misunderstanding, as I will now show, causes us to lose sight of a number of motifs of freedom within the discourse on irony – motifs that cannot be written off as instances of an overly subjectivist ideology. I will only deal in passing with the issue of whether Hegel's critique in fact does justice to Friedrich Schlegel, since the answer to this question (No) plays but a marginal role. Nor will I be dealing with a theory of irony in the narrower sense, as I will not address its rhetorical significance until later (ch. 5, sec. 1). Instead, I begin with the fact that Hegel turns irony – which, as Bohrer has repeatedly emphasized, was in Schlegel's eyes "not primarily a philosophical category, but a poetic concept and rhetorical practice"[42] – into the essence of a kind of freedom he feels we must reject. Obviously, Hegel not only accuses Schlegel of a philosophical self-misunderstanding, but he also criticizes the romantic *zeitgeist*. Neither is his critique of romanticism purely philosophically motivated, nor can it be reduced to a critique of subjectivism. He also rejects motifs of freedom of which, as we will see in closer detail, he gives a distorted description and an improper critique. Therefore, I am not primarily interested in defending romanticism and its conception of irony, but in defending the motifs of freedom that Hegel's critique of romanticism discusses, though only to hastily reject them.

Hegel's critique of irony combines two different strands of argumentation. On the one hand, he rightly criticizes the extremely contradictory conception of an abstract and simply indeterminate ego. On the other hand, he argues that irony favors the particular perspective of individuals over the community and its values. The problems that Hegel sees in romantic irony, however, are located on different levels. Even if we followed Hegel in defining the kind of freedom that places the individual over and against the ethical universal as caprice or arbitrariness [*Willkürfreiheit*], the subject of this freedom would not necessarily be identical to the I of abstract freedom, which wrongly conceives of itself as being absolute. Hegel's critique of arbitrariness, the dominance of subjective freedom over the ethical universal, is not primarily directed against a philosophical and literary conception of freedom and its practical consequences. Instead, it takes aim at the "commonest idea we have of freedom," which "consists in *being able to do as one pleases*" (Rph §15). This notion, which for Hegel indicates "a complete lack of intellectual culture," obviously does not merely deal with a kind of freedom that opposes ethical life due to a false abstraction. Instead, Hegel also criticizes a kind of freedom that is regarded as superior to a concrete form of ethical life.

If we consider irony paradigmatic for this understanding of freedom, then it would no longer necessarily represent a form of alienation from social practices *as a whole*. The consequences, however, would be tremendous, for romantic irony would then – both with and against Hegel – be "essentially secondary, perhaps even parasitic."[43] Ironic consciousness would then be aware that ironic distance "could only be taken up by virtue of valid ethical contents and the real world in which irony lives."[44] In this case "irony would be a position that could never fully be taken, a position to which we could never fully commit."[45] This would mean that, strictly speaking, there could be no ironists, at least not in the sense in which a subject is fully determined – as if a life beyond all social determination were desirable or even possible. Such a self-misunderstanding would in fact lead to the pathologies that Hegel describes.[46] But if we no longer assume that romantic irony abstracts from social practices on the whole and grasp it instead as an element *within* our social practices, then – as I will show in more detail in the following sections – it could be understood as a paradigmatic expression of a historically dynamic notion of freedom. Hegel himself drives toward this alternative conception of freedom when he defines the romanticist's ironic stance not primarily as a practical self-misunderstanding marked by false concepts, but as a certain kind of evil practice. It is no accident that the motifs we saw in our discussion of Plato reappear here. This becomes particularly evident when we look at Hegel's critique, advanced from the perspective of the social order, of the attention the ironist pays to the expressions of his "natural will." The discussion of Hegel's conception of evil is also of particular importance in our context, because, as we have seen, Hegel regards evil not only as the true face of romantic irony, but as systematically marking the point at which morality passes over into its opposite, immorality, thus necessitating a transition to ethical life.

8. Evil and the "Natural Will"

Hegel defines evil as "the arbitrariness" of giving one's "own particularity" precedence "over the universal and realizing it through its actions" (Rph §139). Yet as Hegel repeatedly emphasizes in his critique of the romantics, the particular contents that are set in opposition to the universal (of ethics) can only derive from "the determinations of the natural will, from desire, drive, inclination, etc." (ibid.). This connection stands at the center of Hegel's notion of evil: The "human being is evil insofar as his will is natural ... Insofar as man wills the natural, it is no longer merely the natural but the negation of the good as the concept of the will" (Rph §139, Addition).

It is precisely in this sense that Gilles Deleuze regarded Marquis de Sade as embodying modern irony. He analyzes de Sade's transgression of the laws along with the "discovery of a primary nature which is in every way opposed to the demands and the rule of secondary nature" as being a reaction to the modern view that "the higher principle no longer exists" and that "the Good can no longer provide a basis for the law or a justification of its power."[47] "In all its forms – natural, moral and political – the law represents the rule of secondary nature."[48] Deleuze thus argues that the idea of evil anchored in the first nature is neither identical to tyranny, as the latter presupposes laws, nor to "a combination of whims and arbitrariness." Instead, it is modeled on "anarchic institutions of perpetual motion and permanent revolution."[49] Because the nature asserted against the law is itself no longer determined by laws, the concept of first nature appears to me to be problematic, at least if we understand it in the sense in which it is understood by natural science, as the "embodiment of well-known yet meaningless necessities."[50] This concept of first nature, which refers to a realm of necessity, might be appropriate for characterizing de Sade's excesses; according to the interpretation offered by Adorno and Horkheimer, these excesses characterize the transformation of the freedom from all convention into the brute principles of nature.[51] But in my view, this does not accurately describe Deleuze's intuition. Whether he does justice to de Sade or not is another matter. What Deleuze emphasizes with regard to de Sade, or to modern irony in general, is the relation to a nature that has been fundamentally disrobed of all laws – such that the latter belong neither to our first nor to our second nature. The nature meant here cannot be made into a principle, not even into an anti-principle. It can only give rise to an objection to the law to the extent that it itself is not formulated as a law, and to the extent that it remains radically elusive.

This allows us to pick up on the previous chapter (especially secs 7 and 8), especially with regard to the discussions on the concept of inner nature. In this case the term nature does not mean the opposite of culture, but refers to culturally moderated desires that are not subject to any natural laws. Nor can we derive these desires from the subject's social identity. The expressions of our inner nature are determined neither by a biological purpose nor by a practical norm. They do not come about through the will-formation of a subject guided by practical norms. The concept of inner nature instead refers to those desires that lift the subject out of its social self-understanding and confront it with a dimension of itself of which it could not have been previously aware. The fact that we use the term inner *nature* to describe this phenomenon should not, however, lead us to mistake it for a kind of core personality. Rather, our inner nature manifests itself in specific situations and derives from the subject's mimetic relation to external reality. We cannot objectify this kind of nature in an essentialist fashion as being the subject's "own"; rather, we should grasp it as a kind of potential that only – and repeatedly – becomes a concrete reality through interaction with a changing world. For this reason it can never be entirely absorbed by the subject's social identity. Because the desires and forces of the subject's inner nature – that which is most particular to it – cannot be entirely ascribed to the subject itself, its inner nature remains a source of change and innovation when it comes to interpreting our relation to ourselves and the world, one that is constantly renewed through interaction with the world.

If we grasp what Deleuze misleadingly terms our first nature in this sense, we get a better understanding of why he conceives of it as a permanent revolution. To the same extent that our inner nature cannot be captured in the form of laws, the anarchy that corresponds to it resists any institutionalization. Deleuze writes that anarchy "can only exist in the interval between two regimes based on laws, abolishing the old to give birth to the new." Nevertheless, he goes on to say that "this divine interval, this vanishing instant [testifies] to its fundamental difference from all forms of law."[52] The fact that Deleuze does not reify the suspension or displacement of the law in order to glorify it as absolutely or divinely evil is especially interesting when it comes to the concept of evil that both Deleuze and Hegel associate with irony. For the "divine interval" of the suspension and revision of the law, in its "fundamental difference from all forms of law," indicates for Deleuze a "vanishing instant" in the process of transformation from the old law to the new law. Evil, understood as detachment from the law, would then be a necessary moment of any such transformation.

As we already saw in ch. 1, the structurally anarchical experience of our inner nature, which alienates us from the second nature of our social identity, can move us to pose the question again of what is the best (in both an individual and social sense) and perhaps revise our previous beliefs – or, as Deleuze would put it, to insert a new law. But if this is true, the experience of self-difference – the difference between social identity and inner nature – cannot be rejected as evil or bad in and of itself. At most it is a symptom of a different evil, namely of the compulsion to make identity ascriptions that do not or no longer suit us. To the degree that the experience of self-difference indicates that we are not free toward ourselves and the world, it can represent the beginning of a transformation in our self-understanding. In this sense, as we mentioned above, the discontinuous events of our inner nature can represent an origin for the subject that experiences them. Although it is not an origin in the true sense of the term, i.e. a state prior to all culture, this experience of the self can be described retrospectively as the beginning of a development, as the origin of a transformation (cf. ch. 1, sec. 8). Yet this need not always be the case. The confrontation with desires which I experience in certain situations and which contradict my previous self-image can also lead me to reaffirm my self-image. In both cases, the experience of a divide between our inner nature and our social identity conveys a more or less serious crisis in our self-understanding, which often triggers reflections which aim to restore a feeling of inner harmony.

Hegel is right in assuming that this is how freedom manifests itself psychologically. To use Paul Valery's well-known formulation, the fact that I do not always agree with myself[53] and can be at odds with myself is a necessary element of freedom, because experiences of self-difference are a necessary condition of self-transformation, self-criticism, and self-improvement.[54] By contrast, inconsistency or general indifference toward such a state of self-contradiction can amount to a loss of freedom and could therefore be termed "evil." Indeed, indifference and other forms of suspending judgment – as we saw in the discussion of the life of and in democracy (cf. ch. 1, secs 6 and 11) – constitute forms of evil, constant threats to freedom that we should take seriously. Hegel was right to point out that there can be no freedom without determination, though this should not lead us to regard our capacity to detach from certain determinations as something evil – instead of reserving this concept for the mistake of remaining within this state of detachment or of totalizing indifference. This conclusion would also constitute a violation of freedom and would thus unwillingly take the side of evil. Only if we – ever anew – detach from our determinations can we truly determine ourselves. Only then can we practice (self-)criticism and distinguish between the act of reaffirming our old self (our old principles) from mere conformism. The experience of self-difference, which is always latent and occasionally explicit, is a necessary condition of a self-determined appropriation or transformation of the social practices through which the subject is always already determined. Such an experience is therefore not the other, but a necessary element of a complete concept of practical normativity. After all, even a lived affirmation of one's own beliefs is nothing but the effect of a reflection on "the natural" (Rph §139, Addition).

9. The Dialectic of Freedom

According to our description of the relation between our inner nature and our social identity or second nature, our relation to "the natural" is a necessary function of historical life – a relation that Hegel wrongly identifies with evil. Our inner nature cannot be set in abstract opposition to the various forms of our second nature, but must instead be recognized as a necessary element for potentially transforming or affirming this nature. There is one aspect of this description that must be emphasized with respect to Hegel, an aspect which Deleuze largely passes over because of his focus on de Sade: The transformation of our second nature is always based on reasons. It is never arbitrary, rather it is a reaction to an experience that we cannot control. We never pose the "question of truth" without reason, and it is within the horizon of this question that we seek to transform our respective relation to the world and ourselves; this is the manner in which we change our own social identity, our social nature. Yet we cannot control our reasons for doing so, for our inner nature is never accessible to us as such and cannot be controlled by our will. This is precisely why I use the term "nature" to describe this phenomenon.

If we take romantic irony to be a paradigmatic illustration of our relation to our inner nature, then clearly we will have to make a significant correction to the distorted image Hegel draws of irony. Indeed, contrary to Hegel's assumption, Schlegel's irony is not aimed against all others in the name of a "divine subjectivity."[55] Instead, and this is the crucial point, it rises "infinitely above all limitations, even above its own art, virtue, or genius."[56] It is telling that Hegel makes no mention of the phenomenon of self-irony, and here we see an element of the subject's self-difference which could hardly count as a symptom of hubristic subjectivism elevating the ironic subject to pseudo-divine status. Instead, self-irony conveys a detached relation to the self-images of our second nature – both to our own virtuousness and to our own ingenuity. The self-ironic subject breaks free of such a spell not by assuming a godlike position superior to these self-images, but by distorting them through the comical expressions [*Grimassen*] of its own involuntary vitality. In these expressions, the subject – especially the narcissist subject who is fixated on an overly idealized image of itself – is alienated from itself, and by laughing at itself becomes free for self-images that are new and probably more appropriate.[57]

Contrary to the philosophical tradition that one-sidedly equates freedom with rational subjects' capacity for self-determination, the "dialectic of freedom" (Adorno) romantically integrates non-arbitrary, irrational, anarchic impulses into the concept of freedom. This dialectic represents an antagonism at work in the very core of the concept of freedom, one which combines the capacity for self-determination with a contrary impulse. According to Adorno, freedom is dialectical in the "very strict sense" of a "contradictoriness" that defines the entire concept of what it means to be free. As Adorno puts it, the "concept of freedom could not be formulated in the absence of recourse to something prior to the ego, to an impulse that is in a sense a bodily impulse that has not yet been subjected to the centralizing authority of consciousness; while on the other hand, its trajectory terminates in the strength of the ego itself. In other words, it contains a conflict within itself."[58] According to Adorno, the "mysteries of the concept of freedom in which the extreme exaltation of the ego goes hand in hand in a very strange way with the abyss of the self"[59] is a historical dynamic. The dialectic of freedom is always in historical flux, because our inner nature cannot be experienced and grasped as such, but only emerges in reaction to a changing world as the other of our second nature. For that very reason, our inner nature can bring about new acts of self-determination, making new adjustments to our will and creating new forms of our second, social nature.

This interpretation of romantic irony as an essentially historical and dynamic mediation between the subject's inner nature and its social form runs counter to a further important, not yet discussed aspect of Hegel's critique of morality: his critique of the divide between reason and passion, which he takes to be characteristic of morality in general. His critique even begins with the fact that Socrates transforms virtue into insight to such a degree that he neglects the "alogical," sensible side of virtue. However, his objection is more relevant to the Platonic Socrates than the ironist. I will return later to Socrates' relation to virtue at the end of this chapter (sec. 13) – a relation which cannot be described as one of insight. Hegel correctly regards Kant's rigorism as a dramatic version of a false abstraction of reason from passion. However, according to Hegel, the consequence of this problematic abstraction does not entirely reveal itself until we turn to the romantics. According to Hegel's diagnosis, because the ironic subject rejects all determinations as being merely external, thus attaining the summit of rational self-control, it is left with nothing but its incidental and immediate desires. It is right to problematize the manner in which Kant divides reason into an autonomous and a heteronymous part, but, contrary to Hegel, romantic sensibility is not marked by subjectivism, but by a questioning of the subject in and through an experience of a divide within that subject itself. Therefore, we can formulate Hegel's critique of Kant's rigorism in a way that combines it with a defense of the romantics. This is the aim of the following section, after which I will finally be able to return to the role of romantic experience in developing an alternative understanding of morality (sec. 11).

10. A Less Rigorous Concept of Self-Determination

Kant's principle of morality or autonomy is based on the notion that humans are only truly free if they submit to the universal perspective contained in the categorical imperative. In his most radical formulation of this thesis, Kant claims that humans are only truly autonomous if they are determined not by their individual inclinations, but *solely* by universal, rational reasons. In contrast to this extremely rigorous version of the principle of autonomy, which delegitimizes the following of individual inclinations in general, we could make the more moderate claim that individual inclinations are allowed within a certain framework, i.e. under the condition that they conform to the moral principle. Ingeborg Maus, for instance, has sought out those passages in Kant's work that emphasize that the principle of universality underlying moral judgment does not operate beyond concrete impulses, but in relation to them:

> In the procedure employed by the categorical imperative, the principle of universalization does not (contrary to a common misunderstanding) take the place of concrete motivations; a principle without any substance could never lead to any action. Instead, this principle is only capable of choosing between substantive motives. Analogous to Rousseau's dualism of "amour de soi" and "amour propre," Kant is aware that concrete, particular and "natural" inclinations can coincide with the abstract and universal principle of the categorical imperative. His basic point is that we must examine our reasons for acting before we follow our original inclinations, or as Rousseau puts it: "de consulter sa raison avant d'écouter ses penchants."[60]

Yet even this argument does not entirely refute Kant's legal rigorism.[61] Instead, the argument claims once again that the categorical imperative should extend to our original inclinations – not by suppressing our individual inclinations entirely, but by dictating the conditions under which they are justified.[62]

Regardless of the position of *moral* judgment in self-government, we can already see at this point that romantic irony, at least with regard to the motives discussed here, fundamentally contradicts a model that defines rational self-determination as the domination of presupposed laws that suppress, or at least restrict, our individual inclinations. However, romantic irony does not assert an abstract opposition between the immediacy of individual inclinations and the rationality of universal principles; rather, it brings movement into this relation. The romantic focus on the situational stirrings of our inner nature reveals that we cannot always clearly determine whether a concrete intention constitutes a case of self-obsession or self-love.[63] It is unclear whether my intentions represent a case of (heteronymously determined) self-obsession, in which I lose myself in the satisfaction of momentary desires, or whether they represent a case of (autonomously self-determining) self-love that comes about through my identification, supported by my inclinations, with universal principles (the law).

Here we should revisit[64] those actions that derive from a lack of control or weakness of will, because in these cases my desires not only conflict with my general beliefs, but are also strong enough to motivate me to act upon them. However, just because I act against my principles does not mean that I act without reason. Kant himself accounts for this fact by presenting his "incorporation thesis," according to which desires alone can never cause us to act, but must instead be made into a cause, into a true "motive" to act. This occurs when these intentions are equipped with a reason.[65] Alenka Zupančič has pointed out that even neurotic acts, or acts out of weakness of will, imply a measure of freedom, however unconsciously. The fact that neurotics or the weak-willed make decisions not only entails that they represent genuine subjects (and not the mere plaything of external forces), it is also a necessary condition of our ability – e.g. after psychotherapy – to make choices contrary to unconscious decisions that manifest themselves in compulsive behavior.[66]

According to Kant, the second-order decision by which the subject truly determines its own actions is predicated on the notion of a transcendental subject. The assumption of a position defined entirely by reason and from which the subject chooses its principles implies the very rigorous definition of self-determination in which our individual inclinations might not be entirely suppressed, but certainly restricted by a transcendental law. Due to their sensibility to the occurrences of our inner nature, the romantics manage to conceive of the subject that makes a second-order decision not as a subject that casts judgment from the empty position of transcendental freedom and suppresses (certain) drives, but rather as a subject whose autonomy remains affected by its passions.[67]

Absent this condition there could be neither weakness of will nor the possibility of self-criticism and self-revision – precisely the phenomena that are generally regarded not only as an essential possibility of our practical reason, but also as an essential aspect of our freedom.[68] It is true that the reasons that motivate my weak-willed or uncontrolled actions are illegitimate from the perspective of my principles; they cannot, therefore, be accepted as reasons, rather only as a mere force. That is precisely what makes actions based on weakness of will or a loss of control irrational. Yet there can also be cases in which the strength or insistence of this force leads me to revise my principles and ultimately acknowledge the reason for my deviation from my own principles as a reason in its own right. If one of my principles consists in always remaining in control, then what can appear to be a weakness can move me to recognize that it is necessary to give up the idea of constant sovereignty in order to be human.

Defending the possibility of such self-revision as an important aspect of human freedom also means defending a less rigorous concept of self-determination. The possibility of self-revision shows that even second-order decisions made at the level of reflection, upon which I evaluate my "motives," are affected by the influence of the drives I thereby judge. This also implies that self-determination cannot be viewed as the act of a unified subject that stands above all of its desires. For the decision to change myself always occurs in the name of a self that did not really exist prior to the respective act of self-determination. It is *in* the act of self-determination that I form myself as this or that subject with the constitutive principles of this or that relation to myself and the world.

If we acknowledge that this concept of self-determination is not only immune to the critique of subjectivism, but also entails an objection to subjectivism, since the subject must be re-produced through the experience of self-difference, then we must ask about the consequences of this concept of self-determination for the problem with which we began and which, according to Hegel, is the central (and unresolved) problem of morality: How do we mediate between the particular and the universal? What can romantic irony contribute to our conception of morality?

11. Conflicts with and in Morality

It should be clear that the ironist's reflective reference to the involuntary expressions of "natural will" that life in the world arouses – i.e. "desire, drive, inclination, etc." (Rph §139) – does not in and of itself qualify as evil. Nevertheless, to be aware of these stimuli not only involves being aware of their productive potential for acts of self-determination, but also knowing that the moral stance is not without alternative. The ironist is aware of the source of evil within himself. At the same time, however, this awareness is a requirement for a truly moral stance. We might call a person who is wholly oblivious to the resistance occasionally encountered by the moral perspective holy, but not moral in the proper sense of the term. An awareness of the tense relation between our orientation toward individual happiness and our orientation toward moral universalizability is an essential part of moral consciousness. Like a saint, however, a person whose moral acts are based solely on convention can hardly be called moral either.[69] Romantic irony makes this fact visible as well.

Though Hegel's polemic suggests otherwise, romantic irony does not merely draw attention to the possibility that an individual's orientation toward his own happiness may come into conflict with the moral demand that maxims be universalizable, and that morality may thus be externally confronted with immorality. It also opens our eyes to the possibility of conflicts *within* morality itself. As we have seen, romantic irony is conscious of the fundamental impossibility of a complete and total correspondence between our natural will and the subject's prevailing social identity. And this consciousness gives rise to an essentially historical concept of self-determination which allows for our capacity to either change or actively confirm our understanding of the world and ourselves. Such a historicized concept of self-determination, however, also discloses a source of moral conflicts. Due to their sensitivity for the expressions of the "natural will" and their predilection for aberrations, the romantic ironists point out that what Hegel would call a "splitting" [*Entzweiung*] of the subject from ethical life is in fact grounded in a split within the subject itself. Thus the one "split" is as inevitable as the other. Ethical universality, on account of the self-difference of those who are affected by it – a self-difference that is generally latent but occasionally experienced explicitly – is never immune to critique, never wholly impervious to change. After all, changes in individuals' understanding of the world and of themselves imply changes in the practices in which they are involved. These changes may go undetected and happen without any conflicts arising. However, a conflict can also arise in which those concerned must enter into a struggle for recognition in order to live out their new understanding of the world and themselves.

It is in just this context that Hegel's legitimate critique of Kant takes on an additional moral-philosophical implication. Because a given form of ethical life necessarily influences the categorical imperative, such that moral universality cannot be quite as universal as Kant makes it appear, moral universality must be viewed as something that can be contested, as something historically changeable. Hegel himself, of course, was not in a position to adequately develop this point on account of his critical view of irony. Since there can never be an ultimate and final correspondence between the subject's natural ground and its social role or identity, it is always possible for the two to fall into misalignment, thereby opening up differences in our shared intersubjective understandings of the world and ourselves. This – the "communicative substructure" (Wellmer) of morality – is something that Kant regarded as entirely unproblematic, despite the fact that such differences in our understanding of the world or our self can have ramifications for our moral judgments. The respective cases do not represent an opposition between an individual and a moral universal – as happens when our efforts to fulfill our own happiness conflict with the moral demand that our maxims be universalizable. Such cases instead present us with two opposing moral universals, two different views about what is morally universalizable. For example, if I do not regard homosexuality as harmful, I will reject as immoral the maxim that homosexuals should be subject to legal prosecution and public discrimination. I will see such a maxim as incapable of universalization. If I do not believe that women are irrational by nature, then I will reject the universalizability of any maxim that would prevent them from voting or attending university, etc.

These kinds of moral conflicts, which arise as a result of differences within the collective patterns of interpretation that characterize a society's ethical self-understanding, make a further implication of Socratic reflection on morally complex cases explicit: The moral question of whether my maxim is capable of becoming a universal law is, in the end, equivalent to the question of whether my interpretation of a given situation (i.e. my understanding of the world and myself as expressed in this situation) is appropriate.[70] But the only place where this question (or these questions) can be answered is within an intersubjective practice of truth. For it is only here that we can decide, on the basis of reasons, whether a given view is to be condemned as immoral or evil, or whether it should be defended against prevailing prejudices as moral and good. Yet, the meaning of what we call an "intersubjective practice of truth" takes on a new and more profound significance from the romantic perspective. While Socratic reflection primarily judges the completeness and aptness of given descriptions of situations against the background of a shared culture, the sort of moral reflection involved in romantic irony takes aim at this cultural background itself. When it comes to the adequacy of a description of a given situation, we need to consider the perspectives from which, and the categories with which, the situation is described. The romantic ironist emphasizes – even more strongly than the Socratic ironist – that the categorical imperative presupposes certain commonalities in subjects' understanding(s) of the world and themselves, which should by no means be taken for granted. In bringing this to light, romantic irony makes it clear – contrary to both Kant and Hegel – that the sense and meaning of moral discourse can by no means consist in the production of tautologies.

Because shared understandings of the world and of ourselves cannot simply be presupposed as stable, the significance of moral discourse consists in no small part in disputing and generating the corresponding commonalities. The fact that our communal understanding of the world and of ourselves is not only a presupposition, but also an object and aim of moral discourse thus has the shape of a development, of a process of universalization. This process should not, however, be presented as an incremental approach to a state of total inclusiveness. Rather, it should be portrayed as a discontinuous process in which the hegemony of certain universal formulations must always remain open to the challenges of alternative views. But hegemonic forces do not just open up to challengers of their own accord. This generally requires a political struggle for recognition of those forms of life from which the alternative conceptions of universal moral principles spring.

Yet to the extent that we register how thoroughly Hegelian the idea of such a process of universalization (and the idea of enlightenment connected with it) is, we must also make a decisive correction to certain strands of Hegel's criticism of irony. The same holds for Hegel's project of working out a conception of modern ethical life that preserves a space for subjective freedom. Once we stop conceiving of morality as a progressively radical opposition between subjective freedom and ethical universality, we are faced with the necessity of an ethical universal, which, unlike that of antiquity, "allows individuals [*die Einzelnen*] ... to have freer play." This in turn means that these individuals "[can]not become so dangerous for the universal" (GPh 18:507/1:439). Such an ethical universal would have become reflective. The very concept of the ethical universal would have incorporated into itself the possibility of calling into question any particular determinations of the ethical universal. And the transition from morality to ethical life would no longer involve a triumph over irony. If, as I have argued, irony cannot be reduced to a form of radical alienation from the normative dimension of ethical life as a whole, but can instead be understood as a form of dynamic mediation between subjective freedom and ethical universality, then our modern subjectivity, which is so clearly shaped by and suffused with irony, no longer stands in need of therapy. On the contrary, if my argument holds, irony takes on the productive function it should have had within the Hegelian system itself: It becomes a phenomenon that, from the standpoint of morality, refers to a dimension both before and after morality: ethical life. This phenomenon is comparable to the phenomenon of crime, which similarly plays a crucial role in the transition from abstract right to morality.[71] Irony refers back to the dimension of ethical life insofar as the moral discourse connected with both its Socratic and (even more explicitly) its romantic forms makes reference to shared, intersubjective understandings of the world and ourselves. But as we have seen, this level of shared understandings not only underlies moral discourse as such, but also forms its object and aim. If this is right, then morality also anticipates ethical life. In particular, it anticipates a conception of ethical life that deserves to be called modern insofar as it demands a degree of respect for subjective freedom and difference that compels a change in the very concept of ethical life. The latter must evolve from its "naïve" form into a mode that is truly reflective in the above sense. This would constitute a form of ethical life in which mediating between the universal and the particular is not merely – qua social practices – something whose achievement could always already be presupposed, but something that simultaneously confronts these practices as a task and a challenge. Due to the distorted view of morality in his critique of irony, Hegel was incapable of clearly grasping this implication. This led to a measure of tension in his own theory, for the project of working out a modern conception of ethical life is constantly undercut by conservative arguments which result from his false critique of irony. The rightful place that irony should enjoy can therefore, in a negative fashion, be seen in the arguments that threaten to ultimately turn the project of integrating subjective freedom into ethical life into a project that expels subjective freedom from ethical life.

12. Hegel's Expulsion of Subjective Freedom from Ethical Life

According to Hegel's diagnosis, therefore, the moral standpoint falsely abstracts from universality; and this mistake cannot be corrected merely by returning to a "naïve form of ethics." Although "knowledge brought about the fall," it also "contains the principle of redemption" (GPh I 515/447). The aim is to overcome morality in a way that retains its achievement of having given birth to the principle of knowledge. How does Hegel attempt to avoid falling back behind Socrates while at the same time avoiding the pathologies he ascribes to morality and subjective freedom? To answer this question, I will briefly point out two related and often criticized stages of argumentation in which Hegel responds to this problem in his philosophy of right.

At the first stage of his argumentation, the idea of freedom is bound to the "living good" (Rph §142). Already at this point, Hegel means to do more than correct the subjectivist misunderstanding by recognizing the constitutive role of social practices which precede all subjectivity (and thus all subjective freedom and irony). And this brings about certain problems, for, as Michael Theunissen points out, "the living good occupies a position corresponding to absolute spirit. It no longer stands vis-à-vis the subject, but encompasses self-consciousness and the world as their common ground... The living good is the good life in the Platonic and Aristotelian sense, including the absolute criterion for this good."[72] To the extent that it is grasped as the living good, nothing in ethical life can threaten it; the good universalizes itself. Theunissen thus goes on to say that "this universalization of the good is based on the historical-philosophical premise that reality has essentially become good."[73] This process of universalization, however, is entirely different from the one that we just described as the – fundamentally infinite – universalization of morality. From the perspective of a universal good, evil no longer exists; and even "the self-will of the individual and his own conscience in its attempt to exist for itself and in opposition to the ethical substantiality, have disappeared" (Rph §152). In this context Hegel also writes that individuals must recognize concrete ethical life and accept its validity. The ethical substance attains objectivity in the self-consciousness of the individual; it is "an absolute authority and power, infinitely more firmly based than the being of nature" (cf. Rph §146). Being even more natural than nature, however, the historical becomes as blind as nature: Ethical life confronts the individual as an alien and immutable law.

Once Hegel has thus defined ethical life as the objective good, it is only logical that he then goes on to say that "duty" allows individuals "to attain substantial freedom" (Rph §149), and that virtue is nothing but "the simple adequacy of the individual to the duties of the circumstances to which he belongs" (Rph §150). The mediation between subjective freedom and ethical universality takes place by virtue of an operation in which objectivity is claimed for an ethical order in order to then define the truth of subjective freedom or subjective self-consciousness as the "certainty" of this objectivity (cf. Rph §153). This certainty is anchored in the "self-awareness," i.e. the state of "relationless identity" in which the subject stands to its ethical substance (Rph §147). The idea of an absolute identity between the ethical and individual good, that is, the idea that the "laws and powers" (Rph §146) confront the subject not as something alien to it, but rather as a part of "its own essence" (Rph §147) relies on the fact that our "original nature" has been "transformed into a second, spiritual nature," such that "the opposition between the natural and the subjective will disappear and the resistance of the subject is broken" in the "habitual" character of our second nature (Rph §151, Addition). To the extent that ethical life should present itself as nature, everything natural must disappear from it. Thus it is only logical that Hegel does not associate the passions with our inner nature, but as a "living" expression of our second nature, as an expression of its affirmation. The passions are therefore a part of an Aristotelian conception of virtue, according to which virtue "is determination in accordance with universal, and not particular ends" such that "the whole man, the heart and mind, should be identical with it" (GPh 18:474/1:413). For Hegel, in other words, the passions are merely another way in which ethical universality is realized in the individual (ibid.). By wholly overcoming its natural will, subjectivity appropriates itself in the objectivity of ethical life and in the universality of virtue or second nature.[74] Adorno comments on this feature in Hegel's work as follows: "The Spirit as second nature, however, is the negation of the Spirit, and indeed all the more thoroughly, the more its self-consciousness deceives itself about its being rooted in nature."[75]

Yet, even for Hegel, this certainty does not yet represent knowledge of the objectivity of the ethical. This certainty could also be had at the level of a "naïve form of ethics." And knowledge for Hegel, of course, cannot be understood as reflection. Hegel writes explicitly that the "relationless identity" between the subject and ethical substance expressed in "self-awareness" can be transformed into conviction and faith, into "insight grounded on reasons, which may also begin with certain particular ends, interests, and considerations, with hope or fear, or with historical presuppositions. But *adequate cognition* of this identity belongs to conceptual thought" (Rph §147).

This is where the second stage of Hegel's argumentation begins – which does not merely represent an update of Aristotle's concept of virtue, whose traces have been pointed out in recent research on Hegel.[76] On the contrary, in his conception of that kind of knowledge of ethical objectivity that goes beyond pre-reflective certainty, Hegel reinstalls the very dualism between theoretical and practical subject that he criticized with reference to Socrates – and the entire "philosophy of reflection."[77] This represents a step forward in Hegel's conception of freedom. He proceeds from the conception of freedom as "being with oneself in the other,"[78] which can be developed further by a theory of recognition, to an idea of freedom as freedom of thought. He regards this thought, contrary to the "philosophy of reflection" and in line with Plato and Aristotle, as a kind of sharing in the absolute. As Rolf-Peter Horstmann has shown, Hegel resolves the contradiction between "the individual subject as the finite form of *spirit*" and "the individual subject as the *finite* form of spirit" in two steps. On the one hand, he formalizes freedom by defining it as a pure form of being with oneself; on the other hand, he makes a systematic distinction between the knowing and the acting subject.[79] By formalizing freedom as a pure form of being with oneself, he extracts the very element of the concept of freedom which the notion of "being with oneself in the other" sought to integrate into the concept of freedom – being defined by (the) other (cf. Rph §§22, 23). Furthermore, this formal notion of freedom as being with oneself only represents the freedom of the knowing subject. As an agent that understands itself as an individual, the subject cannot claim its own freedom in the sense of an identity with itself, because Hegel understands action as a determination of the will that remains subjective, trapped in the position of "difference, finitude and appearance" (Rph §108, see also Rph §113).

The first stage of Hegel's argumentation suffers from the fact that Hegel's notion of ethical life as the "living good," which is overburdened by historical-philosophical considerations, fails to move beyond the moral level of reflection. After all, subjective freedom remains in the certainty of the ethical founded on habit rather than knowledge. The difficulty of the second stage lies in the fact that the form of thought with which Hegel attempts to supersede moral reflection comes at the cost of decoupling the theoretical from the practical subject. The latter manifests itself in the praise of the philosopher, who, unlike the crowd of merely reflecting agents, enjoys the privilege of "adequate knowledge." Given these arguments, the project of sublimating subjective freedom into the conception of modern ethical life, freeing it of all subjectivist misunderstandings, must be viewed as a failure.

13. The Riddle of Socratic Virtue and the Historicity of the Good

By contrast, when it comes to the line that both joins and divides Socrates and Schlegel with and from Kant, we saw that it is not necessary to reduce morality to what Hegel regards as its overly subjectivist one-sidedness. Instead, this line illustrates the necessity of truly sublating both morality and its attendant notion of subjective freedom into a form of ethical life that must be conceptualized as both plural and dynamic. What makes this form of ethical life truly modern is that it allows disputes over the substance of the good. Given my considerations on the democratic ontology of the good in the previous chapter, we could call this a democratic form of ethical life.

Therefore, contrary to the role that Plato has Socrates play in *The Republic*, Socrates could be viewed as the first genuinely democratic philosopher. His individual actions are opposed to thinking in philosophical systems, presenting a kind of practice of truth which emphasizes the notion that we can only get sight of the good by knowing that we know nothing. This also means that philosophy cannot claim the privilege of acquiring knowledge of the good, nor can it take up a position, outside of all practices, from which it could then determine the contents of the good. It is only logical, therefore, that Socratic reflection on individual, morally complex cases is at least a latent sign of the fundamental discontinuity between the order of knowledge on the one hand and that of judgment or decision on the other. When we make judgments, we conclude a process that, due to the finite nature of our practical knowledge, can never be truly concluded with final certainty. That is the decisionist aspect of judgments. What I genuinely believe to be morally necessary in one situation can prove to be wrong in the light of an alternative description of the same situation. Perhaps I have overlooked a crucial aspect, or my relation to myself and the world itself proves to be morally dubious. Not only can my description of a given situation be inadequate, the categories I employ can turn out to be wrong in the light of arguments and problems of which I was previously unaware. The plurality of perspectives that come to light in such moral conflicts is unthinkable without the source of difference emphasized by the romantics. The question of the good is posed again and again, both ethically and morally, because there can never be a complete and final correspondence between our inner nature and our social self-understanding. The subject remains susceptible to a changing world, and thus to the possibility of a transformation of its relation to itself and the world.

Ultimately this very modern, romantic insight into the source of the difference between our inner nature and our social self-understanding casts light on what is perhaps the most puzzling feature of Socrates. As Hegel puts it, "though we know what he was, we do not know how he became such" (GPh I 453).[80] For Alexander Nehamas, the last and most complex dimension of Socratic irony is the fact that Socrates was so utterly intransparent to himself that he was uncertain about the possibility of his own oft-praised virtuousness, and that he did not know how his own existence was possible.[81] Though Socrates may have been a model of virtue, he was not an expert on virtue. Apparently he was incapable of turning his virtuousness into a systematic set of guidelines. Just as the philosophical practice of Socratic irony contradicts the conception that we can attain objective knowledge of the good, the puzzle of his admirable life contradicts the notion that virtuousness consists in gaining possession of such knowledge. Socratic virtue does not strive for redemption, rather it uncovers its own historicity. At least, this is how it appears from the romantic perspective.[82] If we give a romantic interpretation of Socrates' claim that he "knows that he knows nothing," then this sentence expresses the truth of an essentially historical existence. The validity of that which we feel we know about the ethical and moral good can never appear except in practice. This knowledge is therefore necessarily fallible.

I hope I have shown convincingly that we can understand the insight into the fallibility of all determinations of the good as an insight into the dialectical movement in which we can experience freedom. If so, then we must defend a democratic concept of ethical life which acknowledges the constitutive possibility of a struggle over the contents of the good. This leads us back to the connection, which we dealt with in ch. 1, between protecting the possibility of inquiring into the good and acknowledging the problem of democracy's indeterminate essence. I will return to this issue in ch. 4, and particularly in part III. But for the moment, I wish to postpone the issue in order to give more contour to the ethical implications of the understanding of freedom attached to the aestheticization phenomenon of romantic irony. To do so I will turn to the work of Søren Kierkegaard, who, quite surprisingly, criticizes irony from an entirely different perspective. For Kierkegaard, irony stands for a kind of subjectivity that is not sufficiently radical in its particularity.

3

The Ethics of Aesthetic Existence: Kierkegaard

It is impossible to mistake the close relationship between Kierkegaard's theory of irony and the work of Hegel. But though Kierkegaard may agree with Hegel's critique of romanticism, his critique of irony has different motives and accents. Kierkegaard does not seek to combat [*therapieren*] irony by reabsorbing the subjective freedom it embodies into the ethical life that has always determined it. On the contrary, his aim is to radicalize the subjective freedom of irony, which should lead via despair to an existential decision in which the subject realizes itself as truly radical subjectivity, i.e. existential inwardness. For my purposes, the distinction between Hegel and Kierkegaard is particularly important because it enables us to view Kierkegaard's critique of aestheticization in an entirely different light. A defense of an aestheticized form of life and the corresponding understanding of freedom must engage with motifs that provide additional contours to the image we have so far worked out – not with regard to the theory of ethical life, but to a theory of existential inwardness. I will thus discuss Kierkegaard's famous theory of stages as a multi-leveled response to the question of what it means to live a free life. The following analysis of Kierkegaard's works and their characters – a failed seducer, a bourgeois [*spießig*] judge, various poets struggling with love, biblical figures, and customary sinners – will present Kierkegaard's stages of aesthetic, ethical, and religious forms of existence as various models of realizing freedom, while discussing the relationships between these various forms.[1]

The Ethics of Aesthetic Existence: Kierkegaard

Although Kierkegaard's critique of the aesthetic form of existence is similar in many respects to Hegel's critique of romantic irony, the difference between them – which becomes more and more explicit as Kierkegaard's theory of stages progresses – is already made apparent by subtle shifts of emphasis in his own critique of romanticism. For instance, Lore Hühn suggests that we regard Kierkegaard's dissertation, *The Concept of Irony*,[2] as "the first document of a separation" from Hegel, "not despite, but because of its obvious terminological and conceptual resemblance to Hegel's critique of romanticism."[3] The question is how we should understand this separation. I believe we must grasp it in terms of a theory of freedom. The very fact that Kierkegaard focuses on the idea of self-realization in his critique of irony marks a departure from Hegel's understanding of freedom, which is grounded in the latter's theory of ethical life. Of course, this separation does not become entirely explicit until the final stage of religious existence, where self-realization is replaced by the more complex idea of religiously founded inwardness. Therefore, we should keep in mind the difference between Kierkegaard and Hegel even when Kierkegaard appears to argue in a Hegelian fashion, i.e. at the intermediate stage of ethical existence. Kierkegaard even warns us to do so by using pseudonyms which cannot be immediately identified with Kierkegaard himself. It is no accident that Wilhelm, the judge, who embodies ethical existence and is clearly modeled on Hegel, occasionally appears to be a caricature. In his portrait of Wilhelm, Kierkegaard isolates and overemphasizes precisely Hegel's more problematic lines of argumentation, which contradict the project of sublating subjective freedom into ethical life. We will, however, have to deal with the question of whether Kierkegaard's alternative to an understanding of freedom reduced to a theory of ethical life in fact rejects precisely that part of Hegel's critique that should be preserved: the idea that we cannot conceive of freedom in isolation from social reality. After all, the discussion of Hegel in the previous chapter dealt solely with the question of how we should conceive of this mediation. The alternative to the alternative "Hegel or Kierkegaard," in which two reductionist accounts of freedom face off against each other (ethical life vs. existential inwardness), lies in an alternative understanding of irony or aesthetic existence.

In order to articulate the distinctions between Hegel and Kierkegaard raised by Kierkegaard's philosophy of existence, however, we first need to establish the common ground upon which these distinctions emerge.

1. The Negative Freedom of Socratic Irony and its Romantic Superseding

Like Hegel, Kierkegaard's interpretation of the early romantic aesthetic contains elements of a cultural critique. For Kierkegaard, therefore, the romantic conception of irony is likewise not merely a matter of philosophical importance; rather, it stands for a phenomenon limited neither to the realm of theory nor to that of art. Here we are dealing with nothing less than the justification of an entire form of life that Kierkegaard terms "aesthetic." Twenty years after Hegel and in a more explicit fashion, Kierkegaard recognized, in the words of Karl Heinz Bohrer, "the power of the aesthetic as a sign of a new age, having felt the effect of this power on his own person."[4] Indeed, Kierkegaard criticized the romantic aesthetic as a vehicle of a new and nihilistic spirit embodied in an equally detached and forcibly subjectivist stance toward the world. But for Kierkegaard the Hegelian, the essence of this stance is embodied by the romantic ironist, whose false self-understanding he equally subjects to a philosophically informed ideology critique. Already in Kierkegaard's dissertation we find the decisive motifs later found in his portrait of aesthetic existence in *Either/Or*. I now want to pick out some of these motifs.

In his text on irony, whose systematic approach resembles Hegel's,[5] Kierkegaard distinguishes between Socratic and romantic forms of irony. He views the Socratic form of irony as a "qualification of subjectivity" (CI 262) in the sense of negative freedom. The Socratic ironist is negatively *free* because he liberates himself from restrictions by negating what exists. And he is merely *negatively* free because he merely negates. Irony is fundamentally incapable of answering the question of what should take the place of what it negates. Kierkegaard thus writes, "Irony establishes nothing" (CI 261). Nevertheless, irony's capacity for negation enables it to become an important motor in times of historical upheaval. If irony is not merely directed against this or that aspect of a given age but against its entire self-understanding, such as was the case with Socrates, then the ironist could even be considered to have revolutionary potential. Even in these cases, the ironic negation of the world does not anticipate a better tomorrow. The Socratic ironist instead combats the world by allowing the world to be turned against himself. Yet this could be precisely the manner in which the ironist becomes, though never consciously, an agent of the world spirit – or rather, of "the irony of the world" (cf. CI 262), according to Kierkegaard's Hegelian formulation. Not only did Socrates view the entire Greek ethical world as having lost its meaning, he also destroyed the Greek self-conception by acting as if he (still) took this self-conception seriously in order to demonstrate its untenability and ultimately to allow it to destroy itself.

Although Kierkegaard already describes Socratic irony as a radically negative concept that is *entirely* foreign to the practices of which it is a part, he characterizes romantic irony as a much more radical form of negativity. While he at least acknowledges that Socratic irony is directed against a certain historical reality, he accuses romantic irony – represented by the works of Friedrich Schlegel and Ludwig Tieck – of turning against reality as such. He characterizes both Socratic and romantic irony as negative forces, though the latter is not directed against anything in particular, not even something as comprehensive as the self-understanding of an entire age. The negative force of romantic irony is instead directed against determination as such. If Kierkegaard's Hegelian diagnosis is right, then romantic irony will have thereby lost its historical justification in relation to Socratic irony. Unlike the latter, romantic irony cannot stand "in the service of the world spirit" (CI 275), for instead of taking aim at the no longer plausible self-understanding of his contemporaries, the romantic ironist withdraws entirely from historical reality in order to "live poetically." According to Kierkegaard, therefore, the romantic ironist does not negate reality in order to explore the possibility of other realities, but for the sake of a reality that is nothing but possibility, nothing but mere "poetry." While he acknowledges the Socratic ironist as having the potential to be a negativist revolutionary, he describes the romantic ironist as a mere aestheticist not concerned with reality at all. Compared to the subjectivity embodied by Socratic irony, the subjectivity associated with romantic irony is, in Kierkegaard's terms, "an exaggerated subjectivity, a subjectivity raised to the second power" (CI 275).

Like Hegel, Kierkegaard also interprets the negativity of the romantic ironist as a symptom of a Fichtean philosophy of the subject, which he criticizes for conceiving of the I as "the constituting entity" (CI 273). And like Hegel, Kierkegaard accuses the romanticists of directly linking Fichtean philosophy and concrete practice, thereby confusing "the empirical and finite I" with "the eternal I," as well as "metaphysical actuality" with "historical actuality" (CI 275). According to Kierkegaard, the romanticists totalize "the subjective freedom that at all times has in its power the possibility of a beginning and is not handicapped by earlier situations" (CI 253) by positing the I as an absolute beginning, without any preconditions, from which the world is then constituted (cf. CI 273–4). Even in the work of Fichte, according to Kierkegaard's Hegelian interpretation, this premise raises a problem, for it claims that the subjective freedom to posit a beginning must ultimately remain a mere pretension, having lost its anchoring in the world: "an exaltation as strong as a god who can lift the whole world and yet has nothing to lift" (CI 274). For the same reason, Kierkegaard claims that the romantic impulse driving the poetic construction of reality must ultimately fail to have any effect. After all, the romantic ironist is to remain in the totalized freedom to begin something, but without ever actually beginning, for that would mean restricting himself. For the ironist, every life plan is merely a further possibility and thus too indifferent and fleeting in order to be truly seized upon and realized. The romantic ironist might flirt with the notion of standing above morality and custom, but he will never actually resolve to take a position above them (cf. CI 283–5).

Yet Kierkegaard does not merely criticize romanticist constructions as being indifferent to all reality and thus mere "poetry," making the romanticist's freedom a merely aesthetic freedom restricted to merely possible, poetic worlds. He goes on to accuse these poetic constructions of being infected by the particular ignorance of their producers. He views the poetic world of the romantic ironist as being radically reduced to the latter's subjectivity. Not only is the world a mere expression of his subjectivity, but it also revolves solely around his merely subjective, i.e. private or incidental, side. In the first instance, this, too, is a Hegelian argument: Because the romantic ironist rejects all determinations, he can only follow the dreary immediacy of his own random impulses. Romantic irony does not set the subject in a free relation to reality; rather, it radically throws the ironist back upon himself. The freedom of poetic life thus proves to be a kind of self-imprisonment, and thus an absence of freedom.

2. Self-Improvement and Forgetfulness-of-Self

Even in his dissertation, however, clear differences between Kierkegaard and Hegel emerge against the background of these commonalities. Kierkegaard gives a different accentuation to his critique of the lack of freedom embodied by the romantic ironist's "exaggerated" subjectivity. While Hegel primarily emphasizes the alienation of the ironist from ethical life, Kierkegaard criticizes the fact that the conception of poetic life associated with romantic irony undermines the formation of something like an independent self:

...by 'living poetically' irony understood something other and something more than what any sensible person who has any respect for a human being's worth, any sense for the originality in a human being, understands by this phrase. It did not take this to mean the artistic earnestness that comes to the aid of the divine in man, that mutely and quietly listens to the voice of what is distinctive in individuality, detects its movements in order to let it really be available in the individual and to let the whole individuality develop harmoniously into a pliable form rounded off in itself. It did not understand it to be what the pious Christian thinks of when he becomes aware that life is an upbringing, an education, which, please note, is not supposed to make him into someone completely different (...). By the phrase 'living poetically,' irony not only registered a protest against all the contemptibleness that is nothing but a miserable product of its environment, against all the commonplace people who, sorry to say, populate the world in such numbers, but it wanted something more. (CI 280)

Kierkegaard views romantic irony as striving to overcome even the limits imposed on poetic life by that which is "peculiar" or "original" about a given individuality (CI 181f). Kierkegaard concludes that the ironist not only lacks any anchoring, but also any substance. By constantly reinventing himself and the world, he does not attempt to form a distinctive personality. Because he can be everything, he cannot truly be anything.[6] According to Kierkegaard, the ironist does not develop "himself," rather he flees into arbitrary roles. By constantly adopting various *personae*, he leaves the potential for his own personality empty and undeveloped. For Kierkegaard this is an indictment of the romantic ironist's self-understanding, since when it comes to the state of his own personality, the romantic ironist converges with his unfree antipode, the "altogether commonplace person" (CI 281). While the latter fails to develop a personality because he lets himself be determined by his circumstances, thus allowing the potential of his own personality to be drowned in conformity, the former fails to develop a personality because he ignores *any* guideline, even that of his own particularity, thus becoming an entirely arbitrary personality. For Kierkegaard, true subjectivity only emerges if reality stands in a dual relation to the subject, "partly as a gift that refuses to be rejected, partly as a task that wants to be fulfilled" (CI 276). In Kierkegaard's view the romantic ironist's worldlessness reflects a forgetfulness-of-self that gets misunderstood as self-improvement. If it were up to Kierkegaard, "living poetically" would not be "the same as being in the dark about oneself, as sweating oneself out in loathsome sultriness, but it means becoming clear and transparent to oneself, not in finite and egotistical self-satisfaction but in one's absolute and eternal validity" (CI 298).

This critique of the romantic ironist, however, is ambiguous. Kierkegaard confounds the Hegelian objection to the romanticist's misunderstanding of his own empirical I as absolute with the objection that the ironist rejects the notion of self-realization altogether. Only in the first case is the ironist taken to be someone who rejects any determination of himself in order to remain – in Hegelian terms – in the loathsome sultriness of being-for-himself. In the second case, by contrast, the ironist can be understood as someone who rejects that particular version of the idea of self-realization according to which the latter must be understood as a process of inner growth or unfolding, as a realization *of something* – a given particularity or an original element of the individual.[7] We must distinguish between these two different cases, even though Kierkegaard suggests that the ironist's aesthetic rejection of this particular idea of self-realization immediately follows from a falsely abstract understanding of freedom. The distinction is necessary because in the second case, life plans can be realized in the world; it is only that, measured against the ideal of a self that is realized in a transparent and eternally valid manner, there are far too many of these ideals, thereby rendering the ironist's plans arbitrary. However, the subject obviously does not retreat from any kind of determinacy, rather it exposes itself to an excessive number of influences and associated possibilities, refusing to be determined by a supposedly original or unique essence. The danger entailed by this understanding of irony does not consist in a narcissistic retreat from the world, rather in exposure to its fullness. And as Kierkegaard saw clearly, this is not the fullness of an organic totality, rather that of an overwhelming variety. If the subject no longer realizes *itself* (as something) in and through the world, then the world itself must likewise be experienced as open and contingent.[8] Romantic irony dissolves the world into individual situations that are not necessarily organically bound together, and to which changing subjective states, determinacies, and determinations can correspond.

Like Hegel, Kierkegaard clearly defines the permeability of ironic subjects to the influences of a likewise open and changeable world in a one-sided manner, grasping it as a relationship of dependency (and thus as a consequence of a false understanding of freedom). However, Kierkegaard's emphasis is different from that of Hegel. Because the ironist also rejects the notion that he is determined by a particular essence, he must give himself over completely to the most diverse influences, thus becoming the victim of the arbitrary moods caused by those influences. Kierkegaard writes that "in a sound and healthy life...the mood is just an intensification of the life that ordinarily stirs and moves within a person," but "since there is no continuity in the ironist, the most contrasting moods succeed one another" (CI 284). The virtuosity with which the romantic ironist cultivates various moods depending on the given occasion cannot conceal his dependence on situations offered by the world. Nor can the intensity of these moods suffice to fill the abysmal emptiness lurking beneath the surface. It is only logical that Kierkegaard regards the boredom that repeatedly emerges from this abyss as the only aspect of constancy and coherence in the ironist's life (cf. CI 285).

According to Kierkegaard, the romantic ironist, who believes himself at the peak of subjective freedom, "drudges along in the most frightful slavery" (CI 284). This existential reformulation of Hegel's critique does not view the romantic ironist as strong and free, but as an exceedingly weak subjectivity prone to the immediacy of moods and the accidents that cause them. The freedom of poetic life is thus not autonomous, but heteronymous; it is in this sense *merely* arbitrary freedom. The subject of this freedom is determined by unintentionally caused moods, rather than controlling their arbitrariness.

Now, control over arbitrary moods is a crucial element of a rationalist concept of self-determination.[9] Although criticizing a both abstract and subjectivist understanding of freedom also means criticizing the suppression of the various ways in which the subject is determined, neither Hegel nor Kierkegaard goes on to integrate the notion of being determined through unintentional constellations and arbitrary strivings into a non-rationalist concept of self-determination. After all, as we saw in the previous chapter (cf. secs 9 and 10), this would presuppose the insight that the experience of something alien within ourselves in no way means that we have lost the capacity for self-determination; it does not mean that we can no longer control our behavior in the face of what changed circumstances and incidental occasions bring about within us. Instead, we should even view this experience as a requirement for the – constantly recurring – possibility and even for the necessity of self-determination in the name of freedom, or rather for the necessity of its dialectical movement.

Like Hegel, however, Kierkegaard is obviously fighting a historical rearguard battle. Similar, though different from Hegel, what Kierkegaard rejects in his critique of ironic, arbitrary freedom – the dissolution of the unity between the subject and the world – is merely the signature of democratic modernity. Unlike Hegel, who attempts to respond to this problem by proposing a mediation between subjective freedom and ethical universality,[10] Kierkegaard attempts to find grounding in the unity of the subject itself in the face of the modern *zeitgeist*, a unity whose own grounding is initially ethical, and subsequently religious.

It is now time to take a closer look at Kierkegaard's theory of stages, for it is here that the difference between himself and Hegel becomes increasingly explicit. This begins in Part I of *Either/Or*, in the first stage (aesthetic existence), where Kierkegaard presents a critique of the romantic ironist (sec. 3). Already at this point it becomes more apparent that Kierkegaard rejects the objection to aesthetic existence on the basis of a theory of ethical life, instead basing his critique on a theory of self-realization anticipated in his work on irony.

Although in Part II of *Either/Or*, he criticizes aesthetic existence by presenting an ethical way of life, he implicitly indicates the problems involved in this way of life in a rather ironic portrait of Wilhelm, the judge, who embodies this stage. In the works that then follow – *Repetition* and *Fear and Trembling* – he becomes more explicit, asserting the right of the – aesthetic – exception against the ethical conception of freedom as the identity of subjective freedom with the ethical universal (sec. 8). However, Kierkegaard meets this challenge not by revising the first stage, i.e. aesthetic existence, but by introducing a third stage: religious existence. The account of this stage is found amongst other writings in *The Concept of Fear*, *Stages Along Life's Way* and *Sickness unto Death* (secs 9–10). We will see, however, that Kierkegaard's solution itself poses a number of difficulties, which can be solved only by re-evaluating the first stage, that of aesthetic existence and its associated morality (sec. 11). But first of all, what is Kierkegaard's own account of this first stage?

3. The Impotent Seducer

The "seducer's diary" is correctly taken to be the systematic core of Kierkegaard's critique of the aesthetic form of life, which he presents in Part I of *Either/Or*.[11] It is no accident that large portions of this work appear to be an illustration of Kierkegaard's critique of irony.[12] We are not dealing here with the document of just any seducer, rather with a portrait of the aesthetic form of life as such, the (fictitious) testimony of a person whose life has been "an attempt to accomplish the task of living poetically" (EO I 304). This seducer is not primarily out for sex but for moods. He is not interested in his object for practical sexual reasons, but for aesthetic-erotic reasons. The girls he seduces (and they are always girls) lose their entire attractiveness for him as soon as they show any sexual devotion. Although the latter is the *telos* of seduction, he is at most interested in devotion as an opportunity to feel the melancholic mood of bidding farewell. For the seducer that Kierkegaard names "Johannes," deriving from Juan or Giovanni, it's all about the process. This is what truly satisfies him, or rather this is his true enjoyment. For it is enjoyment that "his whole life was intended for" (EO I 305). According to Kierkegaard, this life is "aesthetic" in two different senses: first, Johannes takes aesthetic pleasure in reality by experiencing the intensity of moods brought about within him by its changing impulses; second, he enjoys the retrospective aesthetic reflection on this connection in the mode of poetry. In the first aspect of his aesthetic relation-to-world, reality is degraded to a mere occasion for subjective moods; in the second it is "drowned out" in poetry (ibid.).

The moral problem involved in this stance becomes especially clear when it comes to the consequences for love. Like all seducers, Johannes does everything to avoid love. He is not interested in love itself, but in the mood of being in love. He is interested in himself, not in a concrete other. Like everything else, the other is merely an occasion for the subjective experience of various moods – an aesthetic object ultimately entirely robbed of its reality in order to live on as fiction in the mode of poetry. In psychological terms, Kierkegaard's seducer is deeply narcissistic. He shapes the other until it becomes his own. He is not interested in the unique qualities of the girls he seeks out, a precondition for love; he is solely interested in the narcissistic enjoyment of his own projections. Thus Kierkegaard has Johannes say, "Our relationship is not the tender and trusting embrace of understanding," but rather a "repulsion of misunderstanding" (EO I 351). In this sense the girl is strictly "his": a tabula rasa for subjective projections, nothing but an object. For this very reason, the girl can be replaced by other young things. For Johannes, the girls he seeks out do not have an existence of their own. As Kierkegaard has Johannes philosophize in his journal, the girl, who is nothing in her own right, must be thought of "categorically" as "being-for-other" (EO I 429). This theoretical conviction determines his actions: Girls are for him merely (aesthetic) objects, never subjects.

The reifying violence contained in the withholding of subjective recognition is reflected in the name of the girl that stands at the center of the journal. Her name is Cordelia – like King Lear's third daughter. Like Kierkegaard's Cordelia, Shakespeare's Cordelia – as Stanley Cavell has shown impressively[13] – is also a victim of such a strategy of "love-avoidance," manifested in the replacement of ethical by aesthetic relations. The tragedy begins when King Lear forces his daughter to prove her love for him in a public, theatrical manner. How should poor Cordelia, the truly loving daughter, respond to such a demand except to say – to herself – "love, and be silent?"[14] Unlike Lear, however, the last thing Johannes wants is for Cordelia to wear her heart on her sleeve. It is precisely her disposition for non-theatrical virtuosity that he finds aesthetically attractive. Whereas the naïve Lear makes a category mistake, summoning onto the stage something which can only be perverted in the harsh light of the theater – a mistake that will soon spell his doom – Johannes enjoys the virtuous disposition of his chosen one in a purely aesthetic fashion, giving him a cynical kind of happiness (cf. EO I 336f.).

Johannes finds Cordelia's introverted innocence so attractive because he can only fully enjoy something that is not aware of its own aesthetic qualities. He remarks that "a young girl who wants to please by being interesting will, if anything, please herself. From the aesthetic side, this is the objection to all kinds of coquetry. It is quite different with what is inappropriately called coquetry, which is nature's own gesture – for example, feminine modesty, which is always the most beautiful coquetry" (EO I 339). Already in the work of Jean-Jacques Rousseau, the theory of female chasteness stands at the center of his puritan account of a "natural" kind of eroticism which leaves the heterosexist "order of attack and defence" intact.[15] For Rousseau, female chasteness is the ultimate, non-theatrical erotic signal in which defense implicitly invites advance. Of course, the initiative for such an advance must lie with the man. This makes the decadence of the Kierkegaardian seducer become all the more apparent. For Johannes' clever advances are not intended to conquer; a successful hunt is not the point (except for subjective moods). Thus the publisher of the journal writes in the preface:[16] "In the same sense as it could be said that his journey through life was undetectable (for his feet were formed in such a way that he retained the footprint under them – this is how I best picture to myself his infinite reflectedness into himself), in the same sense no victim fell before him" (EO I 307).

The kind of violence to which Johannes subjects Cordelia is obviously of a different kind. Yet it consists neither solely nor primarily in the fact that she is reified as an aesthetic object. Instead, he alienates her by educating her aesthetically, by teaching her to reflect on her femininity and thus on herself. The decisive problem in the relationship between Johannes and Cordelia is not the asymmetry of their gender roles, but their aesthetic perversion: "It is oppressive for her that he has deceived her, but still more oppressive, one is almost tempted to say, that he has awakened multiple-tongued reflection, that he has so developed her esthetically that she no longer listens humbly to one voice but is able to hear the many voices at the same time" (EO I 309). The development of this many-tongued reflection which awakens in Cordelia this intensified sense of possibility, and which also intoxicates the ironic seducer, also becomes responsible for the fact that Cordelia abandons the very idea of femininity that originally made her attractive to Johannes. He is initially pleased at the fact that Cordelia is obviously "an isolated person" (EO I 339). A man cannot be so, "not even a young man, because, since his development depends essentially upon reflection, he must have contact with others" (ibid.). But girls, at least in their youth, should be as self-contented as possible, without, however, having a self that could be content with itself. Whatever causes a girl to be content with herself is therefore, Johannes concludes, an "illusion." Precisely this state of pre-reflective, i.e. illusionary, contentedness is the seducer's ideal of femininity; it is the quintessence of her status as an object. There is nothing more "corrupting" in Johannes' eyes than "associating a great deal with other young girls": "The woman's fundamental qualification is to be company for the man, but through association with her own sex she is led to reflection upon it, which makes her a society lady instead of company...If I were to imagine an ideal girl, she would always stand alone in the world and thereby be assigned to herself, but mainly she would not have friends among the girls" (EO I 340). Ultimately, however, the true crime that the seducer commits against Cordelia consists in seducing her to engage in reflection. Because her relation to him consists solely in latencies, she has nothing but her own power to reflect in order to grasp his unreal reality. Her relation to him is thus necessarily as aesthetic as his relation is to her (cf. EO I 306f.). The seducer is entirely aware of the aesthetic transformation he produces in Cordelia, for it is the loss of her pre-reflective innocence that makes him unattractive to her. As he writes in his final journal entry: "In a man innocence is a negative element, but in woman it is the substance of her being." But it is he who has caused Cordelia to lose her innocence. Thus he writes in a more melancholic than sympathetic note of departure: "If I were a god, I would do for her what Neptune did for a nymph: transform her into a man" (EO I 445).

This is of course a highly interesting turn. Through the process of reflection, the girl transcends the status of object associated with femininity and fulfills a condition for the subjectivity associated with manhood. At the same time, as the publisher notes, the aesthetic education provided to her by the seducer enables her to leap over the possibility of becoming a "complete" subject. Instead, from the origin of her social isolation, she immediately develops an "exaggerated" subjectivity or – as Kierkegaard formulates it in his book on irony

– a subjectivity "raised to the second power" (cf. CI 274f.) which continues to entrap her. She therefore does not acquire subjectivity, rather only a more intense illusion of it.[17] By alienating herself from her "one voice," the voice of her own uniqueness, instead listening to "many voices at the same time" (EO I 309), she fails to attain self-realization. As Kierkegaard suggests, she instead loses herself in a kind of indeterminacy that is also characteristic of the seducer's own empty self. The structural commonality between the self of ironic reflection and the girl's pre-reflective self gives a remarkable gender-theoretical touch to this deficit: first, the subjectivity of the seducer appears to be no less illusory than that of his objects; second, the subjectivity of the seducer, contrary to his own self-assessment, is painted as a not entirely manly, rather effeminate subjectivity. According to the logic of these ascriptions, this subjectivity is largely empty and thus heteronymous; therefore, Kierkegaard's critique of aesthetic existence claims that those who lead such an existence fail to attain self-realization on account of this self-misunderstanding. This is the problem with which the argumentation of the ethicist begins in the part II of *Either/Or*.

4. The "Helmeted" Will and its Desperation in the Face of the Aesthetic

The seducer does not attain "self"-realization and thus, according to Kierkegaard's account, also fails to realize his freedom. Therefore aesthetic freedom is also regarded as deficient. Whoever lives for his freedom, as the Protestant judge Wilhelm in the second part of *Either/Or* writes in a letter to his ironic counterpart, can never lose himself.[18] "Or can you think of anything more appalling," he asks, "than having it all end with the disintegration of your essence into a multiplicity, so that you actually became several, just as that unhappy demoniac became a legion, and thus you would have lost what is the most inward and holy in a human being, the binding power of the personality?" (EO II 160). In Wilhelm's view this is precisely what the ironist does: He destroys the binding power of his personality by giving it over to the centrifugal "obscure forces" (EO II 164), i.e. momentary desires, within himself. It is only logical that Wilhelm, implicitly citing Plato's influential image of the tyrant,[19] cites the Roman emperor Nero as an extreme example of a person who is driven by momentary desires and thus loses himself (cf. EO II 184–8). However, Wilhelm does not directly equate the ironist with the lust-driven tyrant (cf. EO II 204f.). While the tyrant enjoys immediate pleasures, the ironist reflects. While the former enjoys life, the latter enjoys himself (cf. EO II 190f.). But the ironist's reflection in no way enables him to exit the sphere of immediacy to which the life of the tyrant (according to Plato) is restricted. For Wilhelm, reflection is merely another form of enjoyment and, like the immediate pleasure of the tyrant, crucially dependent on contingent circumstances: "The condition for enjoyment is still an external condition that is not within the individual's power" (EO II 190). The ironist can only help himself by repeatedly negating the conditions from which he temporarily allows himself to be determined, taking pleasure in "discarding" them. "But," as Wilhelm argues, "it obviously follows that he who enjoys himself by discarding the conditions is just as dependent on them as one who enjoys them" (EO II 191). Under these conditions – and this is the decisive point for Wilhelm – neither the ironist nor the tyrant will be able to "open the personality" (ibid.).

Given the fact that the ironist is not guided by the idea of an "eternal validity of the personality" (EO II 189, CI 298), a remaining Platonic notion crucial in the eyes of Wilhelm, it is only of secondary importance whether we can assume the ironist – contrary to the tyrant (as Plato conceives of him) – to be capable of reflecting on his contingent desires. Measured in terms of eternity, both the ironist and the tyrant belong to the sphere of mere immediacy. Whoever is guided by his own eternal validity can no longer be shaken in his desires and no longer be susceptible to endless impulses for substantial change; his self is therefore immune to the possibility of becoming other. By taking up this Platonic position, Wilhelm does honor to his name, for as etymology informs us, the name Wilhelm means "he who is helmeted with will."

Because the ironist cannot manage to free his life from finite influences and thus, at least in the estimation of the Kierkegaardian ethicist, ultimately lives an unfree life, the latter regards the former to be evil. For Wilhelm, aesthetic evil consists in incompletely realized freedom. The ironist is evil because he contents himself with the pale shadow of freedom, freely choosing unfreedom. For precisely this reason, however, we must also assume that the ironist has at least an inkling of his own lack of freedom. A symptom for this is the melancholic boredom that, as Wilhelm appears to claim, accompanies all of Johannes's affairs and other episodic aims like a shadow. Wilhelm argues that from the ironist's perspective, every impulse he accepts appears to be a "trivial plaything" (EO II 202) that soon bores him. What makes the ironist evil is thus the self-deceit that consists in not admitting his despair about aesthetic existence, despite his latent awareness of its "nothingness." This self-deceit causes him to fail to transition to a different kind of existence, to freedom, and thus – according to Wilhelm – to a self-determined existence (EO II 194). Thus Wilhelm calls to the aestheticist: "Despair!" (EO II 211).

This, however, makes Wilhelm himself seem somewhat desperate. Wilhelm's lengthy letters ultimately prove futile in the face of the ironist's strange resistance to the demand that he despair, the historical success of aesthetic existence, and the melancholic spirit of the age.[20] This might have less to do with the narrow-mindedness of his contemporaries than with the fact that the Hegelian diagnosis of exaggerated subjectivity, which Wilhelm draws on in order to diagnose the spirit of the age, fails to capture its object. With reference to the deficits of ethical existence that Wilhelm, the Hegelian caricature, represents, we can show that once we no longer identify aesthetic existence with a false, subjectivist understanding of freedom, aesthetic existence in fact implies its own ethic. On the one hand, this agrees with Kierkegaard's own account, as he is aware of the deficits of Wilhelm's ethic; on the other hand, it is contrary to Kierkegaard's account, because he does not regard this consciousness as leading to a fundamental rehabilitation and thus to a renewed conception of aesthetic existence. Rather, it motivates him to introduce a third state, that of "religious existence" (cf. sec. 10). However, let us remain with ethics for a time.

5. Repentance and Duty: The Freedom to Choose What One Already Is

Because the ethicist criticizes aesthetic existence due to its dependence on contingent circumstances, his aim must of course be to overcome this dependence. The first step, despairing at this dependence, has already been taken. According to Wilfried Greve's summary of the idea of the ethicist, this desperation should make the subject aware "that it is identical with its finite states; it shows the self that it is in fact identical with itself *in* all its finite states."[21] The subject, which despairs at its dependence on contingent circumstances and at the "finite states" of itself that react to these circumstances, should now discover itself as being "eternal," identical with itself across all finite states. It should gain an awareness of itself as a "unifying point of all concrete determinacies"[22] and thereby become free. At the same time, however, the full concept of the freedom the ethicist strives to attain can only be had once the subject grasps its "eternal self" in a positive and concrete way. This is because the idea of an eternality of the self – i.e. the ethical idea of freedom – must not be misunderstood as abstract infinity if it is not merely to represent a further version of the problems of aesthetic existence. The ethicist must succeed in mediating between the conception of the eternality of the self that shows up in despair and its concrete and finite existence.

Wilhelm's theory of self-choice is an attempt at just such a mediation. The theory is dialectic because it "makes two dialectical movements simultaneously – that which is chosen does not exist and comes into existence through the choice – and that which is chosen exists; otherwise it was not a choice. In other words, if what I chose did not exist but came into existence absolutely through the choice, then I did not choose – then I created. But I do not create myself – I choose myself" (EO II 215). In the act of self-choice, the I emerges as that which Kierkegaard has Wilhelm term, in an existentialist reinterpretation of Hegel's terminology, the "absolute" (cf. esp. EO II 210, 214). Although the I has always been latently absolute, it only realizes itself as absolute once it becomes conscious of itself as such. Wilhelm thus also states that the I "receives" (EO II 177) itself in the act of self-choice. Furthermore, Wilhelm views the dialectic of positing and being posited as having religious significance, seeing the consciousness of being posited as implying the consciousness of a positing deity (cf. EO II 167f.). Inasmuch as Wilhelm understands God as the source of the absolute in the subject, and thus also as the origin of freedom, he equates the complete realization of freedom with the fulfillment of divine will. Freedom, therefore, is a duty.[23] But again, self-realization can only be a duty in this sense because the act of self-choice requires more than the consciousness of one's self as the unifying point of all determinations. In order for the I not to be directly faced with its finitude and thus to repeat the mistake and the destiny of the romantic ironist, "freedom *from* finitude" must be concretized as "freedom *in* finitude."[24] From Wilhelm's perspective, what the discussion of the ethicist with the aestheticist is supposed to demonstrate is that freedom can only be conceived as concrete freedom. Freedom from finitude, however, can only be concretized as freedom in finitude if the finite is grasped from the perspective of freedom. For Wilhelm, this occurs when the subject takes responsibility for itself as a concrete being. Through this dialectic of positing and being posited, he who chooses must become precisely the person he already is. "He does not become someone other than he was before, but he becomes himself. The consciousness integrates, and he is himself" (EO II 177).

Taking responsibility for one's own concretion, however, means taking up a new perspective on this concretion. It implies "repentance" (cf. esp. EO II 175, 216) for one's previous lack of freedom. And as we have seen, for Wilhelm this also means repenting for the evil of such an existence. After all, the ethicist did not view the ironist as being evil because he opposes collective notions of the good, but because he remains in a sphere of indifference and indecision about himself and the world (cf. EO II 223). The self-choice of the ethicist, his decisiveness toward himself, is a good in itself, which posits a criterion for distinguishing between good and evil: the orientation toward a "true" realization of freedom. Repentance is also accompanied by the recognition that evil "essentially belongs to" human existence (EO II 224). According to Wilhelm, evil not only represents the possibility of refraining from choosing and thus leading an unfree life, rather every life – even that of the ethicist – is unfree prior to the act of choice; every life is guilty. According to Wilhelm's evolutionary thesis, therefore, aesthetic existence represents a necessary transition for the ethicist (cf. EO II 241f.). Choosing oneself means showing remorse for the freedom that had not been realized prior to the act of choosing. For the protestant Wilhelm, the realization of freedom and the acceptance of guilt are both part of one and the same movement:

> Only by repenting himself does he become concrete, and only as a concrete individual is he a free individual.... Not until a person in his choice has taken himself upon himself, has put on himself, has totally interpenetrated himself so that every movement he makes is accompanied by a consciousness of responsibility for himself – not until then has a person chosen himself ethically, not until then has he repented himself, not until then is he concrete, not until then is he in his total isolation in absolute continuity with the actuality to which he belongs. (EO II 247f.)[25]

According to Wilhelm, repentance allows a person to attain the "transparency" (EO II 248) that Kierkegaard holds up to the ironist in his dissertation: "The primary difference, the crux of the matter, is that the ethical individual is transparent to himself and does not live *ins Blaue hinein* [in the wild blue yonder], as does the esthetic individual. This difference encompasses everything" (EO II 258). Although he admits, interestingly enough, that "in every person there is something that up to a point hinders him from becoming completely transparent to himself" (EO II 160), repentance remains the path that can bring an individual close to the ideal of self-transparency. He argues that repentance is capable of joining what was previously heterogeneous into a whole – a history of sin in which the "eternal self" is recognized as its protagonist. It is through this act of appropriating one's past through which "even that which has happened to me is transformed and transferred from necessity to freedom" (EO II 250).

Dieter Thomae, however, points out in his discussion of Kierkegaard that the "willingness to take on one's 'entire existence'" must go together with the "ignorance toward the problem of how this 'entire existence' becomes a model to be adopted."[26] Especially from a psychoanalytical perspective, it is quite naïve to assume that our past is clearly accessible and transparent to us, and yet this is supposed to ensure the authenticity not only of our repentance, but also of the continuity of the "eternal self" with ourselves. Only a self that is fundamentally accessible and transparent to itself in the totality of its actions and strivings can be claimed "eternal." As soon as the history of our sins proves to be merely one version of our self, since there is no neutral point from which we can view our self in its totality, its eternal shape will have already been corrupted by finitude. The history of our sins would then no longer belong to the sphere of ethical repentance but to that of "poetic" construction.

For Wilhelm, however, repentance represents only one dimension of choice, one that faces toward the past. The other, future-oriented dimension of this act carries the term "duty," which in the context of Wilhelm's ethics has a less Kantian and more Hegelian tone. Repentance merely marks the beginning of ethical existence. The context of existence brought about by repentance now becomes the task of self-realization, a task that Wilhelm regards as consisting in the fulfillment of ethical relations (cf. EO II 270). Whereas the ethical conception of repentance aims to retrospectively transform one's own immediacy and accidence into freedom by appropriating the past in its totality as the sinful past of the "eternal self," the conception of duty is focused on leaving behind the immediacy and accidence of our own existence and *becoming* an "eternal self." But this means externalizing the self-transparency that is attained through repentance, which in turn means revealing this self-transparency in practice. According to Wilhelm's Hegelian interpretation, this means that the overcoming of immediacy and accidence is not only the religious duty of the self, it must also manifest itself in the fulfillment of social duties.

Therefore, the accidence and immediacy of aesthetic existence is overcome once the accidental individuality of the individual is sublated into the universality of duty. Although the ethicist's self, like that of all other humans, may be "in its immediacy...defined by accidental characteristics," the "task is to work the accidental and the universal together into a whole" (EO II 256). For Wilhelm, this means that the individual must accept those duties which he finds as a person who is already defined by ethical relations. Accentuating the problematic features of Hegel's account of subjective freedom, Kierkegaard's Wilhelm maintains that duty, to the degree that it is not merely regarded as being externally imposed but as an "expression of his inner-most being" (EO II 254), grants the individual "substantial freedom" (Rph §146). By means of the "unity of the universal and the particular" (EO II 264) attained through the ethical fulfillment of duties, the "highest validity" of a person (EO II 264), the "true art of living" (EO II 256) emerges.

Of course, there is a significant difference between Hegel's and Kierkegaard's Wilhelm, since the latter locates the absolute in the individual subject. Wilhelm defines the conscience, which Hegel problematizes in his critique of morality, as the "secret" (EO II 255) to the identity between the universal and the particular. According to Wilhelm, the conscience is "both the ethical authority of the individual" and "the concrete expression of the objective order."[27] This means that the conscience is no longer interpreted as site of a potential conflict between reflexive freedom and the ethical universal. On the contrary, it is the location of their fundamental identity. For Wilhelm, to choose according to one's conscience *is* to choose the universal. Therefore, Kierkegaard's ethics, despite its anchoring within subjectivity, appears to be less a critique of Hegel's problematic aspects than of their existentialist radicalization. Wilhelm's definition of the existentialist ideal of self-transparency proves to be a corollary of (total) social integration. It is realized in the "revelation" before others, which can only occur through the ethical fulfillment of duties. So it is only logical that Wilhelm views labor and marriage as the privileged spheres of such a revelation, i.e. as privileged spaces for the freedom that is fulfilled through the performance of ethical duties. Kierkegaard, however, in no way presents a true image of Hegel's theory of ethical life. Not only is Wilhelm's ethics restricted to those ethical relations in which the integration of individuals is especially apparent,[28] he also focuses solely on that feature of Hegel's philosophy of right that "drowns"[29] subjective freedom in its ethical substance. As justified as his reference to Hegel's argumentation may be (cf. ch. 2, sec. 12), it cannot do justice to the internal complexity of the conception of ethical life in the third part of the *Philosophy of Right*. This reduction already marks the distance between Kierkegaard and both the ethical pseudonym and its Hegelian model, which will become entirely clear in the writings that follow *Either/Or*.

6. One Sexism for Another

Therefore, the price to be paid for an understanding of freedom in which there is a complete mediation between the individual and the "duties of the circumstances to which he belongs" (Rph §150) becomes especially clear in Wilhelm's ethics. This is already true of Wilhelm's duty-centered conception of work,[30] and even more relevant in this connection is his praise of marriage. Wilhelm views marriage as the paradigm of the kind of freedom which is realized by fulfilling ethical duties, and which can also be understood as the social revelation of the self-transparency achieved through repentance. After all, marriage is an institution that relies on mutual revelation. If we take a closer look at this ethical program, however, we will see that Wilhelm is not, at least not in the first instance, interested in a concrete other (his wife) but in his (literally: his) relation to the universal. When it comes to marriage, revelation is achieved primarily by fulfilling ethical duties, and not – as is sometimes suggested (e.g., EO II 104f., 110f.) – by revealing each individual's singularity in the relation of recognition between lovers. In other words, what is most important about the institution of marriage is not the partner one chooses, but the fact that it enables individuals to take part in the universal. This allows them to overcome the accidental, including their choice of partners, and thereby become free.[31] In Wilhelm's view, the partners to the marriage appear to be wedded more to their marriage than to each other.

Wilhelm's conception of marriage thus occupies a peculiar space between pre-modern and modern conceptions of marriage. On the one hand, the primacy of the institution vis-à-vis individual choice recalls pre-modern conceptions of marriage based not on personalized love but on the preservation of the tradition, power and order of governing or producing households. On the other hand, Wilhelm views the decision for the universal as an element of the modern idea of self-realization. The latter cannot help but bleed into his understanding of marriage, which can no longer be determined by external factors, rather only by subjective decision. The meaning of marriage thus does not primarily consist in fulfilling social roles, but in individual fulfillment, which in this case includes love. Wilhelm must therefore show to his aesthetic counterpart how his conception of marriage also does justice to the modern conception of personalized love. In other words, he must prove that his conception of marriage is accompanied by a convincing conception of love.

Wilhelm attempts to deliver this proof in his first letter, which he dedicates to a defense of marriage. He not only objects to the manner in which the ironic seducer avoids love but, more fundamentally, to a *zeitgeist* in which irony hollows out the ideal of romantic love. Wilhelm initially admits that it is not entirely unjustified to be ironic about this ideal, since the romantic ideal of immediate, immutable, and thus eternal love cannot stand the test of time. And yet, according to Wilhelm's critique of contemporary culture, an ironic stance on this ideal will not lead to a superior ideal. Instead, irony takes on an independent existence, thus leading to a melancholic attitude about love. On the one hand, it derides love's claim to the eternal as illusory; on the other hand, it seeks to redeem this claim in individual moments of euphoric infatuation – in moments already inscribed with their own sobering end. If it were up to Wilhelm, the romantic idea of eternal love would not merely be negated, but transformed into marriage. Yet he regards this transformation as being possible only by means of faith.

Wilhelm insists that only first love is capable of undergoing such a transformation, because here the unity of freedom and necessity has not yet been "disturbed." It is immediate (cf. EO II 45), which in Wilhelm's eyes makes first love "aesthetic." In order to preserve the trace of eternity in the immediacy of first love from the destructive power of ironic reflection, it must be glorified by Christian faith – by lovers' gratitude to the god that, "like all prayer, is united with an element of work," i.e. the "internal" act of seeking to preserve love. According to Wilhelm, "the nature of the first love is not changed thereby; no reflection is involved...it is merely caught up in a higher concentricity" (EO II 47). The crucial role that Christian faith appears to play here nevertheless remains within the limits of Wilhelm's ethic of the will: Because Wilhelm's understanding of god amounts to little more than the consciousness of the duty of self-realization, practiced religion is reduced to a tool for fulfilling duties. With the help of faith Wilhelm replaces the "illusory eternity of imagination," with which the aestheticist glorifies erotic moments' claims to eternity, with the "eternity of consciousness": "will, decision, intention." This is what he calls the "eternity of eternity" (EO II 58).

To the degree, however, that consciousness grasps itself as eternal, it moves away from the concrete other. As Adorno correctly points out in his commentary, Kierkegaard "admonishes the loving person to maintain faith in a once beloved person, even if this faith has lost any rational justification. He ought to believe in the person in spite of any psychological experience which is taboo...as being 'secular.'

Here, the transformation of love into mere inwardness is striking."[32] This resistance to historically lived experience is especially drastic when it comes to Wilhelm's denunciation of the emancipation of women.[33] Remarkably, Wilhelm agrees with his counterpart on this point. Wilhelm's praise of wives and Johannes' praise of girls share the notion that women essentially belong to the sphere of immediacy. And both agree, though for different reasons, that women should remain in this sphere and not become alienated from themselves through reflection, which only causes them to turn into "unfeminine society ladies." Wilhelm puts a correspondingly strict limit on his idealization of the wife: "Woman" is "perfect" for him only in her "imperfection" (EO II 312). Although woman is "more esthetic" than man and in her oft-praised "humility" even closer to god (EO II 66), this is merely an implication of the fact that she, due to her dependence on man, essentially belongs to the sphere of finitude. Because a woman's self is merely relative, i.e. related to man, Wilhelm leaves no doubt about the fact that the "absolute" or "eternal" self is essentially male.

The decisive difference between Wilhelm and Johannes thus does not lie in their respective image of women. Both define femininity as "being for others."[34] Both, though for different reasons, view pre-reflective simplicity as a feminine quality, and both are averse to the emancipation of women. Whereas Johannes turns simplistic girls into the medium of his poetic productions, the simplicity of wives aids the ethicist in gaining a second, "noble simplicity" (EO II 77) through the fulfillment of marital duties, thereby overcoming the reflection associated with aesthetic existence."[35] For Wilhelm, wives have a primarily medial function, similar to the function that young things have for the seducer, which devalues their subjectivity. From Wilhelm's perspective, when it comes to the relationship between the sexes, the decisive distinction between the ethical and the aesthetic life-form lies elsewhere: Ethical existence has the advantage of being able to "maintain" women's subordinate position, while aesthetic reflection necessarily alienates women from the position assigned to them (cf. EO II 92).

As was the case with aesthetic existence, the gender plot also says something fundamental about the understanding of freedom associated with ethical existence. What becomes especially clear about Wilhelm's view of marital love is that the historical quality of concrete eternality, which Wilhelm sets in opposition to the abstract infinity of the ironist, merely entails a constantly repeated affirmation of the will to fulfill one's ethical duties. Neither this will nor the understanding of the corresponding duty is fundamentally put into question by married life. The historical character of marriage is, according to Wilhelm's model, reduced to subordinating shared experiences to the "eternal consciousness," i.e. the previously formulated will to fulfill marital duties. This is what Wilhelm means when he states that spouses' mutual understanding "is all at once just as much as it continually becomes" (EO II 118). Such a concept of marital agreement is just as ahistorical (being trapped within the eternal confirmation of what a will once formulates) as it is inappropriate to the phenomenon of love it purports to explain. It reduces love, which is an emotion, after all, to a mere act[36] (according to Wilhelm, by formulating the intention to hold on to love, the initial, immediate state of infatuation is transformed into love). And it replaces the intersubjective dimension of love with a common relation to the universal, even though the gender roles are asymmetric. This type of "understanding" is no longer an understanding of the other. Love gets replaced by duty. Therefore, Wilhelm's attempt to rescue love from the ironic *zeitgeist* is as much a failure as his claim to reconcile a concept of marriage based on duty with the modern primacy of love.

Already at this point, it makes sense to discuss an alternative that can escape the either/or which Kierkegaard posits between an ethic of duties and a subjectivist aesthetic. The emancipation of women and the attendant conception of love offer an especially striking illustration of a historically dynamic model of freedom – one which overcomes both the lack of freedom associated with the worldlessness of Kierkegaard's seducer and the lack of freedom resulting from the obligation to what exists, as is preached by Kierkegaard's Wilhelm. Now is the appropriate time for a discussion of this alternative, which implies a different interpretation of aesthetic existence and its reflection, since Kierkegaard, as we will see later (secs 8–10) takes an entirely different approach to removing the deficits he sees in both aesthetic and ethical existence.

7. The Love of Divorced Society Ladies

Love cannot be preserved by elevating it to the eternity of the very duty that ultimately destroys it. Love saves itself – that is, to the extent that it saves itself as love – only through the test of time itself, only in lovers' reflection upon the power of their love under changing conditions. Historically, such a dynamic understanding of love goes hand in hand with the emancipation of women, and thus with the denaturalization of asymmetrical gender roles. The consequences of this process, which begins in the Romantic period, for a concept of marriage based on love can be made clear by taking a brief look at twentieth-century cinema. A new genre was born when in the 1930s and 1940s fast-talking emancipated women (all society ladies) took over the big screen, a genre Stanley Cavell has called the "comedy of remarriage."[37] This genre celebrates an understanding of marriage founded on lively relationships between equally entitled spouses – i.e. relationships that include the possibility of separation. "All genuine marriage is remarriage."[38] When the seducer "turns the 'ones' into the narrative principle of erotic love, according to which the first time is the only time that counts, over and over," then the narrative principle of modern marriage, as Gertrud Koch expresses the matter in Cavellian terms, is "not the power of one, but of two, that of remarriage. Love survives the second time at the earliest."[39] This contradicts not only the seducer, but also Wilhelm the patriarch, whose concept of love likewise – though in a different fashion – remains tied to the ones. For Wilhelm, it is the first love that counts – once and for all (with the help of faith and a sense of duty). We might see a virtually utopian element of Hollywood comedies in the fact that the second time is the last. As Cavell emphasizes, these comedies end with a reconciliation between husband and wife that is fundamental because it is based on the recognized emancipation of the woman.[40] For our purposes, these comedies' utopian endings are less important than the development leading up to it. By beginning the love story with a separation, these early twentieth-century Hollywood comedies emphasize the consequences of the romantic topic of change on the understanding of love and marriage. Romanticism brings history into this understanding, ripping apart the corset imposed by the concrete eternality of predetermined duties and social roles. It is no accident that this is an important theme already in romantic literature.

The modern awareness of the historicity of love is also a consequence of what I term the democratic ontology of the good. It is part of an awareness in which the possibility of the question of what constitutes the good (also in terms of our choice of partner) is inscribed into the concept of the good itself. What is decisive for love is not merely the one-time decision to hang on to love, but the question of whether this decision can be confirmed in the course of the partners' life together – that is, whether their love can develop. This means allowing for the possibility that love can come to an end to enter into the horizon of love itself. This, along with the partners' equality, is a condition of freedom. Therefore, not only the existence of emancipated society ladies, but also the normality of divorce in democratic societies should be defended as an expression of freedom, contrary to the pessimistic cultural diagnoses of societal decay. The fact that marriage today, especially given the fact that it is founded on love, is bound within the horizon of the possibility of divorce, does not mean that it has lost its meaning. Instead, it is only within this horizon – i.e. the horizon of possible change – that we see the dramatic nature of the promise to remain true to each other in difficult times. It implies a dynamic, active concept of faithfulness, one that does not rely on the thoughtlessness and complacency of external duty.[41]

Whereas Wilhelm's concept of marriage is focused on the idea of transparency and revelation, the concept of modern love (which, fittingly, is no longer necessarily tied to the institution of marriage) is accompanied by the recognition of an essential lack of transparency – not only of the lovers to each other, but also of each lover to himself or herself. We can never see all the way through ourselves down to the ground – for as Helmuth Plessner puts it, this ground is "eternal potentiality"[42] and as such "foundational (said better, non-foundational)."[43] We can say, picking up on the last two chapters, that because our nature is accessible to us only through a disturbance of our social identity, through an interruption of the habits of our second nature, it is as such nothing more than a potential. This is the foundation – or as Plessner would say, "non-foundation" – of the fact that we can never be fully absorbed by the limited shapes of our social identities, that we are constitutively open for development and change. This naturally affects our social relations as well: "All life with others carries the germ of the capacity of dissolution because souls are more than what they factually are."[44]

The anthropological insight into the potentiality at the base of our existence does not mean that the notion of revelation no longer plays any role in the modern concept of love. Whereas Wilhelm's idea of revelation, as we have seen, is not primarily related to a concrete other, referring instead to the social revelation of the (male) self in and through duty, the notion of mutual revelation between equal partners can certainly be integrated into the historically dynamic conception of love defended here. Revelation, then, is neither the final goal nor the only important element of love, rather it is reduced to an aspect that remains tied to its opposite – reservation, distance. As much as we long for revelation in love, for a recognition of ourselves "as we truly are," just as much would we suffer if our identity was entirely determined, in an "extinguishing"[45] manner, by the judgment of others. We equally need recognition of our potentiality, of the fundamental freedom that we not only have toward ourselves, but also toward the images that our beloved reflect back to us. And we not only love the way the other is (his or her respective determinations), rather love, especially erotic love, always entails the love of the potentiality of the other, his or her unknown sides and latent possibilities. Following Plessner, we should understand "lively" love as a dynamic process that remains in a double movement between "a repulsion that attracts and an attraction which ultimately repulses."[46] Love unfolds as an antagonism between revelation and reservation in a process that represents nothing but the historical life of love. Such a dual movement is presumably the only way we can do justice to the essential "ambiguity" of the soul, its back-and-forth between "potentiality and actuality, process and form."[47] For precisely this reason, love is the relation in which a person experiences the most comprehensive form of recognition.[48]

This kind of living love fits into neither the aesthetic nor the ethical schema. Neither does it avoid determination, i.e. it does not reify the other by mystifying it (or, which essentially amounts to the same thing, by turning it into a blank canvas for our projections), nor does it flee from the possibility that the other might change by obligating him or her to remain the person we have become fond of or accustomed to (which is also a form of reification). This kind of love does justice both to the other and to oneself only insofar as it implies continuous attempts at mutual understanding, as this is what allows the possibility of change and development. Perhaps the secret of so-called true love lies in the fact that it never corresponds to our previous concepts of it. As is often said, by exceeding all our expectations, true love evades the fatal logic of a desire which reduces the happiness that the other is for me to the fulfillment of predetermined conceptions.

Such a conception of love cannot be realized by any life-form that retreats from all determinacy into a space of the merely possible, the space of pure poetry. On the contrary, the only life-form suitable to this kind of love is one that is constantly forced to make new decisions due to the impossibility of a natural social identity. We must not confuse reflective distance from our previously valid decisions with detachment from practices or life in general. The occasionally ironic society ladies do not question the validity of all duties from a position that stands above the level of practices; rather, they reject the validity of certain duties within given practices – such as the duties of the simple and humble wife. Obviously, this is entirely legitimate. We never step back from our previous beliefs and decisions without reason. Instead, this step is often caused by our experiencing desires which do not (or no longer) correspond to our previous beliefs and decisions. This can be the experience of new love, when we suddenly see ourselves in a new light, but also the more gradual experience of no longer feeling the emotions that once lent our decisions substance, a latent aggression toward what we once wanted so badly, a diffuse wish for something else. Experiences such as these convey a crisis – a *krisis*, a turn – in our self-relation, one that can motivate us to truly change our previous relations to ourselves and the world, both political and/or private. Whether these changes actually come about, however, is not up to the individual alone. This is true for changes in the private sphere, but it is especially true when my changed self-image runs into conflict with socially determined roles. The emancipation of women makes clear that the realization of this striving is not decided by the private decision of an individual woman. After all, a broad social movement was necessary to draw attention to individual experiences of alienation as instances of social injustice in order to demand social change.

In any case, the society ladies feared by both Wilhelm and Johannes – women who have not only freed themselves from their subordinate social roles, but also from the one or the other partner – do not share Cordelia's fate. They are isolated neither in the first stage (they have many friends) nor in the second stage (they are not isolated from the world). On the contrary, they repeatedly come to themselves because – and only because – they are open for others and for a changing world. The self of the emancipated society lady is thus never "eternal." Woman's self-determination instead implies a systematic counter-proposal to the ethicist's concept of freedom, a proposal which cannot be discarded on the basis of the ethicist's critique of the Hegelian cliché of the romantic ironist. Here we see again that the critique of romanticism prematurely deems unfree what should be defended as freedom in the name of its dialectic movement. Here we are dealing with a conception of freedom which is not based on the construction of an "eternal self." The latter must be presupposed – contrary to all psychological knowledge – in the retrospective act of repentance, and it is asserted – contrary to all living experience – in the prospective conception of the fulfillment of ethical duties. This conception of freedom can instead become possible, i.e. historically concrete, to the degree that it is able to throw aside the corset of eternal validity. After what has been said, it should be obvious that this counter-proposal is restricted neither to modernity nor to women. The emancipation of women merely provides a clear illustration of what is at stake in general.

On the basis of his conception of freedom, Wilhelm thus not only restricts his wife (by declaring her to be restricted) but also himself, i.e. the ethical life-form in general. This is not only made apparent by his rejection of any experiments in life as being unethical (cf. EO II 253), but also with regard to his theory of exception. The latter once again makes clear that Wilhelm's concept of freedom merely affirms what exists. He views exceptions in which a person "encounters difficulties" in expressing "the universally human in his individual life" (EO II 328) as imperfections which must be overcome at all costs. If this does not succeed, Wilhelm claims that the sadness resulting from such a failure should become the expression of the universal in the heart of the exception (cf. EO II 330f.).

Nevertheless, Kierkegaard's *Either/Or* does hint at the fact that a conception of freedom which posits an identity with the universal is not only extremely bourgeois, but also suffers from a highly problematic kind of idealism. Wilhelm's philosophical complacency is too put-on, and his underestimation of the possibility that individuals could prove "bankrupt"[49] when faced with the demand to become one with the universal is too obvious for us to be able to identify Kierkegaard's position on freedom with that of Wilhelm. This Hegelian caricature instead serves to illustrate the cost of insufficiently integrating subjective freedom into the conception of ethical life. The demand that subjective freedom be completely joined to ethical universality not only remains a mere (idealistic) demand, but the corresponding conception of ethical life proves too static. Kierkegaard's distancing from Wilhelm's ethics, which is already made apparent by the way he is caricatured, is confirmed by the works that follow *Either/Or*.

However, Kierkegaard does not correct Hegel's distorted view of morality, which is most apparent in his critique of romantic irony, in order to then arrive at a more dynamic understanding of the mediation between subjective freedom and ethical universality (and thus at a reformulation of ethical life as democratic ethical life), as we have done in the previous chapter. Instead, Kierkegaard remains largely faithful to Hegel's critique of romanticism. The consequence of his loyalty to Hegel, along with his emphasis of the problems that must result from the idealistic assumption of a total mediation between subjective freedom and ethical universality, is that Kierkegaard chooses an entirely different path.[50] Although (as we will see in the following sections) the focus of his later writings (also under pseudonyms) on the problem of exceptions and sin privileges aesthetic existence over ethical existence, he does not revise his earlier criticism of aesthetic existence, a revision that might then bleed onto the level of ethics. Instead Kierkegaard seeks to resolve the problems he sees in both aesthetic and ethical existence at a further stage, viz. that of religion. The first step in this direction leads us to the problem of the exception.

8. Aesthetic and Aristocratic Exception

"Eventually one grows weary of the incessant chatter about the universal and the universal repeated to the point of the most boring insipidity," notes Kierkegaard's pseudonym Constantin Constantius in *Repetition*. He goes on to say,

> There are exceptions. If they cannot be explained, then the universal cannot be explained, either. Generally, the difficulty is not noticed because one thinks the universal not with passion but with a comfortable superficiality. The exception, however, thinks the universal with intense passion. When one does this, a new order of rank results, and the poor exception, if he has any competence at all, once again, like the girl spurned by the stepmother in the fairy tale, enjoys favour and honour. Such an exception is a poet...[51]

This, however, is something that Wilhelm could have conceded as well. He also allows for the possibility of a case in which an aesthetic existence cannot – despite the best of intentions – be elevated to the universal in an ethical fashion. For this is "a legitimate exception," one that is "reconciled in the universal" (R 227). The young poet, whose fate is narrated by Constantius, is wholly demoralized by the fact that his melancholy disposition prevents him from turning his merely poetic relationship to the girl of his longing into a real relationship. He cannot become a husband on the Wilhelmian model. Yet the cause of this young man's suffering is not so much his own melancholy as the injustice he does to this girl by virtue of his own inability. He feels guilty. Nevertheless, the moment the girl is wed to another, he is relieved of this burden and he is free to lead an exceptional aesthetic existence. This solution to the problem of exception, however, is as incidental as it is harmless, but that is not what makes it a noteworthy case. What is decisive is rather the development that occurs prior to this anti-climactic ending.

At the peak of his development, the young man turns to religion – specifically to the book of Job. He is deeply impressed by the story of this pious and innocent man who loses his entire belongings, his ten children and his health, and yet still refuses to abandon his faith. At first, the young man crudely identifies with Job, as he also regards himself as an innocent victim (cf. R 198). Yet then he takes an interest in the freedom that Job represents, a kind of freedom that emerges when all worldly explanations and thus ethics fail. Whereas Job's acquaintances push him to admit guilt in order to make these horrible sufferings comprehensible as a punishment for his sins, Job insists on his innocence and thus enters into a relationship to God that is all the more profound, transcending worldly rationality and liberating him from the world and his own suffering.[52]

But ultimately, as Constantius later remarks, the young man remains too much a poet to let the book of Job move him to take the step from aesthetic to religious existence. After his suffering unexpectedly comes to an end, his temporary religious inspiration endures as a mere mood (cf. R 229f.). However, and this is the point that interests us here, in Constantius' eyes an exceptional aesthetic existence has the potential to become a religious exception – provided it can be termed "justified" from an ethical perspective, i.e. provided it is oriented toward the ethical universal and seeks to be unified with it. Under these conditions the poet "constitutes the transition to the truly aristocratic exceptions, to the religious exceptions" (R 228). Whereas the "justified" aesthetic exception remains an exception *within* ethics, because it ultimately confirms the ethical universal, the religious exception appears, at least on the surface, to be an exception *to* ethics, because it suspends worldly logic altogether.

The tension between ethics and religion with reference to what Constantius would view as a truly "aristocratic" exception is the subject of *Fear and Trembling*,[53] and it is no accident that this work was published together with *Repetition*. The pseudonym Johannes de Silentio gives an impressive account of the story of Abraham, whom God commands to go to Moriah and sacrifice his beloved son Isaac. Abraham sets off to fulfill God's command, but as he prepares to plunge his knife into Isaac, God intervenes and puts a ram in Isaac's place. According to de Silentio, if we are to understand Abraham, we must not view his story in the light of its fortunate ending as a harmless test (cf. FT 52). Instead we must understand it in the light of the extreme tension or "resilience" [*Spannkraft*] (R 210) in Abraham's situation prior to its happy ending, or we will not understand his story at all.

According to de Silentio, this makes it much more difficult to understand the figure of Abraham than the thought of Hegel (cf. FT 32f.). Abraham's literally inconceivable greatness consists in the fact that his actions cannot be explained in ethical categories, nor with reference to the ethical universal, and thus not at all. Neither can we call his act moral – the ethical term for Abraham's plan is "murdering one's own son" – nor can we generalize Abraham's higher motive of fulfilling God's command that he sacrifice his son. Abraham stands as a radically individual figure before God. Or as de Silentio puts it, "as the single individual" he stands "in an absolute relation to the absolute. This position cannot be mediated, for all mediation takes place only by virtue of the universal" (FT 56). Although Hegel terms the challenge that the particular poses for the universal a "moral form of evil" in his *Philosophy of Right*, he cannot do justice to the phenomenon of the religious exception by falsely equating the universal with the godly, nor by defining as evil everything that cannot be mediated with the universal (FT 54).

When de Silentio attempts to justify the superiority of the individual to the universal upon the premises of Hegelian ethics, his remark that it is only "by means of the universal" (FT 56) that the individual can be superior to the universal is of crucial importance. De Silentio thereby emphasizes repeatedly that the separation between Abraham and the social world is not the expression of an arbitrary abandoning of ethics. After all, Abraham loves his son and his ethical relation to him. And Abraham's faith is not borne by the hope of a better afterlife that could ease the pain of sacrificing his son. He "had faith for this life" (FT 20). At first sight, therefore, an aristocratic exception in the religious sense is, as de Silentio notes, remarkably similar to that of the philistine (cf. FT 38), for he too finds "equanimity" in life (FT 41).

Nevertheless, it is not through mediation with the universal that the aristocratic exception is bound to the world, i.e. not by means of Wilhelmian ethics, but rather "by virtue of the absurd" (cf. FT 37). On the one hand, Abraham resigns himself, coming to terms with sacrificing his son and separating himself from the world and all that binds him to it. On the other hand, contrary to all "human calculation" (FT 34), he believes he will not be forced to sacrifice his son.[54] It is this belief that makes Abraham a "knight of faith" (cf. FT 46). His existence, founded upon faith, is of a kind that believes in spite of all odds, absurdly, in the fulfillment of finite existence. This is what distinguishes the faithful from those who resign in the face of the improbable. This kind of faith is what enables the believer to find his way into the world. The decisive shift of emphasis in *Fear and Trembling* compared to the discussion of Job in *Repetition*, which from the perspective of the aestheticist solely emphasizes that element of faith that resigns from reality, lies in the notion that the faithful not only gain freedom from the world, but freedom toward the world. According to de Silentio's interpretation, Abraham can only continue to live on with his son after the test on the mountain because, "by virtue of the absurd," he never abandoned his son. Because of his absurd faith in God, he who believes is an "heir to the finite," while he who resigns in the face of the improbability of worldly fulfillment must become "a stranger and an alien" in the world (FT 50).

Similar to the case of the young poet in *Repetition*, the case of Abraham in *Fear and Trembling* confirms the premises of ethics – here explicitly associated with Hegel. The exceptional existence of the poet is "justified" because he is oriented toward the ethical universal, and remains filled with the will to the universal even in the face of failure. And Abraham's religiously motivated exceptional existence is only "aristocratic" in the sense that it occurs "by virtue of the universal." Thus de Silentio, following Hegel, emphasizes that anyone who refuses to express his internal existence and reveal it to society, instead wishing to retain it in "the qualifications of feeling, mood, etc." ultimately "trespasses" against the universal. Yet de Silentio also points to the phenomenon of legitimate internality, which "is incommensurable with exteriority" (FT 69).

The admission of such a legitimate, religiously motivated internality also implies a defense of irony. For a further dimension of Abraham's exceptional situation is the fact that his position cannot be mediated and thus cannot be communicated. This is why the author that discusses Abraham's case in so many words carries silence in his name. To be silent in so many words, to leave something unspoken while not saying nothing is one of the rhetorical definitions of irony, which is why de Silentio, just like the ironic seducer in *Either/Or* carries the name Johannes. De Silentio thus mirrors Abraham's irony, while significantly shifting the meaning of irony in the context of the aristocratic exception. Abraham's irony is distinguished from that of the aestheticist because it is employed for the sake of concrete existence and prevailing ethical relations.[55] Like Abraham's religiously grounded inwardness, his irony is also limited in a decisive sense: An individual only receives the "authorization" (FT 111) for hesitant internality and irony if he remains bound to ethical existence "by virtue of the absurd."

9. Common Sinners

We have only moved beyond Wilhelmian-Hegelian ethics once we no longer conceive of religious existence as presupposing the ideality of an ethical mediation with the ethical universal, which could only be exceeded by aristocratic exceptions. This would mean that the religious sphere of existence would no longer presuppose the ethical sphere as a transitional stage, but instead represent an alternative, i.e. an independent type of ethics. It is only at this stage that we see a clear difference between Kierkegaard and Hegel, or rather the idealist of ethical duties that Kierkegaard takes Hegel to represent. The project Kierkegaard formulates in *The Concept of Anxiety*[56] no longer seeks to relativize ethics merely on the basis of aristocratic exceptions, but to shake it to its core by taking up the ethically marginalized reality of sin. "In the struggle to actualize the task of ethics, sin shows itself not as something that belongs only accidentally to the accidental individual, but as something that withdraws deeper and deeper as a deeper and deeper presupposition, as a presupposition that goes beyond the individual. Then all is lost for ethics" (CA 19). Sin is thus no longer regarded as a mere exception that does not undermine the rule of the ethical universal; from the religious perspective it appears instead to be a constitutive element of all existence. Kierkegaard here views Christian dogma as that form of science which is capable of accounting for the fundamental presence of sin in the individual by means of the concept of original sin. This enables the establishment of a "new ethics" which, similar to the "first ethics," turns ideality into a task – but "not by a movement from above and downward but from below and upward" (CA 20). Now, Wilhelm also emphasized that the non-realization of freedom in the aesthetic stage of existence represents a necessary stage in every life, and that it must therefore be repented. We could object that Wilhelm's conception of repentance is also a form of idealism, as it requires that a person be capable of calling to mind the entirety of his previous life and thus capable of becoming entirely transparent to himself.[57] But Kierkegaard is concerned with the idealism of duties, which is supposed to determine the present and the future of the individual, thus replacing repentance, which is directed toward the past. The superiority of religious existence to ethical existence thus concerns its treatment of the *present* of sin, which is underestimated by the idealistic notion of duty.[58]

"In the system," as Brother Taciturnus remarks in *Stages on Life's Way*, "a person repents once and for all in §17 and then goes on to §18."[59] This type of ethics, however, is guilty of a "systematic abbreviation of the pathological elements of life" (S 476), and thus fails to become ethics in the true sense. Like Constantius in *Repetition*, Taciturnus recounts the story of a young man who, due to his melancholy and poetic nature, is simply incapable of being a Wilhelmian husband. Not surprisingly, the young man in *Stages* receives the name Quidam, which essentially means someone or anyone. His case is thus made anonymous, but in a systematic sense. The point is to normalize Quidam's inability to live up to this ethical demand. Unlike in *Repetition*, the problem of guilt facing the merely poetic lover in *Stages* is not solved by means of an external incidence. Quidam instead seeks to work himself out of his guilt – as is documented in his morning diary entries – by concealing his love from his beloved for two months in order to rid her of her feelings for him. From this perspective, what at first sight appears to be an unethical deed – deceiving the object of one's love – in fact proves to be a genuinely moral act, as Quidam seeks to free his beloved from a relationship doomed to be unhappy.

This is a crucial shift away from Wilhelm's conception of conscience, which reduces the latter to a state of unproblematic harmony with the universal of existing ethical life. Conscience is no longer a part of ethical existence but of aesthetic existence. Much closer to Hegel's critique of morality, Taciturnus characterizes conscience as an authority for which the good cannot simply be derived from the general rules of an existing form of ethical life. Instead, it results from the consideration of the particularity of a given situation. Like Hegel, however, Taciturnus also sees an internal connection between the moral consideration of conscience and irony, or rather aesthetic existence. Because moral reflection cannot provide the criteria needed to decide between good and evil, it leads to unfounded considerations which do not lead the subject toward the world and toward action, but rather alienate him from the dimension of practice. Whereas Johannes, the romantic and ironic seducer from *Either/Or*, embodies the climax of this alienation, placing himself in the name of pleasure above "law and thing" (cf. Rph §140),[60] the largely non-ironic poet Quidam represents the problems that Hegel finds in morality. In Kierkegaard's terms, these problems belong to an ethics that is attainable through aesthetic existence. Quidam's fate is supposed to make clear that moral reflection necessarily leads the subject to become entrapped within himself.

His morning diary entries are thus accompanied by evening entries that do away with the author's early morning optimism. Quidam's late night journal entries document his repeated loss of certainty about the moral success of his deception. He is not certain whether he can really protect the girl from unhappiness, nor whether she will actually be able to free herself from him. It remains to be seen whether he will remain guilty in the end. Because the guilt of the author is externally determined, i.e. by the "information from actuality" (S 450), his fate will ultimately be either comic or tragic.

Quidam cannot free himself from the pangs of his conscience on his own. According to Taciturnus' essentially Hegelian argumentation, moral reflection can neither answer the question of guilt nor determine how to compensate for or overcome guilt. Yet this appears to be the best that ethics can do under the conditions determined by aesthetic exceptions. Taciturnus regards whoever cannot manage to reconcile the particular and the universal by performing their duties – which according to *Stages Along Life's Way* is true for everyone – as having no choice but to repent now and in the future: a self-entrapment in endless spirals of moral reflection caused by remorse. Because moral reflection cannot solve the question of guilt on its own, we learn from Quidam that this reflection will ultimately become entangled in interpretations of reality and in the consideration of possible alternatives for action. Ultimately, it will become impossible to act at all. Given the ethical requirement to act, such an alienation from the world of practices is the "highest contradiction" (CA 117). In the final section of this chapter, I will return to the distortions inherent in this Hegelian image of morality – thereby focusing on those motives which are relevant for Kierkegaard's work.[61]

It is important to note that at this point in his theory of stages, Kierkegaard favors morality and the associated aesthetic existence over the idealism of duties that characterizes the first stage.[62] This also explains why Kierkegaard's various pseudonyms, all of whom are critical of ethics, have such a high opinion of Socrates and his irony.[63] They not only view the Socratic earnestness that "tears people out of the doings of 'others' and bustling reality and draws them back into the isolation of the self" as being the "highest form of earnestness that people are capable of outside of revelation," but also as the "indispensable condition for a life of faith."[64] Nevertheless, Kierkegaard retains Hegel's claim that morality necessarily alienates us from practices. He not only seeks to defend morality against Hegel's diagnosis of its pathologies, but also to present an alternative solution for the problems to which morality leads, especially when it is not taken to the frivolous extreme of romantic irony. Kierkegaard finds the solution for the problems of morality in Christian faith, particularly in the concept of sin. As we will see, Kierkegaard thus radically distances himself from Hegel's project of mediating between subjective freedom and ethical universality. This finally reveals the full extent of the difference between Hegel and Kierkegaard, a difference which accompanies the latter's work ever since his study on irony. Kierkegaard sees the task of the second, religiously founded form of ethics no longer in such a mediation, but only in the realization of the "eternal self."

10. The Leap of Faith

From the perspective of the religious consciousness of sin, the fact that moral reflection on our conscience speculates on our innocence is merely the "ingenious sophistry of anxiety" (CA 113). Compared to the ethics that has crystallized into morality (with an either tragic or comic ending), the consciousness of sin is a leap away from the possibility of guilt and toward the reality of sin. Independent of "external circumstances and occasions," the reality of sin, and this is the decisive point, is the "thoroughly sinful existence" of the individual.[65] That is indeed a radical leap, for the reality of sin makes the reality of man – which on the basis of morality must be recognized (repeatedly) in terms of good and evil, true and false – false in its entirety. By its very definition, the leap toward a consciousness of sin cannot be made through reflection. We experience ourselves as "thoroughly sinful" only in our relationship to Christ, and his existence – or rather, the "absolute paradox" (PF 37) that an eternal god at some point in history became man – constitutes the limit of rational reflection. It cannot be understood but only believed, i.e. accepted as that which is incomprehensible. This is also supposed to prove that "belief is not a knowledge but an act of freedom, an expression of will" (PF 83).

In order to grasp just how radical Kierkegaard's shift is in terms of a theory of freedom, we should take a look at Anti-Climacus' discussion of weakness of will in *Sickness unto Death*. He starts by discussing the Platonic notion that there can be no weakness of will.[66] According to Plato we are either aware of what is better and will act accordingly, or we are unaware and will choose the act that is worse.[67] Anti-Climacus rejects this view, for it falsely implies that knowledge of the good automatically leads to a corresponding action. He correctly points out that in reality, "the transition from thinking to being is not so easy, for there is everything at once" (SD 94). The will is "dialectical" (ibid.). The conflict between knowledge and our "lower nature" need not always be carried to the extreme that we do the opposite of what we know is good; usually there is a gradual process of putting off doing what we know is right until this knowledge fades, whereupon we switch sides and recognize that which we want as that which is good (cf. SD 94).

For Anti-Climacus, however, the fact that we sometimes recognize one thing and sometimes another as being good is not a possible expression of a historically dynamic dialectic of freedom – as I have argued in the previous two chapters.[68] The process by which our relationship to the world and ourselves changes, however gradually, merely shows that we have lost our will, ourselves and our freedom – a loss that must be avoided. He is convinced that we not only cannot expect morality to provide us with a solution, but that it also can only be viewed in connection with such a loss of freedom.

Anti-Climacus views the sphere of morality merely as a loss of orientation, giving rise to a form of sophistry through which individuals can deceive themselves into thinking that their "lower nature" is the good. Yet Wilhelm's response to this problem is not an option for Anti-Climacus. He regards it as too idealistic, inferior even to morality. But the implication of this presupposition is that the problems ascribed to morality can only be solved if the particularity of the individual vis-à-vis the ethical universal is recognized and yet remains bound to an objective standard for judging good and evil. This standard is provided by God – thus goes the solution for the second, religious form of ethics. According to Anti-Climacus, "no man of himself and by himself can declare what sin is, precisely because he is in sin" (SD 95).

Inasmuch as the distinction between good and evil is viewed from a Christian perspective as a matter of sin, this is not a problem of knowledge, not a matter of interpreting concrete relations to the self and the world, but a matter of faith that can only be "taught" (SD 95) in and through a relation to God. As Anti-Climacus never tires of emphasizing, sin is a state of being, not an individual act. On the one hand, it precedes, as a state of latent despair, the "act of freedom" that is faith; on the other hand, it follows after this act as the "reality of sin." However, the recognition of this reality through faith in the forgiveness of sin is no longer accompanied by despair. From a Christian perspective, because sin is not an act in either phase, the opposite of sin is not virtue but faith (cf. SD 82). We must have faith, beyond the – in the view of Anti-Climacus entirely groundless – "dialectic of the will" between knowledge and our natural will. The decision to believe is thus a "pure" act of will, for it is founded upon neither knowledge nor natural will, but upon a relation to the "absolute paradox." If we speak in this context of the passion of faith, then we clearly do not mean the immediate passions of the natural will, but a kind of second immediacy that emerges from the relation to the paradox that is God's son (cf. PF 59).

The sheer act of faith, which simultaneously posits the "reality of sin," causes a "breach" by which "the individual becomes another."[69] This is the core of religiously founded ethics. In the consciousness of sin, the individual "becomes conscious of its difference from the humane in general" (UN 297). To allow one's existence to be determined by the category of sin is "sharpened pathos, both because it cannot be thought, and because it is isolating" (UN 298). For "the category of sin is the category of individuality" (SD 199). Inasmuch as humans sin, and this is true of every believer, they each stand before God as individuals (cf. SD 122). The aristocratic exception thus becomes the paradigm of religious existence in general, though not because of its exceptional status, but because of the pathos that goes along with an isolated position toward God. The passion of faith is necessarily accompanied by a passionate inwardness which for Kierkegaard's pseudonyms, unlike for Wilhelm, is the quintessence of successful self-realization. This brings us to the endpoint of the second form of ethics: Faith and self-realization explain each other. Kierkegaard writes: "The greater the conception of God, the more self there is; the more self, the greater the conception of God" (SD 80).[70]

What failed in the first form of ethics should now succeed in and through the passionate inwardness of faith. The latter is (1) understood as a kind of freedom that is not abstract, but concrete, because it concerns individuals in their concrete existence as sinners, though this concretion no longer depends on their concrete actions. The inwardness of faith (2) mediates subjective freedom and reality. Religious inwardness is free from the "bustle" of the social world (into which the first form of ethics sought to "integrate" this inwardness). It is also free toward reality, though this is no longer the reality of ethical life, but the paradoxical reality of God's human son now honored as the only true reality. This means that all forms of appropriating the world, of producing objectivity and evidence, merely appear as forms of appearance of untruth and lacking authenticity. Therefore, the externality of the relation-to-world must constantly be transformed into the inwardness of the relation to God, which in turn means viewing it from the perspective of the all-encompassing "reality of sin." In the inwardness of faith, (3) the mediation of finitude and eternity should succeed – also in a paradoxical form. For according to Theunissen, "the tension between temporality and eternity that prevails over the paradoxically 'assembled' being of God's human son returns in the existence of each Christian who must decide in the course of his life for or against Christ and thus for or against his own eternity."[71] The eternity of the Christian self is nothing but the inwardness gained through a passionate relation to God. In this relation, the faithful self (4) should become transparent to itself by resting "transparently in the power that established it" (SD 14). Faith is supposed to provide the sublime point from which individuals can appear to themselves in their existence as sinners. Through the passionate inwardness of faith, they should acquire that "essential, unchangeable continuity" that they cannot attain through the idealistic notion of duty, nor through the moral reflection that ultimately leads to loss of self.⁷² Because the self can attain itself in transparent continuity and thus as an "eternal self" only through faith, this faith is emphatically defined as a "rebirth" (PF 19).

However, the problem of idealism that afflicted the first form of ethics returns here at the level of the second form of ethics, not least because of a largely "demonic," ironic *zeitgeist* that runs counter to the good defined by religion. Indeed, the separation between this *zeitgeist* and the project of self-realization in religious existence could not be any greater. Far from despairing in aesthetic existence, the *zeitgeist* is entangled in things that are "external" (CA 136–54).⁷³ As Anti-Climacus laments, when it comes to passionate inwardness, even Christianity itself fails to live up to its own essence. The idealism of the first form of ethics, which consisted in demanding that individuals allow their particularity to dissolve into the ethical universal, is countered with a religious idealism requiring individuals to take a leap into the isolation of a relation-to-God through a pure act of will, contrary to all ties to external things. Such a leap, however, can only be demanded and not compelled, for "it shall be believed" (SD 116).

Instead of drawing the conclusion from the failure of the first form of ethics that the distorted image of morality and the attendant aesthetic existence need to be corrected in order to make room for a dynamic concept of mediation between subjective freedom and social practices, Kierkegaard's religious philosophy of existence continues to presuppose the distorted critique of the subjectivism of the moral standpoint, as well as the static image that is opposed to it, which is rather undialectical.⁷⁴ His answer lies neither in reflection nor in the social, with its possible productions of meaning and objectivity,⁷⁵ but in an entirely different order, a (divine) sphere beyond reflection and the social. Yet this is such a radical step, a "leap" into transcendence, that mere mortals can only stare more or less anxiously into the abyss between themselves and the abstract "Thou shalt" of faith.

In fact, the refusal to undertake the "efforts required by earnestness"⁷⁶ is not the exception, but – in the ironic modern age – the rule. Yet, if we take the way that Kierkegaard's pseudonyms criticize the first form of ethics as our model and do not interpret this as a case of cultural decay, but as a symptom for the problematic idealism of this second form of ethics, then we must re-evaluate both the sphere of morality and the aesthetic existence that finds its pinnacle in the works of Hegel and Kierkegaard.⁷⁷ We are thus faced with the fundamental question: Is there an ethics of aesthetic existence?

11. Repetitions

When it comes to sketching the outlines of an ethics of aesthetic existence, it is crucial that we defend aesthetic existence – i.e. the consciousness that we have termed "irony" – against the suspicion of subjectivism that has afflicted it ever since Hegel. But then, as we have already seen in our discussion of Hegel, this consciousness is no longer merely an indicator of alienation from social practices in general. Instead, the sensibility hastily rejected by its critics as being a case of irony points to local experiences of alienation from concrete determinations that do not lead into endless circles of groundless reflection, but rather give us occasion to re-determine ourselves. In this sense, ironic consciousness can be defended as a necessary accompaniment to a historically dynamic concept of freedom; this concept picks up on the fundamental instability of our practical orientations as well as the resulting necessity of deciding on these orientations ever anew. It neither subsumes individuals under the social (which would cause the latter to lose its liveliness) nor does it isolate them from the social in a state of sublime inwardness, a kind of asocial hereafter.

In this context, we should mention that at the end of his dissertation, Kierkegaard himself attempts an ethical rescue of irony, employing the term "controlled irony" (cf. CI 324–9) in order to re-define it as a crucial element of a proper kind of freedom. Ironic detachment from practices is no longer understood as a model for an entire life, rather it is "reduced to an element" (CI 325). As a controlled element, Kierkegaard praises irony. Inasmuch as it "rescues the soul from having its life in finitude," it is not only "the absolute beginning of personal life" (CI 326) but also a "guide" throughout that life (CI 327). The role that irony plays in "personal life" (CI 326) is analogous to the role that doubt plays in science; it has the function of demanding that individuals "balance the accounts" (CI 327). In this sense, irony is even defined as the path to "truth, actuality, content" (CI 326). By casting doubt on beliefs adopted from science or elsewhere, irony moves individuals to take up a position on these beliefs, either rejecting or adopting them. In this function, Kierkegaard writes that irony is "extremely important in enabling personal life to gain health and truth" (CI 328). Irony "manifests itself in its truth precisely by teaching how to actualize actuality" (ibid.).

As convincing as it might seem to define ironic detachment not as a model for the subject but as a productive aspect in its practical life, we must recognize that Kierkegaard reconciles irony and ethics by referring to "controlled" irony. In order for irony to fulfill such a crucial function, it requires the control exercised by a life that is "rounded off" (cf. CI 325), one that is "positively free in the actuality to which he belongs" (CI 326). It is only to this kind of "master" (CI 325) that irony can be a "serving spirit" (CI 325). The fact that Kierkegaard presupposes that which is yet to be achieved by means of irony is perhaps the most obvious indicator of the problems that arise for an attempt to reconcile irony with the idea of a controlled, "rounded off" self.

According to Kierkegaard's Hegelian account, by contrast, romantic irony represents the quintessence of the permeability of the subject to externalities that will ultimately alienate the subject from itself. As Paul de Man formulates the matter, a "discontinuity and a plurality of levels within a subject"[78] asserts itself in romantic irony, which conflicts with the notion of a controlled and well-rounded subjectivity: Subjectivity is divided into the conception it has of itself and its "nature," whose immediate expressions stand in a tense relation – and occasionally even in contradiction – to such conceptions. De Man – along with Baudelaire – thus makes the experience of "falling over," which is simultaneously a "falling out of" the false conception of a total mastery of nature, the paradigm of ironic consciousness.[79] However, the ironic consciousness of the tension between the self-image and the nature of humans only produces an "unhappy consciousness"[80] if – like de Man – we conclude that every relationship to self and the world can only be a "deception" or "illusion." If this were true, only an ironic "fiction," which would only negatively relate to empirical reality, could assert itself against the "empirical reality" that proves "inauthentic" on the whole. The "permanent parabasis," as de Man says citing Schlegel,[81] the permanent marking of the "radical difference"[82] between reality and fiction, would then appear to be the only acceptable possibility. This would confirm the impossibility of finding a way back to reality through irony. Under these conditions, only the gods could help such an unhappy consciousness.[83] Already in the case of instrumental reason, which for de Man is paradigmatic, this consequence only comes about if we make the implausible assumption that all discursive reason is necessarily instrumental. This would entail that any positive self-enlightenment of reason would ultimately prove to be a further deception, for which there is no worldly alternative, rather only ironic detachment.

This is not a plausible assumption.[84] By rejecting it, we get a different image of the relation between irony and reality. If we do not view the experience of alienation, which is constitutive for irony, as an alienation from social practices as such, rather as an aspect of social practices, then we do not deny that in principle every determination can be affected by this experience. Yet we should not define this experience as being directed – simultaneously and independent of a given context – against all elements of our relation to ourselves and the world, i.e. against our practices, our "empiricism" as a whole. This is to take seriously that the critique of irony (in the ethical dimension that interests us here) emphasizes irony's connection with an experience of the other, an experience that the subject cannot control. Such an experience cannot come about constantly and everywhere, it is merely one of the possible effects of the permanent exchange between the subject and a fundamentally changeable world. The crisis in our self-relation brought about by an experience of the inner discrepancy between our self-image and our eccentric desires does not alienate us from articulated relations to self and world in general; on the contrary, it leads us back to these relations. For a crisis in our self-relation is a prominent occasion for re-posing the "question of truth" in an existential sense, for taking account of our principles and, if necessary, making corresponding changes in our life – with the aim of recovering the feeling of inner harmony, i.e. a feeling of realized freedom.

Such changes, however, appear to put an end to irony to the extent that we associate them, following de Man, one-sidedly with the experience of dissonance within the subject. But the consciousness captured in the term irony is not exhausted by this experience; what fickle ironists demonstrate is that a certain way of dealing with this experience is also implied. An ironist constantly redefines himself on the basis of his experiences of both himself and the world. Ironic consciousness is not nihilistic, contrary to what this critique hastily concludes by falsely equating the ironist's situational re-definitions with indifference toward what he situationally defines. Ironic consciousness is instead fallibilistic: It is aware of the possibility that what it regards to the best of its knowledge as the better option today might prove to be the worse option tomorrow. An awareness of the fundamental fallibility of all determinations does not, however, relieve us of the task of making them – unless we are willing to give up our freedom. The ironist, who does not remain in the "loathsome sultriness" of being-for-itself, but rather constantly redefines himself in the course of his interactions with the world, obviously does not pay this price. His acts of self-determination, however, unlike what Kierkegaard claims with his notion of "controlled irony," are not acts of a well-rounded subject who is in control of itself. Instead, it is only in and through such acts that the subject (repeatedly) acquires its self in this or that determination.[85]

Therefore we could also say that the ironic path to freedom consists in repetition. Repetition, however, is not to be understood in the Kierkegaardian sense as a transition to a higher stage (from immediacy to spirit), but more loosely as a procession of multiple acts of self-determination in which immediacy and spirit are brought together ever anew. Precisely because our inner nature is never transparent to us as such, only revealing itself in our interactions with a changeable world and thus remaining, as potentiality, a source of possible change, we are forced to constantly face the challenge of defining ourselves in our interactions with the world. That which Kierkegaard longs for simply does not exist: a single conclusive repetition in which we attain true self-determination. There are only repeated acts of self-determination which can never eliminate the fundamental instability of our practical orientations. From the perspective of the ironic consciousness that is aware of this condition, as de Man emphasizes, though for the wrong reasons, there can never be a conclusive "reconciliation between the ideal and the real." For Friedrich Schlegel, as de Man points out in this connection, the "spirit of the ironic mind" is characterized by a "dialectic of the self-destruction and self-invention which...is an endless process that leads to no synthesis. The positive name he gives to the infinity of this process is freedom, the unwillingness of the mind to accept any stage in its progression as definitive, since this would stop what he calls its 'infinite agility'."[86]

Because of its recognition of the fundamental fallibility of all concrete determinations of the good, ironic consciousness is indeed suspicious of all claims of eternality; its very essence consists in being open to the future. As Kierkegaard recognized, therefore, the "concept of irony" is related to the "concept of anxiety." In *The Concept of Anxiety*, Kierkegaard writes, "The possible corresponds exactly to the future. For freedom, the possible is the future, and the future is for time the possible. To both of these corresponds anxiety in the individual life. An accurate and correct linguistic usage therefore associates anxiety and the future" (CA 91). Ironic consciousness is accompanied by an awareness of the finitude of all decisions and of all the knowledge upon which we base our actions. It is thus also aware that our actions can tragically contradict our own intentions. The fundamental indeterminacy that defines Quidam's guilt in *Stages* must therefore be generalized. Everyone has the possibility of becoming guilty in spite of our best intentions. Whether this is the case or not is not entirely under our control. The success of our actions depends on factors that can never be completely controlled, at least not by finite beings. Ironic consciousness (in the sense that I wish to defend it here) recognizes the possibility, which under certain conditions can be frightening, that a turn of fate can make us guilty in spite of our best intentions, and that this is a constitutive possibility of all our actions. In this sense, ironic consciousness lives in the presence of tragedy.[87] Yet the recognition of the possibility that our actions can fail – and that in extreme cases our good intentions can have the worst effects – is not the end, but the beginning of ethics and morality. Just because the good does not merely depend on our own will is no reason to abandon all praxis, but to be sensitive to history and context. The morality of ironic consciousness thus does not lead to self-contradictory alienation from all practices, such as Kierkegaard suggests in line with Hegel; instead, it is accompanied by a proper understanding of moral action, one that is aware of its own finitude. The attentiveness to concrete situations, constellations and developments protects this consciousness from the false self-certainty with which many self-declared philanthropists bluntly claim to *be* just or good.[88] Thus Adorno writes in *Minima Moralia* that "it is part of morality not to be at home in one's home."[89] And as Alexander García Düttman comments on this passage:

> To not be at home in one's home [… means that …] if fallibility is constitutive for moral action and makes action moral, then not only because ethical life – as an unreflected being-at-home, as an obvious fact about behaviour and action – is not genuinely moral, but also because no rational principle and no rational rule, no conviction and no decision can create the unity of moral action.[90]

Irony is when we nevertheless act – again and again – to the best of our knowledge and with the best of intentions. To recognize that fallibility is a constitutive element of action, not least moral action, due to the finitude of all the knowledge upon which we base our actions, does not contradict the experience of freedom. On the contrary, it is only because the world is given to us in the restrictedness of our finite perspectives that we can discover and think something new, to change our views and act differently. This obviously corresponds to an understanding of freedom that does not confound freedom with the rule of an "eternal self." The ironic subject, with its repeated acts of self-determination, contradicts both an ethical reduction of freedom and one that is based on the notion of inwardness. It develops in lived interaction with the world, in which there is always the possibility of freely appropriating the practices in which it is always already involved – not least in those moments that tear the subject out of its familiar relations to itself and the world. These are moments in which there is no "well rounded" subjectivity and thus no "sovereign" self.

Carl Schmitt's critique of romanticism shifts the discussion of freedom in the last two chapters in a decidedly political direction. Not only for chronological reasons, and not only because this critique once again summarizes motifs of the tradition of such critiques, but also because it is tied to a critique of (liberal) democracy, I have placed the discussion of Schmitt at the end of part II. Schmitt's political critique of romanticism leads us to the connection between a critique of aestheticism formulated in the name of freedom on the one hand and a theory of democracy on the other. This issue will also stand at the center of the discussion in part III, though with explicit reference to the theory of democracy.

4

Sovereignty in Romanticism: Schmitt

Far too little theoretical attention has been paid to Carl Schmitt's critique of political romanticism. After all, this critique represents an important element of Schmitt's diagnosis of the liberal era, which he views as an age of "neutralizations." As such it also represents a crucial element of his critique of liberal democracy, which is a particularly significant part of the history of the discourse on aestheticization, given that Schmitt's work represents an especially striking continuation of Hegelian and Kierkegaardian motifs in the ethical and political thought of the twentieth century. The theory of freedom found in Schmitt's work is of even greater systematic importance, for he thereby demonstrates the close connection between subject-theoretical reflections on the freedom of aesthetic existence and the problem involved in the freedom of political self-government. This is particularly true when it comes to the ambivalence of Schmitt's critique of romanticism, which is made apparent by the fact that he locates this critique within the more general framework of a critique of the liberal "neutralization of the political." Here we find a combination of two different critiques – both of the aesthetic-romantic and of the rationalist neutralization of the political. We will see, however, that Schmitt's argument against the rationalist neutralization of the political draws on the romantic insistence on the inscrutability of the subject. Contrary to Schmitt's own theoretical intentions, this argument allows us to inject an entirely different, dynamic meaning into Schmitt's central concept of sovereignty. Especially with regard to his notion of popular sovereignty, Schmitt links sovereign decisions to the idea of a homogeneous unity, which is irreconcilable with the idea that subjects are inscrutable. At the same time, however, Schmitt at least implicitly presupposes this inscrutability in his rejection of liberal rationalism. Owing to political reasons and to his own adoption of the premises of Hegel's and Kierkegaard's critique of romanticism, Schmitt was incapable of drawing the proper conclusion from this contradiction. If we, on the other hand, reject these premises and thus the critique of the romantic spirit of liberal democracy, we gain a new (liberal) democratic perspective on the concept of political sovereignty Schmitt sets in opposition to romanticism. This will also allow us to uncover the systematic deficits of Schmitt's aggressive anti-liberalist perspective.

1. Aestheticization and Neutralization

In his preface to the second edition of *Political Romanticism*, Schmitt names the difficulty to which he will attempt to give "an objective answer": the difficulty of categorizing romanticism politically.[1] Contrary to a still influential approach, Schmitt argues that romanticism is not "eo ipso a counterrevolutionary movement," nor is it a kind of "political Catholicism."[2] Instead he claims that romanticism is characterized by a peculiar ambiguity: "It is just as romantic to glorify the state because it has a beautiful queen as it is to idolize a revolutionary hero as a 'colossus'" (PR 10). If every thinkable political position can be termed romantic, then the indeterminacy of the concept seems to betray something about the essence of romanticism. Schmitt concludes that in order to get a sense of the "indefinability" (PR 8) of political romanticism, we must go beyond the study of those political positions that define themselves as romantic.

Schmitt first takes a sociological approach to the problem. If we are to understand the political meaning of the diffuse image of romanticism, then we must address "the social character of the persons who were the bearers of the movement" (PR 10). The latter, as Schmitt cites the French historian Hippolyte Taine, consisted in "the new bourgeoisie. Its epoch begins in the eighteenth century... The new romantic art develops along with democracy and the new taste of the new bourgeois public" (PR 12). For Schmitt, this suffices to explain part of the romantic movement's invincibility. He argues that like romantic art itself, the "liberal, bourgeois democracy" which produces such art must be understood as an "intrinsically and radically self-contradictory" "phenomenon" (PR 13). Perched precariously between the "traditional monarchy and the socialist proletariat," the liberal bourgeoisie has not yet found its own determinate form, and thus has no substantial social form. Instead, liberal, bourgeois democracy has merely led to "the dissolution of the old society and the development of contemporary mass democracy" (PR 13). Over the course of this development, the rule of the bourgeoisie has also been "eliminated," yet without having removed the indeterminacy of liberal democracy that has always characterized its existence. "Today," as Schmitt writes in 1925, "the dissolution of traditional culture and form has continued in a radical fashion, but the new society still has not found its own form" (ibid.).

It is interesting that Schmitt refers to the process in which all traditional forms have been dissolved, but without the establishment of any new forms, as a process of "aestheticization." The "expansion of the aesthetic" (PR 15) introduced by romanticism in the eighteenth century and continuing to dominate the twentieth century within the liberal democratic framework proceeds proportionately to the disappearance of its substantive form. Although Schmitt does not deny the "distinctive aesthetic appeal" of romanticism's "productivity," he views romanticism "as a whole" as "the expression of a time that – in art as in other intellectual spheres – has not brought forth a grand style, a time that, in the pregnant sense, is no longer capable of representation" (PR 14f.). Therefore, everything becomes aesthetic, but nothing is representative in the strict sense of the term.[3] Art has become absolute to the degree that it is freed of any representative function and dedicated only to itself. Every "grand and strict form of manifestation...is rejected, and precisely on account of art." "In this way, it becomes possible for art to sympathetically appropriate all forms in a tumultuous disorder, and yet to treat them only as an insignificant model" (PR 15). Because art is no longer subject to any superior authority (neither god nor the state), it can only be a parasite on previously representative forms. At the same time it thereby points to a new source of justification: private taste.[4] Romanticism puts an end to the unquestionably binding character of all that was previously valid, instead leaving it up to the individual to judge art's aesthetic impact. For Schmitt, this development is politically relevant because the undermining of previously representative forms is no merely formal matter. Instead, the thing itself is undermined along with its form, which means in turn that our consciousness, dominated by the romantic movement, is no longer capable of perceiving anything of substance. He thus comes to the following diagnosis of the romantic *zeitgeist*: "To a great extent, all ecclesiastical and state institutions and forms, all legal concepts and arguments, everything that is official, and even democracy itself since the time it assumed a constitution form are perceived as empty and deceptive disguises, as a veil, a façade, a fake, or a decoration" (PR 14). Although this perception is occasionally accompanied by a longing for the essential truth behind the veil, even this cannot produce anything of substance. Instead we must understand even this longing in terms of its aesthetic nature, as the entirely unpractical longing of a "beautiful soul."

Due to its aestheticizing effects, Schmitt views romanticism as marking an important stage in the so-called successive "stages of neutralizations." This is a succession we could regard – in a first general determination – as a procession of spiritual and moral loss. "In reality," as Schmitt writes in "The Age of Neutralizations and Depoliticizations,"

> the romanticism of the nineteenth century signifies (if we want to utilize the moderately didactic word romanticism in a way different from the phenomenon itself, i.e., as a vehicle of confusion) only the intermediary stage of the aesthetic between the moralism of the eighteenth century and the economism of the nineteenth century, only a transition which precipitated the aestheticization of all intellectual domains. It did so very easily and successfully. The way from the metaphysical and moral domains is through the aesthetic domain, which is the surest and most comfortable way to the general economization of intellectual life and to a state of mind which finds the core categories of human existence in production and consumption.[5]

For Schmitt, however, these "stages of neutralization" do not merely represent a successive loss of spiritual and moral substance in favor of the economic. They also represent an increasing decay of the state and the political, starting with the absolutist state of the seventeenth and eighteenth centuries and proceeding to the liberal state of the nineteenth century up until the totalitarian state of the twentieth century. While in totalitarianism state and society collapse completely, Schmitt argues that the liberal state loses its contours to the extent that "what it has to guarantee is taken to be a rational matter of course."[6] In the first instance the neutralization of the political does not mean that the political is replaced by the economic, but that political power is concealed by an overly neutralizing ideology of the law. Political power thereby subjects itself to an overly rationalist notion of law, according to which the law does not only proceed neutrally from the nature of things, for it is something that merely needs to be found through a procedure based on rational consensus. Furthermore, the application of the law to individual cases is supposed to follow neutrally and unproblematically from the nature of things. By contrast, when it comes to both the creation and the application of the law, Schmitt aims to prove that both dimensions imply an irreducibly performative aspect: a decision. It has already been pointed out that we should not so hastily equate Schmitt's recognition of the performative aspect of decision as an intricate part of democratic discourse with his own anti-liberalist stance.[7] The same is true for his warning about the conquest of the political by the economic.[8] Whether we can incorporate this insight and this warning into the framework of a theory of (liberal) democracy, however, depends on whether we can present a convincing rejection of Schmitt's claim that the liberal age as a whole represents an age of neutralizations.

To do so, we must take a closer look at his critique of aestheticization and romanticism, which are supposed to lead to both the economic and the legal neutralization of the political. Schmitt views the romantic movement as the intellectual avant-garde of liberal democracy and as the epitome of an existentially unserious *zeitgeist*, one that has no "perception of an either-or" (PR 65).[9] Based on what has been said in the previous chapters, however, we could argue that, contrary to what Schmitt suggests, the romantically influenced *zeitgeist* characteristic of liberal democracies in no way stands in abstract opposition to the drama of existential decision. But if the diagnosis of neutralization cannot be applied to the liberal age as a whole, there is the basic possibility of criticizing specific forms of neutralization within its own framework. This would allow us not only to reject Schmitt's anti-liberalism, but also to give a genuinely political – non-neutral – meaning to the indeterminacy of (liberal) democracy.

Due to this possibility, which results from an alternative interpretation of the romantic spirit, my first step will be to discuss Schmitt's critique of romanticism in more detail (secs 2–4). Similar to my discussion of Hegel and Kierkegaard, I will begin with Schmitt's theory of the subject and freedom.

2. A Look at an Orange

According to Schmitt, "the definition of the romantic" must "proceed from the romantic subject" and its "relationship to the world" (PR 3). Schmitt formulates this relationship as follows: "Romanticism is subjectified occasionalism. In other words, in the romantic, the romantic subject treats the world as an occasion and an opportunity for his romantic productivity" (PR 17). Schmitt explains further that

> romanticism is subjectified occasionalism because an occasional relationship to the world is essential to it. Instead of God, however, the romantic subject occupies the central position and makes the world and everything that occurs in it into a mere occasion... A world that is ever new arises from ever new opportunities. But it is always a world that is only occasional, a world without substance and functional cohesion, without a fixed direction, without consistency and definition, without decision, without a final court of appeal, continuing into infinity and led only by the magic hand of chance. (PR 19)

Schmitt follows Hegel and Kierkegaard in claiming that romantic consciousness excludes any genuine and serious form of commitment, instead favoring a merely experimental relation to the world in which all orientations are entirely superficial. They are only effective as long as the next influence has not yet come about.[10] Every understanding of the self and the world is built on the sand of fleeting impressions, and is therefore too unstable and too indifferent to become a lived reality, identity, and position. Similar to Hegel and Kierkegaard, Schmitt's account of romanticism is dominated by his polemic against a "poetic" understanding of freedom that alienates subjects from the normatively structured practices of the life-world. Instead their life is guided – in an ultimately regressive manner – by nothing but their own coincidental moods.

Schmitt thus defines alienation from social practices, the fundamental distance between the subject and the relations of meaning established in the world, as the condition of romantic occasionalism. In order for coincidence to play the leading role it plays in the life of romantics, a consciousness is required which abstracts from the relations of meaning within a life-form and "punctuates" reality (PR 74). For this consciousness every moment in time and every detail in space is a potential beginning, a "point in a structure," within which a poetic world can be built on moods and imagination (ibid.). This renders the actual reality of the given occasion irrelevant, for romantic consciousness is only interested in itself, its own moods and poetic productivity, not in the reality of the given object toward which it directs itself. These objects are not of interest in and of themselves, nor due to their practical significance, but rather only as an incidental occasion. Having been robbed of their reality in this fashion and degraded to an occasion "without substance, essence, and function" (PR 84), they are entirely interchangeable. On the basis of a merely occasional stance toward the world, Schmitt concludes that any qualitative difference between these occasions is ultimately insignificant: "What the king and the queen are in reality is intentionally ignored. Their function consists instead in being a point of departure for romantic feelings. The same holds true for the beloved. From the standpoint of romanticism, therefore, it is simply not possible to distinguish between the king, the state, or the beloved. In the twilight of the emotions, they blend into one another" (PR 126).

According to Schmitt, however, occasionalism not only engenders a "deflation of the reality of the world" (PR 74) by taking elements of reality as merely incidental and arbitrary occasions for "impressionistic experience" (PR 100); rather, it also intensifies and processes this experience with imagination. The object brought about by the romantic mood and the imagination that alters it stand, in Schmitt's view, in no causal relation to its effect. Although we can describe the concept of *occasio* with terms such as "occasion, opportunity, and perhaps also chance," it derives its "real significance" from its opposition to the concept of *causa*, "the force of a calculable causality" or a normative context (PR 16f.). Although the concrete occasion is taken up by romantic consciousness, thereby negating the external world (cf. PR 98), the effect this occasion has on the romantic subject is absolutely incalculable and evades any causal description. An "absolutely inadequate relationship obtains between *occasio and effect*. Since any concrete item can be the *occasio* of an incalculable effect – for Mozart, a look at an orange can be the occasion for composing the duet *Là ci darem la mano* – this relationship is completely incommensurable, devoid of all objectivity, and non-rational. It is the relation of the fanciful" (PR 83).

On the one hand, Schmitt asserts that there is a productive or active element in the reaction to *occasio*: He describes an event – an incalculable occurrence – that cannot be derived from *occasio* itself or from its accidental nature. Instead, it is grounded in the specific productivity or activity that follows from this occasion: "All the accidents of our life are materials of which we can make whatever we want" (PR 74), as Schmitt claims quoting Novalis. However, because Schmitt ascribes this process of "making" to a merely "poetic" interest in intensifying the experience of moods, he denies that this activity has any practical significance: "The reaction to a stimulus that stresses pleasure and aversion is not an activity. A person does not become an active personality in the moral sense by feeling pleasure and aversion, regardless of the intensity; nor does this happen when one's condition induces one to make impressive paraphrases" (PR 100). Romantic ironists merely clothe incidental moods with "philosophical and scientific raiments and words rich in associations" (PR 107). Romantic productivity thus appears to be a way of evading the sphere of praxis as such by cloaking itself in worldly substance: "He (the romantic) was never resolved to leave the world of his impressionistic experience and change anything that occurred in commonplace reality" (PR 100). This, after all, would imply decision, commitment, restriction and thus the abandonment of the very same abstract position of subjective infinity that Schmitt, following Hegel and Kierkegaard, views as the essence of romantic consciousness.[11] If one clings to this position in a world that is de facto concrete, then the inevitable result will be an (occasionalist) stance for which the world is merely a means "to avoid any definitive position" (PR 73). Inasmuch as romantic productivity means retreating from the world of practices, while remaining dependent upon impulses with respect to the moods upon which it is based, romantic productivity can at best be termed a kind of "rational resonance" (PR 107), "the affective echo of an activity that is necessarily not his own" (PR 94).

The only kind of productivity that the romantic subject can develop is "of an aesthetic sort" (PR 104). Its result is a world changed "not by means of an activity, but by mood and imagination" (PR 84). The true location of romantic productivity is therefore the world of art. Although Schmitt accords romantic productivity a certain justification in this sense (even though romantic productions stand in clear opposition to his ideal of representative art),[12] he regards the effect of this productivity as being all the more problematic in non-aesthetic spheres: In the theoretical sphere, romantic productivity produces nothing but "quasi-argumentation" (PR 101), whose "empty formulas can be adapted to any state of affairs" (PR 103). In the world of practices, it corresponds to a kind of quasi-action for which opportunism and intrigue are paradigmatic. Schmitt writes that "the problem of occasionalism is not merely metaphysical; it is just as much an ethical problem. It concerns the ancient question of human free will: the question of the status and content of human activity" (PR 94). This problem of free will now leads us into the true core of Schmitt's critique of political romanticism.

3. Alien Power

According to Schmitt, the "essence" of romantic productivity is "passivity" (PR 115). The idea of romantic activity is a *contradictio in adjecto* (cf. PR 160) because "every political activity – regardless of whether its content is merely the technique of conquest, the claim or the expansion of political power, or whether it rests on a legal or a moral decision – conflicts with the essentially aesthetic nature of the romantic" (PR 158). But above all, romantics are passive and, as

Schmitt tellingly remarks, "effeminate" (PR 128), because their freedom from reality remains tied to their subjection to the accidental nature of *occasiones* in reality. As we already saw in Kierkegaard's Hegelian analysis, the romantic-ironic seducer is anything but sovereign, a "king without a country" (EO II 252), whose falsely understood freedom ultimately exposes him to the accidental influence of others and otherness. Schmitt also seeks to show that upon closer – especially political – inspection, romantics, for whom everything is merely an intellectual means for "strengthening the sovereignty of the ego" (PR 65), prove to not be sovereign at all, but rather weak and dependent. Not only is their productivity, due to its aesthetic character, completely irreconcilable with any moral, legal, or political standard (cf. PR 127), romantics are also incapable of moral judgment due to their poetic and occasionalist convictions (PR 117). They lack "the ability to make a decision between right and wrong" and thus also "the principle of every political energy" (PR 116). Schmitt's final verdict is that "where political activity begins, political romanticism ends" (PR 160). "Everything that is romantic is at the disposal of other energies that are unromantic, and the sublime elevation above definition and decision is transformed into a subservient attendance upon alien power and alien decision" (PR 162).

It is quite logical that Schmitt sees the most direct political expression of this problem to lie in "a thoroughly devious opportunism" (PR 127). But this is not a kind of opportunism that is merely out for its own advantage, but an opportunism that consists in a weakened ability to make decisions, an opportunism that even lets itself be told how to interpret its own advantage. Schmitt's damning verdict on romantics: "Lacking all social and intellectual stability, they succumbed to every powerful complex in their vicinity that made a claim to be taken as true reality. Thus lacking all moral scruples and any sense of responsibility other than that of a zealous and servile functionary, they could allow themselves to be used by any political system..." (PR 106). Schmitt also interprets the romantics' penchant for intrigue in this manner. Although he claims that romantics' self-consciousness is not least based on the conviction that they are in control and can make others the tools of their will (cf. PR 79), they remain dependent on the incidents they rely upon for their fanciful intrigues. Although the romantic schemer believes that he is playing with the world, in reality coincidence is playing with him (cf. ibid.). This interpretation describes romantic activity as a manner of adapting to given situations, which implies at least a fleeting will, as well as some kind of strategic decision making. But Schmitt combines this interpretation with a further interpretation, according to which we cannot assume that romantics have a will at all. According to Schmitt, romantics' scheming is not due to the fact that they seek to satisfy a certain interest in a given situation, but to the fact that they do not seek to satisfy any interests at all in reality. Romantics' scheming merely "plays one reality off against another in order to paralyze the reality that is actually present and limited" (PR 72). Instead of creating a new reality, they are merely interested in making the present reality contingent. That which takes place "in another place and another time" (PR 92), in the name of which romantics distance themselves from reality, is for Schmitt entirely interchangeable; its function consists solely in the "negation of the present" (PR 71). The "impression of inner untruthfulness" that such a subject makes therefore has less to do with the presumption of strategic cunning than with the fact that a person, "in the organic passivity that belongs to his occasionalist structure, wants to be productive without becoming active" (PR 159).

Consequently the "game of intrigue that is played with realities" (PR 92) is politically problematic not for certain definable political reasons, but for politics as such. According to Schmitt, romantic intrigue is never political intrigue, rather an aesthetic intrigue against the political. It replaces political activity with pseudo-activity, just as it does not replace previously valid principles and forms with any new ones, instead only suspending what exists. All decision, all acting confrontation with the world is evaded, neutralized. Whereas romantic opportunism amounts to a pure affirmation of the prevailing reality, romantic intrigue is, according to Schmitt's interpretation, only capable of subverting what exists. It puts nothing new in its place and is indifferent about whether what exists really deserves to be undermined or relativized. Therefore, the romantic's productivity never leads to another reality, merely to a "deflation" of the reality of the world, all the while remaining dependent on the world, or more specifically: on the demands of an "activity that is necessarily not his own."

4. The Other in the Own and Decision

In the previous two chapters, I have offered an alternative interpretation of romantic irony to the critique of romanticism. This interpretation focuses on motifs of freedom that Hegel and Kierkegaard associate with romanticism, but which cannot be captured by their reservations about romanticism's subjectivism. Because Schmitt merely repeats and condenses those features of the critical image of romanticism that he criticizes as cases of subjectivism, we need to give an abbreviated and condensed reminder of a few elements of my previous argumentation. Similar to my discussions of Hegel and Kierkegaard in the last two chapters, I am less interested in defending historical romantics, especially since Schmitt's main opponent is not Friedrich Schlegel but Adam Müller. Instead, I argue that Schmitt's polemic against romanticism prevents a more productive interpretation of a colorful and thus aesthetically dazzling life. The freedom to revise our orientations cannot be equated with the loss of orientation in general; it cannot be characterized as a kind of nihilistic indifference toward what we maintain in a given situation; rather, it represents an acute sense of fallibility. Schmitt's blindness toward this alternative interpretation is also relevant here given the fact his critique of romanticism is also directed against the cultural self-understanding of liberal democracies. As we have seen, Schmitt views the romantic spirit of liberal democracies as the epitome of an age of neutralization of all decision. Contrary to Schmitt, we should no longer view the romantically inspired concept of freedom inscribed in the self-understanding of liberal democracies as the practical consequence of a wrongheaded philosophy of the subject, but – as I have proposed in the previous chapters – as grounding, in an anti-subjectivist manner, the possibility of self-determination in the experience of a difference within the subject itself. If we do so, we will get an entirely different picture.

For we will then no longer be dealing with a subject whose detached and selective view of reality allows it to gain control of the events he regards as meaningful, but with a subject that is always already involved in contexts of practices and, due to its basic mimetic openness to the world, can be affected by impulses that are new and unfamiliar. Such impulses can give rise to desires that stand at odds with the subject's previous self-understanding. This does not happen constantly and, as we have seen, it does not always cause us to alter our previous orientations. Contrary to Schmitt's critique of the subjective occasionalism of romantic consciousness, we must first emphasize that the subject cannot control which impulses can play such a defining role for it. Just as little can it control the effects of these impulses on its own person. In this sense as well, "everything [can] really become the occasion for everything else," such that "everything that will happen and all sequential order become incalculable in a fantastic manner" (PR 18f.).

But the fact that the subject is open to "alien powers" in no way means that the subject subjects itself to a decision "that is necessarily not its own." Instead, the subject's ability to detach from its previous self-understanding due to its mimetic openness to others and otherness is a necessary condition for a complete concept of self-determination. Only if I can get distance from myself with the aid of external influences can I pose the "question of truth" and thereby question the validity of the principles that have determined my actions. This can allow me to make a new decision about myself, i.e. about the principles that are constitutive for my self-understanding. Only then can I perform a new act of self-determination. This act then no longer stands in an external relation to my openness to "alien powers," but is motivated by them. Self-determination, however, cannot merely be derived from the influence of "alien powers," for the latter do not directly cause this self-determination. Like the expressions of an inner nature – as I have defined the desires that arise in interaction with the world – that are not derivable from our previous social self-understanding and thus pull us out of our habitual self-understanding,[13] the act of self-determination motivated by these expressions has, in a certain sense, the character of an event. In other words, several points along the way of this process that I have termed (using Adorno's formulation) a "dialectic of freedom" have an event-like character.

If the subject, under the influence of a specific occasion or opportunity, experiences itself in a previously unfamiliar way, this will cause an event-like breach in its prior self-image. Inasmuch as the subject interprets this event, the (re-)discovering of its own self will also be accompanied by an event-like (new) decision about itself. Because of the experience of an inner divide, every act of self-determination is characterized by an interplay of constative and performative aspects. It always occurs in the name of a subject that does not yet or no longer exists prior to the decision. The process of subjectivization is thus strictly speaking not the act of a subject, i.e. of a unified subject in total control of its own perceptions and decisions. It is an event in which, in Derrida's terms, the subject grasps itself "in the moment of an exception from itself."[14] Finally, the act of self-determination is event-like in the sense that no decision on identity, as considered as it may be, can overcome the condition of finitude. In every decision on our identity, therefore, there is an element of haste which leaves that decision open for possible revisions.[15]

This interpretation of self-determination allows us to see a connection between *occasio* and *causa* that remains concealed in Schmitt's polemic against subjectivized occasionalism. Every act of self-determination, regardless of whether I change myself through a new experience or stick to my old principles, has implications for my actions. For example, if I recognize that I or "my situation" has changed, then a whole series of practical measures will follow by which I attempt to bring my actions into line with my changed understanding of myself and the world. By reaffirming my old principles I become more conscious of the practical consequences than prior to my experience of self-difference. However, this also means that the act of self-determination, or rather the interpretation of the situation it implies, posits a *causa*, a normative context which can be derived neither directly from *occasio* nor from the effects that they give rise to in the subject. On the one hand, this normative context remains dependent upon *occasio*, for there could be no (new) decision about myself, no normative (re-)alignment of my actions, without an external occasion that pulls me out of my previous self-understanding. On the other hand, this *causa* does not immediately follow from *occasio* and its incalculable effects, but only from my decision. Furthermore, this act changes *occasio* itself, transforming it from a contingent influence in the world to which I respond without any further consequences into the origin of a new or reaffirmed self-understanding. We could also say that in order to constitute *occasio* in this strong sense, in which it grounds a normative context, the *occasio* must be seized upon. However, here we are dealing with an "originarily affected"[16] decision that is not entirely manly, one in which we determine that we will let ourselves be determined by certain motives, such that the "guiding directives of our life prove to be something that happens to and with our will."[17]

Given this reformulation of the romantic and democratic relation to self and world, *occasio* does not stand in abstract opposition to *causa*, nor does being affected by an "alien power" contradict the power of decision and the normativity it entails. We must recognize, contrary to Schmitt, that *occasio* constantly provokes and re-provokes *causa*. It is only because the subject can never be entirely identical to itself, only because it remains fundamentally open to the world and its diverse impulses that it can detach from the normative practices in which it is involved and thus also from its respective social identity. This distance from ourselves, however, is not something that can be reified into a position (in this sense as well, the idea of poetic detachment from practices remains imaginary). Rather, this self-detachment is experienced as a crisis in our self-relation which challenges us to redefine our own existential situation and confirm or revise our previous normative orientations. Therefore, romantic democratic consciousness is not entirely irreconcilable with "everything that gives consistency and order to life and to what takes place" (PR 17);

rather, it stands in a dynamic relation to consequence and order. This dynamic, according to my claim, represents the sole possibility for lived freedom.

If, therefore, we can grasp the (liberal) democratic understanding of freedom in a way that does not neutralize the "perception of an either-or" (PR 65), then the corresponding self-understanding can no longer be presented as an ideological breeding ground for the neutralization of the political. On the contrary, as I will demonstrate in the following sections, this perspective points to arguments that can be used against the dictatorial anti-liberalism that Schmitt hoped would put an end to the "age of neutralizations."[18]

Several steps are necessary to prove this claim. First I will point out the similarity between the understanding of freedom I have just described and Schmitt's political anthropology (sec. 5). Contrary to Schmitt's own theoretical intention, this opens up a perspective on a (liberal) democratic concept of sovereignty, a perspective Schmitt was incapable of recognizing because of his refusal, for systematic and political reasons, to recognize this similarity. But before we can give more contour to this alternative concept of sovereignty, we must take a closer look at the different facets of his critique of liberalism. I will focus on the relation between his critique of aestheticization and his critique of rationalism, both contained in the thesis of neutralization. This is because, as we have seen, Schmitt's critique of the economic neutralization of the political is merely presented as an implication of his critique of aestheticization. The subjectivism of the romantics whom Schmitt criticizes in the tradition of Hegel and Kierkegaard leads to the "economization of intellectual life," focusing solely on private (consumerist) pleasure. Yet if the romantic spirit of liberal democracies cannot be reduced to subjectivism, then the claim that the "economization of intellectual life" must be seen as a symptom of this spirit is problematic.[19] This undermines the diagnosis upon which Schmitt's claim is based, i.e. the aesthetic-romantic neutralization of all decisions, including political decisions. Now, Schmitt develops his own concept of the political, as well as the concept of sovereignty so crucial to the concept of the political, largely against the background of his critique of the rationalist neutralization of the political. Therefore, a defense of liberal democratic politics cannot content itself with defending the romantic spirit that corresponds to this form of politics. Instead, we must face up to the claim of a connection between this spirit and the other dimension of the neutralization of the political. The latter represents Schmitt's other accusation of liberal democracies: the neutralization of political power by means of an overly rationalist concept of law. We will see that the critique of this neutralization lies on an entirely different level than his critique of aestheticization (sec. 6). Nevertheless, Schmitt argues on two fronts against both diagnoses of neutralization – the aesthetic-romantic and the overly rationalist. It is this two-front argumentation that gives rise to the various versions of his anti-liberal theory of sovereignty – be it the concept of sovereignty found in *Political Theology* (sec. 7) or the concept of popular sovereignty (which is clearly compatible with fascism) developed in *Constitutional Theory* (sec. 9). If we can reformulate the concept of sovereignty within the framework of a theory of (liberal) democracy (sec. 10), then we must first discuss Schmitt's critique of an overly rationalist neutralization of the political (sec. 8).

The first step of my argumentation, however, does not address Schmitt's theory of sovereignty, but rather his ambivalent attempt to ground this theory in a political anthropology.

5. Political Anthropology

"Every political idea," as Schmitt writes in *Political Theology*,[20] "in one way or another takes a position on the 'nature' of man and presupposes that he is either 'by nature good' or 'by nature evil'" (PT 56). For Schmitt, the key players in this dispute are, on the one side, atheistic anarchism with its "axiom of the good man" (PT 57), and, on the other side, the Catholic counter-revolution with its dogma of original sin. The Catholic political philosopher Juan Donoso Cortés, whom Schmitt places at the center of his account, had – apparently provoked by his opponents – radicalized this dogma, turning it into a theory of the absolute sinfulness and depravity of human nature. The result is Donoso Cortés' anti-anarchist political program: "In the face of radical evil the only solution is dictatorship" (PT 66). According to Schmitt, the opposition between dictatorial Catholicism and atheistic anarchy, between Juan Donoso Cortés (and Joseph de Maistre) and Pierre-Joseph Proudhon (and Michail Bakunin), is nothing less than a "bloody decisive battle" (PT 59) between contrary views of good and evil. What appears good from the one perspective appears evil from the other perspective and vice versa:

> De Maistre said that every government is necessarily absolute, and an anarchist says the same; but with the aid of his axiom of the good man and corrupt government, the latter draws the opposite practical conclusion, namely, that all governments must be opposed for the reason that every government is a dictatorship. Every claim of a decision must

be evil for the anarchist, because the right emerges by itself if the immanence of life is not disturbed by such claims. (PT 66)

For Schmitt, when it comes to the "radical antithesis" (ibid.) between authority and anarchy, the political itself is at stake. And in precisely this regard, the conflicting parties are in his eyes anything but symmetrical. According to Schmitt, the anarchist axiom of the good man entails the dissolution of the political: The conception of a "paradisiacal worldliness of immediate natural life and unproblematic concreteness" paralyzes "all moral and political decisions" (PT 65). Anarchism is thus the extreme of an "onslaught against the political" (PT 65) characteristic of the "neutralistic" *zeitgeist* so fascinated by ideas of immanence. This diagnosis, according to which the political is on the retreat, moved Schmitt to show a measure of sympathy for Donoso Cortés' apocalyptic "insanity" (PT 58), which Schmitt regards as an expression of extreme decisiveness. For Schmitt, this is not a conflict between two equal political parties, but between the most extreme proponents of the political against the most extreme representatives of the anti-political struggle. According to this image, it is only because of anarchists' extremism that they can still be considered part of the logic of the political at all. After all, they must decisively decide against decisions (cf. PT 66).

The reason for Schmitt's interest in this struggle is not his own desire to present a decisive anthropological theory, but because it is only here, in the conflict over the true nature of man, that there seem to be any decisive positions at all. In *The Concept of the Political*, Schmitt writes that his relation to political anthropology is more descriptive, although his interest in the latter is not only due to empirical but also systematic motives: "All genuine political theories presuppose man to be evil, i.e., by no means an unproblematic but a dangerous and dynamic being."[21] This assumption is to political theory what the assumption that man can be educated is to pedagogy (cf. CP 63). According to Schmitt, political scientists are, for conceptual reasons, compelled to presuppose that man is evil. Oddly enough, however, Schmitt does not offer a theological justification for this assumption in relation to his own considerations on the concept of the political. Schmitt distinguishes himself from classical political theology, which maintains that man's essentially sinful nature is a decisive reason for dictatorship. He shifts the distinction between good and evil, which is crucial for political theology, to another distinction he claims is essential when it comes to thinking about the concept of the political: "The specific political distinction to which political actions and motives can be reduced is that between friend and enemy," Schmitt famously states in *The Concept of the Political* (CP 26). The distinction between friend and enemy is supposed to have a similar function as the distinction between good and evil. It is meant to indicate the most intense antagonism from which "human life derives its specifically political tension" (CP 35).

However, unlike the distinction between good and evil, which stands at the center of political theology, the distinction between friend and enemy is no longer grasped in a substantive manner: Conflicts can *intensify* and turn into a relation between friend and enemy (cf. CP 38f.), making the latter dynamic categories. The result is a necessary shift in the systematic role accorded to the definition of man as a "dangerous" and "dynamic" being – and thus also of the anthropology upon which it is based. For political philosophy, the role of the anthropological supposition of "evil" is only as a *potential* against "the security of the *status quo*" (CP 94),[22] an incalculable force that allows us to consider the *possibility* of enmity. Schmitt thereby steps back from the extreme alternative he presents in *Political Theology*. For whoever seeks the anthropological source of those differences that can develop into enmity obviously cannot do so by referring to the "axiom of the good man": If "the sphere of the political is in the final analysis determined by the real possibility of enmity, political conceptions and ideas cannot very well start with an anthropological optimism. This would dissolve the possibility of enmity and, thereby, every specific political consequence" (CP 64). However, this does not require a thoroughly pessimistic or even apocalyptic anthropology. Instead, we need an anthropology that regards man as dynamic, one that does not define man as sinful, but that assumes his indeterminacy. Schmitt finds such an anthropology in the work of Helmuth Plessner. If we translate Plessner's determination of man as an essentially indeterminate, inscrutable being into the "anthropological distinction of evil and good and combine Plessner's 'remaining open' with his positive reference to danger, Plessner's theory is closer to evil than to goodness" (CP 60).

Although the concept of "remaining open" tends neither in the one nor in the other direction, Plessner's anthropology, with its emphasis on potentiality, does name the source of social differences that can lead to conflicts with and in morality by making reference to the (non-)foundation of all social identity.[23] These conflicts in turn have the potential to intensify and develop into a relation between friend and enemy. But according to my argument, such an anthropology in no way contradicts romantic sensibility.[24] Such an anthropology cannot be made the object and criterion of the distinction between friend and enemy, as is the case in the dispute between Donoso Cortés and the anarchist. Nor does this present us with an alternative between anarchy and dictatorship. Neither does it presuppose that humans are good by nature and thus do not require government, nor does it assume that humans are morally decrepit in order to derive their "need of dominion"[25] and thus the necessity of dictatorship. Instead, this anthropology seems to have a certain affinity with the indecision of the liberals, though this is certainly not what Schmitt intended.[26] In *Political Theology*, Schmitt remarks that the liberals take no clear position in the "bloody final battle" between Catholicism and Anarchism over human nature. For Schmitt and his informants among the Catholic political philosophers, the liberals are thus "sentenced" (PT 59): "To suspend the decision at the crucial point by denying that there was at all something to be decided upon must have appeared to them [de Maistre and Donoso Cortés] to be a strange pantheistic confusion" (PT 61f.). In *Political Theology*, Schmitt does not discuss the possibility that the refusal to take the one or the other side could be internally connected to a fundamentally different anthropology that evades the naïve distinction between "good" and "evil." Clearly he does not make this claim out of political resentment against the liberals.

Instead, Schmitt goes on to argue that because liberalism refuses to take a position on human nature, it has an entirely contradictory relationship to sovereignty. Liberalism, which for Schmitt represents the epitome of a depoliticized and thus perverted democracy, recognizes sovereignty, including the fact that it cannot be reduced to the declaration of objective circumstances. Yet at the same time, it insists that sovereignty remains dependent upon the consent of the people or its representatives (cf. PT 59f.). As we will see later (sec. 10), this is an accurate formal determination of the (liberal) democratic concept of sovereignty that can and must be defended against the concept of sovereignty in Schmitt's early decisionist phase in *Political Theology* (sec. 7), but especially against Schmitt's later concept of popular sovereignty in *Constitutional Theory* (sec. 9). At this point, however, it is already clear that the "contradictory nature" of liberalism in matters of sovereignty cannot be equated with the theories that Schmitt accuses of neutralizing the political and that seek to eliminate the concept of sovereignty from political theory in general. The latter, however, are the true counterpart to *Political Theology*.

6. Schmitt and Kierkegaard

In *Political Theology*, Schmitt's primary intention is to criticize various attempts to rob sovereignty of the positing aspect [*das setzende Moment*], thus reducing sovereignty to the mere declaration and recognition of objective circumstances. To do so is to abolish sovereignty as such. For instance, Schmitt explains, Rousseau's notion of popular sovereignty and its theory of the identity of the government with the governed conceals the "decisionistic and personalistic element in the concept of sovereignty" (PT 48), for it presupposes an organic unity that does not arise by means of a sovereign decision in the struggle between competing interests. This presupposition is fulfilled by nationalist ideologies and their conception of an organic state whole (cf. PT 49). We will go into Schmitt's critique of this conception of a pre-political community in more detail in sec. 9. For at a significant point in his own theory of popular sovereignty Schmitt takes back this critique. What interests us here, however, is Schmitt's accusation that liberal democracy – clearly at odds with his determination of liberalism as a contradictory theory of sovereignty – eliminates the concept of sovereignty by means of a rationalist neutralization of the political. This accusation is primarily aimed at Hans Kelsen, who attempts to "suppress" (PT 21) the concept of sovereignty by assuming an identity between the state and the legal order. According to Schmitt, this identity can only be construed if "all sociological elements have been left out of the juristic concept" in order to "obtain in unadulterated purity a system of ascriptions to norms and a last uniform basic norm" (PT 18). In the name of objectivity and out of "fear of arbitrariness," "every exception" is "banished" "from the realm of the human mind" (PT 41).

Even before we go into Schmitt's theory of neutralizations in more detail (sec. 8), we can already see that it does not lie on the same level as the theory of neutralization with regard to the critique of aestheticization he develops in *Political Romanticism*. The former is directed against an overly subjectivist misunderstanding of freedom as merely subjective caprice, such that freedom only consists in what the subject can draw from the contingent stirrings of its variable and heteronymous moods. Schmitt's legal-philosophical critique of neutralization begins at an entirely different point. Here he is not dealing with the caprice of the romantic subject, which misunderstands its empirical freedom as abstract freedom, rather with the "fear of arbitrariness" which underlies the rationalist conception of the law. This distinction becomes most apparent when Schmitt makes Kierkegaard an important point of reference in his critique of the rationalism of the liberal system of law. Whereas Schmitt's critique of romanticism refers both to Hegel and Kierkegaard, his critique of rationalism only makes reference to those strands of Kierkegaard's argumentation that are critical of Hegel.[27] In a decisive passage on the "definition of sovereignty," Schmitt, the Catholic, refers to the

"Protestant theologian" who "demonstrated the vital intensity possible in theological reflection in the nineteenth century" (PT 15). The section ends with a bow to Kierkegaard's philosophy of the exception and a collage of quotes from *Repetition*.[28] "Precisely a philosophy of concrete life," as Schmitt formulates the matter while drawing heavily on Kierkegaard's rhetoric:

> must not withdraw from the exception and the extreme case, but must be interested in it to the highest degree. The exception can be more important to it than the rule, not because of a romantic irony for the paradox, but because of the seriousness of an insight goes deeper than the clear generalizations inferred from what ordinarily repeats itself. The exception is more interesting than the rule. The rule proves nothing; the exception proves everything: It confirms not only the rule but also its existence, which derives only from the exception. In the exception the power of real life breaks through the crust of a mechanism that has become torpid by repetition. (PT 15)

The thrust of this legal-political argumentation recalls Kierkegaard's critique of the first (Wilhemian) form of ethics. Against the background of the theory of stages reconstructed in the previous chapter, the distinction between the two different elements of Schmitt's theory of neutralizations becomes clear, i.e. the critique of aestheticization and of rationalism. His objections are not aimed at one and the same ideological complex. Schmitt not only shares Kierkegaard's "nausea" at a "world without seriousness,"[29] which derives from the premises of the critique of romanticism, but also his doubts about any unproblematically presupposed normality. Like Kierkegaard, therefore, Schmitt argues on two fronts: first, against a *zeitgeist* alienated from normative practices in general, and second, against the neglect of the role of the exception in theory. Like Kierkegaard, Schmitt also sees himself forced to take a third path, yet going back to a revision of his critique of aestheticization would have required a fundamental revision of his "neutralistic" image of liberal democratic culture – and thus an alternative interpretation of the "contradictory" stance of liberalism toward sovereignty. For political and systematic reasons, Schmitt chooses a different path, nevertheless developing two varieties of the corresponding alternative. He terms the first "political theology," and the second "democracy," which he understands in a (fascist) dictatorial sense. For Schmitt, dictatorship is not the opposite of democracy, but an authentic case of democracy opposed to the contradictory liberal form of democracy.[30] Before we can defend liberal democracy and its "contradictory" relationship to sovereignty against Schmitt's fascist understanding of democracy, we must first take a brief look at the first path (political theology) Schmitt formulates. That his recourse to theology is ultimately not the decisive point can already be seen in *Political Theology*. For Schmitt, unlike for Kierkegaard, this recourse is anything but religiously motivated. He is not interested in a leap of faith, but in the leap of politics in the unfounded act of absolute sovereignty.

7. Political Theology

"All significant concepts of the modern theory of the state are secularized theological concepts," as Schmitt writes in *Political Theology*. This is true "not only because of their historical development – in which they were transferred from theology to the theory of the state, whereby, for example, the omnipotent God became the omnipotent lawgiver – but also because of their systematic structure, the recognition of which is necessary for a sociological consideration of these concepts. The exception in jurisprudence is analogous to the miracle in theology" (PT 36). The position of rationalism, however, is that the state of exception – be it a violation of the laws of nature or an immediate intervention by the sovereign in the prevailing legal order – can be allowed to exist just as little as miracles. Hans Blumenberg was right to point out that it is "remarkable, methodologically" that Schmitt's argumentation against the rationalist neutralization of the political places so much "value" in this "secularization nexus."[31] According to Blumenberg, it would have seemed more "natural" for Schmitt "to establish the reverse relation of derivation by interpreting the apparent theological derivation of political concepts as a consequence of the absolute quality of political realities."[32] This is especially curious given that Schmitt is interested in the "application" of the analogy of the exception and the miracle by contemporary Catholic political scientists of the counter-revolution, upon which "the personal sovereignty of the monarch" was "ideologically" based (PT 37). Blumenberg comments that "analogies, after all, are precisely not transformations. If every metaphysical borrowing from the dynastic language treasures of theology represented a case of 'secularization' in the sense of transformation, then we would immediately stand before a plethora of products of secularization that would have to be entitled 'Romanticism'."[33]

In fact, the meaning of the corresponding analogies for Schmitt does not derive from the scientific proof of the continued secular existence of theological concepts. Instead it emerges in relation to the political exception. Here Blumenberg writes: "When Carl Schmitt characterizes de Maistre's political philosophy as a 'reduction of the state to the moment of the decision, to a pure decision not based on reason and discussion and not justifying itself, that is, to an absolute decision created out of nothingness' (PT 66), then this is not the secularization of the *creatio ex nihilo* [creation from nothing]; rather it is a metaphorical interpretation of the situation after the revolutionary zero point."[34] Political theology is in truth "theology as politics,"[35] whose analogy between divine power and political sovereignty is supposed to solve the problem that the sovereign, "at the same time that he provides the capacity for decision...must also provide legitimacy for the decision."[36] As Schmitt points out, de Maistre makes metaphorical recourse to the theological vocabulary in order to establish the impression of the "infallibility" of political decisions (cf. PT 55). With regard to such operations, however, Schmitt's theory of secularization has the ideological function of concealing the "cynicism of an open 'theological politics',"[37] by claiming to merely find what it would have had to invent for political reasons: the quasi-divinity of an absolute sovereign that is not compelled to justify its actions and acts, just "as if it were infallible" (cf. PT 55).

As a de facto metaphorical political theology, Carl Schmitt's political theology is not immune to the same objection he raises against the romantics, for Schmitt also resorts to "surrogates" from other times (PR 14) (i.e., a pre-enlightenment vocabulary) in order to give an appearance of substance to the political sovereignty of modernity by secularizing that vocabulary. However, this theological model of an absolute, non-justifying, indivisible and infallible sovereignty could not be further removed from the romantic self-understanding of liberal democratic societies. If we are to defend liberal democracies not only against an anti-liberal political theology, but also against an anti-democratic understanding of democracy (with which Schmitt will soon replace political theology in order to formulate his alternative to the liberal understanding of democracy), then we must gain a more exact understanding of his objection to the rationalist neutralization of the political. In other words, we must pick up on the objective reason for Schmitt's insistence on sovereignty in order to criticize the conclusions that he draws from his critique of the rationalist neutralization of the political. As Christoph Menke summarizes the matter, this reason consists "in the critique of a political order that regards itself as neutral in the sense that it is immune from the confrontation with and the establishment against its other."[38] As Schmitt states in line with Kierkegaard, this other is "concrete life" (PT 15).

8. "Concrete Life" and Decision

The rationalist view of the constitutional rule of law neutralizes the element of sovereign decision by claiming that the normative validity of the law is neither created, but found already in existence. Nor is the law applied, rather it is only tautologically asserted as a valid norm.[39] This corresponds to the notion of a normatively enclosed legal system in which, according to the self-understanding of this system, exceptions can no longer arise. And if exceptions are no longer conceivable, then there is no longer any sovereignty to decide upon these exceptions. For Schmitt, however, this assumption amounts to an ideology. Not only is every system of law based upon a political decision, but concrete life also always entails the possibility of bringing about exceptions that are to be decided upon in the course of the realization of the system of law. The law therefore remains dependent upon sovereign decision – with regard to both its origins and its realization. In an extreme case, or, as Schmitt states, a "serious case" of the exception, this dependency calls upon the authority of the political sovereign. This is what Schmitt refers to when he writes in the first, programmatic sentence of *Political Theology*: "Sovereign is he who decides on the exception" (PT 5). Here we are obviously dealing with the sovereignty of the executive. In this connection, however, we get another hint of Schmitt's political intention of justifying the existence of a "supreme authority" that is "capable of suspending the law": the figure of the dictator.[40] Nevertheless, Schmitt directs his argument against "the normative fiction of a closed system of legality" (LL 6) "not by means of an analysis of political decisions, but of *juridical* decisions."[41] Indeed, Schmitt counters the rationalist understanding of the liberal constitutional state with a theory of law that emphasizes the element of sovereign decision in the creation – the formulation and passing – of laws and, more importantly, in their application in legal practice.

Schmitt begins by referring to the customary case of a judicial decision in which the application of the law does not remove or suspend the rule. Even in everyday cases, the universality of the law shatters in the face of the concretion of life, i.e. the individual case. The legal interest in a decision "is rooted in the character of the normative and is derived from the necessity of judging a concrete fact concretely even though what is given as a standard for the judgment is only a legal principle in its general universality. Thus a transformation takes place every time" (PT 31). "Every legal thought brings a legal idea, which in its purity can never become reality, into another aggregate condition and adds an element." No "juristic deduction" is "traceable in the last detail to its premises," which is why "the circumstance that requires a decision remains an independently determining moment" (PT 30). The legal norm cannot itself determine how it is applied to any individual case, nor its own significance in individual cases. Even the application of the law remains dependent upon the act of deciding. The result is that judicial decisions, as Derrida has shown, always display a certain element of drama. Because no decision can be derived entirely from a legal norm, and because a "fresh judgment" must be made in each concrete case, as Derrida states quoting Stanley Fish, in the moment of decision there is no guarantee that the decision will be just and legitimate.[42] This can only be determined after the fact. The fact that a decision cannot be derived from a legal norm, but must instead rely on interpretations (both of the norm itself and of the case in the light of which the norm is interpreted), means that every decision qua decision, regardless of how it is made, cuts off the process of interpretation. "The decision," Schmitt writes, "becomes instantly independent of argumentative substantiation and receives an autonomous value" (PT 31).

For Schmitt's concept of sovereignty, however, it is crucial that every juridical decision not only implies an interpretation of the norm, but also of the situation to which it is to be applied. A decision must be made not about *how* a norm should be applied to a given situation, but also about *whether* it should be applied at all. An exception does not arise in the case that one norm instead of another, or one law instead of the other must be applied, but in cases in which *the law as such* does not apply.[43] In the latter case, the decision not only refers to the possibility of the transformation of the law in light of individual cases, but also to the suspension of the law, i.e. the removal of the practice of law as such. Such a decision, therefore, is not a juridical but a political decision; it is a decision to be made not by a judge, but by the political sovereign.[44] Inasmuch as the sovereign political decision concerns the question of whether the juridical practice can be applied at all, this decision relates the application of the law "reflexively"[45] back to its own preconditions. Schmitt calls this precondition "normality"; and if normality is no longer given, the exception arises:

> The exception appears in its absolute form when a situation in which legal prescriptions can be valid must first be brought about. Every general norm demands a normal, everyday frame of life to which it can be factually applied and which is subjected to its regulations. The norm requires a homogeneous medium. This effective normal situation

is not a mere "superficial presupposition" that a jurist can ignore; that situation belongs precisely to its immanent validity. There exists no norm that is applicable to chaos. For a legal order to make sense, a normal situation must exist, and he is sovereign who definitely decides whether this normal situation actually exists. All law is situational law. (PT 13)

Interestingly enough, here Schmitt is no longer speaking of political sovereignty in the legal-theoretical sense as a supreme authority or an unjustified power. He does not define sovereignty as power – "power proves nothing in law" (PT 17) – but with reference to that upon which sovereignty decides: the situation.[46] Due to its connection to a pre-existing situation, we might regard this as a rather occasionalist determination of sovereignty – just to emphasize the distinction between this definition and what is called decisionism and associated with the unconditional power to decide.[47] However, sovereign decisions are not made with arbitrary situations in mind, and are thus not arbitrary themselves. Not every situation qualifies as an exception. Yet sovereignty is more than the perception of exceptional situations. The recognition of the exception also has a performative element: the decision about whether an exception is at hand remains "a decision in the true sense of the word" (PT 6).

A sovereign decision on the exception is "in the true sense of the word" a *political* decision, because it links the validity of the legal order to the precondition of the normality of a social order as its "homogeneous medium." It is endangered once it is unclear "what constitutes the public interest or interest of the state, public safety and order" (ibid.), because the unity and homogeneity of the community no longer exists. The paradigmatic case of an exception is therefore a civil war. To declare a civil war means, according to the categories found in *The Concept of the Political*, deciding upon who is friend and who is enemy. The declaration of "enemies of state is possibly the sign of civil war, i.e., the dissolution of the state as an organized political entity, internally peaceful, territorially enclosed, and impenetrable to aliens" (CP 47). This tells us what constitutes the normality or homogeneity of a political unit: It can be equated with a peaceful situation of "tranquility, security, and order" (CP 46); it is indicated by the absence of the enemy (ibid.). This does not mean that no conflicts can arise in the state of normality, but they take place on the basis of shared fundamental beliefs, which means that they can be resolved within the framework of a legal order that is accepted by both parties to the conflict. This is no longer the case in a state of exception or emergency, where the situation is characterized by a conflict that has attained an "existential" (Schmitt) dimension in which it "can neither be decided by a previously determined general norm nor by the judgment of a disinterested and therefore neutral third party" (CP 27). Whoever does not accept the normative framework of the existing legal order within which the conflict could be resolved is the enemy. The declaration of the state of emergency, however, goes beyond dissolving the social unit. There is always an anticipation of certain measures that will put an end to this exceptional situation. To declare a state of emergency therefore means, on the one hand, abandoning the previously valid normative order; on the other hand, it implies actions that aim to restore this order and thus also normality. In this sense, although the sovereign decision "stands outside the normally valid legal system," it "nevertheless belongs to it" (PT 7). This is what separates a state of emergency from "a juristic chaos, from any kind of anarchy" (PT 14).

Schmitt's objection to liberalism is not that it is blind to the possibility of a state of exception in general. On the contrary, he states, citing Lorenz von Stein: "In a constitutional state, the constitution is the expression of the societal order, the existence of society itself. As soon as it is attacked the battle must then be waged outside the constitution and the law, hence decided by the power of weapons" (CP 47). He thus objects to liberalism's blindness to the consequences for the idea of the value neutrality and coherence of the liberal system of law. The essence of Schmitt's accusation is that liberalism ignores the normative dimension that it implicitly presupposes. This means that liberals entangle themselves in the contradiction of claiming that the "principle of equality of opportunity" is a universal principle, while also having to restrict this principle in reality:

> For it is self-evident that one can hold open an equal chance only for those whom one is certain would do the same. Any other use of such a principle would not only be suicide in practical terms, but also an offense against the principle itself. Due to this necessity, the party in legal possession of power, by virtue of its hold on the means of state power, must itself determine and judge every concrete and politically important application and use of the concept of legality and illegality. (LL 33)

The ruling party, however, runs into conflict with the other "essential content of the principle of equal chance," i.e. the fact that "its concrete interpretation and use is not one-sided, but rather that it is taken up by all parties under full legal equality" (ibid.) The equality claimed by liberal democracies is therefore not an indeterminate universal equality, but a limited and determined equality. It contains a normative dimension that remains concealed by the neutralist self-understanding of liberal democracies. This becomes particularly apparent in a state of emergency. Here "the simple truth of legal scholarship becomes evident through all the normative fictions and obscurities: that norms are valid only for normal situations, and the presupposed normalcy of the situation is a positive-legal component of its 'validity'" (LL 69).

Schmitt's own – dictatorial – perspective on the problem of political unity can be seen in the fact that he understands the unity upon which "every democracy, even the parliamentary variety, fundamentally rests" as a "presupposed homogeneity that is thorough and indivisible" (LL 41). The unity necessarily presupposed by every legal order – and which is to be restored in a state of emergency through a sovereign act – is supposed to be a *substantive* unity.[48] This is where we must locate Schmitt's anti-liberal theory of democracy. In obvious contradiction to the objection he makes in *Political Theology* to Rousseau's notion of a presupposed and pre-political organic unity, he now explicitly – especially in *Constitutional Theory*[49] – steps into line with Rousseau.

9. Schmitt's Rousseauism

In this connection, the source of true political legitimacy, which is opposed to the neutralist legality and completeness of the liberal constitutional state, is no longer the political sovereign (neither in the absolute nor in the occasionalist sense), rather the sovereignty of the people. In a democracy, as Schmitt states explicitly in *Constitutional Theory*, "state power must derive from the people and may not be set in motion by a person or from a position that is outside of the people and standing above it... At least so long as the possibility exists that another besides the people itself decides definitively what in concreto God's will is, the appeal to the will of God contains a moment of undemocratic transcendence" (CT 266). True democracy is therefore founded on the "rejection of all political influences and effects not originating from the substantial homogeneity of the people themselves" (CT 267). According to Schmitt, however, the idea that sovereignty derives from the people does not entail an identity between the government and the governed: "For the difference between those governing and those governed, between those who command and those who obey, remains in place so long as there are government and commands generally, that is to say, as long as the democratic state as state exists" (CT 265). "Compared to other state forms," this differentiation "can even be enhanced and increased extraordinarily in *material* terms" (ibid.). What is decisive is that "*persons* who govern and command are still rooted in the substantive similarity of the people. If they receive the consent of and have the confidence of the people, to which they belong, their rule can be stricter and more intense, their government more decisive than that of some patriarchal monarch or a cautious oligarchy" (ibid.). As long as the "*factual* difference between governing and being governed" does not "become a qualitative distinction" and does not "distance governing persons from those governed" (ibid.), Schmitt regards (therein precisely: fascist) dictatorship – to be a democratic option.

Schmitt obviously does not make explicit reference to Rousseau's idea of an identity between the government and the governed; rather, he re-interprets this identity as a substantial unity between the leader and the people. Schmitt's explicit reference to Rousseau's concept of popular sovereignty is thus found elsewhere, where he picks up on Rousseau's conception of the people as unrepresentable presence. Because the idea of popular sovereignty implies that the people stand either prior to or above the constitution, "compared to all such normative frameworks, the people continue to exist as an entity that is directly and genuinely *present*, not mediated by previously defined normative systems, validations and fictions" (CT 271). In this negative determination with regard to norms, however, the people, if it is to be considered sovereign, must represent a substantial unity. Schmitt thus does not justify the fact that the people cannot be represented by arguing that the people must be understood as an essentially heterogeneous entity that could never be fully represented and subsumed under a single norm. Rather, he argues that a people only represents a people in the true sense if it is present as an assembly. "The genuinely assembled people are first a people, and only the genuinely assembled people can do that which pertains distinctly to the activity of the people. They can *acclaim* in that they express their consent or disapproval by a simple calling out, calling higher or lower, celebrating a leader or a suggestion, honoring the king or some other person, or denying the acclamation by silence or complaining" (CT 272). "The correct idea that supports *Rousseau's* famous thesis that the people cannot be represented rests on this truth" (ibid.) that the people is only present as a people in assembly: "They cannot be represented, because they must be *present*, and only something absent, not something present, may be represented" (ibid.).

According to Schmitt, therefore, liberal democracies characteristically ignore "the assembled people as such, because, as already often discussed, a distinctive feature of the bourgeois Rechtsstaat [constitutional state or rule of law] constitution is to ignore the sovereign, whether this sovereign is the monarch or the people" (CT 273). Although liberal democracies allow for the freedom of assembly, the assembled people is not the people that the constitution recognizes as the people. In liberal constitutional democracies, the people are only sovereign in elections and referenda, i.e. in procedures in which the people are not assembled as a people at all. A genuinely popular will cannot be constituted by the individual casting of ballots, especially given the fact that these ballots are secret; this cannot bring about a *volonté générale*, rather only a sum of individual wills, a *volonté de tous* (cf. CT 274). In *Legality and Legitimacy*, Schmitt points out that he only regards "the method of will formation through simple majority vote" as "sensible and acceptable when an essential similarity among the entire people can be assumed. For in this case, there is no voting down of the minority. Rather, the vote should only permit a latent and presupposed agreement and consensus to become evident" (LL 27f.). If we can no longer assume an indivisible national homogeneity, then the "abstract, empty functionalism of pure mathematical majority determinations is the opposite of neutrality and objectivity. It is only the quantitatively larger or smaller, forced subordination of the defeated and, therefore, suppressed minority" (LL 28).

Schmitt thus accuses liberal democracies of nothing less than replacing the true shape of popular sovereignty with procedures that are neutral in appearance only, and that can hardly conceal the fact that they result in a relation of power that contradicts the principle of equal opportunity. In 1932 Schmitt thus sees a "fundamental alternative: recognition of the substantive characteristics and capacities of the German people or retention and extension of functionalist value neutrality, with the fiction of an indiscriminate equal chance for all contents, goals, and drives" (LL 93f.). It is well known on which side Schmitt stands.

Nevertheless, the assumption of "substantive characteristics and capacities of the German people" stands in marked contradiction to Plessner's anthropology, to which Schmitt resorts in *The Concept of the Political* in order to explain how "associations and disassociations" can arise within a political unit. Now Schmitt simply assumes this unity in his Rousseauian concept of popular sovereignty; this unity is not the result of a political decree, rather it is pre-political and, tellingly enough, only requires "recognition." This thesis, however, presupposes an entirely different anthropology, according to which man is substantively determined by his belonging to a community, if the unity of the people is to be maintained. After all, the people can only be sovereign if they are unified. Correspondingly, in the revised third edition of *The Concept of the Political* published in 1933, Schmitt writes that "man is entirely and existentially caught up in political participation."[50] This formulation is diametrically opposed to Plessner's determination of man, according to which "man is 'primarily a being capable of creating distance' who in his essence is undetermined, unfathomable, and remains an 'open question'" (CP 60).

Given the similarity – which Schmitt could not see because of his anti-liberal premises and his critique of Romanticism – between Plessner's anthropology and the romantically inspired, liberal democratic self-understanding, I will now conclude by returning to Schmitt's critical diagnosis that liberal democracies are defined by their "contradictory" relationship to sovereignty.

10. Politics as a Critique of Politics

In his study on the *Limits of Community*, Plessner also formulates a critique of Rousseau's "social radicalism." Although he does not explicitly distance himself from Schmitt, he warns of the potential danger entailed by Schmitt's claim that an element of decision and thus of subjectivity is always involved in the establishment of a political unit. He argues that this should not cause us to retreat into utopian conceptions of pre-political communities:

> The return of the human at the highest stage of societal abstraction – this subordination of the whole under the irrational violence of life for the sake of its inner rationalization – awakens hopes for a restructuring of politics in a communal-ethical sense. And it is, however, simultaneously the strongest counter-argument against utopia. For it is the case that a majority of positions, perspectives, and insights; therefore, it signifies the loss of time required in order to balance the differences, a balance that is, on its part, necessary in order to set free the power to initiate action.[51]

According to Plessner, it is precisely this "balancing of differences" that requires decision. And unlike Schmitt's polemic against the liberal "illusion" of a "dissolution of all relations of power in relations of discourse," even a liberal democracy cannot put off this decision until all those affected have reached an agreement. "There must be a decision."[52] This is not only due to the constant urgency to act, such that one cannot wait until a rational consensus has come about, but also to the structural finitude of even the most cautious practical decision within the horizon of – in Plessner's terms – the "unforeseeability of reality,"[53] i.e. its openness to the future. It is above all this openness that conflicts with the "probability of a final balancing."[54] Every decision of this kind is therefore a necessarily *sovereign* decision.

This reveals the connection between the romantic concept of self-determination defended in this chapter (cf. sec. 4) and the problem of political sovereignty dealt with in the previous sections. Because self-determination can never be complete due to the fundamentally mimetic openness of the subject to a mutable world, meaning that individuals are repeatedly faced over the course of their lives with the task of self-determination, a "balancing of differences" can never be had once and for all. Changes in individuals' self-understanding can have social consequences that call for a new "balancing of differences." Precisely because of the irreducible potentiality in the (non-) foundation of all social identity, however, the political, sovereign character of every decision on such a balancing necessarily comes to the fore. What is also revealed is that the sovereignty of the political, understood properly, is not anti-democratic; rather, it constitutes an essential structural determination of (liberal) democracy. From this perspective, the sovereignty of the political proves to be the exact correlate of the democratic subject and its freedom.

This reference to the incalculable dynamic of "concrete life," which, according to Plessner, lies at the foundation of all social identity and demands a decision, simultaneously contradicts the notion of a popular sovereign in agreement with itself. For the insight into the indeterminate, unfathomable, and "open" essence of the individual members of the polity implies that the popular sovereign cannot be thought of as being present in an unmediated and positive way. Instead, as I will show in more detail in the following chapter on Rousseau, popular sovereignty constitutes itself only in a mediated fashion – through the medium of representation, which at the same time produces a "balancing of differences." This also means that there is a structural difference between the people and its political representations, which always has the potential to turn into conflict.

Just as the internal connection between the anthropological insight into the indeterminacy at the foundation of all social identity and the problem of sovereign decision conflicts with a substantialist notion of popular sovereignty, it also contradicts the fiction of a system of legality free of all power relations, due to its absolute neutrality and thus self-enclosed nature. Yet if the connection between a dynamic anthropology and political sovereignty is characteristic for liberal democracies, then the rationalist misunderstanding of democratic politics is, strictly speaking, a self-misunderstanding. Although it may characterize certain spheres of (liberal) democratic discourse, it does not define this discourse as a whole, and certainly not (liberal) democratic practices as such. Schmitt himself concedes that this self-misunderstanding is not ubiquitous when he criticizes liberalism, not for robbing the political of the concept of sovereignty, but for its "contradictory" relation to sovereignty. Liberalism, to repeat Schmitt's characterization, recognizes the necessity of sovereignty, including that element that cannot be reduced to the declaration of objective facts; yet it insists that sovereignty remains dependent upon the consent of the people or its representatives (cf. PT 59f).

Indeed, the (liberal) democratic system of law – as Schmitt is right to emphasize, though he draws a false conclusion from it – must be understood as a system that is "normatively *concretized* in a system of institutions and practices"[55] and stands in a relation of structural tension to the universalism of the principle of equality of opportunity, to which this system of law is nonetheless committed. But this only results in a contradiction if we misunderstand the (liberal) democratic system of law as being neutral and self-enclosed. What does indeed contradict the idea of the self-enclosed nature of (liberal) democratic practice is the connection of legal and political decisions to the democratic public sphere, where the concretions of democratic equality can be disputed by other, competing conceptions of their realization.

Schmitt, however, could only perceive a "duality of two divergent systems of justification" (LL 66) as an "unsystematic incompleteness" (LL 65) that contradicts both the rationalist idea of the legalist self-enclosedness of the system of law and his own conception of popular sovereignty, and which therefore dissolves both sides. By contrast, the double coding of democratic discourse – "as a network of institutions and formally organized decision-making procedures on the one hand, and as a network of publics on the other hand"[56] – in the sense of the institutional permeability of the democratic legal system and the politics that supports it, can be defended with regard to its other. This other is not a self-enclosed popular sovereignty conceived of as being present, which Schmitt conceptually puts in the place of the sovereign; rather, it is a popular sovereignty which, due to its incalculable potentiality, is an unrepresentable, open, and pluralized public sphere. This is not a situation in which two sovereigns are locked in a "struggle between two forms of law" (LL 66); rather, the public sphere is the medium that binds the sovereignty of legal and political decision making to the legitimating principle of democratic participation. Because the public sphere cannot be reified as the substance of a people, conflict over the meaning of democratic representation and participation, of democratic equality, is always possible. As a result, the legal and political decisions that make these meanings concrete are always capable of revision. In their very different forms of appearance which – contrary to Schmitt, who subsumes the concept of the public sphere under his concept of popular sovereignty (cf. CT 272) – can in no way be reduced to the form of assembly alone, the public sphere not only has an influence on decisions still to be made. Rather it is also a medium for examining and criticizing decisions that have already been made: "The public sphere is the sphere in which discourse can also be extended beyond the moment of decision, such that the communicative power of public opinion can also force decisions to be revised."[57] In *this* sense, Schmitt is right to point out that there can be "no liberal politics" as such, rather "only a liberal critique of politics" (CP 70), for the possibility of criticizing not only political decisions but also the system of law in terms of the meaning of the principle of equality of opportunity specified by that system also amounts to the possibility of (re-)politicizing decisions that have already been made.

According to the self-understanding of (liberal) democracy, despite disputes (also and not least) over the question of how political and legal decisions are to be tied back to the public sphere (often the public sphere itself must be won through struggle and certain publics must struggle for recognition in order to be able to influence such decisions), there is the fundamental possibility of this kind of politicization. The consequence for (liberal) democratic legal practice is that the insight into the fallibility of political and legal decisions – be it those of legislation or of its application – is an essential part of that practice. Thus Schmitt writes in *Legality and Legitimacy* that there "are rarely today any parliamentary majorities that still seriously believe that their statutory decisions will be valid 'in perpetuity'. The situation is so incalculable and so abnormal that the statutory norm is losing its former character and becoming a mere measure" (LL 82f.). However, a (liberal) democratic legislative decision differs from the "measures of the administrative state" (LL 14) by virtue of its internal connection to the public sphere and thus to the problem of legitimacy, about which Schmitt assumed, due to his foreshortened conclusion from a legalistic-neutralistic self-misunderstanding of liberal legal practice to that practice itself, that it is getting repressed.

Yet if we can argue against Schmitt that the question of the legitimacy of legal and political decisions is precisely what gives these decisions a sense of fallibility, the immediate result will be a non-neutral meaning of democratic indeterminacy, which Schmitt, in his critique of political romanticism, took as a sign of a general neutralization of decisions. The fact that (liberal) democracy does not find its own form is not so much the symptom of a general indecisiveness as the expression of the fact that it integrates reflection upon the constantly precarious status of the normality assumed in all legal practice into the concept of law itself. Democracy has politicized this status, as we could maintain with and against Schmitt. Because the (liberal) democratic system of law is grounded in a cultural self-understanding, according to which there can be no final "balancing of differences," it is not the state of exception, but the exception that has become the rule.

This, however, does not mean that liberal democracies are only familiar with exceptions and not with states of exception. Yet the state of exception is not defined with regard to a kind of hostility toward a political unit conceived of as a "substantive agreement" (this indeed could only be realized in a dictatorship) but with regard to an existential hostility toward the openness of liberal democratic politics to the future.[58] This problem can be seen today in the fight against terrorism – here we might think of the fundamentalist idea of a theocracy, which fundamentally contradicts the principle of the self-critique and mutability of democratic orders.[59] However, the same fight against terrorism has also demonstrated (think of the inflationary use of the term "terrorist" for all kinds of different forms of radical critique) that the confusing of exceptions with states of exception can lead to, as Derrida calls it, the "autoimmunity" of democracy to its own openness to the future. This would essentially amount to democracy's suicide, which is complementary to the suicide of the political order by means of an excessive openness (cf. LL 33) addressed by Schmitt.[60] This is the tense relation in which (liberal) democracies stand today.

Because of his critique of aestheticization, Schmitt, as we have seen, deprives himself of the possibility of thoroughly conceiving of the motifs of freedom contained in his own concept of sovereignty. This context also shifts the focus of our own investigation. For it has become evident that the subject-theoretical considerations on the aestheticization of freedom in the previous chapters are directly relevant for the freedom of political self-government. They assert themselves in the tension between necessarily hasty decisions and the possibility of retrospective reflection and revision, a tension that is constitutive for the life of democracy. This takes us back to Plato's question about the connection between the relation of the subject to its freedom and the political order. But contrary to Plato, as the discussion of Schmitt has also shown, this relation cannot be defined by the primacy of ethics over politics. Instead, the dialectic of freedom that we have discussed under the name of "aestheticization" asserts itself both in the ethical and the political sphere, though differently in each case. On the premises of a dynamic anthropology, we must continuously re-determine what we want (to be) in living interaction with the world. Because we can therefore never determine once and for all the meaning of social membership, and thus also the meaning of a just order or a "balancing of differences," this meaning is always the outcome of a political decision, which also means that it is always subject to the possibility of change. Yet as we already pointed out at the end of the chapter on Plato, ethics and politics not only each have their own dynamic, they also stand in a relation of tension in which no side can subordinate or gain priority over the other. Because we can neither deduce a just order from a certain concept of the good life nor deduce the meaning of an individual good life from a certain concept of a just order, and because both spheres nevertheless intersect, this gives rise to tensions and even conflicts that must be mediated.

It is no accident that the connection between ethical and political freedom in Schmitt's critique of aestheticization has led us to employ Rousseauian motifs. Like no other modern thinker, Rousseau stands for a theory of democracy that is critical of aestheticization. And the influence of his theory in no way merely extends to the political right wing. Therefore, I would now like to turn to this classic democratic critique of aestheticization, the effects of which can be found in the most various political camps. In this connection the theory of democratic sovereignty, only vaguely sketched in the previous section, will be further elucidated.

PART III

Democracy and Aestheticization

5

The Spectacle of Democracy: Rousseau*

Rousseau's view of democracy differs from that of Plato in that he does not regard it as being synonymous with the aestheticization of ethics and politics. Whereas Plato sees democratic freedom as the root of a process of aestheticization that begins in the sphere of ethics and goes on to infect the sphere of politics, thus regarding theatrocracy as the true face of democracy, Rousseau's theory of democracy makes just the opposite claim. According to Rousseau's influential definition, democracy is the polar opposite of political theatricalization; it denotes collective self-government, whose model is not the theater but the assembly. In an assembly participants do not put on an act or a play for others, rather all engage in a process of joint action. From this perspective, the theater represents an enormous and fundamental threat to democracy, for theater, unlike the other arts, necessarily involves the imitation of action. It thus problematically separates both citizens from their roles and actors from the audience. Rousseau fears that if these separations come to be culturally accepted, our actions in real life will ultimately turn into mere play and the actions of the others will become an opaque spectacle. Rousseau thus regards the theater as undermining the very possibility of collective self-government. Like Plato – though from an entirely

---

* Parts of this chapter were previously published in Juliane Rebentisch, "Rousseau's Heterotopology of the Theatre," in E. Fischer-Lichte & B. Wihstutz, eds, *Performance and the Politics of Space: Theatre and Topology* (New York: Routledge, 2013), pp. 142–65. Translated by Gerrit Jackson. Reproduced with permission of Taylor and Francis Group LLC Books, conveyed through Copyright Clearance Center, Inc.

different perspective – he is convinced that a prospering theatrical culture marks the beginning of the end of a functioning community: "It was by the violence of the theatre," Rousseau believes, "that Athens was lost."[1]

The fact that Rousseau gathered together the last of his strength to prevent the construction of a theater in his home town of Geneva[2] is much more than a biographical quirk that can be brushed aside as being irrelevant to his political philosophy. His famous objection to d'Alembert's intent to construct a theater in Geneva instead leads us directly into the systematic core of Rousseau's political theory. The ideas that motivate this critique have influenced theories of democracy up into the twentieth century; traces of his argumentation can be found in the works of authors as diverse as Hannah Arendt, Jürgen Habermas, Stanley Cavell, Walter Benjamin, and Guy Debord, all of whom argue that the theatricalization of the political represents a threat to democracy. They also agree that the true essence of democracy lies in common action, which overcomes the division of the political into hypocritical agents and the audience.[3]

In what follows I will show that this assumption can lead to a short-sighted conception of democracy. Moreover, I claim that a decidedly anti-theatrical democracy in fact represents the end of democracy. The fact that Plato's equating of democracy with theatrocracy and Rousseau's defense of democracy against the theatricalization of the culture share a common enemy is a first indication of this claim. Given the similarities between Rousseau's democratic argumentation and Plato's anti-democratic argumentation, we can ask whether Rousseau's critique of the theatricalization or the aestheticization of democratic culture represents an excessive reduction of the concept of democracy, thus causing his concept of democracy necessarily to assume a number of anti-democratic features. Yet, despite the surprising agreement between the critiques of aestheticization offered by Rousseau and Plato, it is impossible to overlook the difference between them. In fact, Rousseau's own recycling of Platonic motifs reveals both the enormous historical distance between the two and the distinctions in their understandings of democracy. Whereas Plato's metaphysical ontology of the good sought to preserve the corresponding order with its supposedly natural hierarchies, Rousseau advocated the collective self-government of equals. This approach once again underlines the connection – which is characteristic of the critique of aestheticization in general – between ethical and political motifs, between questions of government and questions of self-government. Because Rousseau equates government with collective self-government, the ethical question of self-government has immediate political relevance. Like Plato, though for entirely different reasons and with an entirely different accentuation, Rousseau also sees the aesthetic alienation of the individual from himself as the primary cause of the dissolution of the political community. And for Rousseau as well, actors are paradigmatic for the evils of such alienation.

1. The Irony of the Actor

"What is the talent of the actor?" Rousseau asks. "It is the art of counterfeiting himself, of putting on another character than his own, of appearing different than he is, of becoming passionate in cold blood, of saying what he does not think as naturally as if he really did think it, and finally, of forgetting his own place by dint of taking another's" (LtA 79). In order to be able to play his role properly, the actor must be able to forget himself; therefore he "annihilates himself, as it were" (LtA 81). But in doing so, he "[abandons] the most noble [role] of all, that of man" (LtA 80). To illustrate what he means by the "role of man," Rousseau compares the actor to the orator, who, unlike the actor, "appears in public...to speak and not to show himself; he represents only himself; he fills only his own role, speaks only in his own name, says, or ought to say, only what he thinks; the man and the role being the same, he is in his place; he is in the situation of any citizen who fulfils the function of his estate" (LtA 81). Rousseau thus calls "man" whoever is identical with his social role. "Man" is the name for those members of society who fulfill their duties to the community. Now, Rousseau emphasizes not only that role-playing will eventually cause the actor to become estranged from himself – i.e. from his social identity or the place assigned to him – but also that his entire existence is pretence. The problem is not that he might turn his theatrical roles into the roles he plays in real life,[4] but that the actor will ultimately only be able to pretend to assume roles, even the roles he plays in reality. Rousseau is thus not as concerned that theater life could become an earnest social identity as he is that the earnestness of social authenticity could be corrupted by the theater. Because the actor always merely plays his roles, the theatrical form of imitation can in a certain respect be called "entirely innocent": Someone who plays a scoundrel onstage is not necessarily a scoundrel in real life (LtA 81). Yet precisely because of its playfulness, theatrical imitation practices "habits which can be innocent only in the theater and can serve everywhere else only for doing harm" (ibid.). For the theater familiarizes actors with the art of dissimulation. Once someone has practiced this art, he is unlikely to restrict its usage to the stage. It would be miraculous, Rousseau speculates, were a gifted actor not to use his abilities to his advantage in other areas of life as well. Rousseau fears that once the acting profession enjoys cultural recognition and the art of acting itself becomes considered worthy of imitation, the art of dissimulation will spread throughout the republic: The actor cultivates "by profession the talent of deceiving men" for all professions (LtA 80).

Rousseau's first problem with the theater, then, is the problem of dissimulation or irony. After all, the rhetorical meaning of irony is *dissimulatio*,[5] which, however, amounts to much more than deception. As Gregory Vlastos emphasizes in a short survey of the history of irony,[6] the connotations of dishonesty, deception, and fraud are indeed central components of the Greek term from which our understanding of irony derives; but at the same time, *eironeia* had another meaning that was to be decisive for the Latin translation of the concept: transparent dissimulation. This is the meaning we attach to the most well-known forms of irony today: both contrary irony, when an utterance is intended to mean the opposite of what is said,[7] and what Vlastos calls "complex irony," an utterance whose meaning differs from its literal signification.[8] Although these are forms of dissimulation, they are obviously not meant to be fraudulent or deceptive. This form of dissimulation is intended to be transparent, at least for those to whom the ironic utterance is addressed.[9] It does not conceal anything; on the contrary, as transparent dissimulation it maintains the presence of the intended meaning.

Yet there are also cases in which an ironic utterance merely intimates that the speaker intends something other than he is saying, without also transmitting the resolution of the irony into a contrary or alternate meaning. In these cases, ironic dissimulation does indeed conceal something, i.e. the intended meaning, but without being deceptive. Ironic concealment, as Alexander Nehamas notes, lies somewhere between deceit and truthfulness. Like a truthful utterance, it does no injury to the truth; like deceit, it does not reveal it.[10] This form of concealment introduces a form of complexity into the concept of irony that far exceeds the complex irony described by Vlastos.[11] Nevertheless, this kind of complexity can also be found in cases in which we only understand an ironic expression enough to know that what is being said is not what is meant, without being able to determine with any certainty just what *is* meant. In these cases irony "conceals the overall intention that shines through more than it is admitted."[12] We know that the ironist is merely showing us a mask, we recognize his irony, but we do not know what he is concealing.

By making apparent that he does not mean what he says, the ironist can suggest a different position without ever revealing it – in fact, without ever having to take a position at all. Therefore, according to Nehamas, the phenomenology of irony would be incomplete if we were to assume that the ironist always knows what it is he is concealing.[13] Irony indicates that the meaning of what has been said is not genuine, but it does not necessarily imply that the speaker himself possesses the true meaning. The figure of irony permits us to play with having another position than the one we present to others – by employing the more or less explicit use of the notorious quotation marks of irony. It allows us to experiment with being something other than what we appear to be, without obligating us to make that explicit.

It is precisely in this regard that Rousseau's actor is more of an ironist than a deceiver. When he is onstage, his deception is "innocent," for he does not conceal the dissimulation he uses to conceal. We know that the actor is not identical with his roles, but we do not know who or what he is in reality. As we have seen, it is already at this point that Rousseau begins to be concerned. Although this does not yet constitute deception, it leads us back to the true core of his critique of the actor. As innocent as such dissimulation may be, someone who achieves mastery in this discipline will eventually lose his own identity. One can be "everything" only to the extent that one is "nothing." That is, in Diderot's famous phrase, "the paradox of the actor."[14] Yet this paradox, as we have already seen in our discussion of Plato, merely illustrates the paradoxical logic of all imitation. The subject of imitation is always a strangely subjectless subject, one whose subjectivity does not exist until it is formed in and by virtue of the act of imitation (cf. ch. 1, sec. 9).[15] Rousseau now expands the discussion about the paradox of the actor, a discussion within the theory of mimesis, and includes its ironic effects. For the actor's imitation, an imitation marked as such, keeps visible the genesis of the concrete appearances of the subject out of the everything-and-nothing of pre-subjective indeterminacy: The actor is not really what he represents, but it remains undetermined what he really is, and whether he is something (a determinate something) at all.

The actor's irony, then, is a figure of potentiality. It points to the everything-and-nothing of potentiality that forms the (non-) foundation of all social identity. Because there is no subject prior to imitation, rather only subjectivity as an effect of imitation, any form the subject takes in socializing imitation retains the possibility of a mimetic opening toward others and otherness, and hence the possibility of change. That is precisely what the actors' innocent imitations,

imitations marked as play, call to mind. This is also why we should not understand the irony of the actor, contrary to what an alternative perspective on the actor might suggest, as evidence that there is something like a true self behind the social roles the actor masterfully takes on and then abandons, as when Martin Wuttke peels off his Hitler moustache after the filming of Quentin Tarantino's *Inglourious Basterds*. The divide we are dealing with in Rousseau's critique of the actor is not a divide between authentic and inauthentic subjectivity, but between subjectivity (identity) and potentiality, determinacy and indeterminacy.

For Rousseau, what is at stake here is nothing less than the concept of man itself. Once a division arises between a man and the roles he plays, then, as we have seen, Rousseau no longer regards him to be a man. In other words, "man" is doomed the moment he arises conceptually, in opposition to the concept of a role. Rousseau thus defines "Man" in a dual manner: as a determinate member of a community, identical to his roles and thus a complete person, and – as is implied by the concealing irony of the actor – as an indeterminate non-member, different from his roles and thus a non-person. The fact that the indeterminacy of the non-member is never directly apparent, as it only appears negatively in the form of irony, indicates that membership and non-membership lie on different levels. Contrary to membership, non-membership is not a determinate position. As we saw in the previous chapters, we can only take up a position of non-membership by employing a conception of freedom that is both one-sided and suggests a false totality: a kind of freedom that is falsely defined as freedom from the social. A life lived in illusory distance from the social would lead to a stance of total indifference – without any determinacy, but without ever being able to rid ourselves of determinacy, since we can only live our lives as determinate lives. We could then only live in constant dissimulation of the self. A life in permanent quotation marks, however, would not be a life in freedom. And contrary to the cliché, actors are aware of this fact; indeed, they are presumably the last people to confuse their roles with their lives off-stage. But as we have also seen in the previous chapters, a person who has never experienced a difference from his social roles could not be called free either. Such experiences are not only necessary if we are to consciously accept these roles, emancipate ourselves from them and arrive at new understandings of our social existence, but they also represent the condition of our being able to appropriate or influence the social practices of which we are a part. The conflicts involved in such changes are conflicts over what it means to be a subject, i.e. a member of a polity. When we demand that others recognize our new self-understanding, then we demand a new understanding of our shared world.

What is characteristic of the actor's concealing irony, however, is not its relation to such conflicts. Rather, concealing irony points indirectly to the potentiality in the (non-)foundation of our social existence, thereby bringing out the condition of the possibility of such conflicts, i.e. the fact that we are never fully absorbed by our social roles. Concealing irony conveys this fact intersubjectively – another reason why Rousseau regards this form of irony as ethically and politically relevant. Yet in order to give a more detailed account of the crucial systematic position of concealing irony in Rousseau's view of the relation between ethics and politics, I will first have to compare Rousseau with one of his fiercest critics: Helmuth Plessner. Surprisingly enough, Plessner shares Rousseau's claim that a functioning community must be founded on the recognizability and transparency of its members to each other. The use of irony, as we will see, undermines this foundation.

2. The Public Expression of Indeterminacy

In the rhetorical tradition, Quintilian and Cicero associate irony with "urbane wit"[16] and, respectively, elegance and urbanity, because irony enables the speaker to conceal his actual position.[17] Irony thrives in an atmosphere of uncommitted lovability, in which disputes do not lead to injuries and invasiveness can be contained through communicative and friendly reservedness. Irony therefore appears especially qualified for "interactions among an indeterminate number of persons unknown to each other, who because of limited opportunities, time, and reciprocal interests can at most establish acquaintances."[18] Indeed irony does appear suited to solving a problem that, according to Plessner, the urbane (large-scale) community causes for individuals, i.e. the "ephemeral and accidental character of human relationships," which "moves each person to arbitrary perspectives and perceptions that distort the individual and force an abbreviation and simplification which gives no space to individuality" (LC 131f.).[19] We could say that irony is a way of preserving our dignity in such situations. For Plessner sees dignity in the "infinity and inviolability of the personal soul" (LC 132). Respecting another person's dignity means recognizing his "rich and perhaps never exhaustible soul" and that means respecting him "in his possibilities" (ibid.). Indeed, concealing irony – the kind of irony that is paradigmatic for Rousseau's actor – is the only form of expression that can provoke this recognition in the urban public, i.e. vis-à-vis strangers. Here we have an intersection between the rhetorics and the ethics of irony.

Plessner himself, however, envisions a different solution to the problem. On his view the objectification of the self in social roles offers the best protection against the injuries we are exposed to in the urban public. The appearance of being an office-holder protects from the "risk of ridicule" that affects every immediate expression of our soul in unfamiliar settings, due to the fact that this expression can only ever be a simplified and coarse representation of something that can never be represented as a whole (cf. LC 117–20). However, as Plessner is well aware, our public immunity is "paid with the price of individuality" (LC 136). The symbolic form of office or, more generally, a social role "rescues dignity in that it offers for the (hard to comprehend) natural dignity the equivalence of one that is unreal, but clearly delimited" (LC 135). Unlike public office, which is only capable of granting dignity (nimbus) to the degree that the office-holder refrains from any individual expression (cf. LC 132f., 136), irony enables us qua negativity to give public expression to the dignity – which is "hard to comprehend" – of an inexhaustible individuality. This expression is protected by its mediacy against the risk of ridicule.

Yet it is no accident that Plessner, the great critic of Rousseau, makes no mention of irony in this context. Instead, he defines the "ironically destructive perspective" (LC 130) which ridicules the unmediated expression of the soul as something the latter must guard against in the urban public sphere. Plessner does not consider the possibility that irony itself could represent a form of protection, because – like Rousseau – Plessner assumes that the ethic of sociality must be essentially based on the fact that "human characters" are "recognizable and, in their purity, also transparent." "Relativizing and diluting" these "ethical ideals themselves" would mean "putting the cart before the horse" (LC 130). It is only logical, therefore, that his solution to the problem of how to preserve the immunity of the individuality of the individual is prestige, the very opposite of irony. Prestige results from "aim" and "constancy of will," which are expressed by our deeds and give our lives the impression of "clarity" that is both honored and feared as a "superior power" (LC 140f.). Ironic ambiguity is thus replaced by the heroic clarity of the will, which only a few especially charismatic individuals and leader-types are capable of achieving. For the rest, there remains the dignity of office. Now, even as an ideal, such a lucid form of life is highly problematic, especially given what has been discussed in the previous chapters. Furthermore, contrary to what Plessner apparently had in mind, neither heroic decisiveness nor the regalia of public office can protect against the "ironically destructive perspective."[20] For our purposes, however, psychological speculation about Plessner's unironic trust in the "armoured I" is not as important as the fact that his emphasis on the morality of office and heroic decisiveness in *The Limits of Community* systematically coincides with the obligation that public officials be recognizable. Plessner claims that "in public life each person sees through the other, though not so far as to see who he really is, but only what he wants [...]" (LC 157). Plessner is obviously aware that even diplomatic relations are not free of deception; on the contrary, it is expected. Yet beneath this deception lies the definable and instrumental intention of a functionary, a clearly identifiable subjectivity. This is absolutely clear to those who are deceived, if only after the fact. Deception is thus distinct from irony not only because it is masked and not apparent, such that it only becomes apparent after the fact, but also because in deception there is always a clearly identifiable intention at work, at least provided the deception is recognized as such. This is what distinguishes deception from concealing irony, albeit not from all forms of irony.

Nevertheless, there is a sphere in which Plessner also accords concealing irony a legitimate place: the sphere of sociality [*Geselligkeit*] which lies somewhere between the public and the private sphere. Alongside a public sphere defined by diplomatic relations between functionaries, there is a semi-public sociality in which ironic relations between "natural persons" (LC 166) prevail. Here we find the "cultivation of innuendo and allusion," a "culture of restraint," an "aesthetic of hide and seek" which, according to Plessner, reveals the "incomparability of a person," its " incomprehensibility" (LC 162). The lines that run between these "spheres of life" are not, as Plessner himself points out, "as neatly separated as the chapter headings referring to them" (LC 164). It is often difficult to tell where sociality ends and the official business of diplomacy begins. But what would that mean for a theory of public life which centers upon the values of the recognizability and transparency of its members?

Concealing irony, after all, introduces an ambiguity into public life that necessarily contradicts the ideal of mutual recognizability assumed by Plessner – in surprising agreement with Rousseau. Concealing irony is not only a way of maintaining distance in what are otherwise only minimally regulated social interactions; rather, it leaves the trace of the "inexhaustibly human" element in official social roles, offices, and functions. Regardless of whether we believe that individuals should find fulfillment in their social roles (Rousseau) or "reduce" themselves behind these roles for their own protection

(Plessner, cf. LC 178); and regardless of whether the public sphere is subjected to the law of authenticity (Rousseau) or of "unrealization" (ibid.), concealing irony subverts the public recognizability upon which both positions are based. This form of irony not only divides persons from their roles while leaving the status of the persons behind these roles undefined (a problem for Rousseau's theory of social authenticity), the indeterminacy of the persons behind the roles also has an effect on the roles themselves (a problem for Plessner's confidence in the dignity of office). If we do not know who the person is behind these roles, nor what his position is on these roles, then it will remain unclear whether these roles can have any validity at all. The ironic mask loses the status of a socially reliable symbolic form, and instead points to an abyss of alternative possibilities.

What the rhetorical tradition values about irony represents a problem for theories guided solely by the ideal of recognizability: the possibility that the speaker can conceal his true intention (or, in some cases, the lack of any intention) from his addressees. But again, this is not a matter of deception, for concealing irony makes apparent that it is concealing something. It therefore introduces a "non-public" element (something concealed from the public sphere) into the public sphere itself.[21] Concealing irony thereby naturally collides with a culture of authentic openness [*Rückhaltlosigkeit*] that seeks to remove the distinction between the non-public and the public. We must not confuse the "non-public" with the private, for as we will see shortly, a culture of openness does not exclude the division of the community into a private and public sphere; moreover, the idea of a perfect identity between persons and their social roles is based on a social order in which everyone "is in his place" (LTA 81). And this place, especially for women, might very well lie in the private sphere. However, there is another reason why that which irony conceals should not be equated with the private sphere: Concealing irony does not allow any conclusions about the genuine and thus private identity of the person behind the social role from which that person ironically distances himself. Irony merely points to an open horizon of other possible meanings or identities behind what has been said or shown. Because irony leaves that which it publicly conceals undetermined, it collides not only with a culture of authentic openness, but also with a culture of symbolic clarity (Plessner), which requires that nobody cast aside their roles on the public stage.[22] Although Plessner, unlike Rousseau, is aware that people are "never entirely what they are,"[23] this cannot be made apparent in public. Plessner assigns the incomprehensibility of man to the sphere of a "more or less obscure private existence."[24] This categorization, however, is implausible not only because the already mentioned susceptibility to irony of those who publicly display their will to be someone, but also because of the image of the private sphere, which ignores the fact that this sphere is in no way free of social roles.[25] By contrast, ironic consciousness is aware of the inevitability of the difference between humans in their incomprehensibility and humans in their social roles, though it does not reify this difference in a sphere-specific manner. It is no accident that Plessner locates irony in the hybrid sphere of sociality that lies between the private and the public.

This defense of an irony-friendly, aestheticized culture clearly has implications for the conception of the relationship between the private and the public sphere. For the discussion of this connection, however, I will concentrate on Rousseau. Unlike Plessner, who due to his anthropological assumptions turns out to be irony-friendly after all, Rousseau is decidedly opposed to urbane-ironic sociality. Even more so than Plessner, he emphasizes the subversive effects of sociality on the division of the community into a private and a public sphere. The figure that is paradigmatic for the destruction of this division, however, is not the actor, but the actress.

3. The Actress and Her Parodies

Because Rousseau is convinced that there are "no good morals for women outside of a withdrawn and domestic life" (LtA 82), the mere presence of actresses in the city already indicates a moral decline. "How [could] an estate," Rousseau asks, "the unique object of which is to show oneself off to the public and, what is worse, for money... agree with decent women and be compatible with modesty and good morals?" (LtA 90). There can be no doubt as to the answer:

> Immodesty conforms so well to [the actresses' estate] and they are so well aware of it themselves that there is not one who would not think herself ridiculous even in feigning to take for her own the discourses of prudence and honor that she retails to the public. For fear that these severe maxims might make a progress injurious to her interests, the actress is always the first to parody her role and destroy her own work. As soon as she reaches the wings, she divests herself of the morality of the theatre as well as of her dignity; and if lessons of virtue are learned on the stage, they are quickly forgotten in the dressing rooms. (LtA 91)

Rousseau's problem with actresses thus differs from his problem with actors. Whereas the actor's irony takes on the complex form we have just discussed – keeping present the genealogy of social roles in the everything-and-nothing of pre-subjective indeterminacy – the irony of the actress takes the shape of parody. The humorous effect of imitating virtues backstage results from the transparency of the imitation. The imitation of virtue, according to Rousseau, conveys the actress's "actual" lack of morals. The kind of parody we are dealing with here is not that of ironic concealment, but of parodic inversion. For the representation of virtue to become a parody, we must be able to identify an intention that is contrary to the representation of virtue. And as Rousseau argues, actresses always possess this intention, if only in a latent form, due to the "dissoluteness" (LtA 81) resulting from the basic nature of their profession. Actresses, in other words, are a "source of bad morals" (LtA 81) not so much because of their stagecraft but because of the social transgression that represents the core of their profession: the fact that they show themselves in public for money.

What makes this transgression especially scandalous in Rousseau's eyes is the fact that it implies a second kind of parody: that of the sexes. For merely by appearing in public, women imitate men. This, Rousseau believes, is an "odious imitation," one by which they "abase themselves" and "dishonor both their sex and ours" (LtA 88). Not only does women's "effrontery" parody the "assurance" (LtA 88) of men; women who have the impudence to appear in public and offer a distorted copy of man do not even leave the original unscathed. The public existence of the actress, then, evinces a parodic quality not only in the eyes of those who insist that the public sphere be reserved for men and who regard the public presence of a woman as both funny and strange.[26] Actresses' very existence evinces a parodic quality because it represents an attack on this same normality.[27] The object of amusement is then no longer a poor imitation, but the original that the parody has rendered "incredible."[28]

Rousseau finds this second effect even less amusing than the first. In fact, he views the theatrical subversion of the order of the sexes as having devastating consequences: "Only two years of theater and everything will be overturned" (LtA 110), he prophesies to the Genevans. Should the citizens be seduced into constructing a theater, it will mean the decline of Geneva; it might begin with the immorality of the actress, but it will soon spread to the entire community. For the institution of the theater abolishes the separation of the sexes not only among the actors and the crew, but also among the audience. Instead of the pursuit of separate distractions, there will be the two sexes meeting daily in the same place; the groups which will be formed for going there; the ways of life that they will see depicted in the theatre, which they will be eager to imitate; the exposition of the ladies and the maidens all tricked out in their very best and put on display in the boxes as though they were in the window of a shop waiting for buyers; the affluence of the handsome young [men] who will come to show themselves off, for their part, and who will soon find it much nicer to caper in the theatre than to exercise on the Plain-Palais. (LtA 111)

Once this decline has reached a point where men and women go to the theater together in order to show themselves off to each other, Parisian conditions will soon prevail in Geneva. The mixing of the sexes will set in motion a play of appearances that will alter the fundamental structures of the community's ethics. Not only does this process lead to a culture dominated by outward appearances, by the "simulacra of fashion" in which everyone seeks to be more than and different from the persons they really are.[29] It also produces a literal perversion of the traditional order of the sexes. The results can be seen in Paris: "Every woman [there] gathers in her apartment a harem of men more womanish than she" (LtA 101). A truly horrible thought for Rousseau!

For Rousseau, the feminization of men is much worse than the rise of women to dominance. In fact, Rousseau's problem with impudent women – actresses and Parisians – is not that they become men's equals; on the contrary, it is their failure to succeed in doing so, making them merely poor imitations of men.[30] For that very reason, women undermine the male original. Because they do not simply switch sides and become "real" men, they bring about a new sphere of society in which the roles of both sexes change and thereby come to resemble each other. A culture in which women are present in public inevitably causes men to become more feminine. The "weaker sex," Rousseau argues, "not in the position to take our ways of life, which is too hard for it, forces us to take on its way, too soft for us; and [...] unable to make themselves into men, the women make us into women" (LtA 100). To the extent, however, that the public culture is male-coded, the feminization of men at once implies a feminization of the culture as such – a clear decline in Rousseau's eyes. More precisely, this transforms the traditional order into what he calls "society." This is made even more apparent by the behavior of those men who now prefer to dance with women in closed rooms instead of exercising in the public square. "But" as Rousseau rants, "in a republic, men are needed" (LtA 101). It needs real men, of course, who spend "their whole lives in the open air" (LtA 101) and who therefore have not yet lost the soldier's virtue, that of "ruggedness" (LtA 112); men who do not hesitate to serve "the country in their hearts and blood to spill for it" (LtA 112).

Rousseau is thus alarmed not only at the plan to construct a theater in Geneva, but also at the new ideals of education beginning to spread there:

> I am told that the education of the young is generally much better than it was formerly; however, this can be proved only by showing that it makes better citizens. It is certain that the children know how to bow better, that they know how to offer their hand more gallantly to ladies and to say an infinity of charming things to them for which I would have them beaten [...] In order to restrain them with the women whom they are destined to divert, care is taken to raise the children exactly like the women. (LtA 111f.)

From Rousseau's perspective, such efforts are entirely wrongheaded. They only make men indistinguishable from women, except for the fact that "since nature has refused them women's graces, they substitute for them ridiculousness" (LtA 112). "On my last trip to Geneva," as Rousseau reports, "I already saw several of these young ladies in jerkins, with white teeth, plump hands, piping voices, and pretty green parasols in their hands, rather maladroitly counterfeiting men" (ibid.). What others regard as the pinnacle of cultivatedness, Rousseau sees as a clear sign of the decline of civilization: an inverted world, a "crime" against nature (cf. LtA 85). But Geneva is not yet lost, for there are still customs that make men men and women women.

4. The Golden Mean

The ideal of naturalness that Rousseau preaches in this connection is anything but merely natural. Rousseau is not really interested in whether chasteness can really be said to be a naturally female characteristic. Instead, he argues that it becomes their second nature:

> Even if it could be denied that a special sentiment of chasteness was natural to women, would it be any the less true that in society their lot ought to be a domestic and retired life, and that they ought to be raised in principles appropriate to it? If the timidity, chasteness and modesty which are proper to them are social inventions, it is in society's interest that women acquire these qualities; they must be cultivated in women, and any woman who disdains them offends good morals [manners]. (LtA 87)

The same is true of the ruggedness, bravery and solidity characteristic of men. Here, naturalness is the result of education – though of a kind of education whose aim is to eliminate any trace of education and produce the illusion of a natural lack of contrivances.[31] The danger represented by the women and men of Paris, who have been educated by the theater in the art of gender parody, is that they will effectively denature this appearance of naturalness, because gender parody exposes the "imitation structure" of "gender identity as such."[32] The awkwardness of the "ladies in jerkins" makes apparent that men also imitate men. There is no genuine femininity or masculinity, rather only imitations; therefore, there is no reality behind these appearances.[33] On that basis, the parodying of gender roles embodied by the actress intersects with the irony which the actor only learns through the practice of his art. While the actress's parodic existence brings the imitation structure of all social roles to the fore (even those that seem entirely natural), the actor's irony preserves the presubjective indeterminacy that is both the ground and the abyss of all imitation. Both figures emphasize contingency. Precisely because there is no subjectivity prior to imitation, rather only through imitation, the possibility of imitating otherness remains, and thus also the possibility of distancing ourselves from our respective social identities and changing them. This remains true in spite of all ideologies about natural and/or social determinacy.

For Rousseau the contingency of social roles is unacceptable, though this is less due to his ideal of naturalness than to his ideal of a republic. According to Rousseau, gender differences form only after humans have exited the state of nature.[34] Still, the morality of the Genevans, whose naturalness Rousseau defends against the decadence of Parisian society, far from conforms to the state of nature.[35] It instead resembles, if distantly, what Rousseau calls the "true youth of the world" (DI 115) in the Second Discourse, a "happiest" and "most lasting" epoch maintaining a "golden mean": On the one side of this mean lies the state of nature, in which neither the difference between the sexes nor community nor morals exist as yet, and in which man has not yet developed the historically conscious and hence specifically human "faculty of self-improvement" (DI 88). On the other side lies a society in which this faculty has been developed to such an extreme degree that self-love degenerates into *amour-propre*, a craving for recognition, and in whose culture, dominated as it is by appearances, there are no longer (real) differences between the sexes, community, or morals. In his fight to prevent the construction of a theater in Geneva, Rousseau seeks to defend the summit of culture from its transformation into a "new state of nature," which, unlike the original state of nature, is no longer of "pure form," but instead "the fruit of an excess of corruption" (DI 134f.). Every step that humans take beyond the culture developed during the "true youth of the world" for the sake of the "improvement of the individual" (DI 115) is in Rousseau's estimation one step too many. And for all the steps that already divide the Geneva of Rousseau's time from the "true youth of the world" he praises in the Second Discourse, it is above all the cultivation of the "useless" and "pernicious" (DI 134) art of the theater that leads Geneva once and for all into decline.

Here we see a return of Plato's critique of affluence and the associated excess of freedom. In both cases the critique takes aim at an excess of means and freedom, which seduces the members of a community to abandon their social roles, thus hollowing out the community from within. But contrary to Plato, the problem that Rousseau sees here is not primarily a case of "busybodiness" and "meddlesomeness" that leaves nothing unchanged (i.e. in its place), though as we have already seen and will see again, this is also a problem for Rousseau. What primarily concerns Rousseau about this possibility is the gap that underlies it: the gap between persons and their roles, which causes nothing to appear as it is. Neither do we see the true face behind the appearances, nor – for that very reason – do we know the status of the appearances themselves. This corresponds to the image of the (salon) society: Given the play of appearances cultivated there, there are neither real men nor proper women, neither genuine privacy nor a truly public sphere. Everything turns into a diffuse mixture within a feminine and oriental atmosphere of emphatic artificiality. Here we see the fulfillment of what Rousseau regards as the decline of Western civilization: the fact that "we never know with whom we have to deal" (DSA 7). For Rousseau, this means the end of freedom. Defending society against Rousseau's idea of the community thus means, contrary to Plessner, defending its more shady elements: concealment, inversion, and distortion. To do so, we must take a look at Rousseau's idea of the community itself. What, then, is the alternative to urbane (theater) society?

5. "Thy Magic Powers Reunite What Custom's Sword Has Divided":[36] The Feast of the Brothers

Rousseau's response to the impenetrable twilight of urban salon and theater culture is fairly literal: It consists in dragging everything into open daylight. The people are to have their spectacles, but without actors and without theater buildings, instead with popular festivals under open skies. "It is in the open air, under the sky, that you ought to gather and give yourselves to the sweet sentiment of your happiness" (LtA 125). The model for the amusements Rousseau envisions for Geneva are the "modest festivals and games" (LtA 133) of Sparta, which lack all ironic concealment and dissimulation, all parodic inversion and disfiguration – and thus all forms of play.[37] In this sort of spectacle, then, nothing is produced or presented onstage. "But what then will be the objects of these entertainments? What will be shown in them?" The answer is obvious: "Nothing, if you please" (LtA 126). In the Genevan spectacle, no one is to represent anything, no one to put on an act for the others. "In Geneva, there will be only men" (DI 66). "Only men," i.e. *not* actors. Whereas the latter, Rousseau argues, bring about the demise of man's humanity by alienating him from his social role, the upstanding citizen is defined by his identity with his social role. The Genevan spectacle gathers together a community that is transparent to itself in that everyone is found "in his place." The festival, therefore, is to be a spectacle in which identity is not represented but presented, thus also presenting the social order, as everyone demonstrates the place where they belong. The object of these festivals, then, is not nothing, but rather the experience of a community that recognizes itself in the order of places it assigns: "Plant a stake crowned with flowers in the middle of a square; gather the people together there, and you will have a festival. Do better yet; let the spectators become an entertainment to themselves; make them actors themselves; do it so that each sees and loves himself in the others so that all will be better united" (LtA 126).

Good spectacles in this sense, Rousseau writes, include public military reviews and military and athletic competitions in the summer, and balls for young people of marriageable age during the winter. The summer games serve the (self-)presentation of the male populace fit for military service; the winter festivities – when the daylight is a little less bright and people prefer "the private association of friends" (LtA 127) – are reserved for the spectacle of the sexes. In order for this spectacle to avoid the twilight of theatricality, it is of decisive importance that it take place under the watchful "eyes of the public" (LtA 128) and that the young people do not employ the ruses of fashion to deceive each other about their genuine appearance (LtA 128). The provision of such "decent meeting places" is intended to prevent the youth from seeking out "more dangerous ones."[38] The balls scheduled for the winter are to compensate, moreover, for "the intervals [devoted] to occupations and pleasures which are fitting to [each sex]," during which the sexes are "deprived of the continual company of the other" (LtA 130). They thus become a decisive instrument in the effort to sustain and affirm the order of the sexes, including the sex-specific division of labor and the assignment to separate spheres. Whereas the balls allow the community to recognize itself as a "big family" (LtA 131), the festivals and games in the summer enable it to recognize itself as a polity, as a republic. Women, accordingly, are largely excluded from the festival scene, at most they can hope to serve as claqueurs who are to give "new zeal" to the male actors (LtA 135). The paradigmatic republican festival in Rousseau's eyes is, tellingly, the dance of a regiment. Even as a child, the old Rousseau confesses, little Jean-Jacques was carried away by the spectacle of "the harmony of five or six hundred men in uniform, holding one another by the hand and forming a long ribbon which wound around, serpent-like, in cadence and without confusion, with countless turns and returns, countless sorts of figured evolutions" (LtA 135). "'Jean-Jacques'," as the zealous father says to his son, "'love your country. Do you see these good Genevans? They are all friends, they are all your brothers; joy and concord reign in their midst. You are a Genevan; one day you will see other peoples; but even if you should travel as much as your father, you will not find their likes'" (LtA 135).

The very particular charm of such spectacles may even be appealing to foreigners, whom they might entice to Geneva, Rousseau speculates; but of course he at once recognizes in "this influx [...] a problem far more than [...] an advantage" (LtA 132). For the spectacle at Geneva is a spectacle by and for Genevans, at which there are to be no spectators who do not themselves play a role in the community. Whether male actors or female claqueurs, they all are part of a polity, a unity that should not be undermined by foreign spectators. Outsiders – potential enemies – are in their absence indeed indirect addressees of the Genevan spectacle of unity, and hence also of its sovereignty; under the eyes of foreigners with amicable intentions, by contrast, it would degenerate into theater, which would directly contradict the entire purpose of the festival. For the theater separates not only men from their roles, but also actors from the audience and, ultimately, even the individual spectators from each other. "People think they come together in the theater, and it is there that they are isolated. It is there that they go to forget their friends, neighbors, and relations in order to concern themselves with fables, in order to cry for the misfortunes of the dead, or to laugh at the expense of the living" (LtA 16f). This last separation is the consequence not only of the theatrical arrangement, where the audience of spectators is united "indirectly, by mediation of the scenic action,"[39] but also of the theater's effects upon the community's moral ties. Theater not only undermines virtue by familiarizing the audience with the passions it imitates – Rousseau adopts this inverted theory of catharsis from Plato[40] – it also reduces pity, which for Rousseau is the opposite pole of self-love,[41] to a "fleeting and vain emotion which lasts no longer than the illusion which produced it" (LtA 24), because it ultimately only serves self-pleasure (and thus self-love). In the theater, therefore, pity is either suppressed or made "sterile" (LtA 57) by the voyeuristic stance toward what is being represented.[42]

The republican festival, by contrast, is to be a demonstration of the community's moral unity, of the ties that bind it together. Its mode is shared joy, not solitary pleasure. But Rousseau does not simply contrast the theater and the festival as, respectively, institutional forces of separation and unity. Instead he delineates a chiastic structure: Where the one separates, the other unites, and vice versa. For the unity of the republican spectacle implies separations as well, which the theater abolishes: the separation between the sexes and between locals and foreigners. Not only do men and women mingle at the theater, the theater also attracts foreigners. The Genevan republic, by contrast, reveals itself to be a community of brothers – as Derrida would put it, a "fraternocracy"[43] – that excludes women and foreigners, each in a different way: Women cannot even metaphorically be called brothers, and while foreigners can under certain circumstances become friends, they can never become brothers. The spectacle of republican unity is an outward demonstration of "martial spirit" (LtA 135) and an inward demonstration of male dominance.

6. All Brothers are also Men: The Problem of Male Self-Difference

For Rousseau, therefore, the regular festivals have the "explicitly performative function"[44] of manifesting the unity of the republic, confirming and thus sustaining it. A whole series of measures is necessary in order for the festivals to fulfill this function. Not only must the foreigners be excluded and the women excludingly included, but the relationship of the brothers to each other must also be controlled. Here we might recall the ambivalence of the image of a community assembled around a large tree in the *Discourse on the Origin and Foundations of Inequality*. In a community for which, as described in the *Letter to M. D'Alembert*, the festival is its highest expression, the seed of destruction has already been planted. Rousseau describes the transition from the state of nature to society in the second discourse in the following way:

> The human race became more sociable, relationships became more extensive and bonds tightened. People grew used to gathering together in front of their huts or around a large tree; singing and dancing, true progeny of love and leisure, became the amusement, or rather the occupation, of idle men and women thus assembled. Each began to look at the others and to want to be looked at himself; and public esteem came to be prized. He who sang or danced the best; he who was the most handsome, the strongest, the most adroit or the most eloquent became the most highly regarded, and this was the first step towards inequality and at the same time towards vice. From those first preferences there arose, on the one side, vanity and scorn, on the other, shame and envy, and the fermentation produced by these new leavens finally produced compounds fatal to happiness and innocence. (DI 114)

Rousseau goes on to explain that to the same degree that "the rank and destiny of each man" also came to depend on social recognition of qualities such as reason, beauty, virility, and skill, "it soon became necessary either to have them or to feign them. It was necessary in one's own interest to seem to be other than one was in reality [...] Being and appearance became two entirely different things, and from this distinction arose insolent ostentation, deceitful cunning and all the vice that follow in their train" (DI 119).

According to Rousseau, the social esteem accorded to individual deeds also contains a form of inequality in which, on the one hand, the victors regard themselves as more important than the others, thus awakening within them the principle of the love of self (*amour-propre*),[45] and, on the other hand, the losers resort to deception in order to achieve recognition despite their lack of talent. In the long run, according to Rousseau's diagnosis, a culture of recognition that focuses on individual achievement will lead to the decline of the republic. For soon the brothers will no longer know who they are dealing with, at which point brothers will no longer be able to be brothers.[46]

It is true that if we can no longer be certain of others' identity due to our inability to situate them socially, then we must rely on the impression their "performance" makes upon us. We have already seen in the first chapter, however, that our difficulty in categorizing others does not necessarily correspond to a state of skeptical alienation from others, but rather to an insight into what Stanley Cavell has termed the "truth of skepticism": We can never conclusively determine who someone is, rather we can only recognize again and again what they show us of themselves.[47] And the mere fact that we do not let ourselves be pinned down to what tradition has determined for us is not in and of itself a sign of inequality, contrary to what Rousseau suggests, linking the discovery of individual differences to the existence of a competition over already established values. Instead, this merely formulates conditions for social change – for changes that can also affect the values according to which public recognition is granted. I will return to this issue in secs 9 and 10.

What is interesting at this point is the fact that in the second discourse, Rousseau sees the culture of festivals as the source of an ambition that pushes humans' capacity for self-improvement beyond what is necessary for preserving the community. In order to be able to celebrate festivals, therefore, a particularly solid set of morals is required. In *Letter to M. D'Alembert* we find a telling passage in which morals are referred to in the very moment that, on the occasion of the Geneva Summer Games, various shooting and other victors are crowned:

> Good morals [manners] depend more than is thought on each man's being satisfied in his estate. Deceit and the spirit of intrigue come from uneasiness and discontentment; everything goes badly when one aspires to the position of another. One must like his trade to do it well. The disposition of the state is only good and solid when, each feeling in his place, the private forces are united and co-operate for the public good instead of wasting themselves one against the other as they do in every badly constituted sate. This given, what must we think of those who would wish to take the festivals, the pleasures, and every form of amusement away from the people as so many distractions which turn them away from their work? (LtA 126)

For the festivals not to have the corrosive effects described in the Second Discourse, then, all must generally be satisfied with their respective position and their place in the community, for otherwise the spirit of competition will turn into "devouring ambition," and the "dark propensity" of jealousy (DI 119). On the other hand, in order to ensure that such competition does not endanger society's morals, strict attention must be paid to the object of public praise and recognition. A particular type of competition is required in which the battle is not primarily one against another, but rather for the common good – hence the emphasis on military games. Any form of individuation that might develop out of the dynamism of competition is thus contained under the banner of the polity.[48]

That is also why the Genevan festival is about the presentation not of personalities but of personifications.[49] The uniform worn by the soldier during the regiment's dance indicates all too clearly that the republican man who shows "himself" in the festival shows himself as the "individual universal": as citizen/brother. At the same time, the personification, the male embodiment of the militant citizen, should be viewed by Geneva's citizens as something which, as Bettine Menke puts it, "Goethe, Creuzer and others termed symbol."[50] Symbolic perception relies "in a de-rhetoricizing manner on the visibility of the whole in the individual as its appearance."[51]

By contrast, the kind of perception trained by the theater, or the way that strangers or tourists perceive the world, is allegorical. It sees in personification a relation of representation; it recognizes the difference between person and role, signifier and signified. The fact that the symbolic perception of the Genevan festival can be allegorically distorted at all points to the fact that the personification of republican brotherhood is fundamentally threatened by a difference not from an other, but from onself: a division of the male subject into the personification of the universal qua military virtue on the one hand, and that which eludes subsumption under this universal on the other. Rousseau is clearly aware of the self-difference of Genevan men, which is why he regards it as crucial that this difference be kept under control. It is this difference that the rigid republican order of the sexes, with its strict separation between the private and public spheres, seeks to bring under control by externalizing it in a peculiar fashion. For this difference is first projected onto the image of woman, and this image is then banished into the private sphere. Interestingly enough, woman here relates to man not at all as nature does to culture, but instead as allegory does to symbol.[52]

Accordingly, though *Émile* begins with a definition of the difference of the sexes according to which men are "strong and active" and women "passive and weak,"[53] this diagnosis of a "natural" asymmetry immediately leads Rousseau to a second one: Because of her weakness, woman, unlike man, is dependent on social recognition:

> By the very law of nature women are at the mercy of men's judgments. It is not enough that they be estimable; they must be esteemed. It is not enough for them to be pretty; they must please. It is not enough for them to be temperate; they must be recognized as such. Their honor is not only in their conduct but in their reputation; and it is not possible that a woman who consents to be regarded as disreputable can

ever be decent. When a man acts well, he depends only on himself and can brave public judgment; but when a woman acts well, she has accomplished only half of her task, and what is thought of her is no less important to her than what she actually is. From this it follows that the system of woman's education ought to be contrary in this respect to the system of our education. Opinion is the grave of virtue among men and its throne among women.[54]

From Rousseau's perspective, it becomes all the more necessary for women, who in their "naturally" external orientation throne over public opinion, be relegated to the private sphere. Because women by their very nature embody the difference between person and role, their impudent entry into the public sphere represents the beginning of the end of male virtue. Ultimately women will infect men with the feminine principle of the dissociation of reality and appearance, person and role, in short, with the bottomlessness and the shallowness of public opinion. This is precisely what Rousseau means when he remarks that the licentiousness of the actor (his lack of substance) will ultimately follow "in the wake" (LtA 81) of the licentiousness of the actress (her immodesty). Having been plunged into the allegorizing, feminine light of public opinion, it can be plainly seen that even men – the true citizens of Geneva – have never only or never completely been brothers/citizens. That is the true scandal for Rousseau. The reason that immodest women are a threat to the community is not because they try to be like men, but because they expose the latter's latent self-difference.[55]

Various critics have pointed out the proximity between Rousseau's vision of the festival and that of the polity.[56] A passage in the First Discourse (in the famous oration of Fabricius) that is emblematic of Rousseau's oeuvre in general accordingly calls the "assembly of two hundred virtuous men, worthy of commanding Rome and governing the Earth," "the most noble sight [*spectacle*] that has ever appeared beneath the heavens" (DSA 11). Like Rousseau's ideal of the republican festival, his ideal of collective self-government presupposes that there are no false bottoms, that everyone knows with whom he is dealing – with a brother/citizen whose sole interest is in the common good. For sovereignty is predicated on a strict separation between the individual's particular will and the citizen's general will. The sovereignty of the republic (which the festivals celebrate and affirm) thus depends not only on the exclusion of the foreigners' allegorical gaze and the women's exhibition of self-difference, but also on the separation of general will and particular will: "For either the will is general," Rousseau writes in *The Social Contract*, "or it is not; it is either the will of the body of the people, or that of only a part. In the first case the declaration of this will is an act of sovereignty and constitutes law; in the second case it is merely a particular will."⁵⁷ No remainder of the private man is to cling to the citizens as they assemble. Instead, the particular will and the general will must be relegated in a completely transparent manner to two different spheres. It is there that they can have their place; they should attain objectivity in the private and the public sphere. But then everything depends on whether the one can indeed be "distinguished clearly" from the other (SC 61). This is the question *The Social Contract* addresses – and the problem that besets it.

7. The Two Paradoxes of the Social Contract

The human being in the state of nature, who is subjected only to the law of self-preservation, still lacks "the faculty of self-improvement" (DI 88). This also means that human beings in the state of nature are only good to the degree that they are still subhuman.⁵⁸ The formation of the specifically human "faculty of self-improvement" (or the discovery of humans' perfectability – *perfectibilité* is Rousseau's term) only emerges upon humans' exit from the economy of pure self-preservation. Although it derives from the dynamic of the satisfaction of needs, this dynamic drives human beings to attain a new level of existence. For the moment that nature places obstacles in the path of the simple satisfaction of needs, human beings, as Rousseau claims in the Second Discourse, are forced to be inventive and cooperate with others. The moment that humans discover their freedom in relation to nature is also the moment of their association, the birth of their consciousness of history, and thus also their consciousness of possibilities.⁵⁹ Now, according to Rousseau, the capacity for perfection need not only be viewed as a specifically human capacity, for humans also differ from merely instinct-driven animals by virtue of their freedom to "deviate from the laws" (cf. DI 87). On Rousseau's view, therefore, this must also be recognized as a danger for human beings, for they can also suffer a "prejudice" (ibid.) as a result of their deviation from the rules. "There are," as Leo Strauss summarizes the problem with which Rousseau's *Du contrat social* begins, "no natural obstacles to man's almost unlimited progress or to his power of liberating himself from evil. For the same reason, there are no natural obstacles to man's almost unlimited degradation. Man is by nature almost infinitely malleable."⁶⁰ This dangerously malleable, unlimited, and indeterminate freedom goes hand in hand with the danger of social inequality (and hence of the reversal of freedom into unfreedom – the danger that the social contract seeks to avert. The aim is to "find a form of association that will defend and protect the person and goods of each associate with the full common force, and by means of which each, uniting with all, nevertheless obey only himself and remain as free as before" (SC 49f.). The attainment of this end requires that unlimited and indeterminate or, as Rousseau also says, "natural freedom," be transformed into a limited and determinate, a "civil freedom" (SC 54, cf. also 56).

The "act of association" (SC 50) meant to resolve this problem accordingly consists in nothing less than the "total alienation of each associate with all of his rights to the whole community" (SC 50). According to this act, freedom can only mean collective freedom; the individual is from this point on subordinated to the community.[61] Rousseau concedes that man may have a "particular will contrary to or different from the general will" (SC 52); however, Rousseau does not search for the solution to this problem in a dynamic mediation between both sides, but in a strict hierarchy. In this regard, the social contract is without both irony and mercy: "For the social compact not to be an empty formula, it tacitly includes the following engagement which alone can give force to the rest, that whoever refuses to obey the general will shall be constrained to do so by the entire body: which means nothing other than that he shall be forced to be free; for this is the condition which, by giving each Citizen to the Fatherland, guarantees him against all personal dependence" (SC 53). A man's particular will shall thus be subjected to the general will of the citizen, or, if need be, forced into subjection. This means that "what man loses by the social contract is his natural freedom and an unlimited right to everything that tempts him and he can reach; what he gains is civil freedom and property in everything he possesses" (SC 53f.).

Yet a logical problem arises already with regard to the act of association, a problem even the spontaneity and immediacy supposedly characteristic of this act[62] cannot quite cover up: How is the individual supposed to give himself over to the community when this community does not yet exist? The act of alienation from the polity presupposes the existence of the same general will that supposedly only comes into being as the result of this act.[63] The individual would have to already possess the general will the association is supposed to engender. Rousseau himself remarks upon this problem in a later passage,[64] where the issue is no longer the act of association but the maintenance of the body politic by means of laws: "For a nascent people to be capable of appreciating sound maxims of politics and of following the fundamental rules of reason of State, the effect would have to become the cause, the social spirit which is to be the work of the institution would have to preside over the institution itself, and men would have to be prior to laws what they ought to become by means of them" (SC 71). Here we are dealing with a paradox similar to that of Kant's moral principle, which I discussed in ch. 2.[65] The origin of this problem, however, is found in the work of Rousseau. And because Rousseau, contrary to Kant, conceives of the principle of self-government collectively, this principle appears on two levels: first, on the level of the constitution of the general will that must precede the individual and yet also follow from the act of association; second, on the level of its preservation through collective self-legislation: The collective is presupposed as a lawless agent who lays down laws for himself on the basis of laws that precede legislation and yet are also supposed to follow from this legislation. The paradox thus appears to concern both the foundation of the association and the latter's justification.

Indeed, as Rousseau himself admits, a metaleptic inversion of cause and effect would be required to dispose of two problems, one of which arises, he writes, during the constitution of the general will, the other during its legislative maintenance: "Individuals see the good they reject, the public wills the good it does not see" (SC 68). So even if the first paradox, that of foundation, had been overcome by a developmental leap, even if the state of civil freedom in which the individuals disregard their particular wills in the name of a presupposed general will, there would be no guarantee that the public thus formed would already be capable of good government. "For the initial act by which this assumes form and unity still leaves entirely undetermined what it must do to preserve itself" (SC 66). Problems arise at this level as well: "How will a blind multitude, which often does not know what it wills because it rarely knows what is good for it, carry out an undertaking as great, as difficult as a system of legislation? By itself the people always wills the good, but by itself it does not always see it" (SC 68).

Rousseau regards education as the solution to this problem – even "tutelage," which is certainly surprising for a theorist of popular sovereignty: "The first [the individuals] must be obligated to conform their wills to their reason; the other [the public] must be taught to know what it wills" (ibid.). This proposal for solving both paradoxes appears at first sight to amount to an inversion of autonomy in heteronomy. As Jean Starobinski remarks, "we can indeed say that it is a ridiculous form of freedom to be the master of what one *wills* when others determine *what* we should will and prescribe the object that our will is to pursue."[66] In the precarious figure of the legislator, an external authority is called upon to rescue the internal sovereignty of the people (to form and preserve it).

The fact that Rousseau felt that an entity – a crowd or a public – resolved to form a general will could still want the wrong thing shows just how conscious he was of the sweeping power of legislation when it comes to actually constituting the general will, to the association of a people as a people. For what is a will without its object? Can a diffuse good intention already be called a "will"? It seems logical to conclude that there is no general will (rather only a blinded crowd or a public that does not know what it wants) beyond the representation of the general will in the form of the constitution. Only by the act of legislation, by the substantive commitment to the general will, does a people constitute itself as a people. Only through this act of commitment does a people that is presupposed as the author of a constitution actually become a people. This is true in spite of the fact that Rousseau initially presents this matter just the other way around: The transformation of natural freedom into civil freedom presupposes laws that give substance to the general will. The general will does not, therefore, first exist and then lay down laws for itself; rather, a legislator dictates laws which then bring forth the general will. It is thus no accident that Rousseau also charges the legislator with the task of educating the individuals to subordinate their particular wills to the general will. "Although law does not regulate morals, legislation does give rise to them" (SC 141).

It is also because of the primacy of laws over the volonté générale that the legislator must perform the superhuman act of, "so to speak, changing human nature...of substituting a partial and moral existence for the independent and physical existence we have all received from nature" (SC 69). To do so, the legislator must

> take from man his own forces in order to give him forces which are foreign to him and of which he cannot make use without the help of others. The more these natural forces are dead and destroyed, the greater and more lasting are the acquired ones, and the more solid and lasting also is the institution: So that when each Citizen is nothing and can do nothing except with all the others, and the force acquired by the whole is equal or superior to the sum of the natural forces of all the individuals, the legislation may be said to be at the highest pitch of perfection it can reach. (SC 69)

For the legislator to be capable of effecting this enormous transformation in his pupils, he himself must of course not be determined by his particular will. This, Rousseau writes, would strictly speaking "require a superior intelligence who saw all of man's passions and experienced none of them, who had no relation to our nature yet knew it thoroughly" (SC 68). As Rousseau himself sees clearly, this is a condition only a god could meet. For this task to be performed by a human being, then, requires not only extraordinary "genius" (SC 44), but also an institutional provision: The office of the legislator must have "nothing in common with human empire."[67] For if the legislator were at once also prince, Rousseau argues, "he could never avoid having particular views vitiate the sanctity of his work" (SC 70). Yet of course the question remains: How can we know that no trace of a particular will, of passions in fact remains in the legislator? He, too, is after all a mere human being. Who educates the educator?[68] The paradox of the foundation of the general will thus recurs in the figure of the legislator. And this problem affects not only the status of the laws for education, but even the act of legislation itself.

8. The Sovereignty of the Legislator and the Judgment of the "Common Man"

The legislator, Rousseau emphasizes, should have "no legislative right" (SC 70) himself; this right rests with the people, or else it would no longer make sense to speak of popular sovereignty. The legislator, then, is dependent on the judgment of the people as the agency that exercises this sovereignty. The legislator can merely convince the people, which are to decide on the legislative proposal by "free suffrage" (ibid.) of the positive qualities of his draft. And here arises the "further difficulty" that such a draft is animated by "a thousand kinds of ideas [...] which it is impossible to translate into the language of the people" (ibid.). In order to nonetheless persuade the people of his work, the legislator must employ sleight of hand. To secure the recognition of the "vulgar men" (SC 71) for his legislation, the legislator should "have recourse to an authority of a different order, which might be able to rally without violence and to persuade without convincing" (ibid.): the divine. The legislator must place his decisions "in the mouth of the immortals, in order to rally by divine authority those whom human prudence could not move" (ibid.). This rhetorical operation is the "instrument" that the legislator uses so that "people, subject to the laws of the state as to those of nature, and recognizing the same power in the formation of man and in that of the city, freely obey the yoke of public felicity, and bear it with docility" (ibid.).[69] The willing obedience of the people is therefore nothing but the result of manipulation. By masking the human text to make it appear as the word of God, the finite and contingent work of one or more human beings takes on the appearance of eternal and unchangeable law. The laws of the state appear as laws of nature with divine origin. In the name of God, what is and should be, perception and prescription, fact and law, become one.[70]

There is thus little room for the judgment of the everyday citizen; judgment is reserved for the supreme authority. In reality, the rhetorical subterfuge of placing the human word "in the mouth of the immortals" – here we are dealing with *prosopopoeia*[71] – aims to exclude, or at least constrain, the possibility that the conception of the social good held by the "vulgar man" might deviate from that of the legislator. For interestingly enough, the "vulgar man" in Rousseau's construction, though interested in the general will, is incapable of seeing the "true good." In other words, he has not yet made the full transition from the particular to the general will. As we have already said, without a substantive determination, the common will does not (yet) exist; rather, there is only a blind multitude of "vulgar men" with good intentions at best. By allowing the wording of the law to appear as a divine commandment, the unreliable judgment of the "vulgar man" can be eliminated and the blind multitude transformed into a people, the particular wills into the general will. Only to the degree that individual judgments on the social good have been eliminated – which are potentially heterogeneous since they may not have been fully detached from particular wills – can the multitude congeal into a people. In the constitution authorized by God, the blind multitude should recognize what it should always already have willed. By recognizing its own will in the "sacred" constitution, it recognizes itself, and thus the "blind multitude," the ignorant public, becomes a people: the sovereign.

Yet this means that the popular sovereignty that finds expression in the general will is – and this cannot be emphasized enough – nothing but the result of an act of rhetorical subterfuge of which, as Rousseau himself notes, any vulgar demagogue is capable: "Any man can carve tablets of stone, bribe an oracle, feign secret dealings with some divinity, train a bird to speak in his ear, or find other crude ways to impress the people" (SC 71). Whether the manipulation of the people is justified or not is ultimately dependent on the "great soul of the Lawgiver"; this soul is the "true miracle," which, moreover, must first "prove [its] mission" (ibid.). Yet the good legislator who seeks to deceive the people into the truth nevertheless employs sleight of hand, no less than the vulgar demagogue. What this sleight of hand achieves is not merely the repression or concealment of a sovereignty on which popular sovereignty rests – that of the legislator – but also the repression or concealment of the problem of this sovereignty's legitimacy.

The legitimacy of the legislator and its laws does not seem to be a problem for Rousseau, because he simply posits the legislator as a divine authority which possesses the knowledge of what is truly good. He thus cannot see that there is a second rhetorical operation at work beneath this rhetorical operation. Rhetoric, after all, is in play not only where the work of a human mind is presented in the guise of divine provenance, but already when this work, be it of one or a few, signs in everyone's name – in the name of the ("good") general will. This, too, is a sleight of hand, a subterfuge of sorts: For to speak "in the name of the people" is also "nothing but" rhetoric. It is another instance of the rhetorical figure called *prosopopoeia*. This "constitutes the speaking subject that appears in retrospect to have been there all along."[72] The people that is supposedly the "author" (SC 68) of the laws, and that thus exists before the laws, only receives a unified face and voice through the law. The *prosopopoeia* of legislation functions effectively to the extent that the term "voice of the people" is taken to be literally referential, that is, as it appears to speak in the word of law. This suppresses the performative dimension of *prosopopoeia* – the act of constituting the subject in the word of the text – or shows it to be a false referential conclusion. Although *prosopopoeia* creates the fiction of a people's voice that is merely (re)presented in the text of the constitution, as a figure, by virtue of its figurativeness, it at once points up what it dissimulates: the inarticulate noise of the vulgar crowd, which can only be heard as an articulate voice through this figure.[73] As a figure, *prosopopoeia* preserves a "veiled reminder" [*Deckerinnerung*][74] of the faceless foreignness of the vulgar multitude that its operation simultaneously dissimulates.

This *prosopopoeia* can obviously be shielded against the disfigurative impulse implicit in its own figurativeness only to the extent that it places the performative act by which the legislator posits the people as his own authority in the mouth of yet another, higher authority: a *prosopopoeia* of *prosopopoeia*. This protective measure, however, is not entirely sufficient. After all, an attitude of disrespect is possible, such as Rousseau recommends at the beginning of *The Social Contract*: "All power comes from God," as Rousseau admits, "but so does all illness. Does this mean it is forbidden to call the doctor?" (SC 44). In our context, to call the doctor would mean calling on another legislator, perhaps because poor and unjust laws demonstrate that the general will formulated by these laws is not merely identified (represented) in the totalizing metaphor of the voice of the people,[75] but arbitrarily identified (posited).[76]

The sovereignty of the legislator, which rhetorically gives the people its voice and face, corresponds to a theatrical setting to which Rousseau is completely opposed. The problems of fictionality, of artificiality, of masks, of (theatrical and political) representation thus appear in the very place where, according to Rousseau, representation must be excluded. For the general will of which Rousseau says that it "cannot be represented" (SC 114) turns out to be the fiction of a legislator. It exists, we might say, only in and by virtue of the performative momentum of its representation, which also means that the "moral person" (SC 61) of the people exists only as a *persona*. Yet this also inevitably reopens the problem of the right of the strongest, which Rousseau's *Social Contract* was designed to resolve in the first place. A constitutive tension obtains between the act of the legislator – insofar as the latter is no more than human and an individual, at best masking his work as the commandment of God – and the universalism that is at the heart of the concept of the general will. This tension cannot be removed from the lives of democracies. At most it can be concealed by second-order deceptions.

For sovereign power and authority are presumed the moment someone steps forward and claims to speak for everyone. Yet the "vulgar men" are helpless against this presumption of power only to the extent that they are blinded by measures designed to conceal the elements of sovereignty and rhetoric entailed by this act. These measures, after all, aim to evade its judgment. The measures intended to deceive the people could only be justified if the legislator truly retained divine superiority over mere mortals. This would justify any trick that would lead the blind out of the darkness of the cave and into the light of the sun. But if we do not agree to this premise, then there is only one way out: an offensive way of dealing with the fact that the general will can only be posited.

The antidote to the principle that "might makes right," to an irreducible presumption of authority at the founding moment – even and especially – of democratic societies, consists not in denying this presumption, but in staging it publicly. It is inevitable that one person speak for all, for without this act, as we have seen, there can be no general will. There can be no general will without rhetoric and sovereignty (in the sense of the presumption of power and rule). But this act can be obligated to respect the democratic principle of participation if he who speaks for everyone else must do so in front of everyone else. He must expose himself and his production to the fearless judgment of the "vulgar man," who has lost his fear of God and who might possibly base his judgment on an alternative conception of the general will. The "vulgar man" is thus also a potential rival to the legislator: an alternative candidate for interpreting the general will. For Plato and for Rousseau, this is what is so scandalous about "theatrocracy." The latter is democratic to the extent that sovereignty is no longer presented as a transcendentally justified power, and thus opens up the question of its legitimacy.[77] As soon as sovereignty speaks to a heterogeneous crowd to which it must justify itself, it loses its immunity and indivisibility. As Derrida writes, "as soon as I speak to the other, I submit to the law of giving reason(s), I share a virtually universalizable medium, I divide my authority."[78] Even under these conditions, a possible miracle of legislation can only be seen after the fact. Whether a miracle has occurred or not depends on whether this legislation is *recognized* (in an enduring fashion) as being legitimate or not.[79] The production of the general will (the *volonté générale*) continues to depend on being recognized by the accumulated individual interests of the crowd or the public (the *volonté de tous*, the collective will) (SC 60). This also means making explicit that there is always a measure of flexibility in the space between representation and the represented, between the will of the people as it is defined by legislation, and the concrete crowd or public represented in this legislation. Democracy stands in a relation of tension between the *demos* as the "vulgar crowd" and *kratia*, the power or strength of sovereignty which continually gives the *demos* its political form, its face. The crowd, as an authority to which sovereignty must justify itself, always has a tense relation to sovereignty.[80] The irreducibly theatrical dimension of this image of democratic politics, in which one person speaks for everyone and produces himself in front of everyone, thereby remaining dependent on the recognition of a public consisting of potential rivals, can only be avoided if the people already possess direct sovereignty, a clear general will.

This, however, can only be the case if the morals, customs, and opinions that should represent the result of legislation are already established and stable, if they are already "graven [...] in the hearts of the Citizens" (SC 81), i.e. only if cause and effect are reversed. This would make the paradox of self-legislation a tautology, for every act of legislation would appear to be identical to the already established morals. Rousseau could not arrive at this solution, for he saw too clearly how unstable morals are. He knew that in real life, women, two-faced by nature and full of love of self (*amour-propre*), come before the sphere of "moral, customs, and above all of opinion" that is so crucial to the "State's genuine constitution" (SC 81). Women are clearly the ones on the "throne of public opinion," and for Rousseau it is more than uncertain whether they will be able to prove themselves over time as the "guardians of our morals" (DI 65). This is just one reason why the commitment of men to the common good is no sure thing in Rousseau's eyes. Rousseau notes resignedly that democracy as he understands it (non-theatrical) is for the gods; it is not suited to men (cf. SC 92). "Even the happiest people in the world" (SC 121) – Rousseau is of course referring to the Swiss – is threatened by decline, which derives from an "inherent and inevitable vice" whose ultimately fatal effects on the political community can never be stopped, only delayed: "Just as the particular will incessantly acts against the general will, so the Government makes a constant effort against Sovereignty [of the people]" (SC 106). When it comes to defending the theatrical aspects of democratic politics, the fact that there can be tension between the particular will and the general will, between the government and the population, is not to be traced back to the downfall of human civilization; rather, it has structural reasons that cast a more optimistic light on democracy's chances of survival. It is true that because the general will cannot exist beyond political representation, it can never exist beyond the simultaneously established division between representatives and the represented, the governors and the governed; it can never exist outside of relations of power and domination. Yet this does not mean that democratic society is doomed to one-dimensional decay; rather, the rhetorical constitution of the general will is also the possibility of its perfection.

9. Another Kind of Equality

If we abandon the premise that the legislator knows the contents of the true general will, then what is true for "vulgar men" is also true for the legislator: Even if we assume the latter to have the best of intentions, it is never certain whether that which the legislator truly believes to be the general will has not in fact been corrupted by a particular will. Since he is also a finite being, he has just as little access to the definition of the true general will as the "vulgar man." His limited, finite perspective on himself and the world necessarily implies the possibility of error. The legislator can be mistaken. It may be that the metaphysical authority in all its shapes must be removed from the act of legislation, that we must renounce the legislator's divinity as well as the lie that his work is in fact the word of God. This does not, however, imply a kind of relativism. In a post-metaphysical and thus openly theatrical democracy, whether a given construction of the general will in fact fulfills its claim to generality can be determined, on the one hand, according to the recognition, or lack thereof, that the positing of the general will receives among the heterogeneous public; on the other hand, it can be determined according to whether this recognition of a given version of the general will endures. In this sense, every claim to generality refers to the dimension of intersubjectivity and historicity. To the extent that morals can change, so can the concept of the general will.

Now, Rousseau knows all too well that if one is not careful, morals can change faster than one thinks – due to the construction of a theater, for instance. But that is more than just an example, for, as we have seen, there is more at stake in the transformation of the republican festival community into an urbane theater society than just some change of morals. For this is a change of morals in which the principle of changeability itself gains recognition. As soon as respectable Genevan women follow the example of the immodest actresses and show themselves in public – outside of the republican balls – they will infect the men with the feminine principle of self-difference. Citizens will turn into ironists, and nobody will know anymore whether everyone is truly in their rightful place, or whether in fact they secretly long to occupy an entirely different position. The social order of the republic, with its clear assignment of positions and the correspondingly clear identifiability of its members, thereby encounters a potentiality that exercises internal pressure on the order.

This potentiality finds public expression, as we have seen, in concealing irony. Concealing irony allows us to publicly demonstrate that we are not at one with our social appearance. It is a way of distancing ourselves from our social identities, for which we have educated ourselves and without which we would in fact be nothing, i.e. not subjects, yet without committing ourselves to an alternative identity. By merely demonstrating that we are not what we say and show, concealing irony points to the everything-and-nothing of pre-subjective potentiality in the (non-)foundation of all social identity. We could also say it points to the fact that humans are "infinitely malleable," to humans' potential to change their position or invent new identities and thus reconstruct the social – all because they can be influenced by their environment. In other words, concealing irony stands for humans' "faculty"– which Rousseau both admired and feared – for improving themselves and their society (cf. DI 88).

Irony is not, therefore, an expression of egomaniacal pride (which for Rousseau is the psychological complement to a society defined by inequality), nor is it a necessary part of love of self (*amour-propre*). Irony, again, is not a form of deception; when we are ironic we do not lie for our own advantage; we do not misrepresent the truth. Irony – like the possibility of deception – is instead the hallmark of a society in which an individual's social position is no longer determined by tradition. The fact that we can no longer know in advance where to locate others in the social hierarchy only makes explicit that we do not grasp others in the mode of knowledge. We can only recognize, again and again, what others show us of themselves (however ironically distorted such displays might be). These conditions do not suffice in and of themselves to form an unequal society.[81] On the contrary, the insight into the (non-) foundation of all social existence implies a figure of equality, which, however, is diametrically opposed to the republican model of fraternal equality, for it represents human beings' equal potentiality. This is a radical kind of equality that includes all human beings, regardless of their social determinations (thus also including foreigners and women). But it is at the same time a radically indeterminate equality that can never appear positively and thus cannot be accounted for as such in the concretion of legal or political decisions. As unconditional equality, however, it remains the condition of the possibility of changing the conditional, finite, and determinate concepts and forms that equality takes on in democratic practices.

Because we are equal in the sense that we can never determine in advance what our subjectivity is and can be, but can only form it through a mimetic relation to others and otherness, every community of brothers also remains confronted with the dimension of the other in itself. The possibility of the event of the other in oneself – both in the individual member of the republic and in the political community as a whole – does not depend on the size of the republic, as Rousseau suggests when he repeatedly describes his ideal of a small community in which everybody knows everybody (cf. e.g. SC 73f., 91; DI 57). Because the members of a community are always potential non-members, the equality of social membership, whether it be determined by the principle of fraternity or by another principle, can always be put in question. This possibility is always there, even in the smallest province somewhere at the foot of the Alps, for as Rousseau was well aware, it is an implication of the fact that humans are "infinitely malleable" beings. Now, we can view this possibility in different ways. We can, like Rousseau, do everything to keep it under control, or we can explicitly recognize it as the possibility of change and historicity.

10. A Politicizable Boundary

It is by recognizing this fact that, in my view, democracy begins. It begins with the insight that we can never completely know our neighbors, our brothers, nor even ourselves, because we are influenced in a discontinuous manner by changing circumstances and accidental opportunities. We not only let ourselves be affected by them, we can also adapt to them. Democracy begins with the awareness that we can only achieve unity of self through repeated experiences of self-difference. In this self-difference, the social identity we have adopted by means of imitation becomes open to an external impulse which faces us with an other in our self, i.e. with desires we can neither derive from our previous self-understanding nor simply integrate into it. We have already discussed the desires that fulfill these conditions in previous chapters by employing the term "inner nature."[82] The relation of our inner nature to our social identity is not the relation of a genuine nature to an artificial appearance. It cannot be conceived of as an object (as a kind of core personality); rather, as we have seen, our inner nature only refers to disruptions or irritations in our respective self-understandings. Therefore it is not revealed to us through introspection (as if we only needed to listen within ourselves long enough to hear it), but only in a constellation, i.e. in our interaction with the world. For this reason the expressions of the subject's inner nature, which always have an event-like character, can challenge it to examine and even correct its current self-interpretation. Regardless of whether our experiences of self-difference lead us to reaffirm or revise our previous self-understanding, at this point it is important to recognize that without experiences of a difference within ourselves, there could be no self-determination, rather only blind imitation. The experience of self-difference is a constitutive element of our freedom (though it should not be equated with freedom itself).

We therefore understand freedom in a sense that contradicts what Rousseau regards as the indicator of freedom in the "civil state." In this state, "the voice of duty succeeds physical impulsion and right succeeds appetite" (SC 53). This kind of rigorousness is undermined by the understanding of freedom I have just outlined.[83] Unlike Rousseau's citizen, the modern democrat defended here does not first "consult his reason before listening to his inclinations" (SC 53), rather he listens to his inclinations before he consults his reason. "Listening to" does not necessarily mean following his inclinations – the democrat is not a slave to impulse.[84] Instead, he is always already involved in an ethical life that provides him criteria for judging his own desires. These criteria, however, are not stable, transcendentally confirmed truths enabling the subject to decide, sovereignly and categorically, to abandon his desires. Instead, the criteria, beliefs, and habits we adopt from others can be affected by other, new and foreign influences. That is why there can be cases in which a desire that has been set free by an external impulse can lead to a reflection at the end of which we might (not must) revise these criteria.

Furthermore, this implies that in the course of a self-determined life, we constantly stand in a tense relationship to the social practices in which we are involved.[85] Because human rationality cannot be kept free of its nature without robbing humans of the freedom necessarily bound up with the idea of rational self-determination, not only are the respective principles and moral beliefs by which individuals determine their actions essentially contested, but so is the concept of the social good that defines the practices in which they are involved. This also contradicts Rousseau's intuitions, for it entails that the particular will in a democracy can never be wholly separated from the general will, nor the private sphere from the public sphere. Instead, the border between both is always up for renegotiation. It can be politicized from two different directions: not only by the State that occasionally defends and enforces its concept of the general will against particular wills, but also by individuals who occasionally assert a different concept of the general will against that of the State.

Concealing irony, which publicly introduces something non-public into the public sphere,[86] also points to this fundamental politicizability. For precisely this reason, Rousseau judges concealing irony to be just as scandalous as the society that cultivates it. In the irony-friendly and theater-friendly Parisian society, Rousseau sees what happens when what was previously relegated to the private sphere now enters into the public sphere. This does not merely lead to a change of positions, but to a fundamental restructuring of the entire order, altering the meaning of both the private and the public sphere. Precisely this possibility of a position-change revealed by concealing irony, and thus also the possibility of shifting the border between the private and the public, between particular wills and the general will, is an essential characteristic of democratic societies. The fact that democracy allows this possibility "like freedom itself,"[87] is the reason why democratic government, as Rousseau is aware, "tends so strongly and so constantly to change its form" (SC 92). Contrary to Rousseau, who concludes that under these conditions the virtuousness, constancy, and strength of a god is required to preserve the original form of democracy (ibid.), we must take seriously that mutability and flexibility are essential characteristics of democratic societies.

To say that the border between the private and the public, the particular will and the general will can shift, and that the content of what this border divides can also change, does not mean that this delineation itself is obsolete and can make way for a diffuse zone in which nothing can be clearly distinguished from anything else. There can be no political equality and no justice if there is no defined border between public and private affairs. However, this border – like the general will upon which it is based – is always merely the product of a sovereign decision: "[T]he sovereign is alone judge" on the question of which "portion of his power, his goods, his freedom" "each man alienates" and which "the community" is then "able to use," and which portion he may retain for himself (SC 61). As we have seen, the people are not the true sovereign here, rather the legislator. The people appear in two different shapes, both as the product of the constitution that gives the people a face and a will, and as the "vulgar crowd" in which each individual element (in the best case) may follow the general will, but (like the sovereign itself) cannot know once and for all what the genuine, truly general will is. This means that what is taken to be the general will in each case can be influenced by the different particular wills. To the extent that sovereignty remains dependent upon the recognition of the crowd, this is the condition of the possibility of its transformation.

11. The Two Bodies of the People

"It is initially the people, and not the king, that has a double body," as Jacques Rancière's suggestive formulation goes.[88] It is, of course, standard procedure in a democracy to bring the sovereign onto the stage; this is also how Claude Lefort distinguishes between the democratic and monarchical understanding of sovereignty.[89] Whereas the sovereignty of the monarch is based on the fictitious unity of his divine-human double body, a unity that gives its sovereignty "transcendental reality, objective truth and godlike existence,"[90] in a democracy this unity is constitutively fragmented. In a democracy the position of sovereign power is occupied by mortals who must justify their claim to power to an audience of other mortal, potential rivals. Here the justification of power of the sovereign is solely based on its performance and how it represents itself. In an insightful reading of Shakespeare's King Richard II, Ernst Kantorowicz describes this development as a "metamorphosis from the realism to the nominalism" of sovereignty.⁹¹ The "reality" with which a monarch justifies its sovereign power with regard to an absolute, otherworldly pole that legitimates both the position of the king and the hierarchical order and unity of the kingdom, pales in a democracy "to a nothing, a *nomen*."⁹² We could also say that reality is degraded into a second-order rhetorical trick. Claude Lefort sees here the outlines of "the revolutionary and unprecedented feature of democracy," which consists in the fact that "the locus of power is an empty place," such that "no individual and no group can be consubstantial with it."⁹³ Due to the collapse of faith in a transcendentally legitimated power and a quasi-natural order based on an absolute foundation, sovereign power in a democracy can only be seen as a "purely symbolic" authority, that is, as a rhetorical authority.⁹⁴ Nevertheless, as Lefort emphasizes, this authority remains the "agency by virtue of which society apprehends itself in its unity."⁹⁵ Now the society views itself in the mirror of its political representation and it is aware of this mediation. Democratic society is thus a society that "undermines the representation of an organic totality" and is aware of the "social nature of society": "[N]either the state, the people nor the nation represent substantial entities. Their representation is itself, in its dependence upon a political discourse and upon a sociological and historical elaboration, always bound up with ideological debate."⁹⁶

Rancière cautions, however, that we should not conclude that democracy already begins with the overthrowing of the monarch. After all, there remains the temptation of putting the people in the position of the deposed sovereign, with a fictitious totality and with the praise of the "glorious body of the people" that inherits the transcendent power of the monarch.⁹⁷ Democracy, according to Rancière, begins with the end of this more or less openly totalitarian fiction. It begins with the consciousness of an "original division"⁹⁸ of the people in a politically constituted popular body on the one hand, and its necessary supplement on the other hand, which in Rancière's terms "displaces any social identification."⁹⁹ What is being referred to here is the indissoluble duality between the face of the people, which it receives in and through political representation, and the facelessness of the "vulgar" people in its (non-)shape as "indefinite plurality."¹⁰⁰

The surplus of the "vulgar people" over all of its political determinations, which Rancière defines formally as the "count of the uncounted – or the part of those who have no part"¹⁰¹ – would remain unexplained as long as we did not reconnect it to the anthropological fact of the two bodies of its (non-)members. The reason that the people cannot completely be congruent with its political representations is that its individual members cannot simply be identified with certain places, positions, or roles. Therefore, there can only be a political unity, which always implies a certain social order, in the form of political representation. For the same reason, there is always a possibility of a change in the criteria according to which the general will is determined, and thus also according to which it is determined what or who has which significance for the community and what or who has none. As necessary as it is to determine the general will, for without such a determination – in the mode of indifference – there can be no equality and no justice, its content nevertheless remains fundamentally disputed. Because the freedom of social membership is always related to elements of a freedom from social membership, and because only a life that knows both sides and mediates between them can be viewed as truly free, the democratic value of equality must also be regarded as having a dual character. On the one hand, equality signifies the equality of the members of a community that is determined by the general will (in their roles as citizens and in their corresponding role as private persons); on the other hand, equality refers to the equality of their potentiality (the possibility of distancing themselves from their public and private roles).

This last form of equality (potentiality) can, as we have already indicated, never appear in a positive form. For such an appearance would imply a definite shape that would contradict the notion of potentiality. The equality of potentiality thus only manifests itself in the moments of uncertainty that arise when the given determination of the general will and of political equality is shaken by the emergence of a new political subjectivity, a new politicization of the line between particular will and general will, the private and the public. Such moments are, with regard to the political determination of the polity, just as event-like as the expressions of inner nature with regard to the self-understanding of its members. What appears publicly and with a public claim here is something that can be neither derived from the concept of the general will nor integrated into it, because it previously counted as something of merely private interest, or at least not of general interest – be it the interests of workers, women, or other "queers," in the sense that they do not fit in with the given determination of the general will.

The fact that democracy accounts for the possibility of reformulating the general will, and thus re-determining the *demos*, can also be seen in its commitment to human rights. The history of human rights, in my view, conveys this structural tension, for human rights refer to humans in a way that goes beyond their given determinations. Even if human rights can only be realized as civil rights, this does not mean, contrary to Giorgio Agamben's claim, that human rights are de facto identical with civil rights and thus necessarily corrupted by the nation-state. It would be more accurate to say that the effects of human rights can only unfold on the level of civil rights. Because the equality of human potentiality can never assume a positive shape, it cannot be taken account of as such. The only way we get sight of human rights is in the highly indirect manifestations of this equality, which can be seen when a given determination of political equality is shaken by the claim to recognition raised by those who have been previously excluded. This means that the discourse on human rights always marks a crisis of civil rights. The way out of the crisis, however, can only lead us back to the level of civil rights, to their re-definition (be it of their content or their scope). Whereas Agamben takes the ambiguity in the title of the declaration of human rights in 1789 – *déclaration des droits de l'homme et du citoyen* – as an indication of the fact that human rights can only be accorded to humans to the degree that "man is the immediately vanishing ground (who must never come to light as such) of the citizen," I understand this ambiguity as the expression not of an ideologically concealed relationship of identity, but as a relationship of tension that keeps the concept of the citizen open for the possibility of its political renewal.[102]

Just as their inner nature can move individuals to undergo a process of self-critique and self-transformation, which can not only lead to a new self-understanding but also to its politicization in the struggle for recognition, the event-like emergence of a new political subjectivity can lead to a reformulation of the general will. Both at the level of self-government and at the level of government, however, this is not necessarily always the case. It can also happen that the old meaning of the general will is successfully defended against the political demand of a new subjectivity – such as in the case of the fundamentalist idea of a theocracy that contradicts democracy's openness to the future and its perfectability.[103] And there can also be misestimations and false decisions that must later be revised. However, this reminder of the revisability of decisions does not deny the finality that political decisions may have for those affected (e.g., the imprisoned or the deported).

Nevertheless, it is an essential structural feature of democracy that the general will remains open to efforts to perfect it and that the *demos* can always take on new faces. If such transformations take place, then they belong neither in the "beyond" of civil rights nor to the civil order. Instead they characterize a shift of or in this order. This is the dynamic of democratic politics, provided it deserves this name at all.

12. Representation and the Coding of Contingency

Democracy is a form of government that has abandoned the idea of a "good order of rule." A democratic society is a society that no longer upholds the claim to ever be able to be completely "in agreement with itself."[104] This is not only made apparent by the fact that governments are aware that they depend on the consent of a heterogeneous public – which means that the legitimacy of a democratic government does in fact stand and fall with its popularity (a horrible thought for critics of aestheticization). I will return to this issue in the following chapter (sec. 7). In terms of system theory, it can also be seen in the "re-coding of political power," by way of what Niklas Luhmann calls the "code" of government and opposition.[105] Whereas the monarchical system cannot allow the supreme power to be undermined in any way and must veil the character of power as power (through second-order lies), power in democracy is apparent as such. Whereas in the monarchy any weakening, i.e. any characterization of power as mere power, would necessarily provoke its violent overthrow, modern democracies have included the possibility of a change in power in the form of government itself. Democracy, according to Luhmann,

> grasps the pinnacle of the system as the starting point for integrating other possibilities, for making the entire system contingent, because it is at the pinnacle that the crucial decisions are made (and of course always will be). Therefore, this is the point at which the incumbent rulers *or other rulers as well* can be considered. What is important is that the change in government be peaceful and regulated by procedures.[106]

What is remarkable here is not just the fact that in a democracy the problem of succession is resolved in a peaceful manner. Even more remarkable, as Luhmann emphasizes, is the "*simultaneous* presence of government and opposition in all political decisions."[107] This does not, of course, relativize the power of the government; it occupies all offices in which collectively binding decisions are made. Nevertheless, the opposition "reflects" the contingency of these decisions by representing a constant alternative to them.[108] What is decisive here is the fact that contrary to an absolutist monarchy, in which the divine-human double body of the monarch has the sole privilege of invoking the values of justice and the well-being of the people, in a democracy both the government and the opposition can make such appeals. In a democracy, therefore, different interpretations of the general will compete – a fact that Rousseau had to reject due to his assumption of the possibility of an unmediated general will.[109] In other words, it is crucial that the form of the parliamentary duality of government and opposition reflect the possibility of disagreement about the general will. Yet the description of the form of this opposition or this disagreement tells us nothing about its quality. In fact, here, the main point is the structural (not substantive) meaning of parliamentary opposition. The point is that in democracies, the principle of this dispute about the meaning of the general will is kept present whenever the government makes decisions. This is what distinguishes a democracy not only from a monarchy, but also from one-party states, in which the contingency of political decisions is at most reflected by a non-state opposition. But in these cases, the reflection remains external to the decisions of government and is unwanted. Because democracies institutionalize the possibility of a dispute over the general will, they give non-parliamentary opposition a different status, viz. that of a further authority that is allowed and even expected to publicly embody the contingency of the decisions made by the government. It is only logical, therefore, that the line between non-parliamentary and parliamentary opposition is blurry.

This should already make apparent that when we refer to the parliamentary double-headedness of government and opposition, we are not claiming that they reflect two different bodies of the people. The indeterminate *demos* cannot be represented. Instead, it upholds the tension between itself and all possible versions of the general will, which is why independent political positions represented neither by the government nor by the parliamentary opposition can always arise. Furthermore, this is the structural reason for why all interpretations of the general will remain fundamentally open to revision. Yet, the reflection of the contingency of all political decisions, be it by means of an institutionalized parliamentary opposition or in the form of an explicitly permitted non-parliamentary opposition, keeps this fact present at the level of government. Moreover, the government must be regularly confirmed by the people, which takes place in elections. Complementary to Rousseau's dream of regular public assemblies in which the – presupposed – "sovereign body" confirms and stabilizes itself with total transparency (cf. SC 111, 112), modern democracy is borne by the institution of periodic free – and secret – elections. Precisely because the people can never completely coincide with the representations of its will by the government, the – in Luhmann's terms – "decisionary deeds" of the government and the alternative demands of the parliamentary opposition must periodically subject themselves to the judgment of a heterogeneous public.

The fact that elections are secret is what protects them from being controlled by those in power, thus securing the openness of the system as a whole to the future. Elections prevent the justification of the preservation of power by the exercise of power, or the attainment of power by the critique of power. Due to regular free and secret elections, "politics is confronted with an uncertain future."[110] This is also what preserves the political nature of the political system. It is by means of elections, according to Luhmann, that the system guarantees "the unknown quality of its own future, thus assuring that political operations cannot be calculated, but must be made in the form of decisions."[111]

The fact that democracy reckons with an uncertain future and is therefore necessarily defined by "fluctuations," does not mean that democracy can no longer be understood in terms of "the concept of domination, i.e. as the enforceability of a will," as arbitrariness.[112] Perhaps this is true if we understand arbitrariness to mean absolute arbitrariness – such that the question can arise "whether 'arbitrariness' empirically exists at all."[113] Every political decision intervenes in a given framework (and thus under certain conditions); it is always subject to a certain amount of time pressure and must justify itself. But these conditions cannot relativize the element of decision inherent in political and legal decision-making. The element of decision or, in precisely this sense, arbitrariness cannot be removed from a democracy.[114] Democracy replaces sovereignty not with the management of contingency – democratic politics does not abandon sovereign rule and "refound itself" on fluctuation.[115] Rather, the reflection on contingency and the openness to the future, and thus the mutability of democratic societies, are a sign of the fact that the inevitable element of sovereignty at the foundation of every political decision is clearly recognized as such in the dimension of its structural arbitrariness.

Individual governments, however, must represent their decisions as being as non-contingent as possible in order to be able to legitimate them. The individual or the group of individuals who claim to articulate the general will must erase any trace of their particular will; they must therefore distinguish themselves from the rest of society. In order to stabilize this difference and thus itself, power seeks "to be perceived as an *other*"; it "multiplies the signs of its transcendence. It seeks to glorify itself and to embody the majesty of the law, the greatness of the universal and the legitimacy of force."[116] This manner of marking difference is also expected of those who hold power in a democracy – these are entirely inevitable rhetorical and theatrical operations. But in a democracy, the staging of the power of the state as an authority of the general will always remains in a relation of tension to the public observation and marking of its factical particularity. Yet, there can of course be a case in which power, in its effort to occupy the space of generality, falls for the staging of its own prestige and affirms itself up to a point at which it itself believes that it does truly "realize or embody the ultimate stage of the social existence [of the true general will]."[117] This is the point at which democracy turns into totalitarianism.

This transformation has its own kind of aesthetic that must now be illuminated more clearly. For it is precisely the aesthetic of totalitarianism that we most likely associate with the talk of the aestheticization of the political. This association goes back to Walter Benjamin's discussion of fascist mass assemblies in his famous essay "The Work of Art in the Age of Mechanical Reproduction." The fact that there can be various constellations of the aesthetic and the political, even constellations that conflict with an openly theatrical democracy, once again explicitly indicates that the critique of aestheticization is not merely a critique of the aesthetic in general, but an argumentative complex in which specific aesthetic, ethical, and political motives are combined. To investigate this complex not only means decoding the problems underlying the intertwining of these motifs, i.e. uncovering the theory of freedom at the core of the critique of aestheticization. Such an investigation also requires that we take a closer look at which kind of aesthetic is affected by the critique of aestheticization. We have already seen in different ways that the anti-aesthetic discourse only problematizes certain types of aesthetic practices, while viewing others as beneficial to the community. Plato, for instance, praised epic narrative for its form, as it – diametrically opposed to theatrical role-playing – preserves the identity of the narrator, and because its virtuous content educates the listeners to develop an identity that conforms to the given order.[118] As we have also just seen, a similarly anti-theatrical, anti-aestheticizing aesthetic can be found in Rousseau's vision of a "Genevan spectacle," which he conceives of not as representation, but strictly as presentation. According to his theory of the festival, its alternative temporality serves to reinforce the social order that it appears to interrupt. Due to the significant influence that Rousseau's critique of the theater has had on twentieth-century theories of democracy, it is no surprise that his anti-aestheticizing aesthetic has also managed to reach into recent modernity. This anti-aestheticizing argumentation has been especially significant in influencing the great avant-garde aesthetic of the theater, for example in Bertolt Brecht's "epic theater" or in Antonin Artaud's "theater of cruelty." Both conceive of a kind of theater which, in different ways, turns against its own theatricality. Again it is Walter Benjamin who develops this connection in his writings on Brecht, thereby employing a perspective that itself is influenced by the anti-aestheticizing tradition. A more detailed discussion of Benjamin seems appropriate, not only because he – along with Schmitt, but almost certainly more prominent – represents a defining figure in the twentieth-century critique of aestheticization. Not least due to his political position, which is contrary to that of Schmitt, Benjamin challenges us to define more precisely the relationship between an accurate critique of the fascist aestheticization of the political and the defense of an openly theatrocratic democracy.

6

The Anaestheticization of the Political in Fascism: Benjamin

The aestheticization of the political cannot be defended as a feature of democratic societies without explicating its relation to the most well-known twentieth-century critique of aestheticization. Of course I am referring to Walter Benjamin's critique of the "aestheticizing of politics, as practiced by fascism."[1] Benjamin views the fascist staging of the crowd as the pinnacle of an "aestheticizing of politics" which responds to the "right" of the proletarian masses "to changed property relations" with an "expression" of the masses (WA 121f.). On the basis of what has already been said, the fascist crowd is supposed to lend expression to the unity of the political community. Everything should serve the ideological expression of the unity between the leader and the people. All distinctions must be eliminated, both the vertical distinction between the representative (leader) and the represented (the people), as well as the horizontal distinction between individual members of the community. Such a totality, however, which excludes any kind of division, can only be realized at an extraordinarily high price. To the degree that power succumbs to the "madness," as Lefort and Gauchet write, of embodying the position of generality and articulating the true general will, power necessarily passes over into the particular: "Instead of the universality to which it lays claim, we only perceive the arbitrariness of rules and decisions, the narrow bias of judgment and the constant resort to brute force."[2] The claim to totality can only be realized through tyranny. This also means that to the same extent that power claims to let the community "appear in its truth," it also drives the community toward "the limits of its dissolution."[3] The contradiction of totalitarianism consists in the fact that "the sought-for elimination of all divisions within society requires a power that separates itself from this society and thereby divides itself between the claim of its transcendence and its [factical] social immanence."[4] The fact that totalitarian rule is "doomed" in spite of "all the compulsory measures at its disposal"[5] does not, however, eliminate the possibility that the totalitarian vision can succeed in reality – even if only temporarily (as history has shown, even that is far too long).

Totalitarian mass assemblies lend expression to the illusion of a society that is identical with the image that power paints of it. It makes the rhetorical production of the community literal, so to speak. The people are supposed to become one with their representation, which is a false referential conclusion. Correspondingly, the people should no longer take up a reflective stance toward the representations of their will (of their self as a people), but perceive themselves in the immediate evidence of the unity created by this representation. In the chapter on Carl Schmitt, we saw (ch. 4, sec. 9) that the ideology of such immediacy does not necessarily contradict the principle of leadership. In our context, we need to recognize that such an ideology does not renounce every form of theater and spectacle; rather, it produces a particular form of theater and spectacle which eliminates the principle of division: The people no longer represent a heterogeneous "vulgar mass," an incalculable multitude which judges politicians' performance, but a homogeneous mass at one with its leader. If there is an audience for this spectacle at all, it stands entirely on the outside – an enemy who can witness such stagings of sovereignty through the media, but not in the ambivalent form of a present stranger. The latter is just as unwelcome here as he was in the case of the military company assembled as an ornament of Rousseau's crowd – a spectacle whose closed unity already bears a resemblance to the frightening image of a totalitarian community.

I will use the term *an*aesthetic to describe the operation which seeks to transform the representation of the people and its will into the immediacy and literalness of a factical community. The phenomenon of desensitizing connoted by this term is entirely intentional. For here we are not only dealing with an aesthetic strategy that desensitizes its own aesthetic nature, i.e. the differences which are a necessary part of any relation of representation. Rather, this aesthetic strategy is also accompanied by an ethical and political desensitizing of the other in one's own.[6] The reason I refer to fascist stagings of unity as a case of anaestheticization rather than of aestheticization is in order to distinguish Benjamin's observations on the fascist expression of the crowd from his overall critique of aestheticization. As I will show in the following, although Benjamin makes an interesting attempt to modify this tradition's central motifs so as to make them compatible with a critique of capitalism and fascism, his loyalty to the tradition of the critique of aestheticization entails problems which once again underline the necessity of taking a differentiated view toward what is termed the "aestheticizing of the political."

1. Charisma versus Ratio

Benjamin's critique of fascist mass assemblies begins somewhat differently than I have described, for it updates Plato's image of the theatrocratic crowd that is fascinated by rhetoric and charisma. What Benjamin criticizes about the fascist crowd is above all their "reactive moment."[7] The problem that arises when the crowd is put under the spell of the leader derives, in the eyes of Benjamin, who makes explicit reference to Plato, from the theatrical arrangement itself, or more specifically, to the separation between the (political) actors and a passive audience. This constellation, as Benjamin writes in an essay on Brecht, is "what the ancients used to call 'theatrocratia': the use of theater to dominate the crowd by manipulating its reflexes and sensations."[8] According to Benjamin, regardless of whether the crowd is spectacularly arranged to face the eyes of the leader or is directed toward a theatrical spectacle, the reactively arranged crowd is by definition "the exact opposite of responsible collectives freely choosing their positions" (ET I 10). The crowd is to remain entrapped in a constellation in which the intellectuality of the individuals can be manipulated by "reflexes and sensations."

As was already pointed out in the discussion of Plato, there are good reasons to question the claim that we can trace the passive stance of the spectator to the theatrical structure of the separation between the actors and the audience.[9] The fascists could make use of the phenomenon of the crowd whose members mutually infect each other with their affects because fascist stagings of unity dim the aesthetic quality of the theatrical scene with its relations of representations and implicit separations. I will return to this point later (sec. 7). Unlike Plato, Benjamin's critique of theatrocracy does not derive from aristocratic reservations about the judging multitude, but rather in the name of this multitude. Benjamin's rejection of aristocratic thought is even more radical than that of Rousseau, whose "Lawgiver" represents a kind of disguised continuation of such thought. Whereas Plato's critique of theatrocracy is combined with an elitist critique of the crowd, which stands in contrast to the idea of the rule of the best (*aristokratia*) defended in *The Republic*, for Benjamin the "vulgar masses" pose no problem whatsoever. On the contrary, it is upon the latter that he sets his revolutionary hopes. He does not view the theatrocratic rule of the crowd as entailing the problematic rule of a fearlessly judging multitude, but as a kind of rule through whose influence the judging multitude can be turned into a passive mass, a pliable material lacking any will at all. The type of rule that Benjamin has in mind here, picking up on early crowd psychology,[10] can be called (using Max Weber's term) "charismatic" authority.[11] If there is to be any chance for the emancipation of the proletariat, Benjamin argues that the revolutionary power of charisma, which helped fascism to power, must be countered with a different kind of power, that of "ratio." Correspondingly, the reactive fascist crowd is set off against "the antithesis of the proletarian cadre, which obeys a collective ratio" (WA 129). Proletarian class consciousness, according to Benjamin, "loosens" the masses. They "[cease] to be governed by mere reactions" and make "the transition to action" (WA 129).[12] Benjamin's plea for reason against charisma is obviously not, contrary to Plato, meant as a defense of the elitist rule of philosophers, rather it aims to emancipate the masses. Therefore, we must ask what the implications of this distinction are when it comes to the concepts Benjamin employs in his own critique of theatrocracy. Does Benjamin maintain something like a democratic concept of practical reason which could represent a plausible alternative to the other theories that have been presented in this book? There is no evading this question, nor the question as to the status of charismatic authority in a democracy. The answer we give to these questions is what will decide upon the legitimacy of a critique of the critiques of aestheticization.

2. Politicizing Art

We can best approach the question of whether we can propose an alternative concept of practical reason by undertaking a closer reading of Benjamin's writings on art. For it is here that Benjamin sketches an aesthetic-political counter-model to theatrocracy. Like Plato and Rousseau, Benjamin links (which is characteristic of the critique of aestheticization in general) aesthetic and political arguments, even where he seems to be focusing solely on art. What is at issue here is nothing less than the political right of art to exist.

"The aestheticizing of politics as practiced by fascism" should, as Benjamin puts it in the famous concluding sentence of his essay on the work of art, be countered by "politicizing art" (WA 122). Benjamin spells out that he means by this not so much in his work on the cinema, which stand at the center of his essay on the work of art, but in his work on the theater, i.e. Brecht's theater. Although in his essay on the work of art he expresses his optimistic claim that the cinema has changed the relationship of the masses to art so much that "[t]he progressive attitude is characterized by an immediate, intimate fusion of pleasure – pleasure in seeing and experiencing – with an attitude of expert appraisal" (WA 116). Yet this assessment does not correspond to the "reception in distraction" (WA 120) which is based on tact and habit, and which Benjamin observes in the cinema audience. Instead it reminds us of the aim of Brecht's theater. Despite his brief references to Chaplin and to Russian film, Benjamin's essay on the work of art fails to develop a theory of film which differentiates between techniques and effects – in precisely the place where Benjamin's aim is to mobilize the progressive potential of cinema to further proletarians' "understanding [of] themselves and therefore [of] their class" (WA 115) against their capitalist exploitation and fascist utilization. For Benjamin, it seems completely obvious that the old institution of the theater, unlike the new institution of the cinema, cannot be called progressive. After all, this is an institution which has been a paradigm for theatrocracy ever since Plato; from the perspective of a critique of aestheticization, it must be combated politically. Inasmuch as Benjamin adopts the anti-theater premises of this critique and seeks to counter the aestheticizing of politics by politicizing art, he obviously cannot be recalling traditional theater, but must assume the possibility of revolutionizing its structure. Brecht's theater stands for just this possibility.

Brecht's primary aim was to transform the audience into an assembly of interested persons. The interest of the individuals should not, however, be awakened by means of the "effect registered by the nervous systems" (ET I 10). For paradoxically, in Brecht's eyes, it is the individuation resulting from empathy with the actors that turns the crowd of spectators into the false totality of an audience. Empathy for the dramatic events on stage, in other words, communicatively disintegrates the spectators and turns them into an audience in the first place. It is precisely in this sense that the audience, however, does not yet represent a "crowd" in the psychological sense. For the psychological crowd, as we saw in the first chapter, largely derives from the process in which individuals affect each other. The excitability of the crowd results from affective feedback among its members, from the pleasure the crowd takes in its own existence.[13] The crowd, therefore, is compact in a different sense than the audience is. Yet both phenomena, the crowd and the audience, consist in assemblies of unfamiliar individuals which do not necessarily reflect the social differences between the individuals.[14] The differences between the audience and the crowd depend on how this social lack of preconditions gets used. This depends on whether it allows for individual judgment, regardless of the individual's social status (this is the model of the democratic audience or public sphere), or whether this lack of preconditions is used to level and eliminate individuals' judgment by the logic of the crowd. Therefore, we need to distinguish between different forms of staging and different politics of representation. Benjamin's claim, which is plausible at first sight, is that there are transitions and transitional phenomena at work: audiences which have not yet become a compact crowd trapped in an internal feedback loop, but which suppress the individual's judgment rather than challenging it. It is here that Benjamin locates the ideological function of the traditional, bourgeois theater. The latter employs the empathetic relation of individuals to what is presented on stage in order to eliminate social differences. Far from emancipating the audience from these differences, it suppresses them and thus allows them to be reproduced all the more smoothly. Benjamin therefore hopes that the "false and deceptive totality called 'audience'" will begin "to disintegrate," thus providing "a new space for the formation of separate parties within it – separate parties corresponding to conditions as they really are" (ET I 10).

3. Astonishment, Not Sympathy

This is the project of Brecht's theater. His assault on the "false and deceptive totality" of the bourgeois theater audience is the criterion he uses to distinguish epic theater from the concept of empathy practiced in the Aristotelian tradition. For Brecht believes that the empathy of the audience in the theater cannot be politicized. He even regards it as immoral to transfer this empathy to non-aesthetic contexts: Instead of moving the audience to put an end to the suffering of others, it merely causes the members of the audience to put themselves in the place of those who suffer in order to suffer themselves.[15] According to Brecht, if true empathy is not transformed into political rage, it is worthless; it must be put into practice or it will go up in smoke. Interestingly enough, and unlike other prominent critics of the theatrical spectacle such as Stanley Cavell, Brecht's critique is not primarily aimed at the fact that theater aesthetically distracts the audience from the content by directing its attention to the form. On the contrary, he criticizes the element of empathy for the content, the dramatic events, and the characters.[16] Therefore, Brecht's spectators are to adopt an attitude of "smoking and watching" so that they cannot so easily be "carried away."[17]

Nevertheless, Brecht does not employ theatrical means of representation merely for their own sake, but strictly in the service of the content. This is a basic intuition of critics of the theater, one that we can also find in the work of Stanley Cavell.[18] However, the reflective use of theatrical means and the arrangement of the audience should not aim to produce empathy, but a relationship of knowledge to what is being represented, instead of detaching from the latter. Unlike the naturalistic stage, which, as Benjamin writes, "must repress" its own "awareness that it is theatre" in order to "pursue undistracted its aim of portraying the real," epic theater "incessantly derives a lively and productive consciousness from the fact that it is theatre" (ET I 4). This is not meant as a rejection of the project of the traditional naturalistic stage, which consists in showing what is real. Instead, epic theater gives this project a philosophical and political renewal. Showing reality thus no longer means merely mirroring reality in a naturalistic way, but discovering reality, i.e. "alienating" it in a way that reveals the true "state of affairs" to the audience. Due to this orientation toward (political) insight, as Benjamin clearly emphasizes, the fact that epic theater remains aware of its own theatrical nature should not be understood in the sense of the "skills of reflexion" displayed by the romantic stage. For Benjamin, to reject the seemingly logical analogy between Brecht's technique of performatively (co-) exhibiting his theatrical means and the romantic "dramaturgy of reflexion" as being "mistaken" means nothing less than constructing "a spiral staircase to climb the rigging-loft of Brechtian theory" (ET I 11).

Already at the end of his early work "The Concept of Criticism in German Romanticism," in a peculiar counterposition of romantic and Goethian philosophies of art, Benjamin remarks on the unsatisfying relation of the romantics to the problem of mediating form and content, since they favor form over content. Goethe's answer to this problem is, for Benjamin, just as unsatisfying, as Goethe merely emphasizes the content of art at the cost of form. Therefore, the systematic question as to the relation between form and content remains unanswered.[19] In "The Author as Producer," Benjamin addresses this question himself (again making explicit reference to Plato)[20] against the background of the larger question of the political function of art. Brecht's critical work on the apparatus of theater serves as a positive example that the political tendency of a work of art entails an artistic tendency; therefore, in order for the politically progressive content of a work to have full effect, it must address its own form, i.e. its own use of means of production and their social function. This mediation between form and content, which focuses on political insight, is what primarily distinguishes Brecht's theater from the formalism of the romantic stage, which focuses on infinite reflexion. More important than the question of whether or not romantic reflexion should really be reconstructed as the complement to an empty formalism (I do not think it should) is the fact that Benjamin makes this diagnosis the foundation of a political critique of the romantic aesthetic, thereby confirming the aestheticization-critical line reconstructed in this book, a line that connects Plato to the critique of romanticism.

The question of aestheticization is what separates Brecht from the romantic ironist (Benjamin cites Tieck as an example of the latter). Whereas romantic reflexion tends to aestheticize the world as play – Benjamin writes that the romantic author always keeps in mind that "the world may, after all, be just a stage" (ET II 22) – Brecht aims to bring the world to presence through play. By distinguishing epic theater from the romantic tradition, Benjamin does capture an essential feature of Brecht's theater. For in the rejection of an autonomization of the "incidentals of the old works," i.e. of "poetic and theatrical means," Brecht remains an Aristotelian: "And according to Aristotle – and we agree there – narrative is the soul of drama."[21] It would therefore be a misunderstanding if we took Brecht's V-effects as a tool for emancipating the use of theatrical means from the rule of drama and interpreted Brecht as a pioneer of so-called postdramatic theater. As Hans-Thies Lehmann was right to point out, for Brecht "the *fable* (story) is the *sine qua non*."[22] The only way in which Brecht's drama is anti-Aristotelian is its opposition to Aristotelian catharsis, i.e. to "the purging of the emotions through identification with the destiny which rules the hero's life" (ET II 18). The central category for the effects of the epic theater is astonishment, which "must here be inserted into the Aristotelian formula for the effects of tragedy" (ET I 13). "Instead of identifying with the hero, the audience is called upon to learn to be astonished at the circumstances within which he has his being" (ET II 18).

Epic theater thus grasps itself as a thoroughly moral institution, though this is meant in the strong sense (which requires a good deal of explanation) that theater "does not merely transmit knowledge but actually engenders it" (ET I 11). In epic theater, "real conditions" should not, "as in naturalistic theatre," be recognized "with complacency, but with astonishment. This astonishment is the means whereby epic theater, in a hard, pure way, revives Socratic practices. In one

The Anaestheticization of the Political in Fascism: Benjamin 237

who is astonished, interest is born; interest in its primordial form" (ET I 4). At first sight, what makes epic theater political, similar to so-called contemporary theater, lies in *what* it allows the audience to recognize: "real conditions." But unlike "contemporary theater," it also has a dimension which Benjamin terms Socratic, and which refers to *how* these conditions are given to recognition: It teaches the audience to be astonished and thus awakens interest. It is only by virtue of this second, Socratic dimension that epic theater is capable of overcoming a problem that the political protagonists of contemporary theater fail to understand. For, according to Benjamin, the contemporary plays leave the structure of traditional theater largely unchanged, such that the "proletarian masses" merely occupy those positions "which the apparatus of the theater had created for the bourgeois masses" (ET I 2). The prerequisite for truly political theater thus lies in a kind of theatrical practice that is capable of freeing the spectators from the passive position of an audience, instead putting them in an intellectually interested and thereby philosophical relation to what is represented onstage.

4. The Look of the Stranger

But how does epic theater teach its spectators to be astonished about the conditions under which their heroes live? One of the most well-known means of epic theater for doing so is to interrupt the plot flow. This is the primary means by which epic theater turns against the Aristotelian tradition. Therefore, the loyalty of epic theater to the narrative is not, as must now be explained more concretely, directed toward the course of this narrative; "the suspense concerns less the ending than the separate events" (ET II 17). Instead of unfolding a plot for which the audience could develop empathy, epic theater seeks to produce knowledge about "conditions." Therefore, the relation that epic theater maintains with "conditions" should not be confused with the relation of the naturalistic stage to a given "milieu" (ET I 4). For, unlike social milieus on the naturalistic stage, epic theater does not merely represent real political conditions on the stage; they are what ought to be recognized by the spectators themselves, who should be astonished at recognizing them. The conditions therefore stand "at the end of the experiment, not at the beginning" (ET I 4). They are not so much the object to be mediated as they are the result of the theater – a theater that consequently requires spectators in order to be able to have its full effect. It is only in the astonishment of the audience that the conditions discover themselves. This discovery, however, is initiated by interrupting the plot. For instance, if we take the example that Benjamin himself cites, a family scene might be interrupted by the entry of a stranger. From the latter's perspective, the scene becomes dissimilar to itself; it is alienated, turning into a tableau in which the devastations of bourgeois life are recognized as a "condition." The detached perspective of the stranger is therefore nothing but the perspective of the ideal Brechtian spectator. At first sight, it seems that Brecht's aesthetic of the theater could not be further away from the aesthetic of Rousseau's festival, and indeed, from any kind of anaestheticizing staging of unity. Interestingly enough, however, it is right at the summit of this opposition that we find a commonality between Brecht and the tradition of the critique of aestheticization. This initially concerns the figure of the stranger, as well as the issue of the relationship between persons and their roles, typical of critiques of aestheticization. What makes Brecht's stranger strange is not merely the relation to the bourgeois scene into which he enters. For the audience, he represents the epitome of a new community, viz. the proletarian masses. The stranger is the new man, which is also demonstrated by the lack of differentiation between person and role he embodies. In this sense as well, even when Benjamin inverts the critique of aestheticization, he remains true to its basic intuitions. Let us take a closer look at the figure of the stranger.

5. Alienation

What is remarkable in the first instance is that the detached perspective of the stranger in the aforementioned scene is itself represented on the stage. Brecht often inserts an "impartial third party," a "spectator of high rank" (ET II 17). As a threshold figure between the audience and the stage, as a spectator within the play, this character is in Benjamin's view the true center of epic theater. For this figure mediates not only between the events onstage and the audience, it also represents the figure of the wise man or – as Benjamin puts it, drawing on Brecht's *Stories of Herr Keuner* – a thinker, who observes the events on stage with a detached but keen sight for "real conditions." This essentially undramatic figure is the true hero of Brecht's theater. Inasmuch as this figure, as representative of the spectator on the stage, is supposed to have a greater potential for identification than the other characters onstage, we might presume that the undramatic hero at the center of epic theater is at the same time an undercover agent of traditional theater, subtly demanding that the audience take up precisely that empathetic and identifying stance that Brecht sought to eliminate. Yet, Brecht's hero fends off such empathy with his plain and undramatic manner. To the extent that we can speak of a potential for identification at all, it would consist at the most in Herr Keuner's detached attitude, his stance toward what is (co-) represented onstage.[23]

But, on the other hand, the undramatic hero himself corresponds to the "real conditions" that Benjamin and Brecht seek to understand. At the same time Benjamin views the thinker's prim nature, which eliminates any "humane" potential for identification, as the epitome of modern, alienated man. Unlike Rousseau's critique of alienation, Benjamin's critique is not grounded in a concept of authenticity; rather, he maintains that a consciousness of performance and roles is the inevitable condition of modern subjectivity. Especially in his texts on Baudelaire, Benjamin interprets the modern consciousness of performance and thus of contingency as a side-effect of capitalism. He offers a Marxist critique of the expansion of subjectivity permitted by the capacity to assume multiple roles as an effect of social alienation. So it is telling that, in the context of his commentary on Baudelaire, the central object of this renewed critique of alienation, which is at the same time a critique of capitalism, is once again empathy: "If there were such a thing as a commodity-soul (a notion that Marx occasionally mentions in jest), it would be the most empathetic ever encountered in the realm of souls, for it would be bound to see every individual as a buyer in whose hand and house it wants to nestle. Empathy is the nature of the intoxication to which the flaneur abandons himself in the crowd. 'The poet'," Benjamin cites Baudelaire, "'enjoys the incomparable privilege of being himself and someone else, as he sees fit. Like those roving souls in search of a body, he enters another person whenever he wishes. For him alone, all is open; and if certain places seem closed to him, it is because in his view they are not worth visiting.' The commodity itself," Benjamin comments,

> is the speaker here. Yes, the last words give a rather accurate idea of what the commodity whispers to a poor wretch who passes a shop window containing beautiful and expensive things. These objects are not interested in this person; they do not empathize with him. In the important prose poem "Les Foules," we hear the voice – speaking in different words – of the fetish itself, which Baudelaire's sensitive disposition resonated with so powerfully: that empathy with inorganic things which was one of his sources of inspiration.[24]

The Marxist influence does not lie in Benjamin's interpretation of modern subjectivity as the interiorization of commoditized exteriority, but in the hint at a dialectic dissolution of this connection. Unlike Rousseau, Benjamin excludes the possibility of going back to a supposedly undistorted original situation prior to the commodity. Revolutionary potential can only be found by passing though the commoditized nature of the worker. Benjamin thus writes:

> To be sure, insofar as a person, as labor power, is a commodity, there is no need for him to identify himself as such. The more conscious he becomes of his mode of existence, the mode imposed on him by the system of production, the more he proletarianizes himself, the more he will be gripped by the chilly breath of the commodity economy, and the less he will feel like empathizing with commodities. But things had not yet reached that point with the class of the petty bourgeoisie to which Baudelaire belonged. On the scale we are dealing with here, this class was only at the beginning of its decline. Inevitably, many of its members would one day become aware of the commodity nature of their labor power. But this day had not yet come. (PSE 33f.)

But for Brecht the day had come.

Brecht's undramatic hero is entirely unspectacular and yet also entirely extrinsic. Benjamin not only cites the docker Galy Gay in *Man Equals Man* as a man "who doesn't drink, smokes very little and hasn't any passions to speak of," but also as a man whose guiding principle is "not fidelity to any single essence of his own, but a continual readiness to admit a new essence" (ET I 8f.). This willingness does not, however, derive from the pleasure of empathizing with others, a pleasure whose limits, as Benjamin writes in his commentary on Baudelaire, lie in the fact that it is only a pleasure *within* society, but not a pleasure *in* society (cf. PSE 33). Instead, this willingness derives from the contradictions that society itself imposes on the working class. For precisely this reason, the extrinsic nature of Brecht's hero is an authentic expression not of his own essence, but of the society in which he lives. In the extrinsic nature of man as a commodity, man and his role are joined once again: Man consists in nothing but the various shapes or roles which society imposes on him. Galy Gay, according to Benjamin, is "nothing but an empty stage on which the contradictions of our society are acted out." Furthermore, "following Brecht's line of thought one might arrive at the proposition that it is the wise man who is the perfect stage for such a dialectic" (ET I 8). Benjamin argues even more clearly in this direction when it comes to another of Brecht's heroes, one who, although he is not a dramatic hero, does perhaps represent the model for many of his undramatic characters: Herr Keuner, the "thinker." "Herr Keuner, a proletarian, stands in sharp contrast to the ideal proletarian of the philanthropists: he is not interiorized. He expects the abolition of misery to arrive only by the logical development of the attitude which poverty forces upon him."[25]

As an undramatic figure, Herr Keuner distinguishes himself from other charismatic figures that Benjamin regards as an essential element of the aestheticizing of the political "as practiced by fascism." "And in fact, Herr Keuner is the man who concerns all, belongs to all, for he is the leader. But in quite a different sense from the one we usually understand by the word. He is in no way a public speaker, a demagogue; nor is he a show-off or a strongman. His main preoccupations lie light-years away from what people nowadays understand to be those of a 'leader'. The fact is that Herr Keuner is a thinker." But because of his outwardness, the symptom of his alienation, the undramatic Herr Keuner is also different from the authenticity and virtuousness of the Antique philosophers:

> His entire stance will prevent our confusing this thinker with Greek sages – the strict Stoics or the life-enjoying representatives of the school of Epicurus. He is rather more akin to Paul Valéry's character Monsieur Teste: a purely thinking man without any emotions. Both characters have Chinese features. They are infinitely cunning, infinitely discreet, infinitely polite, infinitely old, and infinitely adaptable. Herr Keuner, however, differs entirely from his French counterpart in that he has a goal he never forgets for a single minute. This goal is the new state.[26]

6. Adaptability and Revolution

Benjamin leaves us in the dark about what this new state is supposed to look like. It seems logical that it would be something like a dictatorship of the proletariat which, according to Marx, represents the transition to communism and which, as Lenin wrote in *State and Revolution*, "for the first time becomes democracy for the people," a democracy for the majority. However, this democracy remains bound up with the suppression of a minority, the bourgeoisie. It is only in the socialist transitional phase that, according to Lenin, we can speak of democracy as a form of state. In fully developed communism (after the actual abolition of class antagonisms), democracy as a form of *state*, i.e. in Lenin's eyes an organ for the suppression of one class by another, will be made consummate by being replaced by another form.[27] Brecht's heroes would in this sense be heroes who pointed the way to socialist revolution. But here we are dealing neither with charismatic revolutionaries nor with ethical role models such as the Antique philosophers who, according to Plato, are to form the political elite. These heroes receive their practical attitude from the outside, from social "conditions." In this sense they are universalizable rather than exceptional figures, neither revolutionaries nor intellectual elites, but prototypes of the revolution by the proletarian masses.

Regarding the concept of practical reason, the question with which we began, it is very remarkable that, according to Benjamin's interpretation of Brecht's heroes, even the emergence of the revolutionary struggle should have nothing to do with ethical or moral motives. Instead, the decision to take revolutionary action should be a nearly automatic result from these heroes' adaptability to the objective conditions of their social determination. In Benjamin's view, this – along with the stance that emerges from this determination – already makes these heroes revolutionary figures, even and especially when they appear to be anything but virtuous. Here we might think of the egoistic Fatzer rather than the thoughtful Herr Keuner or the ascetic Galy Gay. Benjamin remarks in this connection: "Marx, we may say, set himself the task of showing how the revolution could arise from its complete opposite, capitalism, without the need for any ethical change. Brecht has transposed the same problem onto the human plane: he wants the revolutionary to emerge from the base and selfish character devoid of any ethos" (BB 369). Furthermore, Benjamin writes:

> The more closely we analyze the types created by Brecht [...], the more clearly it emerges that for all their vigor and vitality, they represent political models, or, as the doctors would say, phantoms. What they all have in common is the desire to bring about rational political actions that spring not from philanthropy, love of one's neighbor, idealism, nobility of mind, or the like, but only from the relevant attitude. This attitude may be essentially dubious, unsympathetic, or self-interested. If only the man it belongs to does not delude himself, if only he clings fast to reality, the attitude will itself provide its own correction. Not an ethical corrective: the man does not become any better. But a social one: his behavior makes him useful. (BB 367)

This clearly technocratic perspective on political action can only be understood against the background of the totalizing critique of alienation that Benjamin formulated in his commentary on Baudelaire. According to this critique, after advanced capitalism has reduced commoditized subjects to merely adaptable creatures, the social process remains the only authority that can give their actions the politically *appropriate* form. Once alienation has attained its peak, it automatically passes over into revolutionary action. Practical reason then tends to move from the acting subjects to the objectivity of the social process; it is from the latter that the "correction" comes. In a totalized world of commodities, in a state of absolute exteriority, the transformation of conformism into "rational political action" can only come from the outside, from the developmental logic of the social "conditions" themselves. Benjamin thus answers the question of the democratic concept of practical reason with his faith in history, which he derives from a controversial interpretation of Marx.

7. Charisma and Democracy

As I have argued in the previous chapters, if we seek to defend the possibility of a mimetic opening to otherness and strangeness, the possibility of admitting "a new essence" as an element of freedom, as a condition of a self-determined life, then we must reject the reduction of this possibility to mere adaptability, as is done in the critique of alienation.[28] Moreover, from this perspective it is highly problematic to replace the fascist vision of a community at one with its rulers with a communist vision of a society at one with itself, beyond all rule and representation. The recognition of a dialectic of freedom implies the defense of a society that accounts for the event of the other in oneself and the attendant possibility of self-improvement in its political form, i.e. democracy. This not only results in a different perspective on the theater of politics, but also on the politics of theater.

We have seen that the anthropological insight into the potentiality in the (non-)foundation of all social identity and thus the insight into the dual bodies of the people are accompanied by the recognition of sovereignty at the basis of all determinations of the people and its will. The *demos* of democracy can never exist outside of its representation, which means (once again) that it cannot exist outside of the *kratia* of sovereignty. It cannot exist outside of relations of power and domination. In a democracy, however, this fact is not concealed but exhibited; we could even say that it is staged – and thereby relativized. The position of power no longer conceals itself by referring to a transcendental authority, but is marked as such. For this reason, every political claim to power, every claim of one or more individuals to speak for the community, must legitimate itself in front of an audience of potential rivals. And this can only occur through a performance, through an act of decision and self-presentation on the part of the government or those who seek office. On the side of the audience or public that judges this performance, there is a corresponding type of judgment that no longer rationalistically stands in sheer opposition to other dimensions of experience such as desire or emotions. Instead, the latter penetrate judgment and remain a constant source of possible change. Yet as has become clear in the previous chapters, this does not mean that judgment gets replaced by immediate desires, rather only that the permeability of the subject to new influences, which is conveyed by such dimensions of experience, must be understood as an essential requirement for examining one's own principles. The democratic subject, as has already been said, is not without rules; rather, it is capable of changing these rules under certain conditions – based on the experiences it has in interaction with the other, the new, the particular.

Without a doubt, this also means that charisma must be grasped as a constantly possible, albeit not necessary, element in the theater of democracy. Indeed, according to Weber, charismatic authority must be understood as a secular result of a previously religious concept. The superhuman quality of the monarch is secularized into the "extraordinary" quality of a personality that seems appropriate for a position of power.[29] This is the manner in which charisma becomes relevant for democracy. Unlike the authority of the monarch, charismatic authority is not derived from previously established authorities or conventions. In this sense it is, as Weber writes, "foreign to all rules," unlike traditional authority, which is bound to the "precedents handed down from the past and to this extent is also oriented to rules. Within the sphere of its claims, charismatic authority repudiates the past, and is in this sense a specifically revolutionary force. It recognizes no appropriation of positions of power by virtue of the possession of property, either on the part of a chief or of socially privileged groups. The only basis of legitimacy for it is personal charisma so long as it is proved; that is, as long as it receives recognition."[30] Therefore, the quality of this charisma is also not predetermined. Weber thus writes: "How the quality in question would be ultimately judged from any ethical, aesthetic, or other such point of view is naturally entirely indifferent for purposes of definition. What is alone important is how the individual is actually regarded by those subject to charismatic authority, by his 'followers' or 'disciples'."[31] This also means that charismatic authority can only be maintained as long as it justifies itself. Because it is dependent on the consent of its addressees and because of the necessity of proving itself to them, the originally extraordinary charisma necessarily becomes "routinized."[32] In this sense, as Gertrud Koch summarizes the matter, charismatic authority represents a "transitional authority on the way to rational or legal authority."[33]

Because charisma, like the assumption of sovereignty, must be recognized by – and prove itself to – the audience to which it addresses itself, it is impure from the beginning. It must be connected with contents that give constancy to its authority. Charismatic self-presentation is always bound to the (co-)presentation of specific contents and to the continued proof of decisions to which the audience can consent. The "extraordinariness" of political charisma, however, is not only linked internally to the phenomenon of its "routinization," but also externally. For especially in the mass media,[34] it must prove itself in competition with other charismatic figures (other politicians, public intellectuals, and other celebrities), who are also a part of the public. Therefore, we can only understand charisma from a democratic perspective as a relation of communication to the audience upon whose consent and support it continues to depend. For this reason, it can also disappear. We need only think of Barack Obama's charisma, initially celebrated worldwide, though the honeymoon with the American people came to a quick end, giving way to the demand that he back up his charisma with action.[35]

Therefore, if charisma, like sovereignty, is democratically tied to relations of recognition, then the threat to democracy does not lie in charisma as such, but in its illusory substantialization as an objective quality existing independent of its being recognized by an audience. The tendency to such a substantialist self-misunderstanding of charismatic authority, even if it is not fully unleashed, can be seen in the case of Silvio Berlusconi.[36] One of the main reasons this self-understanding represents a threat to democracy is that it is an ideological component of that totalitarian madness according to which an individual could in fact embody the site of power, the site of the general. We can see in the case of German fascism that to the extent that the relation of recognition that binds charisma in a democracy was being suppressed, charisma no longer appeared as a temporary and transitional authority, but as a substantial, "inherited charisma of a 'race', viz. a supposedly superior 'arian' race."[37]

If, against this background, it could become clear once more that it is not the aestheticizing of the political, not the theatrical dimension of democratic politics that represents a problem, rather tendencies of their anaestheticizing, then this will obviously have implications for an assessment of political theater.

8. Political Theater

If it is true that the general will, the face of the *demos*, can never exist outside of its political representation, never outside the separation between the representatives and the represented, the governors and the governed, and thus never outside of relations of power and authority, then the theater has the political task of maintaining awareness of this fact.[38] For the theater is capable of playfully exhibiting the separations which underlie any relationship of political representation: The separation between persons and their roles (the representatives of the people always have two bodies, both in politics and in the theater), and the separation between the actors and the audience. Due to its ability to show forms of political representation as representation, the theater has a potentially denaturing, i.e. critical essence. Theater, for instance, can take aim at myths of community which are supposedly pre-political and free of representation, and which, as we have seen, are therefore so suitable to the spectacles of unity practiced by fascism. Christoph Marthaler has done an excellent job of dissecting the latter's claustrophilic design. One of Christoph Schlingensief's projects was to use the theater to bring politicians onto the stage and thus their strategies of representation in front of the same audience they claim to represent. Theater can also be self-critical and reflect on the illusionist techniques with which earlier forms of dramatic theater sought – and contemporary film seeks – to combat its own theatrical nature. This is one of the projects pursued by René Pollesch. His piece *Capucetto Rosso*, for instance, begins with a comical and intelligent reflection on portrayals of Hitler in the work of Bernd Eichinger, Oliver Hirschbiegel, and Heinrich Breloer. Pollesch's actors play actors preparing for the rehearsals of the stage version of Ernst Lubitsch's film *Sein oder Nichtsein* – a film about actors who play Nazis in order to escape from the real Nazis. Backstage, which in *Capucetto Rosso* is the actual stage, the actors discuss the dubious work of Bruno Ganz, who completely took on Hitler's personality in his performance, as well as Tobias Moretti's problem that Hitler can never appear together with a German shepherd, for his image would then immediately resemble the partner of Kommissar Rex. As Sophie Rois says later in the play, it is impossible to be political in these never-ending portrayals of the Nazis. Whoever wants to be truly political must study law. "Go!," she says to the audience, "go out and study law!" Of course, everybody remains in their seats and follows the other kind of politics that is unfolding as a different politics of representation on the stage, on Pollesch's stage.

In the work of all three directors, the political dimension of the stage reveals itself to the same extent that the theater no longer conceals its structures, that is, to the extent that it becomes – to use the term coined by Hans-Thies Lehmann – *postdramatic*.[39] This is a kind of theater that recognizes the political potential of its own aesthetic nature. Unlike the manner in which Brecht, for Platonic motives, turned theater against its own structure, avant-garde theater today emphasizes its own theatricality. It thus picks up on those elements of Brecht's theater that – contrary to his own project – had not entirely abandoned their relation to the romantic tradition: the exhibited reflection on the means of representation and the arrangement of the audience. Postdramatic theater demonstrates that the emancipation of the means of representation from the rule of drama (or of narrative), which goes beyond Brecht, does not imply a decision for a one-sided privileging of form over content. It does not imply an empty formalism. Instead, the form enters into a tense relation with the content, which keeps the audience in a detached, reflective relation to the events onstage. We could say that this also keeps the audience *alienated* from what is presented onstage. I believe that herein – in the effect of this reflective detachment from what is presented onstage – lies the ethical-political potential of art in general and thus also of non-theatrical artistic forms of representation.[40] But when it comes to the specific art of the theater, which is the sole object I am concerned with here, we must realize that postdramatic theater, which is the most enlightened form of theater today, no longer aims to create community. It neither constructs it nor anticipates it. On the contrary, and as Plato and Rousseau were right to point out, it separates both persons from their roles and the represented from the aesthetically detached audience – an audience of (in this aesthetic sense) strangers.

Yet precisely because of this (allegorizing) feature, theater works *against* the anaestheticization of the political "as practiced by fascism." For this is neither the ultimate truth about democracy (rather it is an immanent threat to it), nor is it the truth about the political effects of the theater. Anaestheticization must instead be understood as the truth about the representative dimension of absolute and thereby undemocratic sovereignty. For the latter is essentially characterized by the fact that it conceals its own rhetorical and performative operations. Democracy, by contrast, is marked by the logic of representation found in the theater: Democratic sovereignty is relative in that it points to or exhibits its own decrees as such, and thus exposes them to the recognition of a heterogeneous audience.

7

Post-Democracy and the Anaesthetizing of the Political: A Look Forward

As we have seen, given our experiences of totalitarianism throughout the twentieth century, the problem of our time does not consist in the aestheticization of the political. In fact, a society completely in agreement with itself – the utopian notion which critics of aestheticization oppose to theatrocracy – bears latent or even overtly totalitarian features. This is even true when such a utopia defines itself as democratic, for which Rousseau is certainly the most obvious example. Yet there is another, quite different problem the critique of the aestheticization of the political seems entirely incapable of addressing: the danger that democracy can be transformed into a "post-democracy."[1] "Post-democracy" is one of the slogans that contemporary social criticism has employed to capture the increasingly undemocratic character of Western democracies that have come to be dominated by economic constraints. Jacques Rancière writes that "post-democracy is the government practice and conceptual legitimization of a democracy *after* the *demos*, a democracy that has eliminated...the dispute of the people and is thereby reducible to the sole interplay of state mechanisms and combinations of social energies and interests."[2] Rancière goes on to say that post-democracy equates the permanent statistical recording of public opinion with the "body of the people."[3] This corresponds to the "regime of the all-visible" which eliminates the distinction between image and reality. The conflation of algorithmic polling of public opinion with the *demos*, which is thereby reduced to a statistical average, eliminates the very possibility that a self-difference within the *demos* could appear at all; in other words, it eliminates the possibility of a dispute over the notion of the *demos* itself: A people "in the form of its statistical reduction is a people transformed into an object of knowledge and prediction that sends appearance and its polemics packing."[4]

This corresponds to a kind of politics that abandons its own sovereignty to define the common good and instead merely manages economic necessities and constraints – or even relegates its sovereignty to private courts of arbitration.[5] Post-democratic politics therefore tends to deny its own power, thereby repressing the sovereignty of the political. What is notable in the context of our investigation is that the post-democratic repression of sovereignty is accompanied by the ideological conception of a polity at one with itself, of a complete and total agreement between the forms of the state and the state of social relations.[6] In a post-democracy, however, this notion takes on a much different shape than it does in totalitarianism. Post-democracy is the name of a social formation which pretends that it is no longer necessary to debate the shape of the *demos*, the meaning of community and the forms of its institutionalization, since each citizen has already been granted the possibility of individual self-realization. The political issue of the preconditions of freedom thus gets distorted by inclusiveness, to which corresponds a culture of visibility that, unlike totalitarianism, is not shaped by an anaesthetic of unity, but by an anaesthetic of disintegration: It is precisely the endless openness of this culture which proves to be especially inclusive. This is true of the way that statistics neutralize political differences, but it also holds for an individualization of appearing, which thereby tends to lose both its political and its public character. In the state of post-democracy, all citizens are granted the opportunity to present themselves and their individual particularity, but they are no longer met with the expectation of a demand for political representation. By granting each person the possibility of individual visibility, post-democracy claims that it has given each person his or her just due. In both aesthetic and political terms, this recalls the nightmare of a society that has taken on the form of an afternoon talk show in which there are nothing but individual fates, stories of individual success or failure – and the latter do not challenge the rest to show solidarity, but invite them as individual consumers to take pleasure at other's mischief.

The self-denial of power characteristic of post-democracy is ideologically linked to the equally abstract and subjectivist model of freedom justifiably rejected by the critique of aestheticization in the tradition of Hegel, which is obviously of particular significance in our investigation.[7] Precisely this misunderstanding of human freedom as a kind of self-realization free of all social preconditions and relations seems to have gained in social influence at the very moment that Western democracies appear to be moving toward post-democracy. To the degree that power legitimates its actions by invoking its own powerlessness, the responsibility for the state of society and the situation of each individual is pushed onto the post-democratically governed (and no longer onto the government). Each individual should see himself "as his own militant,"[8] as a bundle of energy that can be moulded to fit into continuously new contexts with new contracts, all the while viewing themselves as being in pursuit of their own pleasures. You just have to want it. Power thus tends to become equated with the image of a – neoliberal – classless society which embraces even the poorest of the poor by according them the potential for creative self-realization. Even the libertarian and anarchist's anti-law and anti-state impulse find their place in this ideological formation, as independence, initiative, and creativity become crucial social demands. They have replaced the disciplinarian tradition without having abolished discipline. Instead of normalizing subjects according to socially predetermined roles, we have the compulsion to creative self-realization in competition. Citizens no longer obey by subjecting themselves to a given order and by following rules, but by fulfilling tasks in a self-responsible and creative way. "Artistic critique" – the term employed by Luc Boltanski and Ève Chiapello for individualist revolt against the law[9] – therefore seems to be becoming the new social paradigm, though still within certain bounds.[10] Even and especially the subjectivist myth – now discredited by contemporary artists – that genius derives from the inner depths of an individual's personality remains; the only difference is that everyone is now considered capable of pioneering innovation, though only in moderate, economically viable proportions.[11]

Clearly, the corresponding discourse – which, by the way, denies having anything to do with ideology – conceals both economic, political, and other forms of social inequality. According to this supposedly anti-ideological ideology, the place an individual occupies in society is entirely up to him. The freedom of self-realization is therefore accorded to the individual to the same degree that it ignores the social conditions of this freedom. Not only does this reduce social antagonisms to a mere social fact, thus eliminating any potential for conflict, but the individualizing perspective on poverty also goes along with a naturalization of the differences produced by the social order[12] – a fact that must be understood as an "ideological-political process par excellence."[13]

Obviously, the demand that individuals realize themselves under these conditions leads to anything but emancipation. Indeed, wherever this ideology takes hold, social pathologies only change shape, as the French sociologist Alain Ehrenberg has shown.[14] While neurosis demonstrates the personal costs of the fact that society expects us to identify with the roles that make up a specific social order, depression shows the costs of the demand that individuals should invent and continually reinvent themselves – entirely blind to social preconditions. Oedipus, who runs into conflict with the law of the father, thus gets replaced by Narcissus, who falls sick with an idealized image of himself. Depression is a narcissist pathology that reveals the difficulties individuals encounter whenever they seek to live up to an ideal of themselves, according to which the ego is supposed to have the capacity to determine the way they live their lives "freely," regardless of social preconditions. Depression represents the other side of this demand: an uncertainty with regard to one's identity, which is not only accompanied by a sense of inferiority, but also by indifference and apathy, perhaps even by a serious lack of motivation and the difficulty of undertaking any action at all.

When it comes to the danger that democracy may turn into post-democracy, it is crucial to criticize the ideological notion of an abstract freedom whose conceptual preconditions and problematic consequences are conceived of independent of social conditions, but without falling back into the problems suffered by critics of aestheticization. When opposing the compulsion to permanent self-transformation, we should not succumb to the temptation to call for a stable order in which everybody has his place. Indeed, the rise of both Islamic and Christian fundamentalism in Western democracies can also be interpreted as a symptom of post-democratic tendencies. In opposition to this kind of one-sidedness, the aim of this investigation has been to defend a concept of self-determination that accounts for the constitutive role that a detachment from the social plays when it comes to the notion of freedom. Given the static conceptions of social order that remain today, this means supporting the possibility of a dynamic social order. In view of the post-democratic ideology that plays an ever more prominent role in Western democracies, this can mean rejecting the competitive demands for constant self-transformation as something alien to our self-relationship, and insisting on slowing down.[15] In other words, we must defend a concept of self-determination that puts experiences of self-difference to use – which can occasionally include the experience of being alienated from socially encouraged images of ourselves – in order to liberate ourselves from these images. With regard to the intensely constructivist model of freedom entailed by post-democracy, this also means putting the ideal of creative self-realization back into a social context and recognizing its ideological function. As Ehrenberg shows, even the healing of the depressed can only succeed to the extent that a person abandons his hypertrophic ideal of himself and recognizes the real limits of his powers. Such an insight is at least the precondition for politicizing these limits. Of course, by politicizing these limits and addressing various inequalities, we also recognize the false equality of a kind of freedom without social preconditions as being a political imposition. This also allows us to regain distance between power and society – and with it the accompanying political possibilities. At the same time, this means grasping the sovereignty of the political as a necessary component of democratic life.

Indeed, as we have seen at various points in this investigation (contrary to Carl Schmitt and Rousseau), the sovereignty of the political must be grasped not in opposition to democracy, but instead as one of its essential – and unique – structural determinations. This reveals the connection we have been dealing with since the first chapter on Plato between the understanding of the subject and its freedom on the one hand and the political order on the other. For the sovereignty of the political is an exact correlate of the democratic subject and its freedom. Because every member of the *demos* is never wholly absorbed by his social identity and remains constantly open for new and foreign influences, and thus for the possibility of transforming his life and his understanding of both self and world, there can be no conclusive determination of the common good, no conclusive – as Helmuth Plessner put it – "balancing of differences."[16] For that very reason, however, every decision on such a balancing is necessarily a sovereign decision. Sovereignty thereby takes on a significance that cannot be grounded in a presupposed understanding of the *demos*; after all, the need for sovereignty derives from the fact that the popular sovereign can never appear for itself; rather, it can only be constituted through political representation. Nor can sovereignty be grounded in transcendence, as long as its decisions remain clearly bound to the condition of finitude, to the "unforeseeability of reality."[17] Given these conditions, sovereignty must become visible as political power, thereby removing any appearance of purity, unconditionality, or divinity, for as soon as power becomes visible as such, it must justify both itself and the political order in which the *demos* is supposed to recognize its own will. And since nobody who presumes to speak in the name of all, or at least the majority, can be assumed to have privileged access to the universal, every political actor must face up to potential rivals and alternatives. The representatives of the *demos* must justify themselves to those whose will they wish to represent; their representation is never undisputed.

But we must not draw the conclusion that such representations should be avoided. On the contrary, if it is true that the *demos* of democracy, that the self of collective self-government cannot merely be presupposed, but must be produced by means of political representation, then this also implies that the stance on the problem of political representation vis-à-vis the critique of aestheticization must be changed. If the *demos* can never appear as such, then it follows directly that the *demos* must be represented. Instead of "making a demand on representation that it cannot possibly fulfill, i.e. representation without any *re*-presentation, without any provisional claim, without any unfinished proof, without any opaque layer of translation, interpretation, betrayal, and without any complicated machinery of assembly, delegation, proof, argumentation, negotiation, and resolution,"[18] as Bruno Latour has emphasized, we must paint a realistic picture of the work of representation – and thus have a certain respect for the political mediators who perform this work. Yet this respect, as always, often appears in the form of critical discussion. Although, according to Latour,[19] we should cast doubt on the capacity of the mediators to speak in the name of their clients, we should not discount it entirely.

The public sphere acts in this context as a medium that binds the sovereignty of legal and political decisions to the principle of democratic participation, while ensuring that decisions are subjected to examination and critique, which can also lead to a revision of these decisions. On the one hand, this function can be fulfilled by the press and the media. They can give a voice to minorities not represented by the institutions; they can contribute to correcting the mistakes made by the government and, if all goes well, eliminate injustice. But as Jacques Derrida was right to emphasize, we should not conclude that this kind of "democratization" will necessarily represent "public opinion" in a legitimate way, without "filtering or screening."[20] Even the most liberal media landscape cannot eliminate the element of power entailed by the determination of what counts as an issue of public interest and what does not. Therefore, democratic freedom of the press must also entail freedom *from* the press, that is, the right to respond and present opposing opinions, which allows the "citizen to be more than the fraction (the private, deprived fraction, in sum, and more and more so) of a passive, consumer 'public,' necessarily cheated because of this."[21]

Such a critique of the public sphere also necessarily concerns the structures that, due to constraints in terms of both time and format, seriously restrict the right of the public to respond. At the same time, however, this critique is made *within* the theatrocratic setting in which all those who claim to represent public opinion are judged by a heterogeneous audience that is not always in agreement with the way it is represented. Instead of a generalized critique of media spectacle, therefore, we should take a closer look, and practice critique in the original sense of the term, i.e. as differentiation: First of all, we must distinguish the anaesthetic of totalitarian stagings of unity and of post-democratic disintegration from the political stagings in which democratic power justifies itself before the *demos* that it claims to represent. Furthermore, from this perspective, we need to consider various different broadcast formats and locations, strategies of political communication, or the role of new technologies and media when it comes to forming public spheres, both mainstream and alternative. Such debates will have to address a whole series of aspects, but what this investigation has made clear is that they will necessarily have to be accompanied – more or less explicitly – by a defense of the theatrocratic structure of democracy. The power to represent – both in politics and in the media – is democratic to the extent that it recognizes that it itself must be recognized, that is, to the extent that it remains exposed – according to its own self-understanding – to possible responses. However, this does not automatically entail that we must agree with a given response. If we take a look at the comments section of online journals, we will see that the responses of interested citizens do not necessarily bear witness to a greater amount of reason. What is decisive, however, is that power – that of both politics and of media – be compelled by the possibility of response to justify itself, thus fundamentally creating the possibility of transforming a given concept of public opinion.

The impulses for such transformations, however, do not always have their origins in the media. They can also emerge from demonstrations and protests upon which the media then report. Every demonstration is also a demonstration of the public sphere, normally as a result of the sheer size of a demonstration. It is crucial that a significant number of people be involved in order for the cause of the demonstration to not remain merely a quasi-private affair but become a public one instead. And the crowd, *as* a crowd, always has the potential to unfold its specific affective dynamic[22] and turn into action – thus the notorious police presence. Sometimes all that is needed is a spark. Because of the crowd's potential to encourage its members to overcome their inhibitions, the transition to action always means a transition to violence. Crowd psychology often addresses the crowd's will to destroy – this is what is most striking about revolutionary masses. When a crowd makes the transition from demonstration to action, it likes to smash windows and start fires. The power of the crowd articulates itself in these cases – as Elias Canetti has pointed out – literally in the form of transgression.[23] Yet even peaceful demonstrations aim to cross the line, so to say. They seek to redefine the border between the public and the private, to change society's perception of the majority opinion or of what is publicly relevant. Given this recognition of the demonstrating crowd's potential for violence, it is all the more important to point out the distinction from the fascist crowd. The difference between the demonstrating crowd on the one side and the fascist crowd on the other side concerns the fleeting character of the former and the permanence of the latter. The former crowd has a merely negative function, disturbing a presumed consensus and interrupting the social order in the name of an alternative order that it cannot yet embody or anticipate. The fascist crowd, by contrast, translates its dynamic into positive social forms. Whereas the demonstrating crowd is extinguished along with the fires it sometimes sets,[24] the fascist crowd makes the torch its very symbol. The truly decisive difference therefore consists in the fact that the demonstrating crowd does not replace the political order with its own logic, but remains in a tense relationship with that order – to the extent, that is, that it necessarily presupposes an order in which the cause it presents is already considered relevant. That is the paradox of a demonstration, so to say. It must presuppose the result it aims to achieve.

This becomes especially apparent in those cases in which the political status of the demonstrators is at stake. The political subjects of the demonstration appear here in the mode of "as if," as Jacques Rancière puts it.[25] For in these cases the demonstrators must act as if the political order in which their speaking and acting counts already exists; they must act as if their speaking and acting is intelligible and generally comprehensible – in short, that it is perceived as publicly relevant speech and action. But it would be misleading to reduce such speaking and acting to this "as if," perhaps even confusing it with an affair that was in some way unreal. A demonstration's anticipation of an already transformed political order occurs by means of the actors' very material and embodied insistence, who are kept out of the public sphere not least due to their specific corporeality. When the public appearance of specific bodies is not accepted by the hegemonic power, or if it is even criminalized, then the mere presence of these bodies in places they should not be represents a shift in the political order and the corresponding social perception, which often gives the police cause to defend this order's original shape. The state force usually involved in defending the order confirms the hegemon's unwillingness to view the demonstrators as anything but potentially violent bodies, to hear anything but noise in their statements – in short, to perceive them politically as all. Therefore, the body is the location for the occurrence of the self-difference of the *demos*. Their sheer public presence aims to transform the people's institutionalized form – a transformation that simultaneously frees the demonstrators from the reified perception that reduces them to mere corporeality. But precisely this change of status anticipated by publicly insistent bodies can be denied to them. The members of demonstrations constantly undergo the risk of being pushed back into the pre-political sphere of the non-public, of being pushed back onto their own corporeality.

With regard to both demonstrations and the official reactions they often provoke, we see a very clear self-difference in the democratic *demos*. In spite of the – occasionally very dramatic – argument over the question of whether and how the demonstration of such a self-difference leads to an actual transformation of the political order and the social perception it underlies, there can be no doubt that the concept of democracy crucially depends on whether it allows space for the appearance of such self-difference. As we have seen, self-difference is present in different and partially overlapping ways in a democracy. It not only appears in the relation between the government and the non-parliamentary opposition, but also in the relation between the government and the parliamentary opposition, between politics and the media, between the media and the citizens, and finally, between citizen and man – which becomes especially relevant at the limits of democratic communities in the discourse of human rights. Those cases in which one or more of these differences are absorbed or ignored then appear to be a problem, that is, whenever human rights are equated with the civil rights granted by nation-states, or when the relationship between the government and the opposition is eliminated in favour of a one-party state, when free speech and the right to protest are restricted, or when the influence of economic and/or political power blurs the line between politics and the media. Defending the levels of democratic life that bear witness to a conflict over various views of what is publicly relevant, of what constitutes the common will, means abandoning the conception of democracy as the final, good form of rule in which the problem of sovereignty has been overcome, just because "the people" itself takes up the position of the sovereign. For this conception presupposes the problematic fiction of an identity of the *demos* with itself. In a democracy, as we have seen, there is no such thing as a pure, indivisible sovereignty, nor something like pure participation free of all sovereignty. We could only conceive of such a thing if the *demos* truly possessed direct sovereignty, an indivisible will, *one* voice, *one* mind. But given the unforeseeable heterogeneity of the *demos*, this is a structurally totalitarian notion.

A concept in contemporary philosophy that is meant to capture this kind of heterogeneity is that of the multitude. This term is usually employed according to the definition provided by Antonio Negri and Michael Hardt, where it is linked to the concept of the so-called "absolute democracy," which I would like to address by way of a conclusion. Although Negri and Hardt view the multitude as the other of sovereignty, which – as they are correct to point out – due to its heterogeneity cannot itself be "the sovereign,"[26] they do not conclude that there is a necessary tension between sovereignty and the multitude, around which – as I have argued – the historical life of democracy revolves. Instead, they dream of a "full and absolute democracy,"[27] in which sovereignty and thus the difference between the government and the governed has been abolished and replaced with the self-government of the many. This utopia is based on the idea of an *absolute* immanence in which there is neither external, i.e. transcendentally legitimated authority, nor hierarchy, nor asymmetry. All elements are to interact at the same level.[28] When the authors speak of the "destruction of sovereignty in favour of democracy," then they mean it in this absolute sense: not just as a democratic transformation of sovereign power into a recognition power, as I have sketched it. Rather they are referring to the abolition of *all* relationships of power and domination. Of course, this is nothing but the utopia of a socially realized form of universal equality. Under these conditions, according to Negri and Hardt, the multitude can emerge in a fully emancipated, pure form. For example, as Negri and Hardt argue, gender difference can only become a "creative, singular power" when "every discipline of labor, affect, and power that makes gender difference into an index of hierarchy is destroyed."[29] The same must be true of all other differences. To transform them into new singularities means allowing them to appear against the background of ultimate equality.

However, the problem or the crux of this utopia of ultimate equality in which every distortion is removed and a state of fundamental understanding has been attained – such that the end of politics coincides with the freedom of unrepresentable individuals – lies in the fact that it can ultimately only be conceived of as the negation of historical life, only as a state outside of history. For the idea of ultimate equality, i.e. a state of complete and total justice, implies eliminating the possibility of error, of deception and self-deception, which, as Albrecht Wellmer has repeatedly pointed out, "is a structural part of all finite beings; as beings with limited and particular perspectives on themselves and the world, they are caught up in a history that is open to the future."[30] The idea that we can overcome the possibility of error means overcoming the multitude, whose unforeseeable plurality of perspectives derives from the conditions of finitude. Only because the world is given to us from a finite perspective do we have the possibility of discovering new things and thinking new thoughts, of changing our own views and acting differently. To the degree that we apply this condition to the multitude, whose unforeseeability reaches beyond all unity and all difference, there can be no final perspective, no final and total integration. In other words: Humankind that has become "all multitudinous"[31] in the sense of an absolute democracy would be none at all – it would no longer be a multitude, but also no longer humankind.

Now, one might argue that this objection fails to recognize the status of Negri and Hardt's use of the term absolute democracy, which is that of a regulative idea for praxis. To this it must be objected that the democratic multitude should neither believe in this idea nor hope for its realization, because the idea of an absolute democracy distorts the essence of democratic policy from the very beginning. For democracy does not take aim at the singularity of the individual as a result of its politics; it is its starting point. This is based on the experience that a structurally unbreachable gap exists between the political determinations of *the demo*s and its corresponding conceptions of equality on the one hand, and the multitude of an unforeseeable diversity of singularities on the other. Democracy begins with the insight that under the condition of finitude, equality can never be absolute, rather only conditional and limited, which means that it never exists independent of power relations. In other words, the recognition of an element of sovereignty at the very foundation of democratic societies is not the unfortunate end, but the beginning of democratic politics. But this is a kind of politics whose dynamic derives from the experience of the self-difference of the *demos* and therefore can be adequately described neither in terms of absolute transcendence, nor in terms of absolute immanence. This is the dynamic of the constitutively historical self-transgression of democracy, in which the latter does not asymptotically approach a regulative idea, but in which democracy is realized only by means of a constant struggle over the nature of its concept.

We have seen just how close the connection is between an understanding of democracy that emphasizes its differential logic and motifs that have been all too hastily rejected in the philosophical tradition of the critique of aestheticization – in terms of both ethics and politics. In both dimensions we have seen that what is rejected as aestheticization is in fact constitutive for a democratic culture of freedom: a democracy that has become immune to the aestheticizing transformation of its own ethical-political self-understanding would no longer be a democracy.

Notes

Introduction: Aestheticization – An Apologia

1. Wolfgang Welsch, "Ästhetisierungsprozesse – Phänomene, Unterscheidungen, Perspektiven," in *Grenzgänge der Ästhetik* (Stuttgart: Reclam, 1996), pp. 9–61, here: p. 20f.
2. A similar discussion could also be had about theoretical philosophy, where "the aesthetic" is criticized as a distorting influence on the functioning of concepts and knowledge. The focus of this investigation, however, is on the question of the meaning of this problem for practical philosophy.
3. For this position, see Rüdiger Bubner, "Ästhetisierung der Lebenswelt," in *Ästhetische Erfahrung* (Frankfurt/Main: Suhrkamp, 1989), pp. 143–56, here especially: p. 150.
4. For this position, see Welsch, "Ästhetisierungsprozesse," especially p. 55.
5. This is Axel Honneth's justified objection to this past discussion: See Axel Honneth, "Ästhetisierung der Lebenswelt," in *Desintegration: Bruchstücke einer soziologischen Zeitdiagnose* (Frankfurt/Main: Fischer, 1994), pp. 29–38, especially pp. 29f.
6. See Gerhard Schulze, *The Experience Society* (London: Sage, 1995).
7. For a critique on Schulze, see Honneth, "Ästhetisierung der Lebenswelt," especially pp. 37f.
8. For the more recent tendency, see Luc Boltanski and Ève Chiapello, *The New Spirit of Capitalism* (London: Verso, 2007).
9. See ch. 2, sec. 7, as well as ch. 7.
10. See Terry Eagleton, *The Ideology of the Aesthetic* (Oxford & Cambridge, MA: Blackwell, 1990), especially pp. 102–19.
11. On the justified critique of a reduction of life to the "disposable material of an individual who is proud of his autonomy," see the discussion in

Wolfgang Kersting & Claus Langbehn, eds, *Kritik der Lebenskunst* (Frankfurt/Main: Suhrkamp, 2007), here: p. 8.
12 See Michel Foucault, "What is Critique," in S. Lotringer, ed., *The Politics of Truth* (Los Angeles, CA: Semiotext(e), 2007), p. 44.
13 See Axel Honneth, "Diagnose der Postmoderne," in *Desintegration*, pp. 11–19, here: pp. 18f.
14 Thus the title of Peter Bieri's book *Handwerk der Freiheit: Über die Entdeckung des eigenen Willens* (Frankfurt/Main: Fischer, 2003).
15 The meaning of the "art of freedom" intended here therefore also contradicts Kant's mention of a "divine art" according to which we are "in a position...to carry out fully, by means of it, what reason prescribes and to put the idea of it into effect." Immanuel Kant, "The Metaphysics of Morals," in *The Cambridge Edition of the Works of Immanuel Kant: Practical Philosophy* (Cambridge: Cambridge University Press, 1996), p. 373.
16 See Theodor W. Adorno, *History and Freedom: Lectures 1964–1965* (Cambridge: Polity, 2006), p. 213.
17 See the compact determination of "démocratie à venir," in Jacques Derrida, *Rogues: Two Essays on Reason* (Stanford, CA: Stanford University Press, 2005), p. 86.
18 Claude Lefort, *The Political Forms of Modern Society: Bureaucracy, Democracy, Totalitarianism* (Cambridge, MA: MIT Press, 1986), p. 305.

Chapter 1 The Provocative Beauty of Democracy: Plato

1 See Leo Strauss, *Natural Right and History* (Chicago, IL: University of Chicago Press, 1950), p. 136f.
2 *The Republic* is a paradigmatic case of the fictionalization that the historical Socrates undergoes in Plato's later dialogues. Socrates loses his independence and his resistance to the author, melding almost entirely with Plato's system. Therefore, while Socrates plays a rather insignificant role in this chapter, which primarily deals with a reading of *The Republic*, in ch. 2 I will discuss Socrates himself (and his characteristic type of irony).
3 Plato, *The Republic*, trans. Desmond Lee (London: Penguin Classics, 2007). Hereafter referred to parenthetically in the text as Rep.
4 See Plato's *Gorgias* (London: Penguin, 2004), 461e; 462b–467c.
5 See Jacques Derrida, *Rogues: Two Essays on Reason*, trans. Pascale-Anne Brault & Michael Naas (Stanford, CA: Stanford University Press, 2004), esp. pp. 26f.
6 According to Isaiah Berlin's definition, negative freedom indicates an area "within which the subject – a person or group of persons – is or should be left to do or be what he is able to do or be, without

interference by other persons." Isaiah Berlin, "Two Concepts of Liberty," in *Four Essays on Liberty* (Oxford: Oxford University Press, 1969), pp. 118–72, here: pp. 121–2.

7   On the differences and similarities between *exousia* and negative freedom (as Berlin uses the term), see also J.H.M. Solomon, "Exousia in Plato," *Platon*, vol. 37/38 (1967), pp. 189–97, here: pp. 189f, 194.

8   A paradigmatic figure would be Bob Dylan as portrayed in Todd Haynes's film *I'm Not There*.

9   See the distinction between various forms of wanting and caring in Harry Frankfurt, "The Importance of What We Care About," in *The Importance of What We Care About* (Cambridge: Cambridge University Press, 1988), pp. 80–94, here: p. 83.

10 See the portrait of the person who merely "drifts" or is "driven along" [*Getriebene*] and his experience of time in Peter Bieri, *Das Handwerk der Freiheit: Über die Entdeckung des eigenen Willens* (Frankfurt/Main: Fischer, 2003), pp. 84–90, 127–32, here: p. 130.

11 Not only Peter Bieri's "Getriebene," but also Harry Frankfurt's "wanton" bears traits of Plato's tyrant. Because the wanton cannot judge his own desires, he cannot attain the status of a person; according to Frankfurt, therefore, he fails to fulfill the condition of the possibility of free will (cf. Harry Frankfurt, "Freedom of the Will and the Concept of a Person," in *The Importance of What We Care About*, pp. 11–25, esp. pp. 16–19). However, this figure, just like Plato's tyrant and Bieri's "Getriebene" appears to me to be relatively far-fetched, as it appears to presuppose an idea of practical rationality according to which we must be capable of answering the question of how we are to act strategically in a given situation, but without evaluating our desires and thus taking up a reflective stance toward them. For this reason I regard Frankfurt's definition of what it means to be a person, contrary to a "merely" rational being, as being questionable. (A detailed critique of Frankfurt can be found in Anna Kusser, *Dimensionen der Kritik von Wünschen* (Frankfurt/Main: Athenäum, 1989), pp. 139–54.) Nevertheless we are clearly dealing with constructions that aim to (overly) accentuate the notion of freedom discussed above: A life without anchoring in beliefs that allow us to judge the intentions that arise in reaction to the world is not a free life.

12 For such an alternative conception of free will, see Martin Seel, "Ein Lob der Willensschwäche," in *Sich bestimmen lassen: Studien zur theoretischen und praktischen Philosophie* (Frankfurt/Main: Suhrkamp, 2002), pp. 227–45, here: p. 238.

13 Plato, *Protagoras* (Oxford: Oxford University Press, 2009), 358c.

14 In this case the soul does not do what reason – supported by the second, zealous part of the soul – commands, but only what its desires urge it to do. On this interpretation of the problem of *akrasia* in the work of Plato, see Anton Hügli, "Willensschwäche," in Joachim Ritter, Karlfried Gründer, & Gottfried Gabriel, eds, *Historisches Wörterbuch der Philosophie*, vol. XII (Basel: Schwabe, 2004), column 800–9, here: 801.

15 See Derrida, *Rogues*, pp. 21–2, 26.
16 See Seel, "Ein Lob der Willensschwäche," p. 237. We find a similar distinction in Harry Frankfurt, "Identification and Wholeheartedness," in *The Importance of What We Care About*, pp. 159–76, here: p. 165.
17 See Seel, "Ein Lob der Willensschwäche," p. 232.
18 On the relation between weakness of will and self-deception, see Donald Davidson, "Deception and Division," in *Problems of Rationality* (Oxford: Clarendon Press, 2004), pp. 199–212, here: p. 200.
19 This is in contrast to Seel's claim in "Ein Lob der Willensschwäche," pp. 235–8.
20 Therefore, we should not merely confound such problems with *akrasia*, as Amélie Rorty suggests. See "The Social and Political Sources of Akrasia," *Ethics*, vol. 107, no. 4 (1997), pp. 644–57.
21 See Bieri, *Das Handwerk der Freiheit*, pp. 54, 61–5.
22 See Martin Löw-Beer, "Sind wir einzigartig? Zum Verhältnis von Selbstbewusstsein und Individualität," *Deutsche Zeitschrift für Philosophie*, vol. 42, no.1 (1994), pp. 121–39, here: p. 132.
23 See Frankfurt, "Identification and Wholeheartedness," esp. pp. 175f.
24 See Frankfurt, "The Importance of What We Care About," p. 84.
25 See Seel, "Ein Lob der Willensschwäche," p. 241.
26 See Jacques Derrida, "Force of Law: The 'Mystical Foundation' of Authority," in *Acts of Religion* (New York: Routledge, 2002), pp. 228–97, here: p. 255.
27 Derrida, *Rogues*, p. 84.
28 Donald Davidson, "Paradoxes of Irrationality," in *Problems of Rationality*, pp. 169–87, here: p. 186.
29 Ibid., p. 187.
30 Ibid.
31 Seel, "Ein Lob der Willensschwäche," p. 242.
32 See Ernst Tugendhat, *Self-Consciousness and Self-Determination* (Cambridge, MA: MIT Press, 1989), p. 294.
33 Ibid., p. 322.
34 See Bieri's portrait of the "intellectual follower" [*gedanklicher Mitläufer*] in *Das Handwerk der Freiheit*, pp. 93–6.
35 Ibid., pp. 95f.
36 See Gerhard Schulze's critical description of the "milieu of self-realization" that prevailed during the 1970s: Gerhard Schulze, *The Experience Society* (London: Sage, 1995), ch. 6.5.
37 See Tugendhat, *Self-Consciousness and Self-Determination*, p. 196.
38 See Arbogast Schmitt, *Der Einzelne und die Gemeinschaft in der Dichtung Homers und in der Staatstheorie bei Platon: Zur Ableitung der Staatstheorie aus der Psychologie* (Stuttgart: Steiner, 2000).
39 After all, this "adumbration" is not merely foreign to the idea of developing the capacities of the soul, as Arbogast Schmitt argues (ibid., pp. 49f.). Rather, it should complement them in a relation between "external actions" and "inward self" (Rep 443c).

40 Jacques Rancière points out the central role played by this argument against *polypragmosyne* in the *Republic*. See Jacques Rancière, *Das Unvernehmen, Politik und Philosophie* (Frankfurt/Main: Suhrkamp, 2002), p. 31.
41 See Solomon, "Exousia in Plato," pp. 193, 195. Thucydides also addresses "*ploutos kai exousia*" in his *History of the Peloponnesian War*. By contrast, the notion of *eleutheria* signifies not only the freedom from external unfreedom, but also freedom from desires, which is why the term often appears in combination with *eirene* (inner) peace. See Rep 329c.
42 See also Christoph Menke, "Innere Natur und soziale Normativität," in Hans Joas & Klaus Wiegandt, eds, *Die kulturellen Werte Europas* (Frankfurt/Main: Fischer, 2005), pp. 304–52, here: pp. 337f.
43 Events "create cracks in the 'interpreted world'," as Martin Seel writes in his brief phenomenology of the event. Martin Seel, "Von Ereignissen," in *Paradoxien der Erfüllung: Philosophische Essays* (Frankfurt/Main: Fischer, 2006), pp. 11–26, here: p. 18.
44 George H. Mead, *Mind, Self, and Society: From the Standpoint of a Social Behaviorist* (Chicago, IL: University of Chicago Press, 1934), p. 204.
45 See also the discussion of Herder's genealogical concept of nature in Menke, "Innere Natur und soziale Normativität," pp. 340f., as well as Christoph Menke, *Kraft: Ein Grundbegriff ästhetischer Anthropologie* (Frankfurt/Main: Suhrkamp, 2008), esp. p. 68.
46 See Jan Bransen, "Identification and the Idea of an Alternative of Oneself," *European Journal of Philosophy*, vol. 4, no. 1 (1996), pp. 1–12, here: p. 12.
47 See Helmuth Plessner, *Die Stufen des Organischen und der Mensch* (Berlin/New York: de Gruyter, 1975), esp. pp. 298f.
48 Ibid., p. 299.
49 With regard to this structure, acts of self-determination are similar to the founding of a state. See Jacques Derrida, "Declarations of Independence," *New Political Science*, vol. 7, no. 1 (1986), pp. 7–15, here: p. 9.
50 This is what Harry Frankfurt suggests when he proposes a hierarchical distinction between "first order desires" and "second order volitions," the latter of which is located at a higher level, from which the subject should be able to judge the desires at the first level. See Frankfurt, "Freedom of the Will and the Concept of a Person."
51 See Dirk Setton, *Unvermögen: Irrationalität und der Begriff der rationalen Fähigkeiten* (Berlin: August Verlag, 2011), esp. ch. 6, secs 1 and 2.
52 See Bieri, *Das Handwerk der Freiheit*, pp. 49–53.
53 See Dieter Thomae, *Erzähle dich selbst: Lebensgeschichte als philosophisches Problem* (Frankfurt/Main: Suhrkamp, 2007), p. 254.
54 The experience of a divide between natural foundation and social form – or in Mead's terms: between the "I" and the "me" – should therefore

not be viewed as a crisis along the path to a *true* self-identity in which both sides are completely integrated, as Habermas suggests. See Jürgen Habermas, "Individuation through Socialization: On George Herbert Mead's Theory of Subjectivity," in *Postmetaphysical Thinking: Philosophical Essays* (Cambridge, MA: MIT Press, 1992), pp. 149–204, here: p. 181. Instead, we are dealing with a fundamental divide that can remain a latent source of possible change even when we feel at one with ourselves.

55 See Philippe Lacoue-Labarthe's reflections on the logic of mimesis in "Diderot: Paradox and Mimesis," in *Typography: Mimesis, Philosophy, Politics* (Stanford, CA: Stanford University Press, 1998), pp. 248–66, esp. pp. 258–61.
56 Plato, *The Laws* (London: Penguin Classics, 1970). Hereafter referred to parenthetically in the text as L.
57 Ludger Schwarte emphasizes this aspect in his reading of the *Nomoi*: Ludger Schwarte, *Philosophie der Architektur* (Munich: Wilhelm Fink, 2009), p. 152.
58 As Urs Stäheli puts it, the crowd is "a typical phenomenon of a post-stratified society." See Urs Stäheli, "Übersteigerte Nachahmung – Tarde's Massentheorie," in Christian Borch & Urs Stäheli, eds, *Soziologie der Nachahmung und des Begehrens: Materialien zu Gabriel Tarde* (Frankfurt/Main: Suhrkamp, 2009), pp. 397–426, here: pp. 401, 411.
59 On the aspect of affective infection, see Gabriel Tarde, "Le public et la foule," in *L'opinion et la foule* (Paris: PUF, 1989), pp. 31–71, here: p. 57; on the self-organization of the crowd, see Gabriel Tarde, *La philosophie pénale* (Paris: Éditions Cujas, 1972), p. 324.
60 On the role of charismatic rule in a democracy, see ch. 6, sec. 7.
61 Stäheli, "Übersteigerte Nachahmung," p. 403.
62 Gabriel Tarde, *The Laws of Imitation* (New York: Henry Holt, 1903), p. 71.
63 Ibid., p. xxii.
64 Gabriel Tarde, *On Communication and Social Influence: Selected Papers*, ed. Terry N. Clark (Chicago, IL: University of Chicago Press, 1969), p. 171.
65 See Tarde, *The Laws of Imitation*; Stäheli, "Übersteigerte Nachahmung," p. 413.
66 For this reason Tarde does not reserve the concept of imitation for conscious acts: "Nothing…is less scientific that the establishment of this absolute separation, of this abrupt break, between the voluntary and the involuntary, between the conscious and the unconscious." Tarde, *The Laws of Imitation*, p. xiii.
67 Tarde, *Social Laws: An Outline of Sociology* (Kitchener: Batoche Books, 2000), pp. 83–5.
68 See the introduction to ch. 6
69 "One can belong – and in fact one always does belong – simultaneously to several publics, as to several corporations or sects; one can only

be part of one crowd at a time. From this follows the far greater intolerance of crowds, and consequently of nations dominated by the spirit of crowds, because one is completely taken over, irresistibly drawn along by a force with no counterbalance; hence the advantage of the gradual substitution of publics for crowds, a transformation which is always accompanied by progress in tolerance, if not in skepticism." Gabriel Tarde, *On Communication and Social Influence: Selected Papers* (Chicago, IL: University of Chicago Press, 1969), p. 281.

70 On the distinction between representatives and exemplars, see Stanley Cavell, *Conditions Handsome and Unhandsome: The Constitution of Emersonian Perfectionism* (Chicago, IL: University of Chicago Press, 1990), esp. pp. 10f., 50f.

71 Ibid., p. 59.

72 Stanley Cavell points out that in the post-metaphysical world, the perfectionist idea of self-cultivation must be understood in connection with the fact that we are not transparent to ourselves. In this sense perfectionism means attempting (repeatedly) to become intelligible to ourselves and others. See ibid., p. xxxi.

73 Because there is a tension between the individual and the social good, which are nevertheless interwoven, both sides cannot be reconciled with each other by relegating them to two separate spheres, as Richard Rorty suggests when he locates self-creation in the private sphere and solidarity in the public sphere. See Richard Rorty, *Contingency, Irony and Solidarity* (Cambridge: Cambridge University Press, 1989), pp. 13f., 142.

74 Standing up for this possibility implies a general objection to political theories that give too little space to the dynamic of self-perfection. See Cavell's critique of John Rawls in *Conditions Handsome and Unhandsome*, pp. 101–26, here: p. 106.

75 On the democratic relation between sovereignty and recognition, see ch. 5, sec. 8.

76 This should also make clear that the transformation in our understanding of ethics and politics brought about by aestheticization does not merely amount to replacing the ethical foundation of political theory with an aesthetic one. (This is the project of Franklin Rudolf Ankersmit's book *Aesthetic Politics: Political Philosophy Beyond Fact and Value* (Stanford, CA: Stanford University Press, 1996).) Instead, the point is to attain a different understanding of both ethics and politics, which also concerns the relation between the two.

77 It is well known that after the antique experiment with the idea of democracy, it essentially disappeared in both theory and practice for a very long time. When it was discussed at all, it was not regarded as an ideal form of government. Not until the eighteenth century did democracy take on a positive connotation, and not until the nineteenth century did democracy gain broad acceptance. This is the climate in which the romantic movement emerges.

Chapter 2 The Morality of Irony: Hegel

1. Georg Wilhelm Friedrich Hegel, *Werke in zwanzig Bänden* (Frankfurt/Main: Suhrkamp, 1969–1971), vol. 7, *Grundlinien der Philosophie des Rechts*, pp. 285–6, trans. H.B. Nisbet as *Elements of the Philosophy of Right* (Cambridge: Cambridge University Press, 1991), pp. 180–2. Translations have been modified. Hereafter referred to parenthetically in the text as Rph. References are to the numbered sections, common to both editions, here, §140.
2. For a reading of Hegelian irony that thus turns Hegel against Hegel, i.e. by setting the Hegel who interprets *Antigone* in the *Phenomenology* against the Hegel who writes the *Philosophy of Right*, see Christoph Menke, *Tragödie im Sittlichen. Gerechtigkeit und Freiheit nach Hegel* (Frankfurt/Main: Suhrkamp, 1996), esp. ch. 4.
3. For a reading that works out the therapeutic ambition of Hegel's *Philosophy of Right*, see Andrew Norris, "Willing and Deciding: Hegel on Irony, Evil, and the Sovereign Exception," *Diacritics*, vol. 37, no. 2–3 (2007), pp. 135–56, trans. B.N. Nagel & J. Rebentisch as "Wollen und Entscheiden: Hegel über das Böse, die Ironie und die souveräne Ausnahme," in J. Rebentisch & D. Setton, eds, *Willkür: Freiheit und Gesetz II* (Berlin: August Verlag, 2011), pp. 101–40.
4. Georg Wilhelm Friedrich Hegel, *Werke*, vols 18–20, *Vorlesungen über die Geschichte der Philosophie*, 18:404, trans. E.S. Haldane & F.H. Simson as *Hegel's Lectures on the History of Philosophy* (New York: The Humanities Press, 1955), vol. 1, p. 350; translation modified. Hereafter referred to parenthetically in the text as GPh. Page references, separated by a slash, will be first to the German *Werke*, then to the English text. Note, however, that the English edition sometimes omits and reorders passages as they appear in the German.
5. Hegel explicitly groups the two together on this point: "On the one hand, [that which is] is subjective for Socrates and Plato, posited by the activity of thought – this is the moment of freedom, that the subject is with its own, this is spiritual [*geistige*] nature; yet on the other hand [that which is] is equally something objective in and for itself – not external objectivity, but spiritual [*geistige*] universality. This is the True, the unity of the subjective and the objective in contemporary terminology" (GPh 18:444/1:387).
6. According to Hegel, Plato developed the Socratic standpoint into a "science." It is only with Plato that "philosophical science" becomes "science" (GPh 19:11/2:1).
7. Cf. Aristophanes, *The Clouds*, edited and translated by J. Henderson (Cambridge: Loeb Classical Library, 1998). Citations are to the line numbers of the original. *The Clouds* presents the fable of Strepsiades, whose name comes from "strepho," which means to overturn, to upset, to twist, to turn things over in one's mind. Strepsiades is a simple Attic

farmer who attempts to avoid paying the debts he incurred through his son's prodigality by means of a sophistical argument that is supposed to convince his creditors that the law that one must pay one's debts does not apply in his case. In order to educate himself in the art that makes right into wrong (cf. l. 657), he undertakes to study with Socrates. After he proves to be unfit for sophistry, he sends his son to learn from Socrates how the case against his creditors can be won. The son turns out to be an extraordinarily talented disciple – albeit in a manner that quickly works to his father's disadvantage. Instead of practicing as a lawyer in his father's case, the son begins to "scorn established customs" (l. 1400) to such an extent that even the command to respect one's father ceases to appear valid to him. To contradict one's father is just as permissible as beating one's father, the son explains in good Socratic style, having just done both. The father then curses Socratic dialectic, pleads for the return of the old ethics that he himself had turned against, and burns down the house of Socrates.

8 Ibid., l. 1485–92.
9 The conviction of Socrates by no means entailed his being condemned to death. Socrates was simply asked to determine his own punishment. Yet because this would have amounted to an admission of guilt for something that he did not consider wrong, he ruled out this option. It was this new revolt of subjective freedom against the law of "naïve ethics" ("*unbefangene Sitte*") that sealed his fate. Cf. GPh 18:508–9/1:440–2.
10 It is telling that in Hegel's *History of Philosophy*, this issue only comes up again in connection with Plato, with the purpose of indicating a deficiency in the "systematic exposition," which is at the same time a "deficiency in respect of the concrete determination of the Idea itself" (GPh 19:27/2:17).
11 For a fuller version of this summary, see Albrecht Wellmer, *Sprachphilosophie: Eine Vorlesung* (Frankfurt/Main: Suhrkamp, 2004), pp. 247–50.
12 Cf. Theodor W. Adorno, *Negative Dialektik*, in his *Gesammelte Schriften* (Frankfurt/Main: Suhrkamp, 1970), 6:350, trans. E.B. Ashton as *Negative Dialectics* (London: Routledge and Kegan Paul, 1973), p. 357; translation modified.
13 Accordingly, Charles Taylor writes that "the crucial characteristic of *Sittlichkeit* is that it enjoins us to bring about what already is. This is a paradoxical way of putting it, but in fact the common life which is the basis of my *sittlich* obligation is already there in existence. It is in virtue of its being an ongoing affair that I have these obligations; and my fulfillment of these obligations is what sustains it and keeps it in being. Hence in *Sittlichkeit*, there is no gap between what ought to be and what is, between *Sollen* and *Sein*." Cf. Charles Taylor, *Hegel* (Cambridge: Cambridge University Press, 1977), p. 376.
14 The marginalization of the particular case is thus the same operation that prepares the way for the equalization of the distinction between

objective and absolute spirit. The result of this operation, as Michael Theunissen has argued, is ultimately that "all intersubjectivity" gets "separated from the basis of ethical substantiality." The independence of the individual then appears to be just an accident of a self-consciousness that gets attributed to substance itself. Cf. Michael Theunissen, "Die verdrängte Intersubjektivität in Hegels Philosophie des Rechts," in D. Henrich & R.P. Horstmann, eds, *Hegels Philosophie des Rechts. Die Theorie der Rechtsformen und ihre Logik*, (Stuttgart: Klett-Cotta, 1982). In particular, see Section I, "Die Verdrängung der Intersubjektivität aus der Sittlichkeit: Familie, Geist und Selbstbewußtsein der Substanz," pp. 322–9, esp. p. 328.

15 Georg Wilhelm Friedrich Hegel, "Über die wissenschaftlichen Behandlungsarten des Naturrechts, seine Stelle in der praktischen Philosophie und sein Verhältnis zu den positive Rechtswissenschaften," in *Werke*, vol. 2, *Jenaer Schriften 1801–1807*, 461. Translations by Daniel Smyth. Hereafter referred to parenthetically in the text as JS. Page references are to the German text.

16 Immanuel Kant, *Critique of Practical Reason*, in *Practical Philosophy*, tr. M.J. Gregor (Cambridge: Cambridge University Press, 1996), Comment to §4.

17 Cf. Terry Pinkard, *German Philosophy 1760–1860: The Legacy of Idealism* (Cambridge: Cambridge University Press, 2002), p. 59.

18 Cf. Jürgen Habermas, "Treffen Hegels Einwände gegen Kant auch auf die Diskursethik zu?," in *Erläuterungen zur Diskursethik* (Frankfurt/Main: Suhrkamp, 1991), p. 21. But then, as Ingeborg Maus argues, the Kantian moral principle is no longer tautological. For it rests "on the differentiation of two reciprocally applicable processes." On this reading, the moral procedure of evaluating maxims according to the categorical imperative is based on ethical connections between action and experience and arises reflexively from within them. Cf. Ingeborg Maus, *Zur Aufklärung der Demokratietheorie: Rechts- und demokratietheoretische Überlegungen im Anschluß an Kant* (Frankfurt/Main: Suhrkamp, 1992), p. 264.

19 Cf. Habermas, "Treffen Hegels Einwände?," p. 21.

20 This would also be the appropriate level on which to discuss the question whether Hegel's objections to Kant equally impugn Habermas' "discourse ethics." But this cannot and should not occupy us here. I cited Habermas in this context only in order to consider the arguments he advances in direct support of Kant.

21 Wellmer's instructive discussion of Kant is highly relevant here. Cf. Albrecht Wellmer, *Ethik und Dialog. Elemente des moralischen Urteils bei Kant und in der Diskursethik* (Frankfurt/Main: Suhrkamp, 1986), p. 48.

22 Cf. ibid., pp. 26–7.
23 Cf. ibid., pp. 29–30.
24 Ibid., p. 130.
25 Ibid., p. 28 (original emphasis).

26 Ibid.
27 Cf. ibid., p. 131.
28 Cf. ibid., pp. 134, 136. This is what distinguishes what I have termed Wellmer's "Socratic" reformulation of the moral principle from the one advocated by Habermas, who focuses on the problem of the justice of norms. For Wellmer's critical discussion of Habermas on this point, see ibid., pp. 122, 134–8.
29 See ibid., p. 132.
30 Axel Honneth, *Suffering from Indeterminacy: An Attempt at a Reactualization of Hegel's Philosophy of Right* (Amsterdam: van Gorcum, 2000), p. 56.
31 Georg Wilhelm Friedrich Hegel, *Werke*, vol. 3, *Phänomenologie des Geistes*, p. 490, trans. A.V. Miller as *Hegel's Phenomenology of Spirit* (Oxford: Oxford University Press, 1977), p. 405; translation modified. Hereafter referred to parenthetically in the text as PhG. Page references, separated by a slash, will be first to the German, then to the English text.
32 Ernst Behler, "Friedrich Schlegel und Hegel," in *Hegel-Studien*, vol. 2 (1963), p. 206.
33 Otto Pöggeler, *Hegels Kritik der Romantik* (Munich: Fink, 1998), p. 39.
34 Georg Wilhelm Friedrich Hegel, *Werke*, vols 13–15, *Vorlesungen über die Ästhetik*, 13:93, trans. T.M. Knox as *Aesthetics: Lectures on Fine Art*, 2 vols (Oxford: Clarendon Press, 1998), 1:64. Hereafter referred to parenthetically in the text as Ä. Volume and page references, separated by a slash, will be first to the German *Werke*, then to the English text.
35 GPh 20:413/3:506. Here we find a convenient summary of Hegel's critique of Fichte. Cf. also Ludwig Siep, *Hegels Fichtekritik und die Wissenschaftslehre von 1804* (Freiburg/Munich: Verlag Karl Alber, 1970).
36 Ernst Tugendhat, *Self-Consciousness and Self-Determination*, p. 309.
37 Axel Honneth, "Organized Self-Realization: Paradoxes of Individualization," in *The I in We* (Cambridge: Polity, 2012), pp. 153–68.
38 This formulation is taken from Luc Boltanski & Ève Chiapello, *The New Spirit of Capitalism*, trans. Gregory Elliott (London: Verso, 2007).
39 Cf. Alain Ehrenberg, *The Weariness of the Self: Diagnosing the History of Depression in the Contemporary Age*, trans. Enrico Caouette et al. (Montreal: McGill-Queens University Press, 2010), p. 230; Ehrenberg, "Depression: Unbehagen in der Kultur oder neue Formen der Sozialität," in Christoph Menke & Juliane Rebentisch, eds, *Kreation und Depression: Freiheit im gegenwärtigen Kapitalismus* (Berlin: Kadmos, 2010), pp. 52–62, esp. pp. 58f. Cf. also Richard Sennett's reflections on the problem of narcissism in post-Fordism: *The Fall of Public Man* (New York: W.W. Norton, 1974), esp. ch. 14, "The Actor Deprived of His Art," pp. 313–36.
40 Cf. ch. 6, sec. 9.

41 Cf. Karl Heinz Bohrer, *Die Kritik der Romantik: Der Verdacht der Philosophie gegen die literarische Moderne* (Frankfurt/Main: Suhrkamp, 1989), esp. pp. 142–53.
42 Karl Heinz Bohrer, "Das Romantisch-Phantastische als dezentriertes Bewusstsein: Zum Problem seiner Repräsentanz," in *Die Grenzes des Ästhetischen* (Munich: Hanser Verlag, 1998), pp. 9–36, here: p. 9.
43 Ludwig Heyde, "Politik und Ironie," in Andreas Arndt, Karol Bal & Henning Ottmann, eds, *Hegels Ästhetik: Die Kunst der Politik – die Politik der Kunst* (Berlin: Akademie, 2000), pp. 30–5, here: p. 34.
44 Ibid.
45 Ibid.
46 In this sense, we cannot conceive of a culture that "socialized its youth in such a way as to make them continually dubious about their own process of socialization." Yet contrary to what Rorty suggests, we should not take this to mean that we require a non-ironic public rhetoric with an established vocabulary from which grown ironists can distance themselves through the development of their own vocabulary (cf. Richard Rorty, *Contingency, Irony and Solidarity* (Cambridge: Cambridge University Press, 1989), p. 87). Instead, we could defend the project of educating children to be ironically dubious about their socialization process as an important element in learning how to live an autonomous life, precisely because this doubt can never be aimed at an entire form of life. This is due less to psychological reasons than to reasons that concern the question of whether such doubt is even possible: "If you tried to doubt everything, you would not get as far as doubting anything. The game of doubting itself presupposes certainty" (cf. Ludwig Wittgenstein, *On Certainty* (New York: Harper and Row, 1969), §115). The impossibility of having reservations concerning the fallibility of everything at once can therefore be seen best in controversies over terminology with which a society articulates its self-understanding. As Donald Davidson has pointed out, such controversies presuppose a quite broad common ground upon which such a debate can take place at all. (Cf. Donald Davidson, "The Method of Truth in Metaphysics," in *Inquiries into Truth and Interpretation*, 2nd edn (Oxford: Oxford University Press, 2001), pp. 199–214, here: pp. 199–201.)
47 Cf. the section entitled "Humor, Irony and the Law" in Gilles Deleuze, "Coldness and Cruelty," in *Masochism: Coldness and Cruelty by Gilles Deleuze and Venus in Furs by Leopold von Sacher-Masoch* (New York: Zone Books, 1989), pp. 81–90, here: pp. 86–7.
48 Ibid., p. 86.
49 Ibid., p. 87.
50 Georg Lukács, *The Theory of the Novel* (London: Merlin Press, 1978), p. 62. Quoted in Theodor W. Adorno, "The Idea of Natural History," *Telos* 6 (1984), p. 118.
51 The rationalism displayed by de Sade's Juliette, who lacks all emotions and passion, is supposed to demonstrate how "as its final result,

civilization leads back to the terrors of nature." See the chapter "Juliette or Enlightenment and Morality," in Theodor W. Adorno & Max Horkheimer, *Dialectic of Enlightenment* (Stanford, CA: Stanford University Press, 2002), pp. 63–93, here: p. 89.
52 Deleuze, "Coldness and Cruelty," p. 87.
53 Paul Valery, *Cahiers/Notebooks*, trans. Paul Gifford (Frankfurt/Main: Peter Lang, 2000), p. 75.
54 On the relation between self-perfecting and self-difference, see ch. 1, sec. 12.
55 Ernst Behler has shown that Hegel's critique refers more to his own notion of Schlegel's irony than the original. Cf. Behler, "Friedrich Schlegel und Hegel," p. 217.
56 Friedrich von Schlegel, *Philosophical Fragments* (Minneapolis, MN: University of Minnesota Press, 1991), pp. 6–7.
57 For a similar interpretation of romantic irony, see also Jean Starobinski's reading of E.T.A. Hoffman's *Prinzessin Bambilla*: Jean Starobinski, "Ironie et mélancholie: Gozzi, Hoffmann, Kierkegaard," in *Estratto da Sensibilitá e Razionalitá nel Settecento* (Florence, 1967).
58 Theodor W. Adorno, *History and Freedom: Lectures 1964–1965* (Cambridge: Polity, 2006), pp. 213f.
59 Ibid., p. 216.
60 Maus, *Zur Aufklärung der Demokratietheorie*, pp. 267f (trans. Joseph Ganahl).
61 Rousseau's complete formulation is as follows: "Only then, when the voice of duty replaces physical impulse and right replaces appetite, does man, who until then considered only himself, find himself forced to act on other principles and to consult his reason before heeding his inclinations." Jean-Jacques Rousseau, *On the Social Contract*, in *The Social Contract and Other Later Political Writings* (Cambridge: Cambridge University Press, 1997), pp. 39–152, here: Book 1, Chapter 8, Paragraph 1.
62 For a discussion of this problem in the work of Rousseau, see ch. 5, sec. 10.
63 Robert Pippin raises a similar objection to Christine Korsgaard in "On Giving Oneself the Law," in Nalin Ranasinghe, *Logos and Eros: Essays Honoring Stanley Rosen* (South Bend, IN: St. Augustine's Press, 2006).
64 See the discussion of Plato's description of the akratic democrat in ch. 1, secs 4 and 5.
65 On Kant's "incorporation thesis," see Henry E. Allison, *Kant's Theory of Freedom* (Cambridge: Cambridge University Press, 1990), pp. 39f.
66 Cf. Alenka Zupančič, *Ethics of the Real: Kant, Lacan* (London: Verso, 2000), pp. 32–3. According to Kant, the evil subject decides against the possibility of a second decision in which it could consider and appropriate its own – unconscious – decisions. Instead, similar to Plato's tyrant and Frankfurt's wanton, it remains on the level of its immediate decisions without critically examining its impulses and thus becoming a true subject of its own will. Because it contents itself with a minimum of

freedom, it is evil. It is evil, because it chooses unfreedom (cf. Zupančič, *Ethics of the Real*, p. 39).
67 Cf. Gerhard Gamm, "Die Unausdeutbarkeit des Selbst," in *Nicht nichts: Studien zu einer Semantik des Unbestimmten* (Frankfurt/Main: Suhrkamp, 2000), pp. 207–27, here: p. 209.
68 Cf. ch. 1, sec. 5 as well as Donald Davidson, "Paradoxes of Irrationality," in *Problems of Rationality* (Oxford: Oxford University Press, 2004), pp. 169–88, here: p. 188.
69 Cf. Martin Seel, "Über das Böse in der Moral," in his *Sich bestimmen lassen*, pp. 246–57, esp. 249–50 and 252–3. Another forceful set of reflections on this point is provided by Hannah Arendt, "Personal Responsibility Under Dictatorship," in her *Responsibility and Judgement* (New York: Schocken Books, 2003), pp. 17–48, esp. 44–5. If we, along with Michel Foucault, view this understanding of morality, which contradicts here conventionality, as a reformulation of Kant's intentions, then we would have to regard this reformulation as being romantic in the sense used here. Cf. Michel Foucault, "What is Enlightenment," in Paul Rabinow, ed., *The Foucault Reader* (New York: Pantheon Books, 1984), pp. 32–50.
70 For a discussion of the connection between moral judgments and changes in collective interpretive patterns, see Wellmer, *Ethik und Dialog*, pp. 125–6.
71 On this point, see Andrew Norris's conclusion that irony and crime occupy similar systematic positions for Hegel: "Crime makes morality possible in that the criminal who violates the contractual conditions of Abstract Right can only be judged from a perspective that respects but nonetheless transcends that Right. (…) Essentially the same is and must be the case with irony, which… signals the need for Ethical Life as crime signals the need for Morality. (…) But at the same time, it is difficult to see how irony might play the large and productive role Hegel assigns to it. Hegel presents irony as dissolving everything it touches into the arbitrary whim of the subject" (Norris, "Willing and Deciding," p. 139).
72 Theunissen, "Die verdrängte Subjektivität in Hegels Philosophie des Rechts," p. 325.
73 Ibid.
74 One of the main points of Jacques Derrida's reading of Hegel, combined with a text on Jean Genet, in *Glas* (Lincoln, NE: University of Nebraska Press, 1986) is to point out the costs of this operation.
75 Adorno, *Negative Dialektik*, p. 350 (trans. Joseph Ganahl).
76 Terry Pinkard therefore sees the actual point of Hegel's objection to Kant as lying in the fact that the "practical judgments made within *Sittlichkeit* are thus not a matter of the application of principles to cases," rather they concern our skill, acquired by virtue of our social practices, to "discern the normative saliences of particular situations." This acquired skill enables us to make a practical judgment as to what to do in those situations without necessarily being able to state a rule

for it." Pinkard uses the term virtue to characterize this quasi-automatic way of orienting ourselves in social space. See Terry Pinkard, "Virtues, Morality, and *Sittlichkeit*: From Maxims to Practices," *European Journal of Philosophy*, vol. 7, no. 2 (April 1999): pp. 217–38, here: pp. 226f. Yet in truth it is not easy to see to what extent this reference to the fact that we often make automatic judgments in matters of morality (since we have trained such practices) can be an answer to those situations that undermine such automatic responses, situations toward which moral reflection addresses itself.

77 Cf. Rolf-Peter Horstmann, "Subjektiver Geist und Moralität: Zur systematischen Stellung der Philosophie des subjektiven Geistes," in Dieter Henrich, ed., *Hegels philosophische Psychologie*, in *Hegel-Studien*, Beiheft 19 (1979), pp. 191–9, here: pp. 197f.
78 Cf. Honneth, *Suffering from Indeterminacy*, pp. 13–38.
79 Horstmann, "Subjektiver Geist und Moralität," p. 197.
80 Hegel thereby cites the observation of an (often criticized) historian of philosophy, Wilhelm Gottlieb Tennemann.
81 Cf. Alexander Nehamas, *The Art of Living: Socratic Reflections from Plato to Foucault* (Berkeley & Los Angeles: University of California Press, 1988), p. 86.
82 The concept of history implied by this argument is therefore entirely different from the concept we find in the Hegelian perspective discussed in the previous section. Once the "concept of the will" is turned into "the will of the concept" (Theunissen, "Die verdrängte Intersubjektivität in Hegels Philosophie des Rechts," p. 332), it is only logical that history is then understood as a procession of conceptually necessary stages in the self-development of the idea. Acting individuals are then degraded to media of a superior cunning of reason, and this conception of the process of history leaves little room for the unexpected, and thus also for individual events [*das Ereignis*]. Ernst Behler points out the position of Schlegel's philosophy of spirit and history as being systematically and diametrically opposed to (this version of) Hegel, and thus also in line with later objections to Hegel, e.g. on the part of Wilhelm Dilthey. This is true both with regard to its sensibility to the "ineliminable particularity and peculiarity of historical life" in its "infinite abundance" and its insistence on the "creative power of intellectual life" in its "radical unpredictability," untameable by "ex post justifications of truth." It is also true with regard to the role that Schlegel in his later work ascribes to the "living knowledge" and the "personal spirit" of historical persons (cf. Behler, "Friedrich Schlegel und Hegel," pp. 228f.).

Chapter 3   The Ethics of Aesthetic Existence: Kierkegaard

1 My sketch of the relations between aesthetic, ethical, and religious existence thus remains within the limits set by Kierkegaard's pseudony-

mous works ranging from *"Either/Or"* to *"Sickness Unto Death."* I will not be dealing with Kierkegaard's Christian writings.

2 Søren Kierkegaard, *The Concept of Irony with Continual Reference to Socrates*, ed. and trans. by H.V. Hong & E.H. Hong (Princeton, NJ: Princeton University Press, 1989). Hereafter referred to parenthetically in the text as CI.

3 Lore Hühn, "Ironie und Dialektik: Zur Kritik der Romantik bei Kierkegaard und Hegel," in Niels Jørgen Cappelørn, Herrmann K. Deuser & K. Brian Söderquist, eds, *Kierkegaard Studies Yearbook 2009: Kierkegaard's Concept of Irony* (Berlin: de Gruyter), pp. 17–40, here: p. 31. On the ambivalence of the references to Hegel in Kierkegaard's text on irony, as well as on the history of the reception of this text, see also Philipp Schwab, "Zwischen Sokrates und Hegel: Der Einzelne, die Weltgeschichte und die Form der Mitteilung in Kierkegaards *Über den Begriff der Ironie*," in Cappelørn et al., *Kierkegaard Studies Yearbook 2009*, pp. 127–51, here: pp. 134–8.

4 Karl Heinz Bohrer, *Die Kritik der Romantik: Der Verdacht der Philosophie gegen die literarische Moderne* (Frankfurt/Main: Suhrkamp, 1989), p. 157.

5 Kierkegaard criticizes the fact that Hegel, due to his polemic stance against Schlegel's irony, does justice neither to the concept of irony in general nor to that of Socratic irony in particular (cf. CI 265–70). Nevertheless, his characterization of both types of irony is largely Hegelian in all of the features that interest us here. In this context it is remarkable that Kierkegaard, vis-à-vis Hegel, uses Socrates' phrase "I know that I know nothing" to emphasize an ambivalence in order to make apparent that even this phrase should be understood as irony. Although it is true, as Hegel noted, that Socrates meant this statement quite seriously, there is a certain levity in Socrates' insistence on knowing nothing. According to Kierkegaard, Socrates only takes his knowing nothing seriously to the extent that it can be mobilized against a given situation. But he takes his "ignorance" seriously neither in a theoretical nor in a personal sense. In other words, neither does he become a speculative philosopher nor is he afflicted by existential despair (CI 270). Because he is thus both serious about his ignorance (he really was ignorant) and not serious about it (he took neither personal nor philosophical account of his ignorance), Kierkegaard claims that the Socratic standpoint expressed in the phrase "I know that I know nothing" should be called ironic. However, precisely the systematic kernel of this determination of the Socratic standpoint as a kind of negativity toward the world, a negativity which does not takes account of its own deficits, closely resembles that of Hegel (cf. ch. 2, sec. 1).

6 We are familiar with this motif, according to which a person can only be *everything* to the degree that he is *nothing*, from Plato's critique of the theater (cf. ch. 1, sec. 9). It will also reappear in Rousseau's critique of the actor (cf. ch. 5, sec. 1). Denis Diderot uses the term "the actor's paradox" to capture this phenomenon.

7 Rahel Jaeggi, for instance, distinguishes between self-realization in the sense of realizing *something* and self-realization as an act of "active appropriation of the world," in which the subject does not realize *itself*, but realizes itself in what it does. See Rahel Jaeggi, *Alienation* (New York: Columbia University Press, 2014), p. 141. See also Michael Theunissen's related distinction between a Hegelian and a post-Hegelian concept of self-realization: Michael Theunissen, *Selbstverwirklichung und Allgemeinheit* (Berlin/New York: de Gruyter, 1982). I have already (ch. 1, sec. 6) argued why I prefer the concept of self-determination for capturing a notion of freedom localized in the interaction between the subject and the world. For this concept gives an account of the crucial fact that the subject of active appropriation of the world must constantly re-appropriate and thus re-determine itself.

8 On the connection between the crisis of a substantialist concept of subjectivity and the experience of contingency in the world, see Peter Bürger, "Zwischenbetrachtung: Zur Dialektik der Selbstverwirklichung," in *Prosa der Moderne* (Frankfurt/Main: Suhrkamp, 1988), pp. 258–72, here: p. 258.

9 In a passage on the concept of self-determination, Hermann Cohen writes, "Determination [*Bestimmung*] first of all recalls a mood [*Stimmung*] with whose arbitrariness and subjectivity determination must cope." See Hermann Cohen, *Ethik des reinen Willens* (Berlin: Bruno Cassirer, 1907), p. 245.

10 As we saw in the previous chapter, the idea of such a mediation itself is unproblematic. The problem begins with the manner in which Hegel presents this mediation in the light of his critique of irony.

11 Søren Kierkegaard, *Either/Or I* (Princeton, NJ: Princeton University Press, 1987). Hereafter referred to parenthetically in the text as EO I.

12 Adorno has criticized poetry's illustrative relation to philosophy with reference to Kierkegaard's writings in *Kierkegaard: Construction of the Aesthetic* (Minneapolis, MN: University of Minnesota Press, 1989), pp. 6f. Kierkegaard chooses the literary form for didactic reasons. The reader should – in maieutic fashion – be "tricked into" the (ultimately Christian) truth. On Kierkegaard's maieutics, see also Wilfried Greve, *Kierkegaards maieutische Ethik: Von "Entweder/Oder II" zu den "Stadien"* (Frankfurt/Main: Suhrkamp, 1990), pp. 15–34.

13 Stanley Cavell, "The Avoidance of Love: A Reading of King Lear," in *Must We Mean What We Say?* (Cambridge: Cambridge University Press, 1976), pp. 267–353.

14 William Shakespeare, *King Lear*, Act I, Scene 1.

15 Jean-Jacques Rousseau, "Letter to M. D'Alembert on the Theatre," in *Politics and the Arts*, ed. and trans. by Allan Bloom (Ithaca, NY: Cornell University Press, 1960), p. 84. Hereafter referred to in the text as LtA.

16 Here, we are dealing with the aesthete "A," to whom the rest of the writings in the first part of *Either/Or* is ascribed, but who only appears as the publisher of the "journal of the seducer." Viktor Eremita, the

publisher of the collected papers that make up *Either/Or*, regards this as a "literary device" (EO I 9); there are too many indications that A is also the author of the journal. The preface, in which A distances himself from the journal, gives the impression that "A himself had become afraid of his fiction" (ibid.). At the same time, however, the preface mirrors the distanced attitude toward the aesthetic life-form adopted by Viktor Eremita as well. It is thus only logical that Eremita should remark that the preface to the "journal of the seducer" only "further complicates" his "own position, since one author becomes enclosed within the other like the boxes in a Chinese puzzle" (ibid.).

17 This demonstrates that, unlike what Konrad Paul Liessmann claims in his apology of the seducer and his aesthetic lifestyle, Kierkegaard does not regard seduction as a "seduction of the other toward oneself." Cf. Konrad Paul Liessmann, *Ästhetik der Verführung: Kierkegaards Konstruktion der Erotik aus dem Geiste der Kunst* (Frankfurt/Main: Philo Fine Arts, 1991), pp. 82f.

18 Søren Kierkegaard, *Either/Or Part II*, ed. and trans. by H.V. Hong & E.H. Hong (Princeton, NJ: Princeton University Press, 1987). Hereafter referred to parenthetically in the text as EO II.

19 See ch. 1, sec. 2.

20 Wilhelm complains, "This sickness, or more correctly this sin, is very prevalent in our day, and it is under this same sin that all of young Germany and France are now groaning" (EO II 189).

21 See Greve, *Kierkegaards maieutische Ethik*, p. 84.

22 Ibid.

23 However, Wilhelm's conception of God is essentially exhausted by the notion of a duty to achieve self-realization (cf. EO II, pp. 81f.).

24 Ibid., p. 82.

25 On the religious dimension of repentance, cf. EO II 216–18.

26 Dieter Thomae, *Erzähle dich selbst: Lebensgeschichte als philosophisches Problem* (Frankfurt/Main: Suhrkamp, 2007), pp. 49–62, here: p. 51.

27 Greve, *Kierkegaards maieutische Ethik*, p. 108.

28 Nevertheless, Kierkegaard does mention the relation of friendship, which Hegel did not include in his theory of ethical life, but which nevertheless could be plausibly integrated into that theory. For a contemporary, Hegel-inspired view of ethical life including the dimension of friendship, see Axel Honneth, *Suffering from Indeterminacy: An Attempt at a Reactualization of Hegel's Philosophy of Right* (Amsterdam: Van Gorcum, 2000), esp. p. 41.

29 Otto Pöggeler, *Hegels Kritik der Romantik* (Munich: Fink, 1998), p. 221.

30 According to Wilhelm's residually Platonic conception, it does not matter which career a person chooses. As long as the latter corresponds to the individual's "own nature," a person takes part in "a rational order of things" in which each person "fills his place" in order to thereby reconcile the universal with the individual – and thus becomes

free (cf. EO II 292). Such a glorified notion of duty not only contains a naturalizing denial of social injustice, justifying the unequal distribution of "places" in society with recourse to individuals' nature. Furthermore, it negates the historical dimension of lived experience in general inasmuch as it entails the possibility of arriving at a different understanding of our own identity under changed conditions, and thus also at a different understanding of what (e.g., which career) is suitable for us. See my discussion of Plato in ch. 1, secs 7 and 8.

31 Hegel at least recognizes that marriage is ultimately "based only on subjective and contingent feeling" and thus "may be dissolved" (Rph §176, Addition). He points out, however, that – inasmuch as a marriage asserts an ethical relationship in spite of its accidental origins – a third, ethical authority is required in order to dissolve the marriage. This authority must determine whether the ethical relationship in the marriage is merely threatened by "transient moods" or whether a divorce is necessary due to "total estrangement" (ibid.).

32 Theodor W. Adorno, "On Kierkegaard's Doctrine of Love," *Studies in Philosophy and Social Science*, vol. 8 (1939–1940), pp. 413–29, here: p. 416.

33 For a comprehensive collection of the relevant passages, see Céline Léon, "(A) Woman's Place Within the Ethical," in Céline Léon & Sylvia Walsh, eds, *Feminist Interpretations of Søren Kierkegaard* (University Park, PA: Pennsylvania University Press, 1997), pp. 103–30.

34 "A woman's nature," as Wilhelm puts it, is "to pray for others" (EO II 314).

35 Thus Wilhelm writes, "it takes a great soul to save his soul from minutiae, but he can if he will, because to will makes the great soul and the person who loves, wills. This can be difficult, especially for the man, and this is why the woman has such great significance for him in this respect. She is created to deal with little matters and knows how to give them a meaning, a value, a beauty that enchants. They rescue from habits, from the tyranny of one-sidedness, from the yoke of whims" (EO II 68).

36 For a critique of Kierkegaard on this point, see Thomae, *Erzähle dich selbst*, pp. 59f.

37 Stanley Cavell, *Pursuits of Happiness: The Hollywood Comedy of Remarriage* (Cambridge: Cambridge University Press, 1981).

38 Stanley Cavell, *Conditions Handsome and Unhandsome: The Constitution of Emerson Perfectionism* (Chicago, IL: University of Chicago Press, 1990), p. 104.

39 Gertrud Koch, "Man liebt sich, man liebt sich nicht, man liebt sich: Stanley Cavells Lob der Wiederverheiratung," *Texte zur Kunst*, vol. 52 (2003), pp. 110–18, here: p. 114.

40 Cavell, *Pursuits of Happiness*, p. 19.

41 See Hannah Arendt's thoughts on the power of the promise when it comes to securing the future in *The Human Condition* (Chicago, IL: University of Chicago Press, 1998), pp. 243–7.

42 Helmuth Plessner, *The Limits of Community: A Critique of Social Radicalism* (Amherst, NY: Humanity Books, 1999), p. 105.
43 Ibid., p. 109.
44 Ibid., p. 105.
45 Ibid., p. 110.
46 Ibid., p. 114.
47 Ibid., p. 111.
48 It is for this reason that Axel Honneth has corrected his previous claim that social esteem constitutes the most demanding form of recognition. The "most individuated" form of recognition must be captured in concepts such as love and affection. See Axel Honneth, *Gerechtigkeit und Gesellschaft: Potsdamer Seminar* (Berlin: Berliner Wissenschaftsverlag, 2008), p. 67. On Honneth's earlier hierarchy of forms of recognition, see Axel Honneth, *The Struggle for Recognition: The Moral Grammar of Social Conflicts* (Cambridge, MA: MIT Press), 1995, esp. p. 129. Drawing on Plessner, we could add that the particularity of love and affection as compared to "individuation" through social esteem consists in the fact that love recognizes something that by definition can find no space in social esteem: the potentiality of the individual that exceeds his or her social roles. For this reason, love and friendship, which according to Gerhard Gamm "do not have their measure in a generalized other, but in a significant other, i.e. in an other that cannot be entirely interpreted because it is distinct from itself" (p. 223), should not be made the model for *all* forms of recognition, as Gamm suggests when criticizing the distinction between different spheres of recognition as a form of reification. See Gamm, "Die Unausdeutbarkeit des Selbst," p. 219.
49 This Kierkegaardian formulation is cited in Michael Theunissen, *Der Begriff Ernst bei Søren Kierkegaard* (Freiburg & Munich: Verlag Karl Alber, 1958), p. 124.
50 Therefore, the "either/or" with which the reader of this work is faced can ultimately be read as a "neither/nor." Although the fact that the either/or is an ethical category appears to suggest a decision for ethics, its formulation in terms of the Wilhelmian ethic proves deficient. The neither/nor in *Either/Or* demands a third variant. This interpretation is supported by the fact that Viktor Eremita, the publisher of *Either/Or*, writes in his foreword to the book that it is a "a piece of good fortune" (EO I 14) that nothing indicates whether one worldview ultimately triumphs over the other.
51 Søren Kierkegaard, "Repetition," in *Fear and Trembling & Repetition*, ed. by H.V. Hong & E.H. Hong (Princeton, NJ: Princeton University Press, 1983), pp. 227f. Hereafter referred to parenthetically in the text as R.
52 For Job, it is stated, "every human interpretation is only a misconception, and to him in relation to God all his troubles are but a sophism that he, to be sure, cannot solve, but he trusts that God can do it" (R 207).

53 Søren Kierkegaard, "Fear and Trembling," in *Fear and Trembling & Repetition*, ed. by H.V. Hong & E.H. Hong (Princeton, NJ: Princeton University Press, 1983), pp. 227f. Hereafter referred to parenthetically in the text as FT.

54 It is "by virtue of the absurd" that Abraham believes that Isaac will be spared, for "it certainly was absurd that God, who required it of him, should in the next moment rescind the requirement" (FT 35f.).

55 The difference between this second form of irony and romantic irony is demonstrated by de Silentio's interpretation of the dialogue between Abraham and Isaac on Mount Moriah. When Isaac arrives at the mountain, he asks where the animal for the sacrifice is, and Abraham responds that "God himself will provide the lamb for the burnt offering, my son!" De Silentio remarks that this answer has "the form of irony, for it is always irony when I say something and still do not say anything. Isaac questions Abraham in the belief that Abraham knows. Now, if Abraham had replied: I know nothing – he would have spoken an untruth. He cannot say anything, for what he knows he cannot say." At the same time, this irony is different from romantic irony, because in de Silentio's view it is not an expression of separation from the ethical world. Abraham's ironic expression is not an expression of a detachment from his ethical relation to Isaac. On the contrary, it bears witness to Abraham's continued ties to this relation "by virtue of the absurd": "If Abraham in resignation had merely relinquished Isaac and done no more, he would have spoken an untruth, for he does indeed know that he himself in this very moment is willing to sacrifice him. After having made this movement, he has at every moment made the next movement, has made the movement of faith by virtue of the absurd" (FT 118f.).

56 Søren Kierkegaard, *The Concept of Anxiety* (Princeton, NJ: Princeton University Press, 1981). Hereafter referred to parenthetically in the text as CA.

57 Cf. sec. 5.

58 For a discussion of the difference between Hegel and Kierkegaard with respect to the difference between speculation and religion, see Richard Kroner, "Kierkegaards Hegelverständnis," in Michael Theunissen & Wilfried Greve, eds, *Materialien zur Philosophie Søren Kierkegaards* (Frankfurt/Main: Suhrkamp, 1979), pp. 425–36.

59 Søren Kierkegaard, *Stages on Life's Way* (Princeton, NJ: Princeton University Press, 1988), p. 451. Hereafter referred to parenthetically in the text as S.

60 On the connection that Hegel sees between openly evil ironic consciousness and moral reflection, see ch. 2, sec. 6.

61 See also my discussion of Hegel's critique of morality in ch. 2, especially my defense of moral reflection in secs 5 and 11.

62 Peter Fenves even sees a movement "back to Kant" in Kierkegaard's *Concept of Anxiety*. See Peter Fenves, *Chatter: Language and History*

in Kierkegaard (Stanford, CA: Stanford University Press, 1993), p. 70.
63 See especially the discussion of "that ironist who has been admired for millennia," Socrates, in Søren Kierkegaard, *Philosophical Fragments* (Princeton, NJ: Princeton University Press, 1985), p. 111. Hereafter referred to parenthetically in the text as PF.
64 Theunissen, *Der Begriff Ernst bei Søren Kierkegaard*, p. 128.
65 Ibid., p. 172.
66 The fact that Kierkegaard calls this notion "Socratic" is misleading (cf. SD 95).
67 See the discussion on the Platonic notion of weakness of will in ch. 1, secs 3–5.
68 See ch. 1, sec. 5 and ch. 2, sec. 10.
69 Søren Kierkegaard, *Concluding Unscientific Postscript to Philosophical Fragments* (Princeton, NJ: Princeton University Press, 1992), p. 517. Hereafter referred to parenthetically in the text as UN.
70 Self-realization in and through a relation to God cannot, as an essentially anti-social form of self-realization, recognize any difference between the sexes. Anti-Climacus thus remarks in a footnote that "in the relationship to God, where the distinction of man-woman vanishes, it holds for men as well as for women that devotion is the self and that in the giving of oneself the self is gained. This holds equally true for man and woman, although," as Kierkegaard hastens to add in accordance with the line of argumentation from the first ethics, "it is probably true that in most cases the woman actually relates to God only through the man" (SD 50).
71 Theunissen, *Der Begriff Ernst bei Søren Kierkegaard*, p. 130.
72 On the relation between relation-to-self and relation-to-God at the religious stage, see also Michael Theunissen, "Das Menschenbild in der 'Krankheit zum Tode'," in Theunissen & Greve, eds, *Materialien zur Philosophie Søren Kierkegaards*, pp. 504f
73 Anti-Climacus thus writes that the "self" is "essentially different from the environment and external events" (SD 54).
74 For a critique of Kierkegaard's static image of ethics, which allows no exceptions and must therefore be overcome in a higher sphere, see also Elmer H. Duncan, "Kierkegaard's Teleological Suspension of the Ethical: A Study of Exception Cases," *Southern Journal of Philosophy*, vol. 1, no. 4 (1963), pp. 9–18. Duncan, however, does not go on to criticize the picture that Kierkegaard paints of (the) aesthetic existence (of morality).
75 See Adorno, *Kierkegaard*, p. 30.
76 Theunissen, *Der Begriff Ernst bei Søren Kierkegaard*, p. 148.
77 We thus contradict the author of *Sickness Unto Death*, who compares himself to a doctor who follows his own knowledge rather than the speculations of his patients about their own maladies (SD 23).
78 See Paul de Man, "The Rhetoric of Temporality," in *Blindness and Insight: Essays in the Rhetoric of Contemporary Criticism*

(Minneapolis, MN: University of Minnesota Press, 1983), pp. 187–228, here: p. 213.
79 See ibid., p. 215.
80 Ibid., p. 222.
81 Ibid., p. 218. He thereby cites Friedrich Schlegel's formulation "Irony is a permanent parabasis." See fragment 668 in Friedrich Schlegel, *Kritische Ausgabe*, vol. XVIII (Munich & Paderborn: Ferdinand Schöningh, 1963), p. 85.
82 De Man, "The Rhetoric of Temporality," p. 217.
83 "What god will be able to rescue us from all these ironies?," as de Man cites Schlegel's essay "Über die Unverständlichkeit," in *Studienausgabe in sechs Bänden*, vol. 2 (Munich & Paderborn: Ferdinand Schöningh, 1988), pp. 235–42, here: p. 240. In the later work of Schlegel, similar to Kierkegaard, only a leap out of language and into faith can redeem an unhappy consciousness.
84 See Jürgen Habermas' critique of such a radicalized critique of reason in his *Theory of Communicative Action*, vol. 1 (Boston, MA: Beacon Press, 1984), pp. 366–402.
85 On the structure of self-determination, see ch. 1, sec. 8.
86 De Man, "Rhetoric of Temporality," p. 220. See Schlegel, "Kritische Fragmente, nr. 37.
87 In his reading of *Oedipus*, Christoph Menke shows that tragic experiences are founded upon "a deficiency in knowledge that defines all human action": "Oedipus unintentionally commits patricide and incest with his mother because there is something else he does not know. Knowledge does not always and for everyone have to be lacking – not every action is derailed – but at any time and for anyone it can be lacking. Consequently, it is not the deficiency of this action and thereby of this agent, but rather the deficiency of action and thereby of every agent." Christoph Menke, *Tragic Play: Irony and Theater from Sophocles to Beckett* (New York: Columbia University Press, 2009), p. 66.
88 In his reflections on the concept of justice, Jacques Derrida points to the problem that lies in a naïve or immediate application of (necessarily infinite) predicates such as "good" or "just" to practices that are necessarily finite: "One cannot speak directly but, instead, only obliquely about justice, thematize or objectivize justice, say 'this is just' or even less 'I am just', without immediately betraying justice if not law" (Jacques Derrida, "Force of Law: The Mystical Foundation of Authority," in D. Cornell and M. Rosenfeld, eds, *Deconstruction and the Possibility of Justice* (New York: Routledge, 1992), p. 10.)
89 Theodor W. Adorno, *Minima Moralia: Reflections on a Damaged Life* (London: Verso), p. 39.
90 See Alexander García Düttmann, *So ist es: Ein philosophischer Kommentar zu Adornos „Minima Moralia"* (Frankfurt/Main: Suhrkamp, 2004), pp. 67f.

Chapter 4   Sovereignty in Romanticism: Schmitt

1. Carl Schmitt, *Political Romanticism* (Cambridge, MA: MIT Press, 1986), p. 21. Hereafter referred to parenthetically in the text as PR.
2. Karl Heinz Bohrer, *Die Kritik der Romantik: Der Verdacht der Philosophie gegen die literarische Moderne* (Frankfurt/Main: Suhrkamp, 1989), p. 286. See also PR 49f. According to Schmitt, romanticism contradicts both political and religious decision-making. Thus Schmitt maintains that romantics believed "they were becoming Catholics without having to make a decision." To truly decide to become Catholic would in fact bring the "romantic situation…to an end" (PR 65).
3. An influential current of German cultural criticism follows this line of argumentation even today. Although Bohrer criticizes Schmitt in *Die Kritik der Romantik* for his anti-modern concept of art, according to which art is "representative" to the extent that it "mirrors positive content" (p. 292), he appears to refuse to draw the political consequences from this aesthetic defense of romantic disintegration. Bohrer has continuously criticized the "ugliness" of the Federal Republic of Germany, which he – among other things – ascribes to a lack of "aesthetic form" and "societal self-representation" (cf. Karl Heinz Bohrer, *Nach der Natur: Über Politik und Ästhetik* (Munich & Vienna: Hanser, 1988), esp. p. 15). Walter Grasskamp's argumentation is equally ambivalent. He also characterizes democracy as "unaesthetic" because it "produces no consummate aesthetic representations." Although Grasskamp criticizes the "horror" of the aesthetic disintegration of Western democracies, he also warns – following Fritz Stern – of the anti-democratic implications of this critique. Nevertheless, he does not draw the consequence that we must separate the democratic resistance to a unified "aesthetic of the state" from the problem of the capitalist privatization of the public sphere and the way it is shaped. See Walter Grasskamp, *Die unästhetische Demokratie: Kunst in der Marktgesellschaft* (Munich: Beck, 1992), esp. pp. 9, 133f.; Fritz Stern, *Kulturpessimismus als politische Gefahr* (Stuttgart: Klett-Cotta, 2005).
4. Luc Ferry argues that democracy must be understood against the background of a "revolution of taste" that entails the problem of relativism: *Homo Aestheticus: The Invention of Taste in the Democratic Age* (Chicago, IL: University of Chicago Press, 1993).
5. Carl Schmitt, "The Age of Neutralizations and Depoliticizations," in *The Concept of the Political* (Chicago, IL: University of Chicago Press, 2007), pp. 80–96, here: p. 84.
6. This is the striking formulation employed by Hans Blumenberg, *The Legitimacy of the Modern Age* (Cambridge, MA: MIT Press, 1985), p. 92.
7. See especially Jacques Derrida, "Force of Law," in D. Cornell, M. Rosenfeld & D.G. Carlson, eds, *Deconstruction and the Possibility of Justice* (New York: Routledge, 1992), pp. 3–67.

8 See my considerations on a so-called post-democracy in ch. 6, sec. 9.
9 Schmitt writes that "it is remarkable that the European liberal state of the nineteenth century could portray itself as a *stato neutrale ed agnostico* and could see its existential legitimation precisely in its neutrality. There are various reasons for this; it cannot be explained in one word or by a single cause. Here it is certainly interesting as a symptom of a general cultural neutrality because the nineteenth century doctrine of the neutral state belongs to a general tendency of intellectual neutrality characteristic of European history in the last century." Schmitt, "The Age of Neutralizations and Depoliticizations," p. 88.
10 Schmitt gives a number of indications of the tradition to which he belongs. He notes with approval that Hegel "executed romanticism" (PR 73). "With an unerring sense of genius," Hegel recognized the "inadequacy" of Fichte's system, from which the romantic subject's false self-understanding proceeds (PR 82). He regards Kierkegaard, on the other hand, whom he misleadingly confounds with his aesthetic pseudonyms, as the "only great figure" among the romantics. Yet he approves of Kierkegaard's Protestant-Christian "resolution of the romantic situation" (PR 166, note 10).
11 The critique of a both overly subjectivist and falsely abstract (mis)-understanding of freedom, which Schmitt, like his philosophical predecessors, directs at the romantics, also corresponds to his claim that romantics lack self-irony, an assessment that Schmitt also adopts from Hegel. Although romantics take up an ironic stance toward the entire world, they never do so toward themselves (cf. PR 73). At least with regard to Friedrich Schlegel, however, this proves to be a false assessment (cf. ch. 2, sec. 9).
12 This is because romantic art, according to Schmitt, not only comes about by means of an occasionalist relation to the world, it also aims to bring about a "play of associations" on the part of the audience. The ideal romantic work of art is thus found in music, because it is particularly easy to turn music into an occasion for moods and imagination. Every melody, every chord, every tone can be put in relation to an entire world of associations and references. Romantics seek to find "a paraphrase that has no bounds, does not nullify subjective freedom, and preserves an abundance of associative possibilities is found for a content without conceptual limits" (PR 105f.). This desire is ultimately fulfilled by the total work of art which is characterized by "a general blending" (PR 106) of genres of art in musical ambiguity. The opposition between ambiguous and transmedial art forms (in the tradition of which the current state of art stands to the extent that it has even abandoned the total artwork's claim to totality in favor of open works of art) and Schmitt's ideal of a representative and formally closed form of art could not be greater. On Schmitt's insight that artistic modernity represents a continuation of the romantic tradition, as well as on his rejection of this connection, see also Karl Heinz Bohrer, "Das Romantisch-Phantastische als dezentriertes Bewusstsein: Zum Problem seiner

Repräsentanz," in *Die Grenzen des Ästhetischen* (Munich: Hanser, 1998), pp. 9–36, here esp. pp. 293f.
13 On the concept of inner nature, see ch. 1, secs 7 and 8, as well as ch. 2, sec. 8.
14 See Jacques Derrida, *The Politics of Friendship* (London & New York: Verso, 2005), pp. 68f.
15 See ch. 1, sec. 5.
16 See Derrida, *Politics of Friendship*, p. 68.
17 Martin Seel, "Sich bestimmen lassen: Ein revidierter Begriff der Selbstbestimmung," in *Sich bestimmen lassen: Studien zur theoretischen und zur praktischen Philosophie* (Frankfurt/Main: Suhrkamp, 2002), pp. 279–98, here: p. 293.
18 Friedrich Balke expands upon Schmitt's diagnosis according to which we live in an occasionalist age by claiming a fundamental "tranformation of the order of knowledge and communication," against the background of which the concept and phenomenon of sovereignty decay to an extent that Schmitt's theory of sovereignty can only be viewed as a defensive reaction to an actual change in the world. By contrast, I argue that Schmitt's diagnosis of neutralization must be rejected because it distorts the specific meaning of sovereignty in liberal democracies. See Friedrich Balke, *Der Staat nach seinem Ende: Die Versuchung Carl Schmitts* (Munich: Fink, 1996), esp. p. 27.
19 In the conclusion of this book (ch. 7), I will return to the tension between this understanding of democracy and the problem of the economicization of the political discussed under the title of "post-democracy."
20 Carl Schmitt, *Political Theology: Four Chapters on the Concept of Sovereignty* (Chicago, IL: University of Chicago Press, 1985). Hereafter referred to parenthetically in the text as PT.
21 Carl Schmitt, *The Concept of the Political* (Chicago, IL: University of Chicago Press, 1996), p. 61. Hereafter referred to parenthetically in the text as CP.
22 See Leo Strauss, "Notes on Carl Schmitt, *The Concept of the Political*," in CP 97–122, here: p. 119.
23 See ch. 2, sec. 11.
24 This is true once we stop conceiving of the romantic attention to the expressions of our inner nature and its consciousness of the productive role that this nature plays in our lives within the framework of a critique of subjectivism. See my discussion of Hegel's determination of romantic irony in ch. 2, secs 8–11.
25 See Strauss, "Notes on Carl Schmitt," p. 115.
26 This would mean relativizing Rüdiger Kramme's attempt to show that "Plessner's attempt at a political anthropology is capable of filling the 'gap' of a fundamental anthropology in line with Schmitt's political theory." Although the basic concepts of this anthropology help us elucidate the objective reason for Schmitt's insistence on the concept of sovereignty, they do not compel us to accept a dictatorial interpretation of sovereignty. Plessner's anthropolgy and Schmitt's political theory are

not merely mutually translatable, even if Plessner's later essay "Macht und menschliche Natur" might suggest otherwise. Rüdiger Kramme, *Helmuth Plessner and Carl Schmitt: Eine historische Fallstudie zum Verhältnis von Anthropologie und Politik in der deutschen Philosophie der zwanziger Jahre* (Berlin: Duncker & Humblot, 1989), p. 159. On the claim of a similarity between Plessner and Schmitt, see also Friedrich Balke, "Zur politischen Anthropologie Carl Schmitts," in Hans-Georg Flickinger, ed., *Die Autonomie des Politischen: Carl Schmitts Kampf um einen beschädigten Begriff* (Weinheim: VCH, 1990), pp. 37–65, here: p. 42. For a defense of Plessner against Plessner which criticizes the notion of such a mutual translatability, see Axel Honneth, "Plessner und Schmitt: Ein Kommentar zur Entdeckung ihrer Affinität," in Wolfgang Essbach, Joachim Fischer & Helmut Lethen, eds, *Plessners 'Grenzen der Gemeinschaft': Eine Debatte* (Frankfurt/Main: Suhrkamp, 2002), pp. 21–8. For a strong emphasis on the distinction between Schmitt and Plessner, see Hans-Peter Krüger, *Zwischen Lachen und Weinen*, vol. 1 (Berlin: Akademie, 1999), esp. pp. 240–6.

27 Schmitt's agreeement with Kierkegaard's existentialist notion of the exception marks the decisive distinction between Schmitt's political theory and that of Hegel. Jean-François Kervégan points out that despite the commonalities between Hegel and Schmitt (e.g., both claim that a state cannot be conceived of without politics and politics cannot be conceived of without an opponent), they crucially differ over whether the political order is a form of appearance of reason (Hegel) or the result of an existential decision (Schmitt). See Jean-François Kervégan, "Politik und Vernünftigkeit: Anmerkungen zum Verhältnis zwischen Carl Schmitt und Hegel," *Der Staat*, vol. 27 (1988), pp. 371–91; see also his book *Hegel, Carl Schmit: Le politique entre spéculation et positivité* (Paris: PUF, 1992).

28 Schmitt quotes Kierkegaard's claim that the "exception explains the general and itself. And if one wants to study the general correctly, one only needs to look around for a true exception. It reveals everything more clearly than does the general. Endless talk about the general becomes boring; there are exceptions. If they cannot be explained, then the general also cannot be explained. The difficulty is usually not noticed because the general is not thought about with passion but with a comfortable superficiality. The exception, on the other hand, thinks the general with intense passion" (PT 15; see R 227 as well as the beginning of ch. 3, sec. 8).

29 See Strauss, "Notes on Carl Schmitt," p. 116.

30 See his preliminary remarks on the "Contradiction between Parliamentarism and Democracy," in Carl Schmitt, *The Crisis of Parliamentary Democracy* (Cambridge, MA: MIT Press, 1988), pp. 1–17, here: p. 16.

31 Blumenberg, *The Legitimacy of the Modern Age*, p. 92.

32 Ibid.

33 Ibid., p. 93.

34 Ibid.

35 Ibid., p. 98.
36 Ibid., p. 101.
37 Ibid.
38 Christoph Menke, "Gnade und Recht: Carl Schmitts Begriff der Souveränität," in *Spiegelungen der Gleichheit: Politische Philosophie nach Adorno und Derrida* (Frankfurt/Main: Suhrkamp, 2004), pp. 300–23, here: p. 302.
39 See Carl Schmitt, *Legality and Legitimacy* (Durham, NC: Duke University Press, 2004), p. 4. Hereafter referred to parenthetically in the text as LL.
40 Carl Schmitt, *Dictatorship* (Cambridge: Polity Press, 2014), p. xliii.
41 Menke, "Gnade und Recht," p. 301.
42 See Derrida, "Force of Law," p. 251.
43 See Menke, "Gnade und Recht," p. 304.
44 Fracesca Raimondi makes this point very clear in *Die Zeit der Demokratie: Entscheiden und Handeln nach Carl Schmitt und Hannah Arendt* (Dissertation, Goethe University, Frankfurt am Main, 2011). Here I refer to the chapter entitled "Souveränität nach dem Souverän (Carl Schmitt)," esp. sec. II.2.
45 Menke, "Gnade und Recht," p. 306.
46 Ibid., p. 305.
47 See Karl Löwith, "Der okkasionelle Dezionismus von Carl Schmitt," in *Sämtliche Schriften*, vol. VIII (Stuttgart: Metzler, 1984), pp. 32–71, here: p. 40.
48 Although Schmitt claims that the "political world is a pluriverse" (CP 53), which follows from his theory of the relationship between friend and enemy, he does maintain that "within one and the same political entity, instead of the decisive friend-and-enemy grouping, a pluralism could take its place without destroying the entity and the political itself" (CP 45).
49 Carl Schmitt, *Constitutional Theory* (Durham, NC: Duke University Press, 2008). Hereafter referred to parenthetically in the text as CT.
50 Carl Schmitt, *Der Begriff des Politischen*, 3rd edn (Hamburg: Duncker & Humblot, 1932), p. 21.
51 Helmuth Plessner, *The Limits of Community: A Critique of Social Radicalism* (Amherst, NY: Humanity Books, 1999), p. 176.
52 Ibid., p. 175.
53 Ibid., p. 176.
54 Ibid. The insight into the moment of decision, which puts an end to all discourse, is "not essentially modified by the appeal to the legitimacy of the decision-making *procedure*," as Albrecht Wellmer emphasizes in opposition to Jürgen Habermas. "For, first of all, even a legitimate procedure can lead to the wrong decision; second, the procedures are also part of the legal order and thus also must be decided upon. Regardless of which point to which we might resort, everywhere we find – even if it is the constituting act of a constitutional assembly – the moment of decision that *creates* law, which could not wait for a consensus

that would grant it legitimacy 'ultimately', but which nevertheless entails the possibility of a justification of violent sanctions." Albrecht Wellmer, "Menschenrechte und Demokratie," in *Revolution und Interpretation: Demokratie ohne Letztbegründung* (Assen: von Gorcum, 1999), pp. 17–42, here: p. 25.
55 Cf. ibid., p. 29.
56 Ibid.
57 Ibid., p. 30.
58 In this sense, we could say with Thorsten Bonacker that contingency itself gains normative power in a democracy. See Thorsten Bonacker, *Die normative Kraft der Kontingenz: Nichtessentialistische Gesellschaftskritik nach Weber und Adorno* (Frankfurt/Main: Campus, 2000).
59 See Jacques Derrida, "Autoimmunity: Real and Symbolic Suicides. A Dialogue with Jacques Derrida," in G. Borradori, ed., *Philosophy in a Time of Terror* (Chicago, IL: University of Chicago Press, 2004), pp. 84–136.
60 See Jacques Derrida, *Rogues: Two Essays on Reason* (Stanford, CA: Stanford University Press, 2005), p. 156.

Chapter 5   The Spectacle of Democracy: Rousseau

1 Jean-Jacques Rousseau, "Letter to M. D'Alembert on the Theatre," in *Politics and the Arts* (Glencoe: The Free Press, 1960), p. 121. Hereafter referred to parenthetically in the text as LtA.
2 Rousseau writes in the preface of his letter to his readers: "If among the essays issued from my pen this paper is even beneath the others, it is less the fault of circumstances than of myself; I am beneath myself. The ills of the body exhaust the soul; by dint of suffering it loses its vitality. A fleeting moment of fermentation produced a certain glimmer of talent in me. It manifested itself late, and it has extinguished itself early. In returning to my natural state, I have gone back to nothingness. I had only a moment; it is past. It is my shame to outlive myself. Reader, if you receive this last work with indulgence, you will be welcoming my shade, for, as for me, I am no more" (LtA 7).
3 For more on this observation, see Christoph Menke, "Die Depotenzierung des Souveräns im Gesang: Claudio Monteverdis *Die Krönung der Poppea* und die Demokratie," in E. Horn, B. Menke & C. Menke, eds, *Literatur als Philosophie – Philosophie als Literatur* (Munich: Fink, 2005), pp. 281–96, here: pp. 284f.
4 This is also the problem emphasized by Plato, see ch. 1, sec. 9.
5 That, at least, is the translation Quintilian proposes. He immediately adds, however, that "this latter name [i.e., *dissimulatio*] does not cover the whole range of this figure," and expresses his preference for the Greek term. In our context, the essential point is that dissimulation can be described as being at least the central rhetorical import of irony.

Cf. Marcus Fabius Quintilianus, *The Institutio Oratoria*, trans. Harold Edgeworth Butler (Cambridge, MA: Harvard University Press, 1922), IX, 2, 44.

6 Gregory Vlastos, "Socratic Irony," in *Socrates: Ironist and Moral Philosopher* (Ithaca, NY: Cornell University Press, 1991), pp. 21–44.
7 For instance, when someone points at the pouring rain and says, "Nice weather today!" On this figure, cf. Quintilian, *The Institutio Oratoria*, VI, 2,15.
8 Vlastos calls this form of irony complex because it creates the appearance that something is both intended and not intended; that which is intended and that which is not intended are located on different levels, which is why this complexity is fairly quickly resolved. Vlastos' example of complex irony is Socrates' claim that he is beautiful. That is not intended to be literally the case (Socrates looked like a satyr), but it is intended to be figuratively true (with respect to his soul). Cf. Vlastos, "Socratic Irony," pp. 30–1.
9 The intended meaning of an ironic utterance is often apparent only to an audience that is in the know. That is one reason why irony is so often associated with superiority, if not even with elitism.
10 Alexander Nehamas, *The Art of Living: Socratic Reflections from Plato to Foucault* (Berkeley, Los Angeles: University of California Press, 1998), p. 62.
11 To the extent that we can consider Socrates as being paradigmatic for this form of irony (cf. ch. 2, sec. 13), Nehamas is right in claiming, contrary to Vlastos, that "Socratic irony is more complex than 'complex irony'" (ibid., p. 65).
12 Quintilian, *The Institutio Oratoria*, IX, 2, 46.
13 See Nehamas, *The Art of Living*, p. 67.
14 Denis Diderot, "The Paradox of the Actor," in *Selected Writings on Art and Literature* (London: Penguin, 1994), pp. 100–59.
15 See also Philippe Lacoue-Labarthe, "Diderot: Paradox and Mimesis," in *Typography: Mimesis, Philosophy, Politics* (Stanford, CA: Stanford University Press, 1998), pp. 248–66.
16 Quintilian, *The Institutio Oratoria*, VIII, 6, 57.
17 "It is likewise very genteel when your meaning and your expressions differ.... [P]eople who know these things better than I do, say, that Socrates, I think, by far excelled all mankind in the wit and good sense of this *irony* and *dissimulation*. It is indeed a very genteel kind, and when seasoned with a serious air, may be applied both in formal harangues, and common conversation. And upon my word all that I have said upon this subject of humour are not more properly the ingredients of pleadings in the forum, than they are of every ordinary discourse." (Marcus Tullius Cicero, *De Oratore/Über den Redner* (Dusseldorf: Patmos Verlag, 2007), 2.67.)
18 Helmuth Plessner, *The Limits of Community: A Critique of Social Radicalism* (Amherst, NY: Humanity Books, 1999), p. 131. Hereafter referred to parenthetically in the text as LC.

19 The problem that Plessner addresses does not even necessarily derive from a distorted perspective. On the contrary, it can be illustrated with reference to the opposite case: We often become uncomfortable when somebody whom we do not know says something true about us: "You are x." On such occasions we hasten to demonstrate that we are not only x, but much more and much different than that.
20 Helmut Lethen writes that "Plessner fails to recognize situations in which those who appear in the regalia of office often appear unintentionally comical. These are situations in which it would have been more appropriate to present oneself informally, and in which the uniform and appearance of the soldier becomes an indicator of heroic nonsense, because it maintains the ambition of having sense...The fixation on situations in which only the armoured I seems capable of evading the curse of ridiculousness is symptomatic for the Republic's modern intelligentsia." See Helmut Lethen, *Verhaltenslehren der Kälte: Lebensversuche zwischen den Kriegen* (Frankfurt/Main: Suhrkamp, 1994), p. 91.
21 Derrida mentions in the context of irony a "nonpublic public within the public." See Derrida, *Rogues*, p. 92.
22 See Helmuth Plessner, "Soziale Rolle und menschliche Natur," in *Gesammelte Schriften*, vol. x (Frankfurt/Main: Suhrkamp, 1985), pp. 227–40, here: p. 232.
23 Ibid., p. 230.
24 Ibid., p. 231.
25 This distortion complements Plessner's remark in *The Limits of Community* that women are more capable of attaining "dignity and grace" because they are "according to the romantics permanently in tune with their nature and have ambition only for that which they can secure with the aid of men" (LC 123). Women represent the epitome of natural dignity – which, interestingly enough, is suddenly characterized as a rather base quality – that has its place in the private sphere (ibid.). Such clichés, which set the dignity of the female nature that remains nebulously true to itself against the public nimbus of male (character) armor, also make clear that we must interpret Plessner's interesting insight into the specific role of friendship and love for the recognition of the incomprehensibility of humans (cf. ch. 3, sec. 7) in a way that partially contradicts Plessner's own intention. Not only does the loving recognition of the other in his or her possibilities structurally contradict such clichés (with their short-sightedness in both directions); rather, the gender-specific division of public determinacy on the one hand, and private indeterminacy on the other, also contradicts the anthropological insight into the tension between determinacy and indeterminacy, which characterizes both the private and the public existence of human beings. This inevitable tension is a prerequisite for our ability to re-determine our social roles – independent of whether they place us in the private or the public sphere. This also means, by the way, that the meaning of "public" and "private" are variable. To

recognize others in their possibilities means recognizing them in the possibility of self-determination.
26 Fredric Jameson thus defined parody by its reference to an original; it is sustained by the "conviction that alongside the abnormal tongue you have momentarily borrowed, some healthy linguistic normality still exists." Fredric Jameson, *Postmodernism, or, The Cultural Logic of Late Capitalism* (Durham, NC: Duke University Press, 1991), p. 17.
27 Cf. Judith Butler, *Gender Trouble: Feminism and the Subversion of Identity* (New York: Routledge, 1999), pp. 176–7.
28 Cf. ibid., p. 180.
29 "The main objection to large cities," Rousseau writes elsewhere, "is that there men become other than what they are. [...] Accosting a Lady in a gathering, instead of the Parisian you think you see, you are seeing only the simulacrum of fashion. Her height, her size, her gait, her waist, her bust, her colorations, her air, her look, her talk, her manners, nothing of all that is hers, and if you saw her in her natural state, you could not recognize her." Jean-Jacques Rousseau, *Julie, or The New Heloise. Letters of Two Lovers Who Live in a Small Town at the Foot of the Alps* (Lebanon, NH: University Press of New England, 1997), p. 223.
30 Rousseau accordingly commends Spartan women for having "the courage to live like men" – without thereby weakening the men (cf. LtA 103).
31 See Barbara Vinken: "Republic, Rhetoric, and Sexual Difference," in A. Haverkamp, ed., *Deconstruction is/in America: A New Sense of the Political* (New York: New York University Press, 1995), pp. 181–99, here: p. 188. The fact that this effect itself must be produced rhetorically becomes especially apparent with regard to the female chasteness that, as Christine Garbe has pointed out, Rousseau does not regard as a simple expression of chasteness, but as "subtle coquetry." Indeed, Rousseau constantly emphasizes that the chaste concealment of female allures is more tantalizing than their exposure could ever be. Garbe writes that the "'innocence' and 'naturalness' of chaste women are the effects of a dual concealment: the concealment of their allures at the level of the object *and* the concealment of the 'intentionality' of this concealment at the meta-level" (cf. Christine Garbe, *Die 'weibliche' List im 'männlichen' Text: Jean-Jacques Rousseau in der feministischen Kritik* (Stuttgart/Weimar: Metzler, 1992), p. 99.
32 Judith Butler, *Gender Trouble*, p. 175.
33 I have already pointed out that this does not eliminate the distinction between reality and appearance in general. Cf. ch. 1, sec. 9.
34 "It was also at this time that the first differences were established in the ways of living of the two sexes, which had hitherto [in the state of nature] had but one." Jean-Jacques Rousseau, *Discourse on Inequality* (Oxford: Oxford University Press, 1994), p. 59. Hereafter referred to parenthetically in the text as DI.

35 However, Rousseau himself describes the state of nature as one "which no longer exists, which perhaps has never existed, and which will probably never exist." It is nonetheless "necessary," he continues, "to have sound ideas [of it] if we are to judge our present state satisfactorily" (DI 68). The state of nature, Jean Starobinski remarks, functions as a "model of pre-social man, enabling us to take exact measure of all accomplishments of culture and social organization." Jean Starobinski, *Rousseaus Anklage der Gesellschaft* (Constance: Universitätsverlag, 1977), p. 24.
36 A line from Schiller's Rousseauian *Ode to Joy*, which even today has not lost any of its political significance. Beethoven's symphony of the same name is the hymn of the European Union: "Joy, beautiful spark of Gods/Daughter of Elysium/We enter, fire-imbibed/Heavenly, thy sanctuary/Thy magic powers reunite/What custom's sword has divided/Beggars become Prince's brothers/Where thy gentle wing abides."
37 Cf. Jacques Derrida, *Of Grammatology* (Baltimore, MD: Johns Hopkins University Press, 1998), p. 307.
38 "For the permitted pleasures which a lively and frolicsome youth is denied are substituted more dangerous ones. Private meetings adroitly concerted take the place of public gatherings. By dint of hiding themselves as if they were guilty, they are tempted to become so. Innocent joy is likely to evaporate in the full light of day; but vice is a friend of shadows, and never have innocence and mystery lived long together" (LtA 129).
39 Jean Starobinski, *Jean-Jacques Rousseau. La transparence et l'obstacle, suivi de sept essais sur Rousseau* (Paris: Gallimard, 1971), p. 120.
40 Like Plato, Rousseau is not only convinced that the theater, due to its task of entertaining the audience, is limited to spectacular contents, which stand in opposition to aesthetically uninteresting virtues, but also that it produces in the audience an inclination for the irrational passions that theater imitates: "I know that the poetic theatre claims to do exactly the opposite and to purge the passions in exciting them. But I have difficulty understanding this rule. Is it possible that in order to become temperate and prudent we must begin by being intemperate and mad?" (LtA 20).
41 See Rousseau's treatment of "natural pity" (DI 100).
42 I have shown elsewhere that this moralistic critique of the theater is based on a failure to recognize the specific structure of aesthetic experience. See Juliane Rebentisch, *Ästhetik der Installation* (Frankfurt/Main: Suhrkamp, 2003), pp. 25–40.
43 See Derrida, *Rogues*, p. 50.
44 See the section "Das Imaginäre der Republik III: Die Feste" (Lüdermann) in A. Koschorke, S. Lüdemann, T. Frank & E. Matala de Mazza, eds, *Der fiktive Staat: Konstruktionen des politischen Körpers in der Geschichte Europas* (Frankfurt/Main: Fischer, 2007), pp. 267–80, here: p. 267.

45 See Rousseau's distinction between *amour de soi* (self-love) and *amour-propre* (pride or love of self), according to which "self-love is a natural sentiment which prompts every animal to watch over its own conservation," whereas "pride is only a relative, artificial sentiment born in society, a sentiment which prompts each individual to attach more importance to himself than to anyone else" (DI 167).

46 Although Rousseau does not make it explicit, the problem of intransparency is accompanied by a logic of suspicion that necessarily leads to the self-destruction of a band of brothers founded on absolute transparency. On the dialectic of fraternity and suspicion, which only knows brothers and enemies and is constantly in danger of turning brothers into enemies, such that "only a dead brother appears to be a 'good brother', that is, the only one who can no longer become a traitor," see the section "Brüderlichkeit als politisches Modell" (Lüdermann) in Koschorke et al., eds, *Der fiktive Staat*, pp. 280–91, here: p. 291. See also the considerations on fraternity found throughout Jacques Derrida's *Politics of Friendship* (London: Verso, 2005).

47 Cf. ch. 1, sec. 10; on the "truth of skepticism," see Stanley Cavell, "Knowing and Acknowledging," in *Must We Mean What We Say? A Book of Essays* (Cambridge: Cambridge University Press, 1969), pp. 238–66.

48 On Rousseau's idea of the "sublimation" of the striving for social esteem that Rousseau associates with *amour-propre* or love of self, see Frederick Neuhouser, *Rousseau's Theodicy of Self-Love: Evil, Rationality, and the Drive for Recognition* (Oxford: Oxford University Press, 2008), esp. p. 264.

49 On the residues of allegory in the festival, cf. Anselm Haverkamp, "Fest/Schrift – Festschreibung unbeschreiblicher Feste: Klopstocks Ode von der Fahrt auf dem Zürchersee," *Poetik und Hermeneutik*, vol. 14 (1989), pp. 276–96.

50 Anselm Haverkamp & Bettine Menke, "Allegorie," in *Ästhetische Grundbegriffe*, vol. I (Stuttgart: Metzler, 2000), pp. 49–104, here: p. 101.

51 Ibid., p. 100.

52 "Man becomes the figure that denies figurality, whereas woman becomes the figure that incarnates figurality," writes Barbara Vinken: "Republic, Rhetoric, and Sexual Difference," in A. Haverkamp, ed., *Deconstruction is/in America: A New Sense of the Political* (New York: New York University Press, 1995), pp. 181–99, here: p. 194.

53 Jean-Jacques Rousseau, *Émile, or On Education* (New York: Basic Books, 1979), p. 358.

54 Ibid., pp. 364–5.

55 Contrary to Frederick Neuhouser, I believe that Rousseau's theory of gender differences is highly relevant to the "philosophical core of Rousseau's thought" (cf. Frederick Neuhouser, *Rousseau's Theodicy of Self-Love*, p. 25). What is decisive here is not the fact *that* the community of brothers clearly rests on the exclusion of women and

foreigners, but *why* Rousseau views this exclusion (and that of the theater as well) as necessary. The point is to contain the latent difference between person and brother/citizen, which is present in every male member of the community. For Neuhouser, and here he follows Rousseau's definition of man according to his social identity, the conflict between person and citizen is a sign of decline. This conflict is either the result of poor education, due to which individuals become alienated from the community, or of the corruption of the community (cf. ibid., pp. 214, 260). In a functioning community, by contrast, the practical identity gained by proper education should coincide with the values of the community, such that the expression of these values can be recognized by their peers, i.e. their brothers, who have undergone the same education process (ibid., p. 261). The systematic importance attached to the exclusion of women, foreigners, and actors is due to the fact that they exemplify an entirely different meaning of the category "human being": pre-subjective indeterminacy, which stands in structural conflict with social identity. The price for the exclusion of this – other – definition of "human being," the suppression of the knowledge that human beings are never entirely absorbed by their social roles, is quite high – as I will show later. The exclusion of women, foreigners, and actors is not a merely empirical or historically contingent problem, as Neuhouser believes. What is at stake are the ethical-political problems systematically associated with the ideal of the identity of person and citizen.

56 See especially Starobinski, *Jean-Jacques Rousseau*, pp. 120–1 and Derrida, *On Grammatology*, pp. 306–7.
57 Jean-Jacques Rousseau, "Of the Social Contract," in *The Social Contract and Other Later Political Writings*, ed. Victor Gourevitch (New York: Cambridge University Press, 1997), pp. 39–152, here: p. 58. Hereafter referred to parenthetically in the text as SC.
58 Leo Strauss, *Natural Right and History* (Chicago, IL: University of Chicago Press, 1953), p. 271.
59 Human beings thereby develop, in Rousseau's words, an "idea of the future" (DI 90).
60 Strauss, *Natural Right*, p. 271.
61 As individuals, the members of the community "call themselves *Citizens* as participants in the sovereign authority, and *Subjects* as subjected to the laws of the State" (SC 51).
62 Nadia Urbinati has highlighted the enormous significance of the temporal figure of the moment's immediacy for Rousseau's conception of the general will. See Nadia Urbinati, *Representative Democracy: Principles and Genealogy* (Chicago, IL: University of Chicago Press, 2008), p. 90.
63 The act of association, according to Rousseau, shall produce "a moral and collective body made up of as many members as the assembly has voices, and which receives by this same act its unity, its common self, its life and its will" (SC 50).

64 See in this context Samuel Weber's inspiring reading of the *Social Contract*, which, drawing on Paul de Man, emphasizes that Rousseau encircles rather than resolves the problem of the interrelation between the general and the particular; see his "In the Name of the Law," *Cardozo Law Review*, vol. 11 (1989–90), pp. 1515–38. Christine Garbe pursues a similar reading strategy in her *Die "weibliche" List im "männlichen" Text*.
65 See ch. 2, sec. 4.
66 Starobinski, *Rousseaus Anklage der Gesellschaft*, p. 28. On the problem of educating a sovereign people, see Heinz-Hermann Schepp, *Die Krise der Erziehung und der Prozeß der Demokratisierung: Zum Verhältnis von Politik und Pädagogik bei J.J. Rousseau* (Kronberg/Ts.: Cornelsen, 1978), especially pp. 42–4.
67 This last aspect is important for distinguishing the extraordinary character of the legislator from that of a monarch. As Albrecht Koschorke summarizes, Rousseau's legislator grows to become "a threshold hero that forms an entire culture and ultimately attains almost transcendental greatness," thereby "presciently granting that form to the body politic which makes the latter capable of rationality and [...] allows humans to become social creatures at all." But nevertheless, "the figure of the creator does not, unlike the monarch, himself rule over the law that he has found or created. In other words, his authorship of the laws provides him with no privilege." See the section "Die Schrift am Ort des Souveräns: das Mysterium der Verfassung" (Koschorke) in Koschorke et al., eds, *Der fiktive Staat*, pp. 241–50, here: p. 249.
68 Cf. Starobinski, *Rousseaus Anklage der Gesellschaft*, p. 28.
69 For Rousseau this is also the decisive function of religion, as he points out in a later passage (Book IV): It "makes him love his duties" (SC 150). This instrumentalization of religion for secular purposes corresponds to his sharp criticism of Christianity and his plea for a "civil" religion reduced to "sentiments of sociality" (ibid.). The moment that the exercise of religion (such as in Christianity) becomes an aim in itself, it conflicts with the duties of the citizen – and this becomes a problem for the community as a whole: "All institutions which put man in contradiction with himself are worthless" (SC 147).
70 See Jacques Derrida, *Declarations of Independence*, in *Negotiations: Interventions and Interviews, 1971–2001* (Stanford, CA: Stanford University Press, 2002), pp. 46–54, here: p. 51.
71 Quintilian writes of *prosopopoeia* that it enables us "to put words of advice, reproach, complaint, praise or pity into the mouths of appropriate persons. Nay, we are even allowed in this form of speech to bring down the gods from heaven and raise the dead, while cities also and peoples may find a voice." We will return to this last possibility. Cf. Quintilian, *The Institutio Oratoria*, IX, 2, 30–1. For a detailed account of the history of this rhetorical figure, see Bettine Menke, *Prosopopoiia: Stimme und Text bei Brentano, Hoffmann, Kleist und Kafka* (Munich: Fink, 2000), pp. 137–216.

72 See Bettine Menke, "Verstelle – Der Ort der Frau," in Barbara Vinken, ed., *Dekonstruktiver Feminismus: Literaturwissenschaft in Amerika* (Frankfurt/Main: Suhrkamp, 1992), pp. 436–76, here: p. 437.
73 In this sense, the conferral of a mask by means of *prosopopoeia* is at once an unmasking; see Paul de Man, "Autobiography as De-Facement," *MLN*, vol. 94, no. 5 (December 1979), pp. 919–30.
74 Menke, *Prosopopoiia*, p. 192.
75 "Metaphor overlooks the fictional, textual element in the nature of the entity it connotes," writes Paul de Man in his studies on Rousseau. Paul de Man, *Allegories of Reading: Figural Language in Rousseau, Nietzsche, Rilke, and Proust* (New Haven, CT: Yale University Press, 1979), p. 151.
76 As Bettine Menke points out, the latter, an aspect of *prosopopoeia*, corresponds to the figure of *katachrese*, for according to rhetorical tradition this is also termed *abusio*, abuse. "It marks the arbitrariness of the accordance of a face and the formation of meaning." Menke, *Prosopopoiia*, pp. 143f.
77 As Christoph Menke mentions in a related context, "democratic power is a kind of power that recognizes that it must be recognized; that it only exists in its successful representation [...] It is inevitably related to the power to recognize (or to refuse to recognize) those over whom this power rules. Political power in a democracy is a power that is broken by the power of recognition, by the power to recognize or to refuse to recognize." Christoph Menke, "Von der Ironie der Politik – zur Politik der Ironie," in T. Bonacker, A. Brodocz & T. Noetzel, eds, *Die Ironie der Politik: Über die Konstruktion politischer Wirklichkeiten* (Frankfurt/Main: Campus, 2003), pp. 19–33, here: pp. 27f.
78 On the tension between sovereignty and legitimacy in democracy, see Derrida, *Rogues*, p. 101.
79 This is why I also do not believe that there can be no political legitimacy without the appeal to a religious authority, as Simon Critchley suggests "with and against Rousseau" (cf. Simon Critchley, *Der Katechismus des Bürgers: Politik, Recht und Religion in, nach, mit und gegen Rousseau* (Berlin: Diaphanes, 2008), p. 55. It is true that Rousseau emphasizes that the appeal to God historically has played a central role in the legitimation of constitutions, but we should not conclude from this fact that there is a necessary connection between politics and religion. The political instrumentalization of religion is only necessary if, like Critchley (influenced by both Rousseau and the political presentism of Alain Badiou), it is assumed that the "essence of politics consists in the act of association without representation." Although Critchley is aware that this is a fiction, he regards it as a "supreme fiction" that we must believe in in the name of politics. And this fiction "must be reinforced by the authority of a divine legislator and the dogmas of a civil religion" (p. 73). Whereas Critchley is apparently willing to take over the costs for his "supreme fiction" up to the point of calling on the US-American left, though with "little

enthusiasm," to "make progressive use of the power of religion," I believe that given the explosive mixture of politics and religion throughout the world, it would be wise to drop this concept of politics altogether. Instead, we should adopt a concept, as I would like to argue against Rousseau and contemporary Rousseau scholarship, of democratic politics in which the insight that there is no general will beyond political representation is constitutive.

80 See ch. 1, sec. 10.
81 Things look different when it comes to private property, which Rousseau, in the second discourse, recognizes as a second source of inequality alongside the recognition of individual achievements. But that is another topic entirely.
82 On the concept of an inner nature that should neither be confused with a first nature nor be misunderstood as the other of culture, see ch. 1, secs 7 and 8, as well as ch. 2, sec 8.
83 For a correspondingly less rigorous concept of self-determination, see ch. 2, sec. 10.
84 Rousseau writes that the "impulsion of mere appetite is slavery" (SC 54).
85 I have argued that this tension should not, however, be misunderstood as an abstract detachment from the social. In reality every change I make to myself necessarily changes the practices in which I am involved. For that reason, even seemingly private changes to my self-understanding are never, or never entirely, private. The corresponding change to the practices in which I am involved can take place without friction and without much ado. But it can also involve conflicts if the change to these practices implies a breach with values that previously determined these practices. A coming-out, for instance, demands that others recognize an openly homosexual self-understanding – one that not only deviates from the way they have always regarded their son, friend, colleague, neighbor, renter, etc. The stance demanded of others instead involves a breach with an entire worldview, to the extent that the latter was previously marked by traditional gender roles. Changes to the self-understanding of individuals can therefore have far-reaching social consequences. They can lead to conflicts in which the meaning of the social good itself is put into question, to conflicts that can even reach the level of legislation, such as, in Germany, the long-standing conflict over §175 in the German penal code, which punished homosexuality and was not abolished until 1994.
86 See again Derrida, *Rogues*, p. 92.
87 Ibid.
88 Jacques Rancière, *Das Unvernehmen, Politik und Philosophie* (Frankfurt/Main: Suhrkamp, 2002), p. 34.
89 Here the term monarchy is to be taken strictly literally.
90 Ernst H. Kantorowicz, *Die zwei Körper des Königs: Eine Studie zur politischen Theologie des Mittelalters* (Munich: dtv, 1990), p. 52.
91 Ibid.

92 Ibid.
93 Claude Lefort, "The Question of Democracy," in *Democracy and Political Theory* (Cambridge: Polity, 1988), pp. 9–20, here: p. 17.
94 Ibid.
95 Ibid.
96 Ibid., p. 18.
97 Rancière, *Dissensus*, p. 34. We have seen that this indeed is a possibility in our discussion of Carl Schmitt. Cf. ch. 4, sec. 9.
98 Contrary to what Lefort and Gauchet suggest in an unfortunate formulation, we should not identify this with class conflict. For this would mean making class conflict the condition of the possibility of democratic societies, which would be unbearable for any democratic project. For this would mean reducing this conflict to a mere fact and removing it from the movements of democratic politics, which of course Lefort and Gauchet explicitly reject. Therefore, it is more plausible to relate this "original division," with the recognition of which democracy begins, to the two bodies of the people. See Claude Lefort & Marcel Gauchet, "Über die Demokratie: Das Politische und die Instituierung des Gesellschaftlichen," in U. Rödel, ed., *Autonome Gesellschaft und libertäre Demokratie* (Frankfurt/Main: Suhrkamp, 1990), pp. 89–122, here especially: pp. 91–4.
99 Jacques Rancière, *Disagreement: Politics and Philosophy* (Minneapolis, MN: University of Minnesota Press, 1999), p. 100.
100 Friedrich Balke, *Figuren der Souveränität* (Munich: Fink, 2009), p. 138.
101 Rancière, *Dissensus*, p. 70.
102 Giorgio Agamben, *Homo Sacer: Sovereign Power and Bare Life* (Stanford, CA: Stanford University Press, 1998), p. 128.
103 See my considerations on the democratic determination of the exception at the end of ch. 4, sec. 10.
104 Lefort, Gauchet, "Über die Demokratie," p. 93. This, by the way, does not mean – even with regard to complex societies – that we should propagate the "irony of the state" in the sense of an ironic self-reduction of state policy. See Helmut Willke, *Ironie des Staates* (Frankfurt/Main: Suhrkamp, 1992). Although the transition from the realism to the democratic nominalism of sovereignty goes along with an autonomization of social sub-systems. "Once the power ceases to manifest the principle which generates and organizes a social body, once it ceases to condense within it virtues deriving from transcendent reason and justice, law and knowledge assert themselves as separate from and irreducible to power" (Lefort, *The Question of Democracy*, p. 17f.). Yet the role of the state, even in a much more sophisticated society, cannot be reduced, as Willke proposes, to the supervision of autonomous social sub-systems that restrict and coordinate themselves in view of the potential threat to collective goods. As Willke himself admits, this would not only assume a reliable climate of solidarity that Willke derives, suprisingly enough given the transnational dimension

of local contexts of action that he himself develops, from the socially integrative effect of national collective identities. Politics, however, already comes into play as soon as the question arises as to what can be regarded as a collective good with reference to which collective. Willke leaves us in the dark on this matter.
105 Niklas Luhmann, *Die Politik der Gesellschaft* (Frankfurt/Main: Suhrkamp, 2000), p. 97.
106 Ibid., p. 98.
107 Ibid.
108 Ibid., p. 99.
109 Rousseau argued that "when factions arise, small associations at the expense of the large association, the will of each one of these associations becomes general in relation to its members and particular in relation to the state; there can then no longer be said to be as many voters as there are men, but only as many as there are associations. The differences become less numerous and yield a less general result. Finally, when one of these associations is so large that it prevails over all the rest, the result you have is no longer a sum of small differences, but one single difference; then there is no longer a general will, and the opinion that prevails is nothing but a private opinion" (SC 60).
110 Luhmann, *Die Politik der Gesellschaft*, p. 104.
111 Ibid., p. 105.
112 Cf. ibid., p. 429, as well as p. 141: "Decisionism exists [...] only in the imagination of critics of the system, but not as a problem of democracy."
113 Ibid., p. 141.
114 Cf. ch. 4, sec. 10.
115 See Luhmann, *Die Politik der Gesellschaft*, p. 429.
116 Lefort & Gauchet, "Über die Demokratie," p. 98.
117 Ibid., p. 104.
118 Cf. ch. 1, sec. 9.

Chapter 6   The Anaestheticization of the Political in Fascism: Benjamin

1 Cf. Walter Benjamin, "The Work of Art in the Age of Its Reproducibility, Second Version," in *Selected Writings*, vol. 3, 1935–1938 (Cambridge, MA: Harvard University Press, 2002), pp. 101–34, here: pp. 121f. Hereafter referred to parenthetically in the text as WA.
2 Lefort and Gauchet, "Über die Demokratie," p. 102.
3 Ibid., p. 103.
4 Ibid., p. 104.
5 Ibid.
6 This use of the term obviously has little to do with a suspicion against the so-called aestheticizing of the life-world which supposedly, because

of an excess of aestheticism, leads to a "gigantic anaestheticizing." This is the thesis proposed by Wolfgang Welsch, "Ästhetik und Anästhetik," in *Ästhetisches Denken* (Stuttgart: Reclam, 1990), pp. 13f. Although Odo Marquard also sees a connection between the anaesthetic and totalitarian stagings, he discusses this phenomenon with a view to the claim of the artistic avant-garde to create something like a total work of art. He also shares a diffuse reservation against the aestheticizing of the life-world. See Odo Marquard, *Aesthetica und Anaesthetica: Philosophische Überlegungen* (Munich: Fink, 2003), esp. pp. 15–17.

7 See Walter Benjamin, "The Work of Art in the Age of Its Technological Reproducibility," in *Selected Writings*, vol. 3: 1935–1938 (Cambridge, MA: Harvard University Press, 2003), pp. 101–33, here: p. 129.

8 Walter Benjamin, "What is Epic Theatre [First Version]," in *Understanding Brecht* (London: Verso, 1998), p. 10. Hereafter referred to parenthetically in the text as ET I.

9 See ch. 1, secs 10 and 11.

10 See Gustave Le Bon, *The Crowd: A Study of the Popular Mind* (New York: Macmillan, 1896). Benjamin makes explicit reference to Le Bon in order to define the "impenetrable and compact," "reactive" mass in more detail (WA 129).

11 See the chapter entitled "The Types of Legitimate Domination," in Max Weber, *Economy and Society* (Los Angeles & Berkeley: University of California Press, 1978), esp. pp. 241–5. I will return to Weber's analysis of charismatic authority in sec. 7.

12 In a letter to Benjamin, Adorno writes that "the few sentences on the disintegration of the proletarians as a 'mass' brought about by revolution belongs to the most profound and powerful bits of political theory I have read since reading [Lenin's] *State and Revolution*." Theodor W. Adorno & Walter Benjamin, *Briefwechsel 1928–1940* (Frankfurt/Main: Suhrkamp, 1994), p. 175.

13 Cf. ch. 1, sec. 2 and Gabriel Tarde, "Le public et la foule," in *L'opinion et la foule* (Paris: PUF, 1989), pp. 31–71, here: p. 57; Gabriel Tarde, *Penal Philosophy* (Boston, MA: Little, Brown & Co., 1968), p. 362.

14 Yet this is certainly the case in bourgeois theater. There the seating arrangement, with its expensive and inexpensive seating, reflects the class relations of the audience. It is precisely this aspect of the theater that Rousseau picks up on in his critique of theater; he sees this aspect as a further indication for the divisive effects of the theater (LtA 113f.). But Rousseau does not conclude from this fact that class relations must be abolished, rather only that they not be made so visible. This is accomplished not least by festivals (cf. LtA 131). Benjamin is clearly concerned with precisely the opposite problem, arguing against the concealment of the social differences in the audience, or rather among the masses.

15 Hannah Arendt, *Benjamin, Brecht: Zwei Essays* (Munich: Piper, 1971), p. 93. In this accusation we also see echoes of Rousseau (cf. LtA 24).

16 Whereas Cavell employs Aristotelian motifs to criticize the detachment of an aesthetic consciousness which can even enjoy the presentation of the most tragic plot, the Platonist Brecht instead sets an anti-Aristotelian drama against the lack of detachment on the part of an empathetic audience. Cf. esp. Stanley Cavell, "Ending the Waiting Game: A Reading of Beckett's *Endgame*," in *Must We Mean What We Say? A Book of Essays* (Cambridge: Cambridge University Press, 1969), pp. 115–62; "The Avoidance of Love: A Reading of King Lear," in *Must We Mean What We Say?*, pp. 267–353. For a critical discussion of Cavell's argument, see Juliane Rebentisch, *Ästhetik der Installation* (Frankfurt/Main: Suhrkamp, 2003), esp. pp. 30–9.
17 Bertolt Brecht, "The Literarization of the Theatre," in *Brecht on Theatre* (New York: Hill and Wang, 1992), pp. 43–6, here: p. 44.
18 It is only logical that Cavell rightly understands Brecht's modern theater as the continuation of "serious drama" with other means. Cf. Stanley Cavell, *The World Viewed: Reflections on the Ontology of Film* (Cambridge, MA: Harvard University Press, 1979), p. 111.
19 Walter Benjamin, "The Concept of Criticism in German Romanticism," in *Selected Writings*, vol. 1, pp. 116–200, here: pp. 179–84.
20 Benjamin begins his lecture by saying, "You will remember how Plato, in his project for a Republic, deals with writers. In the interests of the community, he denies them the right to dwell therein. Plato had a high opinion of the power of literature. But he thought it harmful and superfluous – in a *perfect* community, be it understood. Since Plato, the question of the writer's right to exist has not often been raised with the same emphasis; today, however, it arises once more." Walter Benjamin, "The Author as Producer," in *Understanding Brecht*, pp. 85–103, here: p. 85.
21 Bertolt Brecht, "A Short Organum for the Theatre," *Brecht on Theatre*, pp. 179–205, here: pp. 182–3.
22 Hans-Thies Lehmann, *Postdramatic Theatre* (London/New York: Routledge, 2006), p. 33.
23 From a strictly Platonic perspective, of course, the construction of epic *theater* is just as paradoxical as the *dramatic* existence of an undramatic hero. Benjamin is aware of this fact: The "thinking man" is necessarily a stranger to the stage. He can at most, as Benjamin says in accordance with Brecht, be "carried on stage lying down, so little is he drawn thither" (ET I 5). Yet the Socratic plea that epic narrative be considered the solely legitimate literary form from a philosophical-political perspective has its own place in a Platonic dialogue. Plato's own dialogues, as Benjamin writes in his study on Brecht, carry the wise man "to the very threshold of drama" (ET II 17). And in *The Origin of German Tragic Drama*, Brecht writes that the "superiority" with which Plato's work stands up to tragedy is ultimately due less to the "rational spirit of Socrates" than to the "spirit of the dialogue itself," such that this superiority "ultimately affected the challenger more than the object challenged." Cf. Walter Benjamin, *The Origin of German Tragic Drama*

(New York: Verso, 1998), p. 118. According to Benjamin, the Platonic dialogues do not disclose the other of theater; instead, they argue for a dramatic genre that could, though only subtly and via an "overgrown stalking path" (ET I 6) lead to the formation of a literary tradition whose most significant stations Benjamin sees in German medieval mysteries and baroque tragic drama. He views Brecht's search for a non-tragic hero as the continuation of this tradition.

24 Walter Benjamin, "The Paris of the Second Empire in Baudelaire," in *Selected Writings*, vol. 4: 1938–1940 (Cambridge, MA: Harvard University Press, 2003), pp. 31f. Hereafter referred to parenthetically in the text as PSE.

25 Walter Benjamin, "From the Brecht Commentary," in *Understanding Brecht*, pp. 27–32, here: p. 28.

26 Walter Benjamin, "Bert Brecht," in *Selected Writings*, vol. 2, part 1: 1927–1930, pp. 365–71, here: p. 367. Hereafter referred to parenthetically in the text as BB.

27 Cf. Vladimir Lenin, "The State and Revolution," in *Essential Works of Lenin* (New York: Bantam Books, 1966), pp. 271–364, here: p. 339.

28 For the distinction between a concept of practical rationality that includes such a mimetic opening of the subject to otherness and strangeness and the conformity to "serving authority," cf. also Theodor W. Adorno, "Anmerkungen zum philosophischen Denken," in *Gesammelte Schriften*, vol. X.2 (Frankfurt/Main: Suhrkamp, 1977), pp. 599–607, here: p. 601. Cf. also Josef Früchtl, *Mimesis: Konstellationen eines Zentralbegriffs bei Adorno* (Wurzburg: Königshausen & Neumann, 1986), p. 35.

29 Weber, *Economy and Society*, p. 241.

30 Ibid., p. 244.

31 Ibid., pp. 241f.

32 Ibid., pp. 246–9.

33 Gertrud Koch, "Unterhaltung und Autorität: Konstellationen der Massenmedien," in Hauke Brunkhorst, ed., *Demokratischer Experimentalismus: Politik in der komplexen Gesellschaft* (Frankfurt/Main: Suhrkamp, 1998), pp. 92–105, here: p. 101.

34 Ibid., pp. 101f.

35 Of course, even before his election, Obama had to prove himself in his election campaign. Bill Clinton put it best in a campaign event for Obama when he stated that an election campaign is the longest job interview in the world; it's about time "to hire the guy."

36 In Berlusconi's case, the fact that this self-misunderstanding could become so politically effective cannot be separated from his power as a media mogul. Therefore, the case of Berlusconi points up the problem of a substantialized charismatic authority under post-democratic conditions. On this problem, see ch. 7.

37 Koch, "Unterhaltung und Autorität," p. 103.

38 Cf. Christoph Menke's considerations on a kind of politics of the theater that criticizes the theater of politics in "Die Depotenzierung des

Souveräns im Gesang," in E. Horn, B. Menke, & C. Menke, eds, *Literatur als Philosophie – Philosophie als Literatur* (Munich: Fink, 2006), pp. 281–96, here: pp. 294–6.
39 Lehmann, *Postdramatic Theatre*.
40 For a more detailed account, cf. Rebentisch, *Ästhetik der Installation*, esp. pp. 276–9; cf. also Juliane Rebentisch, "Realismus heute: Kunst, Politik und die Kritik der Repräsentation," *WestEnd*, vol. 2 (2010), pp. 15–29.

Chapter 7   Post-Democracy and the Anaesthetizing of the Political: A Look Forward

1 This is why I find it misleading that Colin Crouch's book on this issue introduces the concept with reference to anti-aestheticization clichés, according to which election campaigns, due to the workings of the mass media, "degenerate into a mere spectacle" in which "the mass of citizens plays a passive, quiescent, even apathetic part." This overly generalized critique of spectacle distorts the discussion, crucial to a democracy, of various broadcast formats and the influence of economic and or political power on the media. A few pages later, however, Crouch himself admits that the crisis of democracy is not "just the fault of the mass media." Instead, it is linked to the hidden influence of economic elites on politics. Colin Crouch, *Post-Democracy* (Cambridge: Polity, 2004), pp. 4, 6.
2 Jacques Rancière, *Disagreement*, p. 101–2.
3 Ibid., p. 104.
4 Ibid., p. 105.
5 Ibid., p. 113. The self-emasculation of power thus goes along with the naturalization of a specific economic order, a specific form of capitalism.
6 Ibid., p. 102.
7 See ch. 2, sec. 7. The problem with the critique of aestheticization lies in the fact that it subsumes further motifs of freedom under subjectivism. As we have seen, these motifs deserve to be defended against such an accusation.
8 Rancière, *Disagreement*, p. 114.
9 Luc Boltanski & Ève Chiapello, *The New Spirit of Capitalism* (London: Verso, 2007), pp. 461–3.
10 Maurizio Lazzarato correctly points out that, wherever there has been a transition from socieites based on discipline to those based on control, difference and creativity are no longer neutralized and suppressed, but rather "controlled" and "modulated." In other words, not every deviation or novelty is welcome in the world of the project economy. See Maurizio Lazzarato, "The Concepts of Living in the Societies of Control," in M. Fuglsang & B.M. Sørensen, eds, *Deleuze and the Social*

(Edinburgh: Edinburgh University Press, 2006), pp. 171–90, here: p. 178.

11 By contrast, the artistic critique of the artist myth picks up on the very subjectivism that the genius myth shares with the neoliberal ideology of creativity. Contrary to the mythical conceptions of artistic creation and inspiration, artistic critique since the 1960s has directed its attention to the fact that even the most individual artistic act is always subject to the influence of society. It would be an over-simplification, therefore, to regard the artistic critique of the myth of the artistic genius as the art world's own contribution to the "undifferentiation" of creative-economic and artistic practices, as Andreas Reckwitz presumes. (On this thesis, see Andreas Reckwitz, ed., *Kreation und Depression*, pp. 98–117, esp. p. 100.) In truth, this critique has been linked to other developments in the world of art over the last few decades, which have freed the concept of art from the problematic notion of the artist as an exceptionally creative subject. This has not come about in order to dedifferentiate art, but to understand this difference in a different and superior way; cf. Juliane Rebentisch, *Theorien der Gegenwartskunst zur Einführung* (Hamburg: Junius, 2013). Furthermore, and that is the crucial point here, this critique formulates an opposition to the neoliberal democratization of the genius myth – an opposition that does not concern the notion of democratization itself, but that which is to be democratized: an exceedingly abstract, and thus false, image of freedom.

12 Alenka Zupančič sees here a new form of racism which, unlike traditional forms of racism, no longer turns biological characteristics into social characteristics, but rather "tends to 'naturalize' the differences and features produced by the sociosymbolic order." See Alenka Zupančič, *The Odd One In: On Comedy* (Cambridge, MA: MIT Press, 2008), p. 6.

13 Ibid., p. 7.

14 See Alain Ehrenberg, *The Weariness of the Self: Diagnosing the History of Depression in the Contemporary Age*, trans. Enrico Caouette et al. (Montreal: McGill-Queens University Press, 2010).

15 On the connection between self-determination and acceleration, see Harmut Rosa, "Kritik der Zeitverhältnisse: Beschleunigung und Entfremdung als Schlüsselbegriffe der Sozialkritik," in R. Jaeggi & T. Wesche, eds, *Was ist Kritik?* (Frankfurt/Main: Suhrkamp, 2009), pp. 23–54, esp. 38–52; see also *Beschleunigung: Die Veränderung der Zeitstrukturen in der Moderne* (Frankfurt/Main: Suhrkamp 2005), esp. pp. 460–90.

16 See Plessner, *Limits of Community*, p. 176.

17 Ibid.

18 Bruno Latour, *Von der Realpolitik zur Dingpolitik oder Wie man Dinge öffentlich macht* (Berlin: Merve, 2005), p. 39.

19 Bruno Latour, *Politics of Nature: How to Bring the Sciences into Democracy* (Cambridge, MA: Harvard University Press, 2004), pp. 62ff.

20 Jacques Derrida, *The Other Heading: Reflections on Today's Europe* (Bloomington, IN: Indiana University Press, 1992), p. 98.
21 Ibid., pp. 105f.
22 See ch. 1, sec. 11.
23 See Elias Canetti, *Crowds and Power* (New York: Seabury Press, 1978), p. 19.
24 Ibid., p. 20.
25 See Rancière, *Disagreement*, p. 65.
26 Michael Hardt & Antonio Negri, *Multitude: War and Democracy in the Age of Empire* (New York: The Penguin Press, 2004), p. 330.
27 Ibid., p. 353.
28 Ibid., p. 337.
29 Ibid., p. 355.
30 Albrecht Wellmer, *Sprachphilosophie. Eine Vorlesung* (Frankfurt/Main: Suhrkamp, 2004), pp. 247f.
31 Hardt & Negri, *Multitude*, p. 355.

Index

Abraham 129–30, 131
abstract freedom 9, 78, 79–82, 163, 251
actors 40–4, 185–9
Adorno, Theodor 67, 82, 96, 120, 143, 276n, 300n, 302n
  dialectic of freedom 86, 156
aestheticization 1–13
  of the life-world 1, 3, 4–5, 299n, 300n
  meaning 1
  of the political 10, 11, 13, 227, 229–47
    fascism 229–47
    Schmitt on 146–9
Agamben, Giorgio 222–3
Alcibiades 63
alien powers 152–4, 155–6
alienation 1, 150
  Benjamin and 235, 238–41
  Rousseau and 185, 199, 202, 207, 239
Ankersmit, Franklin Rudolf 266n
Arendt, Hannah 184, 273n, 278n, 300n

Aristophanes 63–4
Aristotelian philosophy 95, 96, 234, 236, 237
Artaud, Antonin 227–8
artist myth, the 304n
artistic critique 250

Badiou, Alain 296n
Bakunin, Michail 159
Balke, Friedrich 285n
Baudelaire, Charles 140, 239, 240, 242
Beethoven, Ludwig van 292n
Behler, Ernst 272n, 274n
Benjamin, Walter 13, 184, 228, 229–47
  adaptability and revolution 241–3
  alienation 235, 238–41
  "The Author as Producer" 235
  on Brecht 227–8, 231, 233, 234–47
  charisma
    democracy and 243–5
    vs. ratio 231–2

"The Concept of Criticism in
    German Romanticism" 235
epic theater 227–8, 234–8
fascist mass assemblies 227, 229,
    230, 231
political theater 245
politicizing art 232–4
"The Work of Art in the Age of Its
    Reproducibility" 227, 229,
    232–3
theatrocracy 231–2, 233
Understanding Brecht 231, 233,
    234, 235–8, 240
Berlin, Isaiah 261n, 262n
Berlusconi, Silvio 245
Bieri, Peter 28, 261n, 262n
Blumenberg, Hans 165–6, 283n
Bohrer, Karl Heinz 80, 102, 283n,
    284n
Boltanski, Luc 250
Bonacker, Thorsten 288n
boredom 79, 107, 113
Brecht, Bertolt 227–8, 231, 233,
    234–47
    alienation 235, 238–41
    astonishment 234–7
    epic theater 227–8, 234–8
    Man Equals Man 240
    Stories of Herr Keuner 238–9,
        240–1
    V-effects 236
Breloer, Heinrich 246

Canetti, Elias 255
catharsis 201, 206
Cavell, Stanley 109, 123, 184, 202,
    234, 235, 266n, 293n
charisma 18, 25, 50, 231–2, 243–5
Chiapello, Eve 250
China 19
Cicero 189
cinema 123, 188, 233, 246
Clinton, Bill 302n
Cohen, Hermann 276n
colorfulness 2, 5, 17, 19–20, 51
conscience 64, 65, 76, 95, 118, 133,
    134

controlled irony 139–41
Critchley, Simon 296n
Critias 63
Crouch, Colin 303n
crowd, the
    Benjamin and 227, 230, 231–2,
        233–4, 239
    fascist mass assemblies 227, 230,
        231, 255
    masses and mimesis 49–52
    Plato and 48, 49–52, 53, 231–2
    Rousseau and 209, 214, 220, 230
    the will to destroy 254–5
cultural diversity 2, 5, 17, 19–20, 51

D'Alembert, Jean Le Rond 184
Davidson, Donald 30, 271n
De Maistre, Josephe 159, 162, 166
De Man, Paul 140, 141, 142, 295n
De Sade, Marquis de 82–3, 85
Debord, Guy 184
deception 258
    Kierkegaard and 133, 140
    Rousseau and 186, 187, 191, 192,
        202, 213, 217
    self-deception 26–7, 30, 66, 258
degenerate freedom 7–8
Deleuze, Gilles 82–5
depression 80, 251
Derrida, Jacques 156, 214, 273n,
    283n, 290n, 292n, 293n, 295n
    on democracy 10, 178, 253
    fraternocracy 201
    judicial decisions 168
    on justice 282n
    moments of decision 29
    Plato's *Republic* 25
dialectic of freedom 13, 54, 85–7,
    135, 156, 179, 243
Diderot, Denis 187
Dilthey, Wilhelm 274n
dissimulation 186, 187, 188, 199,
    212
distance 2, 9, 33, 52, 53, 124, 188,
    252
    concealing irony and 191, 192
    ironic distance 81

distance (cont.)
  reflective distance 125
  Romantics and 150, 154
  Schmitt and 150, 154, 156, 157
divorce 122–8
Dominican Republic 19
Donoso Cortés, Juan 159–60, 162
Duncan, Elmer H. 281n
Düttman, Alexander García 143
Dylan, Bob 262n

Ehrenberg, Alain 251, 252
Eichinger, Bernd 246
election campaigns 173, 225–6,
  302n, 303n
epic theater 227–8
  alienation 238–41
  astonishment 234–7
  the look of the stranger 237–8
Eremita, Viktor 276n, 277n
evil 82–5, 90
experience society 3

fable 200, 236, 267n
fascism 229–47
  charisma and 231–2, 243–5
  mass assemblies 227, 230, 231,
    255
  staging of unity 230, 231, 238,
    254
  see also totalitarianism
Fenves, Peter 280n
Ferry, Luc 283n
festivals 13, 198–206
Fichte, Johann Gottlieb 76–7, 79,
  103–4, 284n
film see cinema
Fish, Stanley 168
forgetfulness-of-self 104–8
Foucault, Michel 8, 273n
Franco, Francisco 19
Frankfurt, Harry 28, 262n, 264n
fraternocracy 201
fundamentalism 251

Gamm, Gerhard 279n
Ganz, Bruno 246

Garbe, Christine 291n
Gauchet, Marcel 229, 298n
gender differences 101, 121–2,
  204–5, 257
gender parody 193–6, 197
genius 77, 86, 210, 250
Goethe, Johann Wolfgang von 204,
  235
Grasskamp, Walter 283n
Greve, Wilfried 114

Habermas, Jürgen 184, 265n, 269n,
  270n, 287n
Hardt, Michael 257, 258
Haverkamp, Anselm 293n
Haynes, Todd 262n
Hegel, Georg Wilhelm Friedrich 7,
  13, 55, 59–99, 146, 150,
  249
  abstract freedom 78, 79–82
  Aesthetics 76–9
  conflicts with and in morality 90–4
  dialectic of freedom 85–7
  evil 82–5, 90
  on Fichte 76–7, 79, 103–4
  *Hegel's Lectures on the History of
    Philosophy* 60–5, 67, 78, 93,
    94, 96, 98
  historicity of the good 97–9
  inner nature 83–4, 85–7, 88, 89,
    95, 98
  irony and the practice of
    truth 66–8
  Jenaer Schriften 1801–1807 69–70
  Kant's moral principle
    critique of 68–71, 91
    self-determination 87–90
    Socratic reformulation of 71–4
  Kierkegaard and 100–8, 114, 115,
    118, 126, 127, 130, 131–4,
    138, 139, 140, 143
  Lectures on Fine Arts 76
  "natural will" 82–5, 90, 91, 96
  Phenomenology of Spirit 75–6
  Philosophy of Right 59, 68–9, 76,
    77, 78, 81, 82, 85, 90, 94, 95,
    96, 97, 118, 119, 130, 133

romantic irony, critique of 8, 55, 56, 59–60, 65, 68, 74, 75–99
self-determination 86, 87–90, 91
Socratic irony 60–2
Socratic philosophy 62–5
Socratic virtue 97–9
subjective freedom 59, 60, 64–5, 67, 68, 69, 74, 75, 79–82, 93, 118
  expulsion from ethical life 94–7
Heidegger, Martin 32, 66
Hirschbiegel, Oliver 246
Hitler, Adolf, portrayals of 246
homosexuality 92, 297n
Honneth, Axel 79, 260n, 277n, 279n, 286n
Horkheimer, Max 82
Horstmann, Rolf-Peter 96
Hühn, Lore 101
human rights 222–3, 256

Inglourious Basterds 188
inner nature
  Hegel and 83–4, 85–7, 88, 89, 95, 98
  Kierkegaard and 142
  Plato and 36, 37, 38–40, 43, 47, 52
  Rousseau and 218, 222, 223
  Schmitt and 156
irony
  of the actor 185–9
  complex irony 186
  concealing irony 185–92, 194, 198, 216–17
  controlled irony 139–41
  Hegel and 8, 55, 56, 59–60, 65, 68, 74, 75–99
  Kierkegaard and 55, 56, 79, 102–8, 115, 126, 127, 139–41
  the practice of truth and 66–8
  public expression of indeterminacy 189–93
  Rousseau and 55, 185–93
  Socratic irony 60–2, 102–4
Isaac 129

Jaeggi, Rahel 276n
Jameson, Frederic 291n
Job 128–9, 279n
justice 35–6, 220, 222, 224, 282n

Kant, Immanuel
  divine art 261n
  moral principle 208
    Hegel's critique 68–71, 91
    self-determination 87–90
    Socratic reformulation of 71–4
Kantorowicz, Ernst 220–1
Kervégan, Jean-François 286n
Kierkegaard, Søren 13, 99, 100–44, 146, 150
  aristocratic exception 128–31, 132, 137
  boredom 79, 107, 113
  common sinners 131–4
  The Concept of Anxiety 132, 135, 142
  The Concept of Irony 101, 102–4, 105–7, 139–40
  conscience 118, 133, 134
  controlled irony 139–41
  divorce 122–8
  Either/Or 108–22, 127, 131, 133
  Fear and Trembling 129–31
  forgetfulness-of-self 104–8
  Hegel and 100–8, 114, 115, 118, 126, 127, 130, 131–4, 138, 139, 140, 143
  the impotent seducer 108–14
  inner nature 142
  irony 55, 56, 79, 100–8, 115, 126, 127, 139–41
  Journal of a Seducer 79
  the leap of faith 134–8
  love 109–10, 119–28
  marriage 118, 119–24
  negative freedom 102–4
  religion 120, 128–31, 134–8
  religious existence 101, 108, 114
  repentance 114–18, 126, 132, 134
  Repetition 128–9, 132
  repetitions 139–44

Kierkegaard, Søren (cont.)
romantic irony 55, 56, 79, 102–8, 115, 126, 127, 139–41
Schmitt and 162–5
self-choice 114–18
self-determination 107, 114, 126, 141–3
self-enhancement 104–8
self-realization 101, 106, 108, 112, 115, 117, 119, 120, 137, 138
Sickness unto Death 135–6
sin 116–17, 127, 132, 134–8
Socratic irony 102–4
Stages on Life's Way 132–4, 142
theory of stages 100, 101, 108, 134, 164
women, emancipation of 121, 122, 123, 126
King Lear 109
King Richard II 220
Koch, Gertrud 123, 244
Koschorke, Albrecht 295n
Kramme, Rüdiger 285n
Kroner, Richard 280n

Lacoue-Labarthe, Philippe 265n
Latour, Bruno 253
Lazzarato, Maurizio 303n
Le Bon, Gustave 300n
Lefort, Claude 10, 220, 221, 229, 298n
Lehmann, Hans-Thies 236, 246
Lenin, V.I. 241
Lethen, Helmut 290n
Liessmann, Konrad Paul 277n
love 109–10, 119–28
Löw-Beer, Martin 28
Lubitsch, Ernst 246
Luhmann, Niklas 224, 225–6

Marquard, Odo 300n
marriage 118, 119–24
Marthaler, Christoph 246
Marx, Karl 239, 241, 242, 243
mass assemblies 227, 229, 230, 231, 255
see also crowd

master of the art of living (*Lebenskünstler*) 8, 9, 20
Maus, Ingeborg 88, 269n
Mead, George Herbert 38
Menke, Bettine 204, 295n, 296n
Menke, Christoph 166, 282n, 302n
military dictatorships 19
mimesis 41–2, 187
Moretti, Tobias 246
Müller, Adam 155
multitude, the 257
mutability 2, 9
of democratic societies 178, 220, 226

Narcissus 251
natural will 82–5, 90, 91, 96
negative freedom 19, 63
definition 261n
Socratic irony and 102–4
Negri, Antonio 257, 258
Nehamas, Alexander 98, 186–7
Neuhouser, Frederick 293n
neurosis 89, 251
Norris, Andrew 273n
Novalis 78, 151

Obama, Barack 245
occasionalism 149–52, 155, 156
Oedipus 251

parody 193–6, 197, 199, 291n
philosophy 3–4, 56
Pinkard, Terry 69, 273n
Pippin, Robert 272n
Plato 17–56, 61, 96, 178, 198, 236, 242
actors 40–4, 187
catharsis 201
critique of democracy 5–6, 7, 8, 10, 11–13, 17–56
the crowd 48, 49–52, 53, 231–2
decision making 29–32, 33–4
degenerate freedom 7–8
democratic freedom (*exousia*) 7, 19, 23, 36, 44, 183

freedom and indeterminacy 18–20
freedom toward self 38–40
inner nature 36, 37, 38–40, 43, 47, 52
justice 35–6
The Laws (Nomoi) 45–6, 47
many jobs and much trespassing 35–8
masses and mimesis 49–52
on playwrights 40–4
on poets 40, 41, 42, 45, 51
Protagoras 23–4
The Republic (Politeia) 5–6, 17–56, 97–8, 232
self-determination 34, 35, 38, 39–40, 51
self-difference 52–4
self-perfection 52–4
slavery of the tyrant 21–3, 112–13
on taste 45, 46
theater types 40–4
theatrocracy 44–9, 184, 214, 231
the unfree opportunist 32–4
the unstable democrat 23–5
weakness of will (*akrasia*) 23, 135
  clear-sighted *akrasia* 26
  decision making and 29–32
  freedom from oneself and 29–32
  processual *akrasia* 25–7
  totalized *akrasia* 27–9
playwrights 40–4
Plessner, Helmuth 124, 125, 189–98, 252
  anthropology 161, 173
  eccentric positionality of humans 39, 40
  The Limits of Community 174–5, 189–92
  women 290n
poetry 103, 104, 109, 125, 276n
poets
  Benjamin on 239
  Plato on 40, 41, 42, 45, 51
political anthropology 158, 159–62
political romanticism 144, 145–79

political theater 245–7
politicizing art 232–4
Pollesch, René 246
post-democracy 13, 248–59
postdramatic theater 236, 246–7
postmodernism 3, 4
prosopopoeia 211, 212
Protagoras 63
Proudhon, Pierre-Joseph 159

Quintilian 189, 288n, 295n

racism 304n
Raimondi, Francesca 287n
Rancière, Jacques 220, 221, 248, 255, 264n
Reckwitz, Andreas 304n
religion
  function of 295n
  fundamentalism 251
  Kierkegaard and 101, 108, 114, 120, 128–31, 134–8
  the leap of faith 134–8
  politics and 297n
  Rousseau and 295n
  sin 116–17, 127, 132, 134–8
repentance 114–18, 126, 132, 134
Republican festivals 13, 198–206
rhetoric 2, 63, 80, 131, 164, 186, 189–93, 210–15, 221, 226, 230, 247
Rois, Sophie 246
romantic irony
  Hegel and 8, 55, 56, 59–60, 65, 68, 74, 75–99
  Kierkegaard and 55, 56, 79, 102–8, 115, 126, 127, 139–41
Rorty, Richard 266n, 271n
Rosa, Harmut 304n
Rousseau, Jean-Jacques 11–12, 41, 55, 110, 179, 183–228, 248, 252
  act of association 207–8
  actors
    actresses and parody 193–6
    irony of the actor 185–9
    alienation 185, 199, 202, 207, 239

Rousseau, Jean-Jacques (cont.)
  amour de soi (self-love) 88, 293n
  amour-propre (love of self) 88,
    197, 214, 217, 293n
  catharsis 201, 206
  civil freedom 207, 208, 209
  community 184, 185, 189–93,
    198–227
  community of brothers 201, 217,
    293n
  concept of man 188
  deception 186, 187, 191, 192,
    202, 213, 217
  Discourse on Inequality 197–8,
    201–2, 206
  dissimulation 186, 187, 188, 199,
    212
  education 208
  Émile 204–5
  equality 201–3, 215–20
  festivals 13, 198–206
  gender differences 204–5
  gender parody 193–6, 197
  general will 205, 207–10
    common man 210–15
  the golden mean 196–8
  inner nature 218, 222, 223
  legislator 208–10, 231
    sovereignty of 210–15
  Letter to d'Alembert 185–6,
    193–6, 199–201, 203, 205
  male self-difference 201–6
  manipulation 211
  natural freedom 207, 209
  naturalness 196–7
  parody 193–6, 197, 199, 291n
  perfectibility 206
  a politicizable boundary 218–20
  prosopopoeia 211, 212
  public expression of
    indeterminacy 189–93
  religion, function of 295n
  representation and the coding of
    contingency 224–8
  Schmitt and 171–4
  self-determination 218, 219
  self-improvement 197, 203, 206

The Social Contract 205–15
sovereignty
  of the legislator 210–15
  popular sovereignty 171–4, 208,
    210–12
spectacle 198–206, 227
theater 183–4
  actors and actresses 185–9,
    193–6
  divisive effects of 300n
  two bodies of the people 220–3
  women 192, 201, 216
    actresses 193–6
    festivals 200
    gender differences 204–5

Schiller, Friedrich 6, 292n
Schlegel, Friedrich 75–7, 80, 86, 97,
  103, 140, 142, 155, 284n
Schlingensief, Christoph 246
Schmitt, Arbogast 263n
Schmitt, Carl 13, 144, 145–79, 230,
  252
  aestheticization 146–9, 158, 159,
    164, 178–9
  alien powers 152–4, 155–6, 157
  anti-liberalism 56, 146, 147, 149,
    170
  "concrete life" 167–71, 175
  Constitutional Theory 159, 171–4,
    177
  The Concept of the Political
    160–2, 169, 173–4, 177
  inner nature 156
  juridical decisions 167–71
  Kierkegaard and 162–5
  Legality and Legitimacy 167,
    170–1, 173, 176, 177, 178
  neutralizations 145, 146–9, 158–9,
    160, 163, 165, 166
  occasionalism 149–52, 155, 156
  the other in the own and
    decision 154–9
  passivity 152–4
  political anthropology 158,
    159–62
  Political Romanticism 146–59

political romanticism 55, 56,
    145–59
Political Theology 159–60, 162–9,
    176
politics as a critique of
    politics 174–9
pre-political community 163, 174
Romanticism 55, 56, 145–79,
    284n
Rousseauism 171–4
secularization 165–6
self-determination 155, 156–7, 175
sovereignty 145–6, 158–9, 162–9
    popular sovereignty 145, 159,
        162, 163, 171–7
    subject and freedom 149–52
    totalitarianism 148
Schulze, Gerhard 3, 263n
secularization 165–6
Seel, Martin 25, 31, 264n, 285n
self-choice 114–18
self-deception 26–7, 30, 66, 258
self-determination 243, 251–2
    Hegel and 86, 87–90, 91
    Kant's moral principle 87–90
    Kierkegaard and 107, 114, 126,
        141–3
    Plato and 34, 35, 38, 39–40, 51
    Rousseau and 218, 219
    Schmitt and 155, 156–7, 175
self-difference 52–4
self-enhancement 104–8
self-improvement 197, 203, 206
self-perfection 52–4
self-realization 34, 35, 249–50, 251–2
    Kierkegaard and 101, 106, 108,
        112, 115, 117, 119, 120, 137,
        138
sin 116–17, 127, 132, 134–8
slavery of the tyrant 21–3, 112–13
socialization 50, 271n
sociology 3
Socrates
    Aristophanes and 63–4
    Hegel and 60–5, 97–9
    Kant's moral principle and 71–4
    Kierkegaard and 102–4, 134

Socratic virtue 97–9
    see also Plato
Socratic irony 60–2, 102–4
sovereignty
    post-democratic politics 249,
        252–3, 256–7, 258
    Rousseau and
        popular sovereignty 171–4, 208,
            210–12
        sovereignty of the
            legislator 210–15
    Schmitt and 145–6, 158–9, 162–9
        popular sovereignty 145, 159,
            162, 163, 171–7
Soviet Union 19
Spain 19
staging 2, 45, 234
    of community 7
    mass assemblies 227, 229, 230,
        231, 255
    of state power 213, 226–7, 254
    of unity 230, 231, 238, 254
Stäheli, Urs 265n
Starobinski, Jean 208, 292n, 294n
Stern, Fritz 283n
Strauss, Leo 206
subjective freedom 12
    Hegel on 59, 60, 64–5, 67, 68, 69,
        74, 75, 79–82, 93, 94–7, 118

Taine, Hyppolyte 146
Tarantino, Quentin 188
Tarde, Gabriel 49–50
taste 2, 3, 7
    Plato on 45, 46
    Romantic movement 146, 147
Taylor, Charles 268n
theater
    actors 40–4, 185–9
    the actress and her parodies
        193–6
    epic theater 227–8, 234–8
    Plato and 40–4
    playwrights 40–4
    postdramatic theater 236, 246–7
    seating arrangements 300n
    theater of cruelty 227–8

theatrocracy 248
  Benjamin and 231–2, 233
  Plato and 44–9, 184, 214, 231
  Rousseau and 214
Theunissen, Michael 94–5, 137, 269n, 274n, 276n, 279n, 280n, 281n
Thomae, Dieter 40, 117
Thucydides 264n
Tieck, Ludwig 103, 236
totalitarianism 51, 148, 221, 227, 229–30, 248
  see also fascism
Trujillo, Rafael 19
Tugendhat, Ernst 31, 34

Urbinati, Nadia 294n

Valéry, Paul 84, 241
Vinken, Barbara 291n, 293n
Vlastos, Gregory 186
von Stein, Lorenz 170

Weber, Max 232, 244
Weber, Samuel 295n
Wellmer, Albrecht 71–2, 73, 91, 258, 287n

Welsch, Wolfgang 300n
Willke, Helmut 298n
women
  actresses 193–6
  divorce 122–8
  emancipation of 121, 122, 123, 126
  femininity 121
  festivals 200
  gender differences 101, 121–2, 204–5, 257
  gender parody 193–6, 197
  Kierkegaard and 121, 122, 123, 126
  marriage 118, 119–24
  natural dignity 290n
  Plessner and 290n
  Rousseau and 192, 193–6, 200, 201, 216
  social role 192

zeitgeist 56, 108, 160
  ironic zeitgeist 120, 122, 138
  opportunists and 32–3
  romantic zeitgeist 56, 80, 147, 149, 164
Zupančič, Alenka 89, 304n